P9-APH-189

French Politics, Society and Culture Series

General Editor: **Robert Elgie**, Paddy Moriarty Professor of Government and International Studies, Dublin City University

France has always fascinated outside observers. Now, the country is undergoing a period of profound transformation. France is faced with a rapidly changing international and European environment and it is having to rethink some of its most basic social, political and economic orthodoxies. As elsewhere, there is pressure to conform. And yet, while France is responding in ways that are no doubt familiar to people in other European countries, it is also managing to maintain elements of its long-standing distinctiveness. Overall, it remains a place that is not exactly *comme les autres*.

This new series examines all aspects of French politics, society and culture. In so doing it focuses on the changing nature of the French system as well as the established patterns of political, social and cultural life. Contributors to the series are encouraged to present new and innovative arguments so that the informed reader can learn and understand more about one of the most beguiling and compelling of all European countries.

Titles include:

Jean K. Chalaby
THE DE GAULLE PRESIDENCY AND THE MEDIA
Statism and Public Communications

Pepper D. Culpepper, Peter A. Hall and Bruno Palier (*editors*)

CHANGING FRANCE
The Politics that Markets Make

David Drake
FRENCH INTELLECTUALS AND POLITICS FROM THE DREYFUS AFFAIR TO THE OCCUPATION

David Drake
INTELLECTUALS AND POLITICS IN POST-WAR FRANCE

Graeme Hayes
ENVIRONMENTAL PROTEST AND THE STATE IN FRANCE

David J. Howarth
THE FRENCH ROAD TO EUROPEAN MONETARY UNION

Andrew Knapp
PARTIES AND THE PARTY SYSTEM IN FRANCE
A Disconnected Democracy?

Michael S. Lewis-Beck (*editor*)
THE FRENCH VOTER
Before and After the 2002 Elections

Mairi Maclean, Charles Harvey and Jon Press
BUSINESS ELITES AND CORPORATE GOVERNANCE IN FRANCE AND THE UK

Susan Milner and Nick Parsons (*editors*)
REINVENTING FRANCE
State and Society in the Twenty-First Century

Gino G. Raymond
THE FRENCH COMMUNIST PARTY DURING THE FIFTH REPUBLIC
A Crisis of Leadership and Ideology

Sarah Waters
SOCIAL MOVEMENTS IN FRANCE
Towards a New Citizenship

Reuben Y. Wong
THE EUROPEANIZATION OF FRENCH FOREIGN POLICY
France and the EU in East Asia

French Politics, Society and Culture
Series Standing Order ISBN 0–333–80440–6 hardcover
Series Standing Order ISBN 0–333–80441–4 paperback
(outside North America only)

You can receive future titles in this series as they are published by placing a standing order. Please contact your bookseller or, in case of difficulty, write to us at the address below with your name and address, the title of the series and the ISBN quoted above.

Customer Services Department, Macmillan Distribution Ltd, Houndmills, Basingstoke, Hampshire RG21 6XS, England

---

Changing France

The Politics that Markets Make

Edited by

Pepper D. Culpepper
Associate Professor of Public Policy
Harvard University, USA

Peter A. Hall
Krupp Foundation Professor of European Studies
Harvard University, USA

Bruno Palier
Chargé de Recherches, CNRS, Paris, France

First published in 2006 by
PALGRAVE MACMILLAN
Houndmills, Basingstoke, Hampshire RG21 6XS and
175 Fifth Avenue, New York, N.Y. 10010
Companies and representatives throughout the world.

PALGRAVE MACMILLAN is the global academic imprint of the Palgrave Macmillan division of St. Martin's Press, LLC and of Palgrave Macmillan Ltd. Macmillan® is a registered trademark in the United States, United Kingdom and other countries. Palgrave is a registered trademark in the European Union and other countries.

ISBN-13: 978–1–4039–9696–1 hardback
ISBN-10: 1–4039–9696–2 hardback

This book is printed on paper suitable for recycling and made from fully managed and sustained forest sources.

A catalogue record for this book is available from the British Library.

Library of Congress Cataloging-in-Publication Data

Changing France: the politics that markets make / edited by Pepper D. Culpepper, Peter A. Hall, Bruno Palier.
p. cm.—(French politics, society, and culture)
Includes bibliographical references and index.
ISBN 1–4039–9696–2
1. Social change – France. 2. France – Politics and government – 1981–1995. 3. France – Politics and government – 1995–. 4. France – Economic conditions – 1981–1995. 5. France – Economic conditions – 1995– . I. Culpepper, Pepper D. II. Hall, Peter A., 1950– . III. Palier, Bruno. IV. French politics, society, and culture series.

HN425.5.C45 2006
330.944—dc22 2005049523

10 9 8 7 6 5 4 3 2 1
15 14 13 12 11 10 09 08 07 06

Printed and bound in Great Britain by
Antony Rowe Ltd, Chippenham and Eastbourne

Contents

Part IV

Figures

Tables

Notes on Contributors

Richard Balme is Professor and Head of the Department of Government International Studies at Hong Kong Baptist University. He also teaches at Sciences Po Paris. His research focuses on European integration, comparative government and policy-making in Europe, and the theoretical and empirical aspects of political decision-making. His publications include *L'Action collective en Europe*.

Suzanne Berger is the Raphael Dorman-Helen Starbuck Professor of Political Science at Massachusetts Institute of Technology and Director of the MIT International Science and Technology Initiatives. Her first book dealt with the politics of French peasants. Her most recent book, *How We Compete*, deals with choices under globalization.

Louis Chauvel is Professor of Sociology at Sciences Po Paris and a member of the Institut Universitaire de France. He is the author of *Le Destin des générations, structure sociale et cohortes en France au XXe siècle*, as well as dozens of papers on suicide, inequalities (generational, gender, class,) international comparisons, and the role of the state in social change.

Pepper D. Culpepper is Associate Professor of Public Policy at the Kennedy School of Government at Harvard University. He has published extensively on the subject of institutional change in advanced capitalist countries, including the books, *Creating Cooperation: the Politics of Human Capital Development in Europe* and *The German Skills Machine*.

Michel Goyer is Assistant Professor in the Industrial Relations and Organizational Behavior unit at the Warwick Business School, University of Warwick. He holds a PhD in Political Science from MIT and has held positions at Birkbeck College and at the London School of Economics. He has published in the areas of comparative corporate governance with a focus on France and Germany, institutional theory and diversity in advanced industrialized nations, and on labor relations in France.

Gérard Grunberg is Deputy Director and Vice-Provost for Research at Sciences Po Paris. He is a senior CNRS researcher in Political Science and specializes in European political parties and party systems. He has published extensively in both of these areas and also on French and European public opinion and politics.

Virginie Guiraudon is Chargée de Recherche at the CNRS in France and currently Marie Curie Chair Professor in Political and Social Sciences at the European University Institute in Italy. Her work focuses on the comparative politics of immigration and citizenship and on the Europeanization and externalization of migration control. She has published *Les Politiques d'immigration en Europe* and co-edited *Controlling a New Migration World.*

Peter A. Hall is Krupp Foundation Professor of European Studies and Director of the Minda de Gunzburg Center for European Studies at Harvard University. He is author or editor of many works on European politics, including *Governing the Economy, Varieties of Capitalism* and *Developments in French Politics*.

Michel Lallement is Professor of Sociology at the Conservatorie National des Arts et Métiers (Paris) and co-director of the LISE-CNRS. He has written numerous articles and books on work, employment and industrial relations including: *Les Gouvernances de l'empoli; Temps, travail et modes de vie; Stratégies de la comparaison internationl; Toward Decent Working Time*; and *Le Capital social*.

Patrick Le Galès is Directeur de Recherche of the CNRS at CEVIPOF and Professor of Politics and Sociology at Sciences Po Paris. He has published widely on comparative public policy in Europe, local economic development, urban and regional governance, and urban sociology. He has authored or edited 10 books, including *European Cities, Social Conflicts and Governance* which won the Stein Rokkan Prize for comparative social research.

Bruno Palier is Chargé de Recherche at the CNRS at the Centre d'études de la vie politique française de Sciences Po Paris (CEVIPOF). His research deals with globalization and change in national welfare states, and his books include *Globalization and European Welfare States, Gouverner la Sécurité sociale,* and *La Réforme des retraites*.

Andy Smith is Directeur de Recherche at the Foundation Nationale des Sciences Politiques and works at the CERVL research center in Bordeaux. A specialist of European public policy-making and European Union institutions, he recently published *Le Gouvernement de l'Union européenne*: *une sociologie politique* and edited *Politics and the European Commission.*

Introduction: the Politics of Social Change in France

Peter A. Hall

This book is animated by a problem and a puzzle. The problem is how to understand the dramatic changes that have transformed France over the past 25 years. Accounts of contemporary France often emphasize continuities rooted in the historical features of Jacobinism, Gaullism, *dirigisme* or the social relations of *la société bloquée* (cf. Crozier 1964; Jeanneney 1995). But the economy, society and politics of France have changed so profoundly during the past 25 years that even the most discerning accounts about previous eras, from Hoffmann's (1963) diagnosis of the stalemate society to Wright's (1983) analysis of the Gaullist state, no longer capture crucial dimensions of French life today. Our objective is to chart the most important recent changes in social, economic and political relations in France.

To this task, we bring a perspective that is implicitly comparative. Many descriptions of French politics or society emphasize the nation's uniqueness. Like Dorothy in *The Wizard of Oz*, any observer of a French school, firm or political meeting would immediately recognize that she is not in Kansas anymore. But the problems facing France have unsettled traditional political formulae in other countries as well, and we believe France can be understood best by moving beyond the traditional stress on French exceptionalism.

In that respect, this is a book about political change in Europe. Contemporary Europe has an underlying dynamism that belies persistent images of it as a continent dominated by inefficient markets, interventionist states and sclerotic civil societies. We are interested in characterizing the new patterns of behavior replacing previous ones in politics, society and the economy and in understanding the processes whereby such patterns shift. How do changes in these three spheres intersect with one another to condition the quality of a country's democracy and collective life?

The puzzle behind the book is characteristically but not exclusively French: namely, how to explain why the nation is permeated by widespread feelings of malaise. In economic terms, a majority of French citizens has been pessimistic about the economy and their own prospects within it for most of the past 20 years (OFCE 2003: 12). Their views reflect high rates of unemployment and rates of economic growth well below those of the *trente glorieuses*. But France is now three decades beyond the 'glorious' three decades that followed the last world war. Why have expectations not adjusted? What accounts for such persistent discontent?

The political malaise afflicting France is even more striking. Popular trust in politicians has fallen steadily since 1985. The French are now less willing to trust their government and political parties than the citizens of any other European nation (Duhamel 2001; Turner 2004: 10). In the first round of the 2002 presidential elections, 19 percent of the electorate voted for radical right-wing parties hostile to immigration and the European Union (EU), while another 10 percent voted for anti-system parties on the radical left. In May 2005, a majority of the French electorate repudiated the new constitution for the EU drafted under the aegis of a former French president.

From a neo-liberal perspective, such discontent is paradoxical.[1] France has moved faster than most of her neighbors to open markets, expand services and intensify competition in response to the challenges of a global economy. Since 1980, her gross domestic product (GDP) per hour worked has increased at rates well above those of her principal trading partners. In terms of adjusting to market competition, France is a success story. However, more open markets do not necessarily increase satisfaction. Economic adjustment can have distributional effects from which many emerge as losers. Ten percent of the French workforce is now unemployed.

Dissatisfaction in France has many contradictory dimensions. Among the spate of works on French bookstands decrying the state of the nation, some claim that France has changed too much, bemoaning the loss of a 'disappearing France' (cf. Rouart 2003). Others charge that it has changed too little: 'France has chosen to ignore the great transformation of the 21st century and cultivate a culture of status quo and rigidity' (Baverez 2003).[2] Such laments reflect confusion, as well as debate, about what is happening amidst a complex politics of social change.

The chapters in this volume consider that politics, examining the most important developments in France's economy, society and polity over the past 25 years. In this introductory essay, I summarize their findings and attempt to describe the dynamics of change.

1. Two sets of structural challenges

Although the features of any economy, society and polity are constructed out of a complex layering of responses to successive challenges, for the last 25 years, two sets of structural developments have played an overarching role in western Europe, defining the distinctive problems of the epoch.

The economic climacteric

The first of these developments was the shift from the rapid rates of economic growth and low levels of unemployment experienced during the 1950s and 1960s to markedly lower rates of growth and higher levels of unemployment in the 1980s and 1990s. After doubling between 1958 and 1978, average real net earnings in France grew by less than 10 percent in the subsequent 20 years and the rate of unemployment rose to between 8 and 12 percent (INSEE 2003: 93, 79). The roots of this shift are complex. They lie in declining rates of growth of total factor productivity that followed the exhaustion of Fordist models of production and the productivity gains initially secured by the movement of labor from agriculture to industry (Blanchard and Wolfers 2000; Boyer and Mistral 1981). Most European nations had such an experience.

Four significant effects followed this economic climacteric. Lower rates of growth disappointed many who had hoped to experience continuous improvements in their standard of living. The younger generations no longer have the opportunities their parents enjoyed. Lower rates of growth sharpened the trade-off between public expenditure and personal disposable income, ending an era in which government spending could rise continually without biting into earnings, thereby intensifying conflict about the value of government spending. Across Europe, poor economic performance inspired public disenchantment with the governments seen as responsible for it.

As it began to approach 10 percent of the labor force, unemployment took on new meaning as a public problem. A phenomenon once seen as a temporary side-effect of economic fluctuations affecting a few individuals for brief periods of time was redefined as a structural problem linked to fundamental defects in the economy or its regulatory regimes. By 2003, 43 percent of the unemployed in France had been without work for more than a year. Once an issue of economic management, unemployment became a problem of social cohesion. Many of the young were unable to find routes into stable employment, and joblessness provided the impetus for many shifts in public policy.

Demographic challenges

A second set of developments, broadly demographic in character but with cultural origins and implications, reinforced these problems. Although French women have long been encouraged to take paid employment, the proportion of women in the French labor force increased from 35 percent in 1968 to 60 percent in 1994. This trend has complex roots but double-sided effects on the unemployment problem. On the one hand, in the absence of jobs, women seeking employment swell the ranks of the unemployed. On the other hand, the impact of unemployment has shifted. Now that many households contain more than one breadwinner, the effect on the household of one family member becoming unemployed, while still severe, has declined.

At the same time, in France as in many European nations, the birth rate has been falling and longevity increasing. The ratio of those over the age of 60 to the working-age population is expected to rise from 37 percent today to 63 percent by 2030 (Arthus 2002: 13). This development puts severe fiscal pressure on old age pensions and health care for the elderly, which already consume 70 percent of the public budget for social spending in France, because smaller cohorts in work must bear the cost of programs for the larger cohorts who are retired. The problem is especially acute in France, because French pensions have become more generous over the post-war years, disproportionately benefit those in well-paid jobs, and must be paid from current revenues, since few pension obligations are already funded.[3] The effect has been to increase pressure on French governments to reduce social benefits and increase contributions, tasks that inspire intense political resistance and resentment against the governments that undertake them.

In recent decades, the ethnic and religious composition of the French population has also been shifting. France has welcomed immigrants for many years, but the pace of immigration increased sharply during the 1960s and 1970s. With decolonization, many workers migrated from southeastern Europe and North Africa to meet the manpower demands of an expanding economy. Although expected to return to their country of origin, many of these workers remained in France and were joined by their families. As a result, the number of foreign-born residents of France increased by 70 percent between 1954 and 1975 to reach 9 percent of the population. The proportion of foreigners of African or Arab background climbed from 13 percent in 1954 to about 43 percent by 1994 (Kuisel 1995: 35). As a result, France now has the largest Muslim community in Europe.

As Guiraudon indicates, the significance of these developments is multifaceted.[4] If they find employment, immigrants increase aggregate demand and the labor force available to support an aging population. But, partly because of ethnic discrimination, more than a quarter of immigrants from North Africa were unemployed in 2002 and many are concentrated in urban ghettos whose ethnic character breeds popular resentment (INSEE 2003: 87). Religious diversity poses serious challenges to the traditional republican model of France, which associates social integration with assimilation to the dominant culture and demands a strict separation between religion and the public sphere. The intense controversy surrounding efforts to force Muslim women to remove their headscarves in schools or places of employment is emblematic of the strains that a multiethnic society puts on long-established modes of thought and public action in France. Since 1983, one by-product has been the growth of radical right-wing parties with racist overtones, such as the National Front, whose opposition to immigration and further European integration has attracted between 15 and 20 percent of the electorate since the early 1980s.

2. The trajectory of changes in policy

Traditional portraits of France based on the 1960s and 1970s describe a *dirigiste* state that used national economic planning, its control over flows of funds in the banking system and the close connections between officials and leading businessmen forged during their education in the *grands écoles* to mount an activist industrial policy that modernized the economy (Zysman 1983; Hall 1986). Power was concentrated in the hands of Parisian technocrats and the prefects, their delegates to the provinces (Gourevitch 1980; Grémion 1986). Inside firms, relations were hierarchical and rule bound, and wages were often tied to the minimum wage (SMIC [*salaire minimum interprofessionel de croissance*]) or set by branch-level agreements ratified by the state (Maurice et al. 1986). Social benefits were provided in Bismarckian fashion by a multiplicity of contributory schemes, each covering specific types of workers, financed mainly from social charges on employers or employees and administered by the trade unions and employers federations (Palier 2002). The result was a highly regulated economy in which public officials played an active role, a centralized polity that concentrated power in Paris, and a society accustomed to looking to the state to resolve its problems. Over the past 25 years, each of these features of France has changed significantly.

If socioeconomic developments constitute the structural backdrop for change, the actual process of change was highly political and driven initially by important shifts in policy. Although most accounts of the process begin in the 1980s, the politics of the 1970s set the stage for much of what was to follow. When commodity price increases plunged France into recession in 1974, ushering in an era of stagnant growth, French policy-makers were unaware that this was not a temporary recession; they responded as if it were, increasing industrial subsidies to firms and social benefits to individuals to cushion them against the downturn (Berger 1981). Because the economy failed to expand again as rapidly as in the past, however, the result was a remarkable increase in the share of GDP devoted to public expenditure, which rose from 39 percent in 1974 to 52 percent in 1984. The nation took on an expensive set of new social programs just when it could least afford them, a legacy that would bedevil policy-makers for several decades.

At the same time, an electorate accustomed to prosperity turned against those who were presiding over stagnation in 1981, electing a Socialist president and Socialist-Communist coalition government for the first time during the Fifth Republic. For almost three years, that government responded to continuing economic stagnation in *dirigiste* fashion, raising the SMIC by 15 percent to spur demand, nationalizing 49 major enterprises, and pouring funds into industry on the premise that public investment could be a substitute for lagging capital spending in the private sector (cf. Hall 1986: ch. 8). When the expected upturn in the world economy failed to materialize, the result was not only mediocre economic performance but also intense downward pressure on the exchange rate of the French franc, then pegged to other currencies in the European monetary system (EMS).

Although disillusionment with *dirigiste* policies was widespread among French officials by this time, the exchange rate crises of 1982 and 1983 forced President François Mitterrand to confront their failure. To continue expansionary policies would require leaving the EMS, a symbolic repudiation of European integration. Announcing budget cuts to bolster the exchange rate in March 1983, Mitterrand opted for European integration. This decision and its subsequent affirmation when France supported the Single European Act of 1986 set the stage for much of what was to follow. The government embraced the opening of French markets to more intense European competition and further political integration into what was to become the European Union.

These steps were not only a commitment to Europe but a repudiation of *dirigisme* in favor of economic strategies oriented to market competition. Mitterrand opted for European integration in 1983, not only because he had long supported it, but because he was persuaded that alternative policies would not succeed. Facing what was then termed 'Eurosclerosis', policy-makers became convinced that French firms would prosper in an increasingly global economy only if they became accustomed to more intense competition. The Socialists had found the fiscal resources of the state an inadequate substitute for private investment and concluded that corporate profits would have to increase if private investment was to rise.[5] In this respect, the conversion experience of the French Socialist government was much like that of the British Labour Party. The decision to create a 'single European market' and intensify the competition facing French firms was the international reflection of a domestic 'move to the market' with which some, such as Raymond Barre, had flirted since the 1970s, but which was to be implemented fully only during the 1980s.

The chapters in this volume document many of the developments associated with this initiative. As Goyer notes, most controls on corporate borrowing were lifted and measures taken to make the French stock market attractive to domestic and foreign investors. As a proportion of GDP, the value of its shares increased from 8 percent of GDP in 1980 to 112 percent in 2000 (O'Sullivan 2002). Under the conservative governments of Prime Ministers Jacques Chirac (1986–88) and Édouard Balladur (1993–95), the nationalized industries were privatized on terms attractive to investors, restrictions on mergers and acquisitions lifted, and the hard core of controlling shareholdings in the newly privatized firms gradually dispersed. The Auroux laws of 1982 mandating firm-level consultation between employers and employees strengthened firm-level bargaining, lending impetus to what Lallement describes as the 'contractualization' of French industrial relations. Restrictions on lay-offs were gradually lifted. These steps and persistently high levels of unemployment weakened the capacity of trade unions to resist employer initiatives. In the context of EU restrictions on industrial subsidies, French governments phased out their activist industrial policies in favor of active labor market policies that subsidized training or jobs for workers who had been unemployed (cf. Levy 1999). At the same time, the government's commitment to European monetary union (EMU) and to a high exchange rate during the transition to it put intense pressure on French firms to rationalize their operations. In order to compete in a more open European market at a high exchange rate, many had to secure new efficiencies and concentrate on high value-added production. In this respect, the policies of the 1980s can be seen as an effort at market-led modernization, different from but as consequential as the state-led modernization of the 1950s and 1960s.

The effect of these steps was to increase the competitiveness of French markets for goods, capital and labor. French consumers benefited, as the prices of some commodities fell, but many workers lost their jobs in the course of restructuring, and others began to feel increasingly insecure. The rate of unemployment hit 12 percent in 1997 and levels close to twice that for those at the margins of the labor market such as the young.[6] Older employees were less likely to find another job if they lost the one they had, and many came under increasing pressure to retire early.

In this context, the social benefits of the French welfare state assumed more importance and the orientation of social policy-making began to change. In order to counter rising rates of unemployment, substantial new resources were devoted to active labor market policy, and its orientation shifted. In the early 1980s, the government responded to unemployment with a set of policies designed to reduce the numbers seeking work. By 1984, Mitterrand had tripled the number of employees offered early retirement (to 700,000) and reduced the retirement age to 60 (Levy 2005). The distributive effect was to take many older workers out of the labor force: although 51 percent of French men over the age of 50 were employed in 1975, only 36 percent had jobs by 1990.[7]

Since this approach intensified the fiscal crisis of the pension system, however, by the end of the 1980s the emphasis had shifted to policies designed to create jobs and retrain the labor force by subsidizing employers' social charges when they hired the young or unemployed. Throughout the 1990s, France spent about 3.6 percent of GDP a year on such policies; by 2001, it was subsidizing more than 2 million jobs (INSEE 2003: 81, 85). The 1997–2002 Socialist government under Lionel Jospin also legislated a 35-hour week, in the hope that firms would hire further employees, and it increased public employment, which grew by 10 percent between 1990 and 2001.

From a comparative perspective, the French trajectory is remarkable. On the one hand, the steps taken by the government to liberalize the economy were the most substantial of any nation in continental Europe. On the other hand, after some restraint in the second half of the 1980s, successive governments devoted vast sums to social spending to cushion key groups from the negative effects of market competition, defying the liberal view that economic deregulation should be accompanied by fiscal restraint. Several features of France help to explain this pattern. One is the longstanding structure of the taxation system. France raises more revenue from social charges on employers and employees and less from income taxes than most developed nations. Since social charges impede job creation by raising the cost of labor, but substituting higher income taxes for them is politically costly, French governments have subsidized social charges instead, in order to reduce unemployment. They were encouraged to do so by the republican concept of *solidarité sociale* that holds the government responsible for the welfare of the least affluent. As a result, at 53 percent of GDP, France's public expenditure has reached Scandinavian levels, although the redistributive impact of its tax and transfer systems is more meager (INSEE 2002: 243; Smith 2004: ch. 5).

The government also began to adjust the structure of social benefits. The French welfare state has long had a Bismarckian structure, which provides highly particularistic benefits to specific groups, usually funded by contributions based on their employment status, in schemes supervised by trade unions and employer organizations. However, this system is not well suited to the problem of providing social protection in contexts of high unemployment and market insecurity, because its benefits are rarely targeted on those who most need them, such as people who have never held a stable job, and cost control is difficult. In response to these problems, successive governments began to target more benefits on the most needy, finance more of those benefits from a tax on income (the CSG [*contribution sociale généralisée*]), trim the health and pension benefits to which existing groups were entitled, and transfer more control over benefit systems from producer groups to the state. A minimum annual income (the RMI [*revenu minimum d'insertion*]) established in 1988, covered more than one million people by 2003, and the CSG crept up from 1.1 percent of income in 1990 to 7.5 percent in 1998. Despite social protests, major reforms to health care and pensions were legislated in 1993, 1995 and 2003. French social policy is gradually moving away from a system that privileges insiders with secure jobs toward policies aimed at those without them.

3. The societal dynamics of change

The precondition for many of the most important changes France has experienced was often a governmental decision, whether to embrace the single European market, to shift regulations in an economic sphere, or to take new policy initiatives. But the state has rarely been able to dictate the pace or outcomes of social change. In that respect, what France has been experiencing is not *dirigisme* in disguise but something quite different. Many shifts in policy were largely permissive: what came of them depended on the response of other actors. As Lallement notes, for instance, although the Auroux laws of 1982 mandated closer consultation between firms and their employees and the Aubry laws of the late 1990s required them to negotiate a 35-hour workweek, what came of those negotiations turned heavily on the strategies and resources mobilized by each side (cf. Howell 1992). As Goyer and Culpepper observe, the liberalization of financial markets gave firms new room for maneuver but did not dictate the strategies each would pursue.

The fate of such initiatives often depended on the organization of the relevant social actors. Culpepper (2003) shows that the efforts of the government to encourage collaborative training schemes often failed because regional employer organizations were not robust enough to induce firms to take advantage of the opportunities offered. Le Galès reminds us that the success of local initiatives often turned on the ability of local organizations to coordinate their endeavors (cf. Levy 1999; Smyrl 1997).

In these respects, French society has never been well endowed. Interconfederational rivalries limit the ability of French unions to devise a coordinated response to employer initiatives and, as Lallement notes, their organizational links to the rank-and-file are tenuous. French employer associations have been prone to conflict between large and small firms (Berger 1985). Although there are notable exceptions, visible in the influence the FNSEA (*Fédération nationale des syndicats d'exploitants agricoles*) wields over agriculture, French producer groups generally lack the organizational cohesion necessary to administer neo-corporatist policies of the sort pursued in northern Europe (Keeler 1987; Suleiman 1987). Partly for this reason, although some flirted with the idea of moving France closer to the German model, tentative efforts to do so during the 1980s failed (Albert 1991).

Levy (1999) attributes many of the limitations of French society to the effects of 30 years of *dirigiste* policy. Although French planners encouraged the development of business associations in order to secure interlocutors for the modernization process, they were less willing to promote strong trade unions. Although the unions secured some resources by virtue of their role in the administration of social security, the government's practice of extending contracts signed by one trade union to an entire sector left the unions with few incentives to organize at the grassroots. Many governmental initiatives of the 1980s authorized coordination among social actors without providing them with the resources to secure it.

If unwilling to create powerful interlocutors, however, recent French governments have encouraged the growth of secondary associations dedicated to activities ranging from sports clubs to cultural associations. The past two decades have seen an efflorescence of 'associational life' at the local level, where neighborhood associations have become a popular novelty. By 1990, more than 60,000 new secondary associations were being registered in

France each year (Worms 2002). Moreover, if France does not have neo-corporatist systems of interest intermediation beyond the spheres of social security, agriculture and a few other domains, consultation with outside experts and representatives of those likely to be affected by policy has become a standard feature of French policy-making (Hall 1990; Laurence 2003).

As Le Galès notes, the devolution of power to the regional level has encouraged this type of consultation and 'contractualization' as a mode of policy-making. In a growing number of domains, the provision of public resources is now contingent on the signing of formal contracts between the relevant ministry in Paris and regional actors, including para-public agencies as well as regional authorities. The object is to specify a set of expectations against which the outcomes of policy can be measured and to ensure coordination among the actors who are to implement it. Although the approach often works better in theory than practice, it has encouraged cooperation among a growing number of actors, especially at the regional level. French policy is no longer made by a few officials in Paris but by a host of public authorities and quasi-public organizations. The principal danger is no longer that policies unsuitable to local conditions will be promulgated from Paris, but that, amidst the welter of participating bodies each of whose interests must be satisfied, the efficacy of an initiative may be lost.

Among the actors on whose decisions the recent trajectory of France has turned, business enterprises loom large. In any capitalist economy, the response of firms to shifting market conditions aggregates into overall economic performance. Entry into a single European market and monetary union put intense competitive pressure on French firms, just as the liberalization of capital markets and a weakening of the trade unions gave them new opportunities. The response of French business affected the life situation of many people.

As Hancké (2002) notes, large firms took the lead. Many took advantage of state-sponsored early-retirment programs to reduce their workforce. Between 1980 and 1990, Renault shed half its manual assembly workforce, lowering the average age of its employees and increasing their skill levels. Many firms made equally dramatic changes to production regimes. To increase productivity, they intensified work regimes, hired more skilled employees, moved away from standardized task systems, and eliminated layers of supervisory personnel. An increasing number tied compensation to performance, and branch level wage-setting gave way to firm-level negotiation about wages and working conditions. Some firms used the Auroux laws of 1982 and the 35-hour workweek mandated as pretexts for introducing more flexible working practices. In many cases, large companies not only rationalized their operations but developed new supplier networks that encouraged smaller firms to reorganize production (Casper and Hancké 1999).

As a result, French business is now substantially more efficient than it was 20 years ago. Since 1982, its unit labor costs have increased by only 1.6 percent a year, compared to an OECD average of 4 percent.[8] But the well-being of many workers has been affected. As Lallement observes, many jobs have become more demanding. Those forced into early retirement or unemployment bore the main costs of economic adjustment, but the fate of many workers is now tied more closely to market conditions. Unemployment is an issue of concern to most people. Moreover, the institutions within which the well-being of millions of workers is decided have also changed. Branch-level bargaining has given way to firm-level negotiations in which the unions are often less influential.

In this context, popular mobilization in the political arena has assumed renewed importance. France has a tradition of popular protest, to which its governments have long been sensitive. In this arena, the trade unions act as tribunes for the people, using mass demonstrations or strikes to call upon the state to redress grievances, whether generated by public policy or market forces. In recent years, they have been joined by new groups speaking for causes that do not secure such representation in other societies, such as the unemployed, opponents of globalization, and critics of racial discrimination. Although their tangible victories are rare relative to the number of demonstrations mounted, such groups have kept issues of social solidarity high on the political agenda and forced the government to abandon several projects in the spheres of social and educational reform.

The trade unions also remain influential in the realm of social security. To bolster their reputation for pragmatism, the CFDT (*Confédération française démocratique du travail*) and FO (*Force ouvrière*) agreed with the employer's confederation (MEDEF [*Mouvement des enterprises de France*]) to make benefit systems less costly and more uniform, in return for the state taking on more fiscal responsibility for social programs. MEDEF itself has practiced a politics of brinksmanship, alternately proposing radical changes to social benefits and threatening to withdraw from their administration. The result has been a messy politics but one in which the voices of employer and worker representatives have remained forceful.

Notably absent from these debates have been organized voices for the young. As Chauvel notes, because white-collar positions are expanding more slowly than they did after the war, the prospects for many of the young in France look far worse today than they did for their parents. For those under the age of 30, the rate of unemployment hovers around 15 percent. For those born in 1970, the rate of downward social mobility is twice as high as for those born between 1920 and 1950; and the gap between the average starting salary of 20–5 years olds and the average national salary virtually doubled between 1970 and 2000 (Smith 2004: ch. 8; Chauvel 1998). However, intergenerational issues have rarely been a focus for political mobilization. High-school and college students have agitated for higher spending on education and more steps to counter unemployment. But discrepancies in intergenerational well-being have been largely organized out of politics by the structure of existing interest groups. The trade unions have mounted a defense of pensions much more forceful than their expressions of concern for the young.

The position of immigrants and ethnic or religious minorities in France is more ambiguous. On the one hand, issues pertinent to them have been prominent in French political debate for more than 20 years. On the other hand, the impetus for that debate has come from the radical right, whose partisans oppose immigration, the provision of social or political rights to immigrants, and measures to address racial discrimination. Arrayed against the radical right is an ad hoc set of coalitions drawn largely from the political left, dedicated to improving the living conditions of immigrant communities. However, the measures the government has been willing to entertain are limited by the widespread influence of a republican discourse that sees France, not as a multicultural society, but as a nation to whose culture all residents should assimilate. One manifestation was a refusal until recently even to collect official statistics on racial discrimination (Bleich 2003). This republican vision made governments reluctant to use affirmative action to address the problems of minority communities. But, as Guiraudon notes, the government has begun to approach such problems by treating them as territorial issues, providing funds or special facilities to the poorer localities in which many immigrants reside. Moreover, although they get a chilly reception in the political arena, the claims of immigrants have been treated more sympathetically by French courts and social administrators, who call on an equally republican concept of equality before the law (cf. Guiraudon 2000).

4. Governance in contemporary France

How should the contemporary French system of governance be characterized? By governance, I refer not only to the formal institutions of the political system but to the broader modalities whereby resources are allocated in France. The distribution of well-being is determined by a matrix of institutions in which many interests are represented more or less powerfully. Successive French governments have accorded more influence over the allocation of resources to market mechanisms, but the retreat of the French state is far from complete. It continues to intervene heavily in the distribution of employment, by means of active labor market policies on which some three million households depend. Although the redistributive impact of the tax system is minimal, the state influences the distribution of income via social benefits. More than 10 percent of the populace receives a minimum income set by the state, and millions of others are pensioners. Even where the government has encouraged the development of competitive markets, its role remains substantial. Trumbull (2004) found more than 1,200 kinds of public aid available to start-up firms in France and a public agency certifying the firms eligible for private as well as public funds. However, industrial policy is more diffuse and less directive than it was 30 years ago. Although French officials still encourage one firm to take over another, in most cases, they concede that markets will determine the outcome.

Moreover, the state is now quite different from the one France had three decades ago. As Le Galès notes, substantial levels of authority have been devolved onto the regional governments created by the Defferre laws of 1982. The prefect is now only one among multiple actors with influence over provincial affairs. It is not uncommon for the implementation of policy to be contingent on the agreement of multiple bodies at the regional level, and agreement is often secured only after consultation with groups in the private as well as public sector. As a result, France has a more pluralist and negotiated polity.

There is also a more pronounced market logic to the processes whereby public resources are distributed. Regional governments often find themselves in competition with each other to attract industry, and they respond by providing subsidies and regulatory conditions more appealing to potential investors. As public utilities such as France Télécom were privatized, they moved away from the public service logic on which they once operated, toward market logics that put more emphasis on the profitability of their operations. The subcontracting of public services, such as municipal garbage collection, has proceeded apace, intensifying cost competition among those who commission and provide them. In many cases, the result is more efficient service, but the implications of such steps are far reaching. They reduce the weight given to the concept of 'public service' in debates about public goods. Those with market power are now better placed to demand services, and outlying regions or poorer communities less likely to receive the level of services they might once have enjoyed.

The devolution of authority over policy has also intensified what Le Galès terms the 'territorialization' of public policy-making in France. Key regions have always been in a good position to demand resources from the state by virtue of the *cumul des mandats* that allows mayors and other local officials to accumulate national offices, and the regional policies of the 1960s and 1970s leveled many economic inequalities across regions. But the appearance of influential regional governments, with a grassroots electoral constituency has enhanced the importance given territorial considerations in the distribution of benefits. The regions have emerged as significant centers of decision-making in their own right with jurisdiction over an increasing range of issues. Departments, localities and regions now distribute about 8 percent of GDP, half raised via local taxes and half via grants from Paris, and they have a voice in the implementation of many policies. Local authorities have become actors that interest groups cultivate and national governments cannot ignore.

Equally important for the operation of the French state is its membership in a European Union that became substantially more integrated following the adoption of qualified majority voting in 1986 and the extension of EU jurisdiction in 1992. As Smith points out, it would be a mistake to see European integration as a process that passes jurisdiction over a few matters to the EU level. The EU has had far-reaching effects on all domains of French policy-making. Because France is now imbricated in a European system of governance, the modalities of policy-making have changed even in fields where the EU has no direct jurisdiction. Many policies must be designed to conform to the *acquis communautaire* or to secure approval at a European level, and others are influenced by Europe-wide discussions taking place in many fields. As a consequence, the very terms in which policies are discussed and the criteria by which they are judged have changed (cf. Muller et al. 1996; Fouilleux 2003). To borrow the evocative term of Jobert and Muller (1986), the *réferentiel* has shifted, to privilege European, rather than specifically French, lines of argument; and the locus of influence has moved away from traditional issue networks toward the ministries best connected at the European level and the ministerial *cabinets* charged with shepherding a policy through the EU.

Thus, as Smith notes, the way in which policy is formulated in response to emerging issues has changed. More emphasis is now put on the problem of coordinating among ministries a response that will constitute the French position at the EU level, and less emphasis on forging a compromise among the affected interests in France. This inter-ministerial dialogue is often conducted in quasi-diplomatic terms that privilege the problem of forging coalitions across issue-areas at the EU level rather than the substantive concerns expressed by segments of French society. In this respect, European political integration has set in motion a dynamic at odds with the movement toward more extensive consultation with domestic groups. It has inspired a tendency to justify policy by reference to the exigencies of the EU, at the cost of alienating domestic groups who feel their concerns have not been given due weight.

Although the organizational coherence of the French state even during the heyday of Gaullism should not be exaggerated (cf. McArthur and Scott 1969; Cohen 1989), the days when one could identify two or three officials in Paris with preponderant influence over a particular sphere of policy seem to be gone. Industrial policy is now more likely to be permissive than directive, and the onus to implement a policy left up to regional officials or private sector actors. European terms of discourse loom larger, and even French interest groups have moved to Brussels to press their case.

While laudable in some respects, this system of governance is confusing for those who seek to hold a specific set of officials accountable for the quality of policy. France no longer has a 'state above society' but one in which power is so diffusely divided among local, regional, national and European organs of governance that it can be difficult to establish who is responsible for a specific line of policy, much as it was under the Third Republic for entirely different reasons (cf. Hoffmann 1963). In this context, it is not surprising to find critics on both the left and right calling for a more assertive French state (Séguin 1993). Paradoxically, the same critics rail against French technocracy. But this too makes some sense. Europeanization has tended to depoliticize policy-making in France. The European system of governance privileges technical argumentation and a mastery of the modalities of power within European networks that is the preserve of the higher civil service (cf. Joerges and Neyer 1997).

5. Political representation and malaise

In this context, it is not altogether surprising that the French are dissatisfied with how they are governed. In 2001, barely 30 percent of them expressed trust in the government and just 12 percent said they trusted political parties. Only 50 percent said they were satisfied with the state of democracy in France (SOFRES/*Le Monde* 2001; Turner 2004: 10; Rimac and Stuhlhofer 2004: 316). The result has been frequent alternations of government. In the six sets of legislative elections held since 1980, the incumbent party has never been returned. How are we to understand this level of political discontent?

Some of its roots are material. A move to the market sends shock waves through the lives of ordinary people. To make their operations more efficient, French firms shed labor, but the economy did not create enough jobs to absorb those seeking work. More than 1.2 million people in France today have been without work for over a year, and several million more have left the labor force, often to early retirement, whether they wanted to or not. Others now work part-time, more or less willingly. French firms have become more competitive by holding down labor costs and inducing employees to work harder. As Lallement notes, many jobs have become more difficult and insecure. Real disposable income for the average worker has increased by only 1.2 percent a year since 1980, as companies hold down wages and governments raise taxes to support the unemployed and retired. Although political leaders blame poor economic performance on market conditions, influenced by the Keynesian view that governments should be able to ensure full employment and a republican view of the state as the guarantor of social cohesion, many have turned their ire on the government.

The response they found there has deepened political disillusionment. Although one government after another has been voted out of office since 1980, the main thrust of policy has not changed. Governments of both the left and right have pursued liberal policies, mixed at the margins with support for the poor, the retired and the unemployed. As a result, elections have lost some of their meaningfulness, and the absence of sustained debate between the principal political parties about the basic thrust toward market liberalization has lent credibility to those on the extreme right and left who seem to offer 'a choice rather than an echo'. Many see liberalization as a process taking place over their heads. The result is a gulf between the *pays légal* and the *pays réel* reminiscent of the Third Republic.[9]

Central to this phenomenon, of course, has been the conversion of the French Socialist party to the market. Liberalization was initiated by a Socialist-led government in 1983 and reinforced by another in 1988–93. To be sure, the Socialists also took steps to mitigate the social impact of market competition, but this veneer of social solidarity was pasted onto a platform of market-led modernization. For the past 20 years, the Socialist party has looked more like its conservative rivals than it ever did before. Of course, this phenomenon is not unique to France. Facing the disillusionment with state intervention that followed the failed economic experiments of the late 1970s and forced to restrain social spending in an era of slow growth, socialist parties across Europe have abandoned the interventionism once used to build the welfare state and mixed economy. They have lost the heroic narrative that once sustained them and no longer wear so easily the mantle of tribunes for the working class, presenting themselves instead as more humane managers of a market economy. This is a development that has disorganized electoral politics across Europe.

It has also undercut some of the representational achievements of the Fifth Republic. As Grunberg notes, the French system of political representation has some strengths. Two coherent political blocs have formed, centering on the Socialist party and the UMP (*Union pour la majorité présidentielle*), the succesor to the Gaullists, providing stable majorities in the Assembly, while two rounds of voting have allowed parties speaking for a diverse range of interests to emerge. But, while the party system has become more structured, the political thinking of the electorate has been losing its structure. Political left and right are still recognizable in the National Assembly, but they are increasingly confused in the minds of the electorate. By 2002, 40 percent of French voters were unwilling to say they belonged to a social class, and almost two-thirds considered the concepts of left and right irrelevant to politics – compared to one-third in 1981 (Marcel and Witkowski 2003; TNS-Sofres 2002). The politics of the nation that invented the political left and right is no longer firmly anchored in this distinction. The result is considerable flux in the alignments of French politics. Many workers who once supported the political left now vote for the radical right. Jean-Marie Le Pen secured a majority of the votes of ordinary workers (*ouvriers*) in the first round of the 2002 presidential elections.

Political dealignment is a global phenomenon, rooted in the declining political salience of class in the face of post-war prosperity and the rise of the service sector. But some features of French politics have intensified it. Prominent among these is the experience of cohabitation. France has a semi-presidential regime that apportions a share of power to an elected president and to a prime minister appointed to command a majority in the National Assembly (Skach 2006). For 9 of the last 20 years, the French presidency has been held by one political bloc while the cabinet and legislature were dominated by the other. As Grunberg observes, securing workable governance under such circumstances can be counted as a success. But it is not surprising that the electorate has difficulty distinguishing the policies of the left from those of the right. Like grand coalitions, cohabitation tends to advantage parties at the extremes of the political spectrum, as voters turn to them to express dissatisfaction with existing policy.

The mixed feelings about market liberalization that many express may also have roots in the discursive strategies governments have deployed to defend them (Schmidt 1997). France's political elites have yet to find a persuasive formula to justify the policy regimes they superintend. In the early 1980s, Mitterrand mounted a vigorous defense of the move to the market, associating it with a brave European project designed to revive the economy, famously declaring *'La France est notre patrie, l'Europe est notre avenir'*.[10] But, when mixed results ensued, the governing parties became more reluctant to defend the European market model, even as they let it guide their policies. An effort by the Chirac government of 1986–88 to deploy an assertive defense of economic liberalism, spearheaded by Alain Madelin, was short lived, and subsequent governments have walked a tightrope, facilitating market competition without wanting to be seen as full supporters of the market. Most adopted a rhetoric of modernization, with its favorable Gaullist overtones of advancing France's place in the world, joined to an emphasis on republican values, redefined as support for 'social solidarity' in the face of global markets. Lionel Jospin struck precisely these themes in his inaugural address. As a result, in France, the case for a liberal market economy has not been made with the forcefulness mounted in Britain by Margaret Thatcher and Tony Blair. Instead, liberal measures are often presented as a necessary, if slightly distasteful, response to the imperatives of the global economy – hardly a posture likely to inspire electoral enthusiasm for them.

The character of the EU as a discursive object in the French universe of political discourse has shifted in tandem with these developments. Once presented by de Gaulle as a vehicle for French ambitions in the world and by Mitterrand or Delors as an engine for economic dynamism, in recent years the EU has often been portrayed by the government as a constraint on French policy-making or a terrain on which it battles (cf. Ross 1995). Although French leaders approved all the major steps taken toward European integration, they have developed a tendency to describe painful policies as ones forced on them by membership in the EU (Cohen 1996).

To some extent, of course, these shifting descriptions mirror a changing reality. France endorsed the intensification of European integration in the

1980s and again in the early 1990s, confident that it could continue to dominate the new European Union, only to find that Union as constraining as enabling. The need to assemble shifting coalitions among a growing number of partners leaves France in a position that is far from dominant. Agreements made at the EU level now cut a broader swath across French society, and the organs of the EU have become powers in their own right. At the same time, the European Commission has become fixated on market liberalization, leaving its member states with the task of social protection (Majone 1996; Streeck 1995). The effect has been to blunt the popular appeal of the 'European project' in France. A diffuse cleavage is opening up, loosely along class lines. French business is now deeply invested in Europe and many individuals who have acquired the skills to operate on a European terrain have become more 'European'. But those who lack commensurate market power have begun to associate the EU with an erosion in their quality of life (cf. Duhamel 2001; Stone 1993).

Thus, it is not surprising that some of the political discontent in France takes the form of apprehension about the European Union. Barely 51 percent of French voters approved the Maastricht Treaty in September 1992, after a vigorous campaign in which senior figures from the established right joined radical parties on the right and left to oppose it. Popular support for European integration reached a low ebb in 2003, when only 44 percent of the French thought membership in the EU desirable, a troubling figure for a founding state of the Union; and the EU itself was thrown into crisis in May 2005, when 55 percent of the French electorate voted against the new constitution proposed for it. While 80 percent of managers and professionals (*cadres superieurs*) voted for the constitution, 80 percent of ordinary workers voted against it. Exit polls suggest there were many motivations for opposition. Some simply wanted to express their dissatisfaction with the government, but many feared that an expanding EU dedicated to market competition would bring further increases in unemployment and decreases in social benefits.

This context explains the character of some of the political complaints now being voiced in France. When French officials present the EU as a constraint on policy, they implicitly call into question the capacities of the French state to exercise the responsibilities associated with republican governance, namely, to protect the citizenry and implement the general will. A disjunction has opened up between the rhetoric of national grandeur, still frequently called upon to justify the policies of the Republic, and the perception that France must bow to the edicts of the EU. For many, this disjunction inspires a vague sense of disquiet, born of the feeling that they confront two discrepant realities, both somehow operative but neither entirely credible. Critics of the EU have reinforced such unease with calls for more assertive governance, appealing to longstanding conceptions of a strong French state (Séguin 1993). As a result, in France more than in most countries, contemporary problems are seen as a crisis of the state.

The diffuse sense of threat that permeates French society has been reinforced by the inclination of many public figures to demonize 'globalization' as the major threat against which the nation must be defended. Globalization is an attractive target for the French political class, sufficiently foreign to evoke widespread nationalist sentiment and commercial enough to allow them to show they are not blind supporters of the market. As a rallying cry, opposition to globalization has cultural as well as economic appeal, simultaneously summoning up the loss of jobs to low-wage countries and the invasion of a homogenizing American culture especially threatening to a nation whose capital city was once the cultural capital of the world and whose language its lingua franca. Even during a round of trade talks, it was not atypical for a French minister to say: 'So, it's war and in a war, our nation must stand together' (Berger 1995: 203).

All segments of French society have been affected by the imagery of the anti-globalization debate (Forester 1999).[11] By 1993, an influential Senate commission could claim that five million jobs were threatened by competition from low-wage countries and two-thirds of the French electorate favored limitations on imports (Berger 1995). José Bové, a farmer from Larzac jailed for attacking the local McDonalds, attracted considerable public sympathy. Paris has become the base for ATTAC (*Association pour la Taxation des Transactions pour l'Aide aux Citoyens*), one of the most influential popular movements against globalization, and host to the World Social Forum of 2003 (Ancelovici 2002). Like the *tiers-mondisme* of the 1950s, the anti-globalization movement has provided the French left with a cause linking their domestic concerns about the depredations of the market to the suffering of developing-world peoples at the hands of a Washington establishment (Lefebvre Leclercq 1992). Some see it as a cause that can position France, once again, as the developed nation that speaks for the developing world.

The irony, as Smith (2004) has so forcefully pointed out, is that many of the ills casually attributed to globalization, such as rising levels of unemployment and inequality, have more immediate origins in the structure of the French economy and the government's policies. Less than 20 percent of French imports come from low-wage nations, while 60 percent come from the EU, and many of the developments popularly attributed to globalization are actually effects of more intense competition within the single European market. However, many who are unwilling to criticize that European market because France is now deeply imbricated in it have been tempted to rail against its effects in the name of opposition to globalization.

The results have been subtly corrosive. Dramatic statements about the threat of globalization have deepened popular insecurity and dissatisfaction with a state that seems impotent in the face of it precisely becaue the menace is presented as so vague and inexorable. By promoting market competition at home but deploring the effects of globalization, political leaders have inspired a diffuse sense of hypocrisy that feeds cynicism about the political class. Although there are legitimate grounds for concern about the impact of transnational commerce on France's economy and culture, globalization has been a smokescreen often used to hide the nation's problems from itself.

At the same time, France's political leaders are embroiled in intense debate about how to stretch the republican doctrines long central to the national self-image to cover new realities (Hayward 1990). Despite the changes documented here, it is not uncommon to hear complaints that French political parties lack any clear *projets de société* or grand vision of what the nation should do (Slama 1995: 63). This is a typically French complaint, born of the grandeur of Gaullist leadership and a republican emphasis on the nation's mission in the world. But it taps longstanding conceptions of national identity. The French are accustomed to seeing their national self-image reflected in the projects of the state. But, in recent decades, that mirror has thrown back images that are increasingly fuzzy. The processes that have eroded French exceptionalism inspire unease among those of its citizens who want to see their nation as exceptional. It may be safe for French governments to ignore the nostalgia for what is often called *la France profonde*, because generational renewal has reduced the number of people who remember a pastoral nation in which half the population lived on the land.[12] But, if nations are 'imagined communities' (Anderson 1983), there is no avoiding the fact that France now faces the task of reimagining its own political community.

Many developments now challenge the republican doctrines on which most conceptions of that community have been based. The growing prominence of Islam, a faith that resists the relegation of religion to the private sphere, has inspired a debate about the rigid boundaries republican doctrine draws between the public and the private (cf. Modood 2003). Greater ethnic diversity raises questions about the virtues of a citizenship model based on assimilation to a dominant culture. High levels of unemployment challenge the rhetoric of 'social solidarity'. A system of governance in which policy is negotiated with interlocutors in the EU or the regions no longer corresponds to conventional republican images of policy-making as the expression of an autonomous general will dedicated to the common good. As the European Union becomes larger, France's role in it is less pivotal and in question (cf. Gordon and Meunier 2001). If de Gaulle evinced 'une certaine idée de la France', his successors must also find 'une certaine idée de l'Europe'.

Thus, France confronts a new set of paradoxes (cf. Hoffmann 1963). Over the past 25 years, the nation has succeeded in modernizing its economy to meet the challenges of a single European market, but at the cost of leaving many feeling less, rather than more, prosperous. Social benefits for those at the margins of society have increased, but at the cost of cutbacks in benefits for those in established social positions that lead many to question whether the government is really protecting social solidarity. A once-fragmented political system has seen the emergence of two broad political blocs, but consensus between them on liberalization turned French bipolarity into the fetishism of small differences; and the reaction against it now threatens to fragment those blocs all over again. In both the domestic and international arenas, France is a nation in search of a new vision.

6. The dynamics of social change

Within Europe, France stands out, not only because it has liberalized some domains more fully than its neighbors but because, in so doing, it has dismantled the most forceful system of *dirigisme* in Europe. The French mode of economic governance is no longer so unique. As collective bargaining moves to the firm level and French capital markets become tolerant of hostile takeovers, France has come to resemble a liberal market economy more than it does the coordinated market economies on its borders (cf. Hall and Soskice 2001). After flirting with proposals to emulate the German model in the early 1980s, the nation has moved somewhat closer to the modalities of the British economy (cf. Albert 1991; Levy 1999).

In more general terms, however, the changes taking place in France mirror developments elsewhere in Europe. All western European nations have had to cope with slower rates of growth, higher levels of unemployment, aging populations, and more diverse societies, although the severity of their problems varies (Pierson 2001). Most have responded by trimming social benefits, spending more on active labor market policies, and intensifying efforts to integrate immigrants. All the EU nations have had to adjust to a more competitive single European market. Most have privatized public enterprises and deregulated key markets (Thatcher 2004). Across Europe, firms are making more use of part-time employment and temporary labor contracts and altering their production regimes to secure higher levels of productivity.

Thus, the French case is a good one in which to assess the general character of the processes whereby the European nations are reallocating resources and life-chances as they adjust to international economic challenges. In contrast to works that focus only on the political system, we have deliberately examined the economy, polity and society so as to explore the role that each of them plays in the adjustment process. Although one must be cautious about generalizing from a single case, several features of this one are revealing.

We can begin with the role of the state, which most analysts see as the guiding force behind adjustment and the counterweight to market-led developments. As might be expected, the policies adopted by successive French governments certainly conditioned the character of adjustment. Policies to deregulate markets and reallocate social benefits set the stage for many of the developments that followed. But the process of policy-making itself was far less strategic than might be imagined. Although some decisions were informed by an overarching vision, over the past 25 years, French policy-making is best characterized as an elaborate process of experimentation in the face of considerable uncertainty. Each government tried out putative solutions to the problems it faced, only to revise them later on, when some proved more effective or popular than others, as the retreat from generous early-retirement policies and the torturous trajectory of policy toward immigrants indicate. This is striking in a nation whose state is known for its strategic vision.

However, policy was never a random walk. In many instances, the decisions taken at one point in time set in motion institutional dynamics that limited the government's options in the coming years. In some cases, these followed from the network externalities of policy (Pierson 1996). France's entry into a single European market and then monetary union were fateful steps from which it would have been difficult for subsequent governments to withdraw, even if they had wanted to, not least because so many other social actors made investments that hinged on their continuation. In other cases, new policies shifted the opportunity costs of alternative courses of action. The resignation with which the Socialist government of 1988–93 accepted the privatizations by its predecessor is a case in point.

Here, the importance of the European Union cannot be overstated. It acted as a commitment device, especially with regard to liberalization, locking France into lines of policy from which subsequent governments might have edged away if they had not been backed by the force of EU agreements and institutions. The character of the EU has become especially significant. Because it is equipped with the regulatory capacities to open markets but few resources for intervening to limit their effects, for the past 20 years the EU has exerted consistent pressure to expand the role of markets in the allocation of resources (Majone 1996). The EU is gradually locking Europe into a competitive market model, albeit one that may have room for multiple modes of production regimes and various types of welfare states.

In this process of change, however, it is striking that the French state was by no means the only agent of adjustment. Firms proved equally important agents, even more responsive than governments to shifting market forces. They took many of the decisions that were most consequential for aggregate economic performance and the quality of working life in France. Emboldened by the deregulatory initiatives of the state and the weakness of the trade unions, large firms rationalized their operations in terms that forced changes on many workers and other companies. The character of a firm's response was conditioned by market opportunities and its institutional context (Hall and Soskice 2001). As Goyer notes, many French firms responded to more open markets differently from their German counterparts because they faced a different set of industrial relations and began with different corporate structures.

Although it is conventional to see economic adjustment as a matter of states and markets, organized social actors also played a role in the response to the economic challenges of the 1980s and 1990s. Organized producer groups have more influence in most other European nations than in France. But the popular sympathy that mass mobilization can arouse there acted as a cautionary check on what governments were willing to do. Many of the changes to French social policy were negotiated with the trade unions and the employers' confederation. In this sphere, the outcomes were often driven as much by what would evoke a minimum of protest as by what officials might think desirable. Thus, the shape of French social policy has reflected a series of uneasy compromises that satisfied some interests of each of the bargaining partners, if often leaving them with divergent views about just what the principles behind the policy were supposed to be.

As Palier observes, the resulting dynamic is one in which a set of profound changes in many spheres of French life have been reached through processes of incrementalism. Unlike Britain, where the analogous 'move toward the market' was dramatic and associated with the heated political contests of the Thatcher years, France edged toward even greater changes in incremental steps (Hall 1993; Palier 2005). This is a reminder that the prerequisite for fundamental institutional change need not be political upheaval.

However, the politics of social change put severe pressure on the political system of France, as it has on many European nations. Some of that pressure derives from inauspicious economic circumstances. Reform is politically easier in contexts of prosperity, where the dividends of growth can be shared among those competing for resources, as they were during the modernization of the French economy in the 1950s and 1960s. Slower rates of economic growth and the fiscal pressure on benefits systems generated by demographic trends made the 'modernization' of the 1980s and 1990s a more difficult enterprise. In that setting, reallocating resources across the economy meant holding back the incomes going to some in order to enhance those of others. The result has been a more overt politics of winners and losers – reflected most recently in the polarization of French opinion about the EU.

Moreover, this process of social change took place during an era when the political alignment of left and right that once dominated European politics was eroding, as class divisions lost their salience and the establishment of robust welfare states left socialist parties casting about for new platforms. Across most of Europe the recent politics of social change has accelerated that erosion. It was marked initially by a new political centrism, as mainstream leaders of left and right agreed on the need to encourage market competition, then followed by partisan fragmentation, as dissidents sought new political vehicles through which to express their dissatisfaction. These developments now strain the internal cohesion of many mainstream parties and fuel support for parties on the margins of the European political spectrum.

As a result, in France as in many parts of Europe, party politics is more unsettled, the voices in the political arena more cacophonous, and levels of political dissatisfaction higher than they have been for some decades. It remains to be seen how well the European political systems will cope with these developments. In all likelihood, much depends on the economic prospects of the continent. Renewed prosperity may revive the fortunes of the mainstream parties presiding over it and the faith of electorates in their governments.

However, there are some respects in which contemporary French politics resemble those of the Third Republic, where a tenuous republican consensus kept the regime stable but governments largely immobile in the face of a fragmented electorate (Hoffmann 1963). The EU looks much like the 'state above society' of that Republic and is an increasingly important target for the politics of resentment. National governments are better placed to rally support for themselves and the EU, but it is not clear on what basis they can do so. Electorates are tired of liberal initiatives that have borne limited fruit and the residual political loyalty parties command is low. The potential is there for a self-defeating *politique du pire*.

Whether France and its neighbors will see political stasis or forceful new reform efforts in the coming years, however, cannot be predicted from the structure of the polity or the composition of the electorate. Much will turn on the political visions that can be assembled in these polities. Whether rising political figures, such as Nicolas Sarkozy, can break the current impasse with fresh political programs remains to be seen. But, given volatile electorates, the mobilizing power of their appeals is likely to be important, and the fate of the continent tied as much to contests of political vision as to the ingenuity brought to bear on social or economic problems.

The chapters that follow explore the process of social and economic change in France more fully. Each compares recent developments in the sphere it is examining to previous modes of social regulation, with a view to establishing the character of the changes France has been experiencing. The chapters look for the forces inspiring change and the actors most influential over its direction. They explore the politics of change, asking how it is negotiated and what interests are defended in it. Together, they consider the impact of recent changes on the character of governance and the distribution of well-being in France.

The book begins with three essays documenting the dramatic transformation of the political economy. Pepper Culpepper traces the breakdown of *dirigisme* and the emergence of new modes of economic coordination via a process of firm-led negotiation. Michel Lallement examines changes in workplace relations, industrial bargaining and trade union strategies since the early 1980s, finding new production regimes and a shift in the locus of bargaining that has altered the character of worker representation. Michel Goyer identifies dramatic changes in the sphere of corporate governance, arguing that their distinctive character owes much to the nature of workplace representation.

The second section of the volume considers the challenges that unemployment, immigration and intergenerational inequality pose to the French quest for social solidarity. Bruno Palier documents the reforms to the Bismarckian system of social security that have transformed the French welfare state. Virginie Guiraudon outlines the challenges immigration poses for French society and efforts to adjust a republican model to respond to them. Louis Chauvel exposes the inequalities that have opened up between younger and older generations in France and the dilemmas they pose for policy-makers.

In the third section of the volume, Andy Smith examines the impact of the European system of governance on French policy-making, arguing that it has reinforced the influence of the technocracy but reduced their capacities for intersectoral coordination, biasing policy toward market-oriented solutions to public problems. Patrick Le Galès charts the sweeping decentralization that has increased the power of regional and local authorities over the past 25 years, linking the dynamic of change to the role of local elites within the national parties. He shows that the devolution of power has pushed the nation toward a more pluralistic politics.

The three essays in the final section take up the implications of these developments for political representation in France. Gérard Grunberg argues that the French party system has responded with considerable flexibility to the challenges of a changing society. Richard Balme examines shifts in the attitudes of the French electorate, finding broad congruence between the direction of policy and the preferences of many voters but an electorate polarized into four segments. Taking issue with the view that the French system of representation is working well, Suzanne Berger argues that the French parties have been unable to reconcile the public to the social changes that have transformed their world.

The view of social, economic and political change that this volume presents is not monolithic. The contributors disagree about how to interpret some developments, but together they provide a portrait of France that illuminates the broader dynamics of change in developed democracies during an era of globalization.

Notes

This essay has been influenced by extensive discussions with Pepper Culpepper and Bruno Palier. I am grateful to the Wissenschaftskolleg zu Berlin for support and to Arthur Goldhammer for his comments.

1 Throughout this essay, I use the term 'liberal' in its classical European sense to refer to measures that enhance market competition or individual rights.

2 Bavarez is quoted in Eric Le Boucher, 'Les New Misérables,' *Foreign Policy* (Jan/Feb 2004): 2.

3 France spent 12 percent of GDP on pensions in 1994 compared with 4 percent in 1960, and the value of pensions increased by 260 percent in 1970–85 alone. See the extensive discussion in Smith 2004: ch. 5.

4 Here and elsewhere in this essay, where a citation is not given, the reference refers to the author's chapter in this volume.
5 The share of value added going to labor fell from 68 percent in 1983 to 59 percent in 1995 (Hancké 2002: 12).
6 The proportion of French employees who thought their job was secure fell by 14 percentage points in the decade after 1985 and, by 2001, 22 percent were working without a secure labor contract (OECD 1997). Unemployment among those under the age of 29 reached 17 percent in 2003.
7 On these issues, see INSEE 2003: 77; and Smith 2004: ch. 5.
8 OECD 2004: Annex Table 23.
9 Although 42 percent of the electorate said that politicians pay little or no attention to what the people think in 1977, that figure rose steadily to reach 74 percent by 2002 (TNS-Sofres 2002).
10 François Mitterrand, 'Lettre à tous les Français', *Le Monde* (8 April 1988).
11 When asked their views of globalization in 2003, 36 percent of French respondents expressed a negative opinion, the highest proportion of the populace among the wealthy countries surveyed (Pew Research Center 2003).
12 If half the population of France were still peasants in 1950, barely 5 percent are today (Kuisel 1995).

Part I

1
Capitalism, Coordination, and Economic Change: the French Political Economy since 1985

Pepper D. Culpepper

Introduction

France is no longer a statist political economy; but what sort of political economy is it? In this chapter I show how the major institutions of the French economy have changed since 1985 and consider the character of the current political economy in light of the key actors in this process of change. Many scholars argue that the limits of statism were abundantly clear after the failure of François Mitterrand's experiment with "Keynesianism in one country" in 1983, but the analysis in this chapter shows that the withdrawal of the state from the economy was only consummated in the 1990s. The period between the mid-1980s and 1990 saw French governments attempt to empower various actors in civil society, especially employers and unions (Howell 1992; Schmidt 1996; Levy 1999). These initial policies, which attempted to develop a coherent model for the post-statist political economy, set in motion a process in which national politicians and bureaucrats exercised ever-decreasing influence over the choices of companies and individuals. State signals still matter in the French economy, as they do in all the advanced capitalist countries. The 1990s, though, witnessed the transformation of that economy largely through the uncoordinated action of individual economic actors, in a process made possible by policy choices but neither directed nor fully anticipated by governments. Markets and market power now set expectations in a wide array of fields, while French governments on the left and the right continue to assert their distaste for the market society. This uneasy tension between market reality and state discourse may partially account for the well of public discontent in the contemporary French polity.

The 1990s was a period of turbulent economic change for all the major industrialized economies, one characterized by the growing role of financial markets and the use of information technology across all sectors of the economy. I accordingly embed this discussion of economic change in France in a comparative perspective by drawing on insights from the varieties of capitalism literature, which holds that different advanced economies rely on systematically different means of coordinating the expectations of economic actors, especially those of business firms (Hall and Soskice 2001). Firms in all political economies must develop relationships with their employees, their suppliers and collaborators, and with public actors. These economic relationships pose a variety of problems of coordination, and firms in different sorts of political economies rely on different sorts of institutions to overcome these problems of coordination. In liberal market economies (LMEs), firms rely primarily on the familiar institutions of the market economy: arms-lengths contractual relationships among companies, stock market systems of finance, company or individual-level wage bargaining, and an educational system premised on individual investments in general skills. The United Kingdom and the United States are the exemplars of this model. By way of contrast, firms in coordinated market economies (CMEs) rely to a much greater extent than do those in LMEs on mechanisms of non-market coordination: extensive intercompany relational contracting, strategic shareholding that provides patient capital, powerful and autonomous associations of capital and labor that regulate wages and other company policies, and educational systems that create the conditions for shared investment in specific skill sets. Germany and the rest of northern Europe, along with Japan, approximate to this model.

France has never fitted easily into the conceptual dichotomy between CMEs and LMEs, and its institutions circa 2005 continue to elude easy categorization. Yet the analytical strength of the varieties of approaches to capitalism lies not so much in its typologies as in its focus on problems of coordination and economic change.[1] This approach draws attention to those mechanisms that allow actors to predict how other actors will respond to political, economic, or technical changes. Knowing the likely response of other actors to an exogenous shock to the economy helps actors, in game theoretic terms, understand the game they are playing and to predict the payoffs associated with different courses of action. The functioning of financial, labor, and product markets depends crucially on how the participants in these markets predict what other market participants will do. Their inability to coordinate their expectations can be costly, since they are then unable to make gains from trade that each would like to make if they knew the likely behavior of other actors

In statist France, firms looked primarily to public institutions for information about how to coordinate their actions. As the mechanisms of state control weakened in the 1980s, economic actors began to look elsewhere for their signals about how other actors were likely to respond to any given change in the environment. In LMEs, these actors look primarily to the markets; in CMEs, such actors look primarily to the associational and network mechanisms of non-market coordination. In the late 1980s, policy-makers had attempted to build up the associations of civil society that allowed for non-market coordination in Germany, but those attempts had met with little success (Levy 1999). Thus, the question confronting economic actors and successive governments during the 1990s was the same: how should they get their information about the likely developments in the economy? By what new rules would they coordinate their expectations about economic change?

The questions are central to the politics of economic change. Yet they are not always central to the way political scientists study economic change, because many political scientists take as axiomatic that institutional change must be ratified by public policy. Legislative arenas and outcomes are of course fundamental to democratic capitalism. However, politics encompasses private negotiations that influence, and are influenced by, the prevailing rules of the game in an economy. Governments are not free to set these rules at will; they emerge from a history of private and public interaction. When effective institutions depend on informal practices rather than formal laws—when the law periodically races to catch up to current practice, rather than dictating that practice—then it may not be in legislatures or elections that the politics of institutional adjustment play out. This was certainly the case of the radical changes that took place in the French financial system during the 1990s. While French governments made important policies that attempted to shape institutions of industrial relations and education, the incremental changes that we observe in those institutions in the end resulted less from public policy than from the choices of, and negotiations among, private actors.

To sustain these claims this chapter proceeds in the following way. Section 1 reviews the statist model as it existed circa 1985, focusing on the major subsystems of the economy emphasized in the varieties of capitalist frameworks: finance and corporate governance, industrial relations, and vocational education and training. Section 2 reviews the major changes in each of these subsystems after 1990, along with the shifting balance in economic governance among state, market, and civil society entailed by these changes. The final section concludes with a discussion of how we should characterize the current French political economy.

1. The statist model

To understand the extent to which the French political economy changed between 1985 and 2005, it is important to know where it started. At least until the early 1980s, the principal elements of the statist model of economic governance worked together in a way that was characteristic neither of LMEs nor of CMEs.[2] This section outlines that model in ideal-typical form by considering three principal subsystems of the political economy highlighted in the explanatory framework of varieties of capitalism: the system of finance and corporate governance, by which companies raise capital and owners monitor (or not) the performance of managers; the system of industrial relations that organizes relationships between employers and employees, both within firms and across entire sectors of the economy; and the system of education and training, which determines the sorts of skill sets on which employers will be able to draw for their production.[3]

The statist model of political economy that characterized France during the so-called *trente glorieuses*—the 30 glorious years of post-war economic expansion—comprised substantial state control in all three of the linchpin institutions of the economy. In the area of corporate governance and finance, French governments exercised substantial influence through three connected mechanisms: a large direct ownership stake in the economy, a policy of indicative planning, and a system of credit allocation. Ownership was the most obvious element of the state's presence in the economy. After the last round of sweeping nationalizations by the Mitterrand government in 1981, the state owned 13 of the 20 largest companies in the economy and virtually the entire credit sector (Hall 1986: 204). At its high water mark in 1985, public ownership accounted for 10 percent of the economy (Schmidt 2002: 189).

The role of indicative planning was, as Peter Hall has argued, twofold. On the one hand, it performed a function of "economic triage, letting the more inefficient sectors die—in some cases, from exposure to the global market—and strengthening the sectors with apparent competitive potential in manufacturing and agriculture" (Hall 1986: 163). In setting these priorities, economic planners could use both the links they developed with key leaders in industry and their control of the allocation of private bank credit for investment. On the other hand, planning served a clear political function: to legitimize the choices of state planners, and thereby reduce social conflict, "by masking individual loss with the veneer of common interest, by presenting industrial execution as economic euthanasia, and by tying present sacrifice to future gain" (Hall 1986: 163).

The real bite behind the economic plans, which retained its sharpness even after planning declined in the 1970s, was state leverage over the way in which banks allocated their long-term credit. As argued by John Zysman (1983: 130), "the French financial system [was] a credit based system with administered pricing." Through its mechanisms for the allocation of credit, the French treasury—the heart of the French bureaucratic elite—was for much of the post-war period capable of directing a substantial portion of the flows of capital for investment purposes. As access to finance was administered, so corporate governance was tied closely to the state apparatus, as top managers were recruited from the ranks of state bureaucratic elites (Bauer and Bertin-Mourot 1997). Thus, public influence over the managers at the towering heights of the French economy was secured both by controlling many of the available funds for investment and by the fact that most of these managers came out of the state bureaucratic corps in the first place.

In the second core institution of the economy—the system of industrial relations—public officials were the dominant actors in a field of weak employers' associations and even weaker unions.[4] In the early post-war years government had intervened in industrial relations so as to promote economic growth, with little attempt to involve organized labor in the implementation of this growth strategy. As the economy modernized, though, and especially after the crisis of 1968, the government moved increasingly to incorporate organized labor into a pattern of collective bargaining, if only to prevent labor strife from destabilizing the republic or retarding economic growth (Howell 1992). Even the attempt to construct a system based on collective negotiations among unions and employers still led fundamentally to a system in which the state was the preeminent actor, as reflected in three of the prominent features of the statist institutions of industrial relations. First, given its large ownership stake in the economy, the state was a significant employer, and its negotiations with its employees set standards that influenced private sector negotiations. Second, the minimum wage after 1970 became an increasingly important tool of policy-makers to influence wage levels (Howell 1992: 107–10). The third policy tool of statist regulation was the extension procedure, which allowed the government to extend agreements reached with one union to workers in an entire sector (Traxler et al. 2001: 182–3). Over time, low and falling rates of union density came to be counterbalanced by periodic expansions of the coverage rate, most notably by the socialist government of François Mitterrand; the effective proportion of the workforce covered by bargained agreements grew from 64 percent in 1980 to 94 percent in 1985 (Golden, Lange, and Wallerstein 2002). Although these policies frequently aimed to facilitate the development of an independent role for labor unions in collective bargaining, their joint effect was to divorce the actual development of wages from the negotiating and organizational capacities of unions and employers (Levy 1999).

Wage bargaining institutions lie at the core of industrial relations systems in all advanced capitalist economies. The distinctive features of the statist model of wage bargaining in France, in contrast to those in both liberal and coordinated market economies, did *not* induce unions and employers to develop strong firm-level organizations to support their sectoral wage negotiations. French employers and unions have long been highly involved in the joint management of various social policy schemes, as Lallement discusses in his chapter in this volume. Ironically, though, this involvement in *paritarisme* (joint management bodies) further reduced the incentives for unions to develop their organizational base at the firm level because of the organizational resources with which it provided them (Goetschy 1998). Given their weakness and the proclivity for public intervention, "union officials could gain more from episodic political mobilization, designed to attract the attention of the *dirigiste* state, than from patient negotiations in their narrow arena" (Levy 1999: 243). French unions, historically riven by ideological cleavages, had nothing to gain by developing their ability to promote in-firm discussion with employers, since they could do better by waiting for the inevitable public intervention. Employers' associations, which also knew the likely outcome of any negotiation would be determined by the government, focused on developing their expertise in labor law rather than developing the collective capacities necessary to acquire information from member firms about their in-firm negotiating practices, so as to circulate best practices and coordinate company actions (Culpepper 2003). The statist system of industrial relations thus promoted the development of social organizations whose strengths lay in the law, the street, or the legislature, but not in firms themselves.

The third element of the state-led market economy was its education and skill-provision system. This system emerged in the post-war era from the junction of three imperatives: to produce a meritocratically selected elite to operate the bureaucracy that ran the *dirigiste* economy; to provide for the general education of French citizens; and to furnish the (largely unskilled) labor that was demanded by the modernizing French industry. The first imperative imposed a series of competitive exams that very successfully selected a Cartesian technocratic elite, whose high seminaries were the ENA and Polytechnique and whose Vatican was the French treasury (Suleiman 1978; Ziegler 1997). The mass education system reproduced at a lower level the same set of competitive selection measures to permit mobility through education of the most academically gifted. Those who failed to meet the rigorous demands of academic training in general skills were shunted into a vocational training track that was widely perceived as a track of failure (Comité de Coordination 1996). During the *trente glorieuses*, this group was easily absorbed by French industry, which was predominantly organized along Fordist lines, stressing repetitive assembly line production that made low demands on the skills of line workers (Boyer 1995). French companies tried to compensate for skill weaknesses on the shopfloor by employing a comparatively high proportion of managers with technical education (Maurice et al. 1986).

The end result of these measures was a skill-provision system that was financed by the state and provided by the public school system. From public financing flowed state influence over the educational tracks chosen. By way of contrast, Germany provided for massive private funding of firm-based training through its dual apprenticeship system, as employers paid the costs of in-firm training. Since company participation in German vocational training was voluntary, it was firms themselves that determined the exact composition of the skills certifications taught. In a system such as the American one, which like the French system was overwhelmingly school based, much of the tertiary education provided was partially privately funded, through parental investment and student loans. In this system, students carried some of the credit risk of their investment in their own human capital, and their choices influenced the available degree programs. In international comparison, then, a notable specificity of the French system of education and training was to concentrate control exclusively in public hands.[5] In education as in industrial relations and finance, the statist model functioned on the basis of clear public signals around which private actors could reliably coordinate their expectations.

2. The breakdown of the statist political economy

By the year 2000, the French political economy had changed dramatically. The French government and bureaucracy could do no more to direct the course of adjustment in the political economy than governments of the other major industrialized countries. In this section I examine how the principal institutions of the statist political economy broke down between 1985 and 2000.

Finance and corporate governance

In the area of corporate governance and finance, the statist model is dead. The rightist government of Jacques Chirac, elected in 1986, privatized 13 large groups, including some of those that had been nationalized by Mitterrand's first government in 1981 (Levy 1999: 65). After a hiatus in privatization between 1988 and 1993, governments of the right and the left became equally avid in their privatization of state assets (Holcblatt 2002). Consistent with practice in other OECD countries, the state's direct control of the economy has been reduced to core areas of public service provision.

Public influence over non-state assets has diminished equally dramatically. Following the privatizations of 1986–88, the Chirac government had encouraged the reinforcement of existing patterns of corporate cross-shareholding, creating *noyaux durs*—hard-core owners. These companies held each others' shares and thereby provided mutual takeover protection and patient capital, attenuating the short-term bias of liberal market regulation induced by focusing on share price and quarterly reports. There were two principal shareholding networks: one centered around Paribas and Société Générale (SocGen) and one centered around Suez and BNP (Schmidt 1996; Morin 2000). Table 1.1 demonstrates that the mutual cross-shareholdings held by companies in these two shareholding groups collapsed by roughly equivalent amounts between 1997 and 1999. These interlocking French shareholdings among large French firms were replaced by the growing weight of foreign (mostly British and American) institutional investors, which as of 2003 owned over 40 percent of the outstanding shares in CAC-40 companies (Goyer 2003: 2; Morin 1998). If France were still a form of state-directed capitalism, we should expect to observe some ability of public officials to shape the course of this ownership transformation.

However, the state levers of control that had worked in the past were no longer available by the mid-1990s, had ministers or bureaucrats wanted to use them. Control over credit allocation was a distant memory, as French

Table 1.1 The breakdown of French cross-shareholding

	Average level of mutual cross-shareholdings within the hard cores (as a percentage of shares outstanding)				
	1996	**1997**	**1998**	**1999**	**2000**
SOCGEN Group	2.83	3.12	2.66	1.92	1.89
% of 1996 level	100	110	94	68	66
BNP Group	4.80	4.07	2.99	2.14	2.07
% of 1996 level	100	85	63	45	43

Note: The Socgen Group includes four dyads of mutual shareholding (in which each company holds the other's shares): AGF/Societe Generale, Alcatel/Societe Generale, Vivendi/Societe Generale, and Vivendi/Alcatel. The BNP Group includes five dyads: UAP-AXA/Suez, UAP-AXA/BNP, UAP-AXA/St. Gobain, BNP/St. Gobain, and Suez/St. Gobain.

Source: SISIFE/Lereps Database, University of Toulouse.

firms turned increasingly to equity markets. As demonstrated in the Table 1.2, existing French companies used equity markets heavily throughout the 1990s to raise money; in this respect, they acted more like companies in the American liberal market economy than companies in the German coordinated market economy.

Table 1.2 Equity raised by listed companies, as percentage of GDP

	1990–1996	1997–1999	Change, T2–T1 (%)
France	86.0	117.7	38
Germany	58.4	55.3	−5
USA	98.3	161.0	64

Note: Share buy-backs excluded.

Source: Van der Elst 2000: 12, own calculations.

French managers, cut loose from the supervision of state planners, were able to exercise extraordinary autonomy in developing their strategies. French firms use a variety of unequal voting measures to disenfranchise minority shareholders. As Michel Goyer shows in his chapter in this volume, French CEOs used their concentrated authority to dismantle their conglomerate structures and focus increasingly on core competencies—in marked contrast to the behavior of German large corporations. In other words, following the breakdown of the system of interfirm cross-shareholding French CEOs behaved more like their counterparts in a liberal market economy than those in a coordinated market economy. By the year 2000, more than 90 percent of French large companies were using stock options to compensate employees, which was a higher rate even than in the British liberal market economy (Trumbull 2004). There is nothing egalitarian about the use of stock options in France: they are limited to the very top layers of management, with less than 1 percent of the French workforce eligible for them (Goyer 2003). With strong ownership by American and British investment funds and the alignment of management interests closely with (large) shareholder value, French companies are largely unconstrained in their response to market signals in the area of finance.

Government policy played little role in directing the rapid transformation of French financial markets in the 1990s. The unraveling of cross-shareholdings took place as companies in the main shareholding networks responded to each others' decisions about the future costs and benefits of patient capital (Culpepper 2005). The concentration of power in CEOs, long a feature of the French model, now operates in the absence of countervailing channels through which public officials can exercise significant influence on those managers. The changes in the French financial system in the 1990s were engineered by the calculations of individual firms, for whom the cross-shareholding system showed declining attraction. This was a process of change dominated by private companies, not by public actors.[6]

Industrial relations

In the sphere of industrial relations, firm-level negotiation has vastly increased in importance since 1985. Public policy has not so much driven this change as it has provided the toolkit that companies have used to reorganize production (cf. Hancké 2002). In the early 1980s, wage agreements which covered entire sectors provided the minimum threshold below which wages and other working conditions could not fall. Yet, as argued by Michel Lallement in this volume, a set of legal exemptions first introduced in the 1980s steadily eroded the primacy of the sectoral level, capped by a 2004 law on social dialogue which reinforced the autonomy of firm-level bargainers in almost every domain save wages (Jobert and Saglio 2004; Souriac 2004). While wage bargaining technically remains a prerogative of the sectoral level, this legal fiction often masks different facts on the ground: a study by the French employment ministry suggests that by the early 1990s firms had become the locus of wage flexibility, with average firm salaries undercutting sectorally specified salaries from 1991 to 1994 (Yakubovich 2002: 8).[7]

The 1990s witnessed a massive acceleration of the scope of firm-level bargaining, especially as a result of negotiations over working time. These negotiations themselves resulted from government policies on working time that aimed to increase social dialogue and employment. In their implementation, however, available evidence suggests they did little to improve either social dialogue or employment (cf. Charpentier et al. 2004). As in the case of reforms in the 1980s, the process of change arrived at this destination at least partly due to the weak collective capacities of French unions and employer's associations (Levy 1999). The potential for firm-level negotiations to undermine unions, whose plant strength has always been tenuous, was first exposed widely in the application of the Auroux laws in the 1980s (Howell 1992). The statist industrial relations system had depended on the use of coverage rates to compensate for the anemic organizational capacities of unions. French employers delighted in their ability to use the principle of firm-level exemptions to escape the state-extended system and began to introduce flexibility of various sorts at the workplace level. Available case-study evidence suggests the same one-sided dynamic in the burst of firm-level negotiation mandated by the Aubry (II) Law of 2000 (Charpentier et al. 2004)

Employers in France have their own substantial organizational problems (Bunel 1995; Culpepper 2003). These problems became especially apparent over the course of the 1990s, as firm-level negotiations over working time revealed the inability of either the government or secondary associations to direct the process of economic adjustment. French governments of both the left and right tried to use negotiations over working time to promote employment-friendly, productivity-enhancing negotiations in which workers exchanged the flexibility of working rules for reductions in the workweek. These negotiations revealed the shortcomings of both policy-makers and organized employers. Policy-makers, far removed from the sorts of plant-level specificities that vary from one place to the next, lacked the information to write legislation that imposed an efficient solution on the entire economy. Employers' associations and unions, long responsive to the incentives of a statist system that prioritized lobbying power and knowledge of labor law over shopfloor organization, were equally poorly equipped to assist their local members. The uncoordinated set of firm-level bargains that emerged as the basis of the new French system of industrial relations is the consequence of the weaknesses of both state and civil society.

To see this dynamic in action, consider the three major working-time reforms of the 1990s: the Robien Law and the two Aubry Laws (I and II).[8] The Robien Law of 1996, passed by the rightist Juppé government, urged firms to negotiate individually with their workers to reduce the workweek, establishing a set of financial incentives to encourage that development. The Aubry (I) Law, passed by the socialist Jospin government in 1998, changed the character of the 35-hour negotiations by using the stick of government authority as well as the carrot of government incentive. The incentives were similar to those of the Robien Law, but the new stick was the stipulation that, from the beginning of the year 2000, all firms with more than 20 employees would be compelled to pay employees on the basis of a 35-hour week.

The Robien Law encouraged firms to reduce working time by offering companies the possibility of paying lower social charges if their planned reduction passed a certain threshold and created (or preserved) jobs.[9] More than 80 percent of the accords signed under the Robien Law were based on an explicit exchange of flexibility on work organization for reduced working time (DARES 1999: 5). Yet sectoral employers' associations, given their limited capacities to coordinate company action and circulate information about best practices, proved unable to assist companies in negotiating these accords. A case study of the Robien accords signed in Alsace demonstrated that company managers regretted not receiving more outside help in designing their accords. With Aubry I, the Jospin government recognized this problem and subsidized the use of outside consultants to help with devising firm-level accords. However, the Jospin government's own analysis underlined the difficulties faced by outside consultants in understanding the complex trade-offs in work organization: "the ambition to hold simultaneously to a logic of analysis of the problems of the organization of work and the logic of facilitating social dialogue remains a complex exercise that demands a lot of *savoir faire*" (MES 1999: 35).[10] This is the sort of information that the government hoped secondary associations might provide, but which their weak coordinating capacity left them unfit to deliver.

Unable to rely on private associations to support its initiative, the Jospin government was only able to attract widespread participation in its voluntary measure from state-owned firms. Thus, by January 2000, almost all significant voluntary agreements covered only public-sector firms: firms employing 90 percent of the workers in the private sector had not yet signed firm-level agreements by the time of Aubry II, which imposed the arrangements on them (MES 1999). While the management of state-owned companies clearly responded to the government's incentives, managers in the private sector ignored the government's attempts to incite firm-level negotiations. The government's cupboard of strategies to coerce "voluntary" cooperation was bare, and it fell back on its only remaining lever of influence: binding regulation.

Aubry II reminds us that the French government can still legislate social practices that have significant impacts on the economy. However, particularly given the unilateral way in which the reform was implemented by companies, many workers complain that the law has led to a loss of pay or an increase of work-intensity (Charpentier et al. 2004).[11] Moreover, the law was a rallying point for organized employers, who proposed the *refondation sociale* in a variety of areas subject to government regulation. The animating idea behind this program was to roll back legal regulation so as to widen further the ambit of firm autonomy (Lallement and Mériaux 2003). Although these are the sort of political preferences associated with organized employers in some liberal market economies, such a fundamental challenge to the system of legal regulation was a radical departure from the past practice of French employers' associations. The law lowering working time thus expanded social rights whose implementation was broadly controlled by companies, and it led employers to push aggressively for the expansion of the autonomy of firm-level negotiation. Far from the government's initial goals of boosting employment and reinvigorating sector-based solutions, the second Aubry Law instead accelerated the move to firm-level negotiation in France.

The hallmark of the modern system of French industrial relations is negotiation, rather than either conflict (through strikes) or governmental control (through detailed regulation). It is clear that the market is not the principal mechanism to which economic actors look for their signals of likely outcomes. But neither do they look primarily to the state. Instead, the French model of industrial relations appears increasingly oriented to outcomes that are negotiated and debated at the level of the firm rather than the sector. This trend is likely to continue, and its continuation will highlight the contradictions between the traditional republican commitment to equality and an increasing diversity of situations at the level of the firm.

Education and training

The French system of education and training reveals clearly how decentralized decisions by uncoordinated economic actors have undermined the mechanisms of statist coordination without being able to replace them. In youth vocational training, regional councils have taken over state competencies while being even less capable than the national state of imposing effective coordination. As a result, their policies are largely ignored by individual companies, who use the vocational system primarily to finance firm-specific training with public subsidies (Culpepper 2003). At the level of elite production, meanwhile, student choice has shifted toward earlier departure from the *grand corps* to lucrative private-sector careers. The ENA may now be France's best business school, handsomely underwritten by the government (cf. Bauer and Bertin-Mourot 1997). At both ends of the education system—that is, the aspects in which France has differed most from the other advanced capitalist countries—state financing no longer equates to state coordination.

The most important reform of the system of education and training in the 1990s was the delegation of the nominal right to coordinate all youth professional training measures to the regional councils in the Five Year Law of 1993 (henceforth the FYL).[12] This law and its enabling legislation were the culmination of a decade during which national governments had repeatedly attempted to draw regional councils and social partners into the governance of education and training institutions. The FYL specified a set of jointly managed institutions within which employers and unions were to discuss the problems besetting local labor markets and to devise solutions for them. The FYL not only attempted to effect a substantial increase in the degree of employer investment in the vocational training system, through the *alternance* contracts (apprenticeship and qualification contracts); it attempted to do so through an institutional mechanism that would invigorate social partnership at a regional level, mobilizing the private information necessary for regional councils to design policy that could respond effectively to the problems of local employers and trainees.

In its goal of increasing firm investment in *alternance* training, the reform failed. French employers continue to invest relatively little in the general skills of their young workers. When they use training measures, they use them almost entirely to invest in specific-skills training (Culpepper 2003). While the reasons for this failure are complex, a central obstacle to achieving the goals of the reform was the inability of employers' associations to provide information about future skill demands. Reports of the prime ministerial body charged with evaluation of the project, the Comité de Coordination (1996: 69), repeatedly underlined the "weakness of sophisticated knowledge on the part of sectoral employers' organizations" in limiting the ability of regions to develop appropriate policies to increase human capital investments. Without this knowledge, regional councils had no access to information about the new qualifications that would be demanded, nor how to target the companies most likely to be interested in investing in them. As a result, their policies could not effectively promote firm-level investments in vocational training.

While employers' associations have generally been unsuccessful in developing information about a broad spectrum of company skill needs, large firms themselves have been somewhat more effective. Large employers are able to internalize the cost of collective action in determining their own skill needs. French employers' associations, whose collective capacities are too weak to develop skill predictions that cover large portions of their membership, cannot play this role on their own. Large companies generally dominate the associations, which provide those companies with institutional representation through which they can influence the skill content of vocational certifications. The large firms thus use their influence in expert committees of the Ministry of Education and in employers' associations to develop degree programs that respond closely to their needs (Hancké 2002: 66–7). They are able to do this because both their skills expertise and their material advantages dwarf those of the state bureaucrats and union officials with whom they draft these revisions. In the state system of degree certification development as in the parallel system of social partner-negotiated certifications (CQPs [*contrats de qualification professionel*]), empirical research has demonstrated clearly that large employers were the pre-eminent voice during the 1990s (Charraud 1995; Béret et al. 1997: 17–18).

Where the 1993 reform of the FYL did succeed was in devolving the strategic task of setting priorities for youth professional education to the regional level (Lamanthe and Verdier 1999). However, as we have already seen, the legal institutions that were to enable the regions to assume this authority were incorrectly premised on the ability of labor unions and employers' associations to provide regional officials with information on the skill needs of the economy. There is little the regional councils could do to develop a closer articulation between the educational system and the economy without knowing what skills companies needed in the future. Moreover, the fact that large firms effectively controlled much of the certification process—which is still a national prerogative, both for diplomas and non-state certifications—further removed the regional councils from the core area for which they have the authority (but not the informational capacity) to set priorities. Regional councils lacked the tools to persuade the individual actors in training and education—companies and students—that their coordination generated meaningful signals to which those actors should respond. Priority-setting without effective mechanisms to support those priorities is a weak mandate indeed.

In the domain of vocational education and training, the FYL diluted the capacity of public actors to influence private actors. The architecture of the law was to accord the social partners at regional level greater input into the skill-provision system. This was an attempt by the French government to increase the role of civil society in authoritative decision-making. The collective actors of civil society—in this case, employers' associations and trade unions—were unable to play this role. The weakening of the state opened a greater space for the market, as some regions have tried to make the market the axis of their new policies.[13] Thus, in this policy area, the 1990s have seen a decreasing role for the state, and an increasing role both for firms and for market signals more generally.

The vocational education and training system is part of a national system that provides employers with skills. A particularly French element of this system used to be the production of elites for the state bureaucracy, an important employer in the statist system. During the 1990s, this high end of the training and education system saw an important change in the choices of the highest-achieving French students, who appear to respond increasingly to attractions of the private sector. This is *not* a wider trend among young people in France: a survey of workers aged from 18 to 40 conducted in 2000 showed that 47 percent of respondents would still prefer to work in the public rather than the private sector (Trumbull 2004), and the number of candidates to the ENA has remained stable since 1985.[14]

However, among the students who not only gain admittance to the ENA but who gained a place near the top of their class, there was a marked reduction during the 1990s in the proportion of those whose careers remained rooted in the public sector. A recent study of one of the most striking articulations between the state educational system and the economy—the practice of *pantouflage*, whereby elites circulate from the public to the private sector—shows that the 1990s represented a sea change in the patterns of the topmost elites (Rouban 2002). Luc Rouban has investigated the careers of members of the Inspection générale de finances—arguably the grandest of the *grands corps*—between 1958 and 2000. His results show that, at the very top, the products of state training are increasingly leaving for the private sector, and leaving at an earlier age than in the past. In the heyday of statist French capitalism, *pantouflage* referred to the common practice of these elites' moving into high posts in the private sectors *after* their retirement from the inspection. Their state career led to a second, post-retirement career in the private sector. In the three decades between 1958 and 1989, there were only 7 (pre-retirement) resignations from the corps. By contrast, in the single decade between 1990 and 2000, there were 33 such resignations (out of a corps of less than 200 people).[15] "The fact of having entered the Inspection des Finances is tending to become a simple professional stage, a 'transition (*passage*)' in a career that extends well beyond [it]" (Rouban 2002: 107).

The state continues to be the preeminent actor in French education, but only in its general core. What was most unique about the statist model of education and training and most linked to its model of economic governance was its management of what we might call the lowest (vocational training) and highest (training public elites) rungs of the educational ladder. The domination of the vocational training track by the French education ministry in earlier years had minimized the responsiveness of that system either to skills demanded on the labor market or to the demands of organized employers. As long as employers were able to absorb semi- and unskilled workers into their production processes, the educational bureaucracy was able to maintain its control of the system. With the rising importance of vocational training in France (Béret et al. 1997) has come the recognition by government officials that they cannot effectively manage the development of this system from the center. As a result, it has become more subject to the demands of the market and of the specific demands of large firms.

At the other end of the educational spectrum, as long as the prestige and perquisites of the civil service were able to attract the brightest young elites into bureaucratic careers, the state-controlled system was able to set the criteria of elite recruitment. Although the data are not definitive, the growing attraction of private-sector careers appears to have reduced the capacity of the French statist model to select the best and the brightest. At both ends of the educational system, of course, state financing is still extensive; and in the broad middle—the system of general and university education—the state still reigns supreme. Yet there is nothing unique about governments providing and controlling basic education systems; governments do that in every advanced industrial country. The specificity of the statist model of education and training—controlling curricular development at all levels and ensuring the meritocratic selection of the highest elites to serve the state apparatus—was severely attenuated in the 1990s.

The role of the state and of the European Union in economic change

Each of the three subsystems of the French political economy experienced dramatic change after 1990. In none of these subsystems did government policies determine the outcome of these changes. It is difficult to sustain the claim that France remains a "state-enhanced" economy (Schmidt 2002), or one whose economic difficulties stem from the character of state intervention, rather than its extent (Levy 1999: 292). Both these positions depend on the analytic axiom that the French government still *can* determine the course of adjustment of the political economy. Whether policy-makers stand aside (as they did in watching the transformation of the financial system) or attempt actively to intervene (as they did in negotiations over working time), their intervention will not be decisive in dictating the direction of change, though they may affect its pace.

This is a controversial claim, given the central role of the French case in academic discussions of *étatisme*. The most plausible objection is that this account has omitted important regulatory elements of the political economy: notably, monetary policy and social policy. The French government ceded its monetary policy authority to the European Union during the period under examination. Thus, one objection runs, if French policy-makers do indeed have much less control over the economy than they used to, that partly results from the decision of French governments to cede this power to the European Central Bank, not from decentralized private action. Likewise, in the area of social policy the French state continues to be an important actor.[16] Do the respective roles of the EU and of the government in these policy areas vitiate the claims made above about the death of the distinctive features of statism?

French monetary policy is now made by the European Central Bank in Frankfurt. There is, however, little reason to think that French macroeconomic policy would be dramatically different if it were still made in Paris. More importantly, there is no reason to think that a different monetary policy would itself impinge on any of the aforementioned institutions of the economy. The restrictiveness that characterizes French macroeconomic policy in 2004 is the continuation of a policy that was decided by the socialist government in 1983, following its famous U-turn and adherence to the *franc fort* policy. This policy enabled the government to restrain inflation and to stabilize the price of the franc, but it had a high cost in terms of unemployment (Blanchard and Muet 1993). This unemployment, in turn, led to a massive infusion of public money to the unemployed. Expressed in the terms of the *régulation* school of French economic analysis, "the use of mass unemployment to regulate prices and profits had to be accompanied by a significant rise in social expenditure ... [In this new regime of accumulation] the maintenance of the welfare state coexists with structurally restrictive macroeconomic policies" (Vidal 2002: 373). Successive French governments used the European monetary arrangements as part of their strategy of lowering inflation and stabilizing the franc, and the culmination of this policy was their adoption of the single European currency in 1999.

Both French macroeconomic policy and French social policy have undergone dramatic shifts since the economic U-turn of 1983. Yet those shifts are analytically distinct from the institutions of the political economy discussed in this chapter. When looking at the core institutions of statism circa 1985, it may be seen that none depended primarily on either of these policies. While social policy and macroeconomic policy are both linked to other elements of the political economy—and particularly to the industrial relations system—the evolution of those institutions, which are little directed by policy decisions, should be analytically divorced from those policy choices that governments can make. When French governments tried to use policy to reform institutions fundamentally, as in the episodes of the 35-hour law and the FYL, their policy goals were thwarted by the responses and capacities of private actors. Although macroeconomic and social policy have important implications for the French economy, we should not assume that policy determines the institutions of the political economy. Instead we should examine what has happened empirically in the major areas of the political economy and attempt to establish the causes for observed changes. None of the causal trails examined in this chapter leads to either macroeconomic or social policy.

3. Is there a French variety of capitalism?

In creating the conditions for France to be a competitive economy at the heart of the European Union, French policy-makers have discovered that the widening ambit of markets makes the task of directing economic development exponentially more difficult. As market governance penetrates more aspects of the French economy, many individual actors look to those markets for information about the likely behavior of others. The market is a better source of such information than the state, and individual actors know that. Yet the reach of the free market in France is hobbled by its discursive illegitimacy (Schmidt 2002: 271–87). Thus, there is widespread resistance to accepting the market as the central source of information about mutual expectations. Rather than the emergence of a new French system of coordination for the political economy, the process of change in the 1990s reveals a negotiated *bricolage*: a general move to the firm level combined with a greater role for the market overlaid on an abiding belief that social negotiation, not market regulation, is the heart of the French economy. This *bricolage* is built on the wreckage of failed projects of coherent transformation attempted by governments in the 1980s (Howell 1992; Levy 1999).

France clearly lacks the infrastructure of strong associations of employers and labor to support a CME-style system of non-market coordination. In coordinated market economies, employers' associations and unions pool the power of weaker individual actors with stronger ones to negotiate the course of economic adjustment. Lacking associations with these strengths, the French political economy has seen the strongest individual employers (large firms) and the strongest individuals (public elites and managers) rely increasingly on their individual market power to improve their own relative position. Their inability to act collectively, however, seems likely to remain a defining feature of the French political economy. And it is here that this analysis diverges from that of Bob Hancké, who asserts that large firms in France have become the "central node of political-economic decision-making, a position previously held by the state" (2002: 30). French large firms have indeed opportunistically used their increase in relative power to redistribute costs to their workers, to their suppliers, and to the government, as Hancké argues. Yet these firms lack the collective capacity to convert their individual positions of power into a consistent means of control over the economy: neither associations nor cross-shareholdings were sufficient to the task in 1985, and both those institutions were much weaker by 2005.

Large firms cannot rely on their decentralized market power alone because, for all its openings to the market, France is emphatically not a liberal market economy, at least as of this writing. Companies increased their autonomy over the course of the 1990s, particularly with respect to the influence of state officials. But they did not push for a move toward a market economy. Instead, their objective is an economy based on firm-level negotiation. No major party espouses the movement of France toward free-market liberalism.[17] Even the immodest aim of the MEDEF's *refondation sociale* falls well short of espousing individual-level negotiation. The continued existence of the extension procedure covering more than the 90 percent of the workforce and the robust employment protection that characterize French labor market policy ensure that the market is not the major coordinating mechanism for actors in this economy.

What kind of political economy is France after 2000? It appears on this evidence to be a political economy characterized fundamentally by the uncertainty of expectations of economic actors. This is because there is no organizing principle behind the French economy according to which the principal actors orient their expectations. Employers, whose hand has been most strengthened in the 1990s, are still not free of state control, as the passage of Aubry II reminded them. The government, whose influence has unquestionably weakened in the 1990s, is unable to coerce either employers or even labor unions to follow its lead. In industrial relations, employers and unions have seen their weaknesses highlighted over the course of the decade. Yet any French government ignores the concerns of the unions at its peril, as Alain Juppé learned the hard way in 1995. And organized employers, for all their internal divisions, remained a powerful societal force of opposition against the Jospin government between 1997 and 2002.

It is a truism of economics that markets do not like uncertainty. The varieties of capitalism approach, which puts the firm at the center of its analytical attention, correctly suggests that firms will try to reduce this uncertainty to maximize their efficiency. But politics often creates uncertainty, and the politics of economic change in France has created a system that, at the moment, lacks a coherent way of coordinating expectations among actors. It would be a functionalist fallacy to believe that France will necessarily evolve an optimal set of institutions for coordinating the expectations of economic actors. The varieties of capitalism approach has difficulty classifying the French political economy because that approach looks for a self-reinforcing equilibrium to emerge, based on the interests of companies. The interests of companies have been an important influence on the nature of changes in the 1990s, but so too have the pre-existing political commitments to a regulated labor market and to social negotiation.

The political system—and especially political parties—have been almost absent from the changes of the French political economy in the 1990s. Yet this has nevertheless been a process characterized by continuous negotiation. Firms, both as political actors and as social institutions, have played an expanded role in this process of change. Markets, especially the financial markets, have seen their sway over French business, if not French political discourse, increase. The evidence in this chapter suggests that the shape of the French political economy will be determined by negotiations among social actors, more at the firm level than in parliament. Its evolution will be negotiated and, in the medium term, somewhat incoherent. But incoherence is sometimes the tribute that economics must pay to politics.

Notes

This chapter has been improved thanks to the comments of participants in two workshops of the Changing France project, held at the Center for European Studies at Harvard University in May 2002, and at Sciences Po in Paris in March 2003. In addition, Peter Gourevitch, Peter Hall, Michel Lallement, and Eric Verdier made valuable suggestions. The author thanks Ben Ansell, Jane Gingrich, and Jonathan Laurence for their research assistance.

1 It is for this reason—the microfoundational logic based on problems of coordination—that I adopt the varieties of capitalism framework to analyze France. Other analytical frameworks, such as that of Bruno Amable (2003) or Vivien Schmidt (2002), offer typologies into which France fits somewhat better than it does in the CME/LME distinction of Hall and Soskice. Yet as the rest of this chapter makes clear, the focus on coordination underscores that France also fits uneasily into the "continental European capitalism" of Amable or, a fortiori, the "state-enhanced" capitalism of Schmidt.

2 Even at the high-water mark of state control of the economy, statism was more complex than the features briefly highlighted in this summary. The goal of such a cursory description is to identify the essential features of state coordination as a standard against which to assess the evolution of the French economy since the mid-1980s.

3 The varieties of capitalism framework as elucidated by Hall and Soskice (2001) specifies four main subsystems of the political economy. The fourth subsystem, intercompany relations, refers to the extent and character of technology transfer among firms and the prevalence of relational vs. arms-length contracting.

This subsystem is the most difficult to operationalize and measure in a reliable and comparative way, and so I exclude it from this analysis.

4 As discussed in Lallement's chapter in this volume, French employers' associations and unions have low and declining membership numbers. Given the fact that less than 10 percent of the working population even belongs to a labor union, the state's legal recognition of their "representative" status is an important part of the very legitimacy of the social partners in a way that would be equally foreign to unions in the United States and in Germany.

5 Even its attempt to provide firm-based training through the training tax—which was never widely successful and always concentrated on training already highly-skilled workers—was adopted in 1971 through a coercive state measure rather than voluntary participation by companies.

Some have argued that the system of continuing training in France allows for its workers to catch up on the skills possessed by their German shopfloor counterparts (e.g., Géhin and Méhaut 1993). Econometric results from a study conducted by researchers at the LEST (Laboratoire d'Economie et de la Sociologie du Travail) clearly reject this claim, though, showing that continuing training in France functions essentially as a selection mechanism: in other words, "continuing vocational training would not remedy lacunae in professionalism or increase individual productive capacity, but would do nothing other than demonstrate a skills advantage that is already observed" (Béret et al. 1997: 122–3).

6 It is true that these changes of the French system of finance and corporate governance could not have taken place without the deregulation of French financial markets by the Chirac government in 1987 (Schmidt 1996: 140–1). In this narrow sense, public action was a necessary condition for the changes in cross-shareholding that occurred one decade later. However, the adoption of the legal framework for deregulation explains neither the timing of the breakdown of French cross-shareholding arrangements, nor the fact that similar legal deregulation did not lead to the breakdown of patient capital in Italy and Germany during this time (Culpepper 2005).

7 In their comparative study of labor relations institutions, Traxler and his colleagues observe that wage agreements at higher levels are frequently less relevant than lower-level (e.g., firm-level) agreements in determining wages paid across the advanced industrial countries: "lower levels cover fewer employees but have more influence on actual wages than do higher levels" (Traxler et al. 2001: 112).

8 The Five-Year Law of 1993 also had created the possibility of negotiating work-time reduction as a way to create extra jobs, but that measure was little used by firms until the introduction of the Robien Law.

9 Those firms which reduced their working time by 10 percent (going essentially from 39 to 35 hours) got a 40 percent reduction in social charges for the first year of the accord, then a 30 percent reduction for each of the following six years; those reducing working time by 15 percent received corresponding reductions of 50 percent the first year and 40 percent the following years. For those pacts aimed at job creation ("offensive" as opposed to "defensive" firm agreements), the reduction of charges was tied to new hiring as prescribed by the firm-level agreement (DARES 1999: 10).

10 This problem was not unique to employers. Trade union members similarly complained that they "had not received much practical assistance from their central association" (DRTEFP 1999: 6).

11 In the cases examined by Charpentier et al. (2004: 28), complaints about lower pay are much more likely from blue-collar workers and from women than from white-collar workers and men.

12 A decentralization law passed in August 2004, extended this authority of the regional councils to include vocational training for unemployed adults (David-Aeschlimann 2004).
13 Some regions (such as Picardy) have tried to use the tools of government regulation to make the market of training provision more transparent to individuals and to companies. This sort of intervention can permit better functioning of the market among training centers, of course, but it does not attempt to increase firm investment in skills. It looks, in fact, remarkably like a policy of governments in liberal market economies, making markets as transparent as possible in order to avoid inefficiencies of market functioning.
14 Through its three different entries for examination, the ENA had 1,713 candidates in 1985 and 1,725 candidates in 2003.
15 The Inspection des Finances is very small, recruiting on average only five students per year from the finishing ENA class. Thus, 33 early leavers in a decade means that a number equivalent to 60 percent of the total new recruits left for the private sector. A study conducted for the government in 2003 found that graduates of Polytechnique (X), the other summit of the French *grandes écoles*, had even more departures for the private sector than did those from ENA (Thibault de Silguy 2003: 47a). See also Domart (2004).
16 See the chapter by Bruno Palier in this volume.
17 Alain Madelin, the closest thing to a proponent of free-market liberalism, was eliminated in the first round of the 2002 presidential elections, receiving less than 5 percent of the vote.

2

New Patterns of Industrial Relations and Political Action since the 1980s

Michel Lallement

Introduction: a new institutional rationalization

Industrial relations can be defined as a set of social institutions that link the market, civil society, and public action. Is the French system of industrial relations unique? In international comparisons, researchers tend to stress the role of laws in the making of rules that govern employment and labor relations. Certainly in comparison with the American model, the French state has a very different place in the industrial relations process. Yet the role of the state varies considerably from one sector to another, making it difficult to locate the French case among the categories frequently used in industrial relation theories, such as neo-corporatism or pluralism (Saglio 1990). That is especially true at the present time, since French industrial relations have undergone many fundamental changes over the last two decades.

Recent developments that have increased this sectoral diversity are the focus of what follows. More precisely, this chapter assesses empirically two fundamental issues in French industrial relations: first, the changing relationship between industrial relations, civil society, and the market; and second, the place of the state in reshaping labor relations. In attempting to illuminate these issues, my main hypothesis is that current changes are based on the contractualization of society. Contractualization can be defined as a trend toward consensual negotiation in determining the frames of practices, representations, and interactions that define social life. Following Supiot (2000), I argue that the share of prescribed social ties has been declining in favor of relationships that are negotiated and consensual. This has been manifested in three complementary processes: an obligation for individuals to be genuine and autonomous, the development of procedural rules as tools of social coordination, and, finally, the will to cement social ties according to a contractual solidarity model. As Supiot reminds us, the thesis of contractualization of society is not new. More than a century ago, H. S. Maine, T. Spencer, and L. Bourgeois had already developed the concept of contract to explain social change. In France, however, contractualization has acquired an important new dimension that differs from what we could observe even 30 years ago.[1] After examining how this has occurred, I will conclude with a brief review of the reasons for this change.

In industrial society, and especially during the Fordist era, labor relations were characterized by institutional constraints on social practices. Taylorist management and delegation of workers' collective interests to unions clearly defined both sides of the labor relations system. Initiatives and legitimacy in work organization, such as in collective action, were formalized and placed under the authority of managers on one side and union leaders on the other. The internalization of organizational roles and division of status ensured a relative stability in the industrial order. As the character of the economy and the labor force has changed, however, this model is being replaced by a more fluid and negotiated relationship. Factors such as the rise of the workers' educational level, the emergence of middle-class values, the globalization of the economy, and the development of new services have eroded the formal structures of labor relations. Beyond its traditional role of specifying the rights and responsibilities of workers, the contract has become a tool for managing labor relations. Within the firm, the problem is no longer to specify *ex ante* what workers and employers must do, but rather to set the framework within which negotiations over specific issues will take place (De Munck 2000).

During the 1970s, few French sociologists anticipated the importance of these changes (Reynaud 1973). Although awareness is increasing, no consensus has developed as to the best way to analyze contractualization generally or to understand its consequences for labor relations in particular. Some industrial relations researchers still evoke a crisis of unions; others maintain more generally that institutions are declining, placing greater emphasis in their research on individual actors rather than social systems. From my point of view, institutions in the Durkheimian sense (namely, as a set of rules, formal or not, which puts an external constraint on the individuals) do not disappear, but instead change under constraints of the so-called post-industrial society. Specifically, institutions are becoming more flexible and less centralized. This new institutional rationalization leads to at least three main points I would like to develop.

First, the French state has always played an important role in securing greater autonomy for social actors. This emphasis on the state is inspired by Durkheim's famous 1892 study devoted to the family. In this study, the father of French sociology noted a double movement: on the one hand, a greater intervention by the state in the regulation of family relations; on the other hand, an increasing privatization of family. A similar double movement has characterized the intervention of the state in French labor relations. From the 1980s to the present, labor relations have become more private even as state intervention has increased.[2]

Secondly, the historical pattern of sectoral bargaining between social partners is breaking down, creating a trend toward the consolidation of both fields and actors. The negotiation of procedural rules offers the opportunity to articulate both sector and firm agreements and provide more autonomy at the local level. At the same time, the construction of a "Social Europe" imposes a higher level of regulation. This leads to a second apparent paradox: contractualization of labor relations shifts authority to both higher and lower levels of governance in a joint movement of both "localization" and "globalization." Once again, this trend is not specific to French labor relations. "If one asks, for example, why the Scots want more independence in the UK, or why there is a strong separatist movement in Quebec, the answer is not to be found only in their cultural history. Local nationalisms spring up as a response to globalizing tendencies, as the hold of older nation-states weakens" (Giddens 1999: 13).

Thirdly, even if they can enhance actors' autonomy, contractual relationships may also increase dependency and inequality. This is apparent when observing the way the market is reshaping productive processes and human resources management. In the post-Taylorism era, the demands of work here become more complex and varied. As market pressures increase, employers demand that workers take a greater share of responsibility, that they bring a wider set of competencies and more intensity to their jobs, and that they meet higher qualifications while receiving less job security. The results of bargaining between unions and employers have been subject to similar pressures even though bargaining over social policy remains highly centralized because of the strong presence of unions in jointly managed bodies. But unions are crucially absent at the grassroots level, especially in the small and medium enterprises and in subcontractors' network. In these environments, bargaining is the exception and labor law rarely respected.

Taken together, these trends contain elements that appear inconsistent or even contradictory – privatization and publicization, localization and globalization, autonomy and dependence. The framework of contractualization, however, suggests that all of these trends should be seen as parts of a new institutional rationalization that is reshaping both industrial relations and public action. Contractualization can explain changes in the roles played by various public and private actors and the emergence of new reference frames for negotiations and decisions. To demonstrate this, I will start by describing the major features of the classic industrial relations model that characterized the three post-war decades (section 1). Then, I will point out the changes that, since the 1980s, have upset and reshaped markets (section 2), civil society (section 3), and public action (section 4). In the conclusion (section 5), I will underline the major lessons we can draw from those observations and examine some of the contradictions and possible evolutions they suggest for the field of industrial relations.

1. The industrial relations pattern since 1945

What are the main features of the prevailing labor relations patterns since the Second World War? After 1945, national economic growth and the containment of social conflict were held to be more important than competitiveness and labor market questions. In this context, state action – illustrated particularly by the nationalization of some industrial firms – was shaped by a rhetoric that assimilated national identity, technical progress and trade-union influence. In other words, industrial relations influenced the broader contexts of class and market in the three decades after the war by articulating the will to modernize and the principle of industrial democracy. To use the vocabulary of French regulation economists (Boyer and Mistral 1981), modernization and industrial democracy formed parts of the virtuous circle linking production and mass consumption. The industrial relations system supported a tacit social compromise: on the one hand, employers rationalized work organization in order to achieve higher productivity and, on the other, trade unions gave priority to the fight for higher wages, maximizing their share of the wealth generated by productivity growth.

In the legal realm, the French system of industrial relations has been governed largely by the 1950 law on collective bargaining agreements.[3] This legal framework, however, was only one expression of the social dynamic that linked industrial relations with other social sub-systems. The legal structure was given meaning by three more fundamental aspects of French society. First, during the post-war period, industrial disputes were defined in terms of broader social conflicts. Experienced and represented as manifestations of class conflicts, industrial disputes became mass collective actions orchestrated by trade unions. The power of industrial relations to shape class conflict differed across social and economic sectors. Running the risk of being too schematic, one can distinguish sectors characterized by a strong professional standing (in a power position to negotiate agreements generating differential advantages) from those tied to the secondary labor market, where capacities of mobilization were limited (Jobert and Muller 1987). In part, this segmentation corresponded to the distinction between the private and public sectors. In the latter, the rules of the game were different, since the state acted as both employer and external referee. After 1946, civil servants could not negotiate their terms of employment. Formally, this meant that public-sector unions could not participate in collective bargaining, and that in some segments (such as the military) unions could be entirely forbidden in the name of the public interest. This formal restriction did not mean that public-sector unions had no power. On the contrary, they belonged to "joint commissions" (*commissions paritaires*) that managed career paths and regulated employment. In the labor market divided into distinct social groups, unions also contribute to the defense of professional interests. That is why, even today, the public sector in France is considered a spearhead of social contestation.

A second feature of industrial relations during this period arose from French history. At the end of the nineteenth century, France had recognized the potential of "consultative administration" and created several "superior councils" in policy areas such as work, agriculture, industry, and commerce. These councils formalized the representation of interest groups in specific areas of policy-making. After 1945, this consultative model was expanded to a variety of policy domains (Duclos and Mériaux 1998). Adopting the principle of "management by interested parties," the State granted union, employer, and mutualist representatives important prerogatives in the management of social policy, including seats on the managing boards of the various social security funds (pensions, family allowances, health) at national and local levels. These so-called joint management institutions moved further away from state control with the collective agreements to manage complementary pension schemes for management staff (1947) and for all wage-earners (1961). The expansion of this model to include the social partners in managing unemployment insurance in 1958 was a state initiative. Since 1970, joint management has also been used to implement a continuing vocational training system. In this system, the social partners are entitled to manage the insurance training funds built up by compulsory contributions from firms (Mériaux 1999). In a word, joint management (*paritarisme*) may be analyzed as an important piece of corporatism embedded in the generally pluralist pattern of the French industrial relations system.

A third important feature of the post-war French model involved the management of wages and employment at the firm level. Facing a relatively stable economic environment, large industrial firms relied on internal labor markets to allocate and retain labor. Employers perceived their own interest in stabilizing access to skilled manpower to minimize training and lay-off costs. In exchange for commitment to the tasks set by managers, employers guaranteed employment stability and – importantly – career advancement. In large firms that adopted this strategy, wages did not reflect shifts of supply and demand in various labor markets, but were the result of equivalence agreements that set out formal salary scales (initially of Parodi type)[4] codifying an agreed-upon pattern of career advancement. These scales and the process of collective bargaining that created them made industrial relations a more influence aspect of labor-market regulation. It should be noted that the scales set up by these agreements did not eliminate employers' flexibility: the introduction of new, more flexible salary scales called *à critères classants* at the beginning of the 1970s and the use of small subcontracting firms not subject to negotiated wage scales and therefore able to absorb economic shocks were two significant levers that guaranteed firms some level of flexibility and adjustment capacity.

2. The return of the market

Since the 1980s, the most important development in the field of labor and employment has been the trend toward greater flexibility. Though the term "flexibility" can signify many things (Boyer 1986), it should be understood here as meaning that labor and employment patterns must adapt more quickly and effectively to meet the requirements of an evolving market. This trend explains why firms have gained more autonomy and changed their human resource management strategies at the local level, reshaping collective bargaining into a multilevel system.

When markets reshape human resource management

The market is coming back into French firms, forcing emoployees to react more quickly to satisfy increasingly demanding customers. Over the past two decades, industrial growth rates have increased while the service sector has reduced the time required to respond to customer demands. For white-collar workers, pressure to increase speed and efficiency have been greater than for blue-collar workers, but the trend for both is similar. In 1998, 33 percent of managers declared that the normal limit to satisfy a customer's request was between one hour and one day, compared to 23 percent in 1991 (Bué and Rougerie 1999). At the same time, the number and complexity of the tasks facing employees in some industries (e.g. auto sales, retail sales, health care, and transportation) has also increased. Work intensification has thus been the first noticeable manifestation of market pressure. In the face of increased competition in both quality and reaction times, work organization has been contaminated by urgency. The market has entered firms through "just-in-time" practice, such as eliminating inventories of raw material and manufactured components, many hierarchical levels, and superfluous unskilled labor. As economic relations have become more contractualized both within and between firms (e.g., through the creation and development of "profit centers" and the increased use of sub- and co-contracting), the market has infiltrated all levels of firm operation (*Sociologie du travail* 1996).

As the Aubry laws (1998, 2000) have reduced working time for firms with more than 20 employees, work intensity has increased. This has manifested itself both in higher labor productivity and in more flexible use of labor. "Irregular" work schedules have become more widespread, with more employees starting their working day earlier or finishing it later. Varying the number of working days from one week to another and expanding work schedules to include Saturdays and Sundays have all become more common (Lallement 2003). These shifts in how working time is allocated combined with greater work intensity have changed the world of work in France. Discussions of stress and suffering or harassment in the workplace have replaced the debates on boredom that were common in the 1960s and 1970s. The growing discomfort of many wages-earners has resulted from the strain imposed by competitive pressure and the organization of employees into increasingly interdependent work-teams. Sociological inquiries have also noted less social differentiation and protection among some categories of wage-earners: between blue and white collar, between non-manager and manager (the so-called *cadres*) (Bouffartigue 2001), and between workers with long-term contracts and those with short-term contracts.

The intrusion of market values has also produced greater individualization of wages as competition comes to dominate human resource management. In the Fordist model, two fundamental principles structured wage policies. The first one was the rigidity of nominal and real wages. Under this system, every job was linked to a coefficient included in salary scales that had been negotiated by unions and employers at the sectoral level. This resulted in wages patterns that were not dependent on economic fluctuations. Second, wage levels were set with reference to a given standard of living and anticipated productivity. Since the 1980s, those two principles have gradually eroded. The range of wages has increased as firms have added different bonuses to a basic wage. Those bonuses depend particularly on performance measurements of various kinds such as productivity per employee, assiduousness at work, or the profitability of the firm (Reynaud 1992). For employers, the advantage is obvious: one part of the wage is reversible, making it easier to defer to employees some risks associated with the economic situation. Though this trend toward greater wage dispersion has been spread and innovations like profit-sharing bonuses, stock-options, and wage saving have become more common, wages have not been drastically affected. At the end of the 1990s, individual bonuses represented about 15 percent of the wages of senior manager, 6.5 percent for lower-level manager, and 2 percent for blue-collar workers.

Tradtional salary scales have also been challenged by wages based on a "competency principle." Under the pressure of ever more differentiated and unforeseeable demand, some firms have tried to depart from sectoral wage agreements that give each employee a minimum wage guarantee linked to criteria such as degrees, seniority, or special features of the job. Instead, these firms would like to set wages according to each employee's individual competency. The risks of such a practice (which is still not widespread) are already well known: extremely personalized assessment and salaries, greater management control over each employee, scattered labor communities, and a loss of union control over sectoral wages. Although widely promoted by employers' organizations, this competency-based wage model is more than just an offensive by employers to weaken labor solidarity and improve their bargaining position; it contains the seeds of a new social contract. The effect of such a contract may be a more effective mobilization of labor as wage incentives produce loyalty and commitment to their employer. In exchange, employees might benefit from greater autonomy in the workplace as well as resource guarantees (vocational training programs in particular) that could improve their ability to manage their professional career. Reality remains far from this theoretical promise, however: the first empirical evaluations show that few firms have adopted the whole "competency" principle for their employees and, when they do, there is evidence that arbitrary assessment of individual competence is risky (Colin and Grasser 2003; Segrestin 2004).

Results have been similar in the public sector. The so-called "modernization" of the early 1990s was based on principles shared with the private sector: lean organization, project-oriented structure, contractual relationships between parts of the administration, and fewer levels of management. With increasing emphasis on bringing government closer to the people it serves, new kinds of relationships have been formed between administrative organizations and their publics. These new relationships involved paying greater attention to individual cases and ending the strict division of labor that had prevented public employees from handling problems outside of their strict area of responsibility. The reference to market efficiency has now become so habitual that the word "consumer" has replaced that of "public services' user" (*usager*) in administrative terminology. But difficulties and ambiguities remain. For instance, in many public organizations, performance is still measured with quantitative indicators: number of users' files dealt with, number of phone calls taken, or number of pre-stamped envelopes sealed. The dissonance between the rhetoric and practice of modernization has brought work-related stress to public administration as well.

Lastly, flexibility has created new patterns of employment. The main pillars of the so-called "regular jobs" – full-time status, long-term contracts in employment, subordination to a single employer – have been eroded. Employees, especially young people first entering the labor force, can no longer expect these conditions of employment. In recent years, the fraction of the work force employed in part-time or temporary jobs has increased even in periods of economic recovery. Between 1990 and 2000, people employed with a short-term contract grew by 60 percent, those who benefited from a training period or special contracts with public financing, by 65 percent, and temporary workers by 130 percent. During the same period, employment in "regular" jobs increased by only 2 percent. The victims of this kind of flexibility are mainly found among youth, women, and groups with lower skill populations.

Between local and global bargaining

Changes in patterns of collective bargaining also reveal a more prevalent market logic. The ability of individual firms to modify rules has been given a higher priority. In other words, the firm has become a more important unit for social regulation (Supiot 1989). To understand the significance of this, it should be recalled that the French industrial relations system operates at several negotiating levels. The articulation between those levels depends on a preferential principle (*principe de l'ordre public social*). This means that, de jure, collective agreements negotiated by trade unions' and employers' organizations must improve wage earners' conditions. It also means that, de facto, standards set at the sectoral level are used as a reference to determine the threshold below which negotiators at the firm level cannot strike deals less favorable to workers (e.g., a lower wage).

For many years it has been possible to exempt individual firms from standards set in collective bargaining. These exceptions, which required prior authorization at the sectoral level, were first authorized in the early 1980s to give firms additional flexibility, especially in the area of working time. The inter-professional agreement reached in October 1995 made these firm-level exceptions the rule rather than the exception by declaring that rules negotiated at the sectoral level would be applied only to the firms where local negotiations failed (Tissandier 1997).[5] To understand the revolutionary character of this change, we have to remember that the primacy of collective agreements had not been disputed since the legal establishment of the post-war labor relations system in 1950 (see note 3 above). According to the terms of this law, "in any plant included in the application field of a collective agreement, the provisions of this agreement are essential on individual labor contracts" (Article 31, book I of the Labor Code). By shifting the presumptive level of collective bargaining from the sector to the firm, the 1995 agreement marked a true turning point in labor regulation.

The shift from sectoral to firm level is visible in the continuous growth of firm agreements throughout the 1990s (Figure 2.1). According to the Ministry for Employment and Solidarity, 4,840 local agreements were signed in 1993 compared with almost 35,000 in 2001. Even though these data are not entirely reliable, the increasing importance of local regulations is obvious in fields such as wages and vocational training (Lanfranchi and Sandoval 1990; Lamanthe and Verdier 1999; Tallard 2004). Since the 1980s, negotiations on working hours have been decentralized, giving firms the

Figure 2.1 Collective bargaining at the firm level

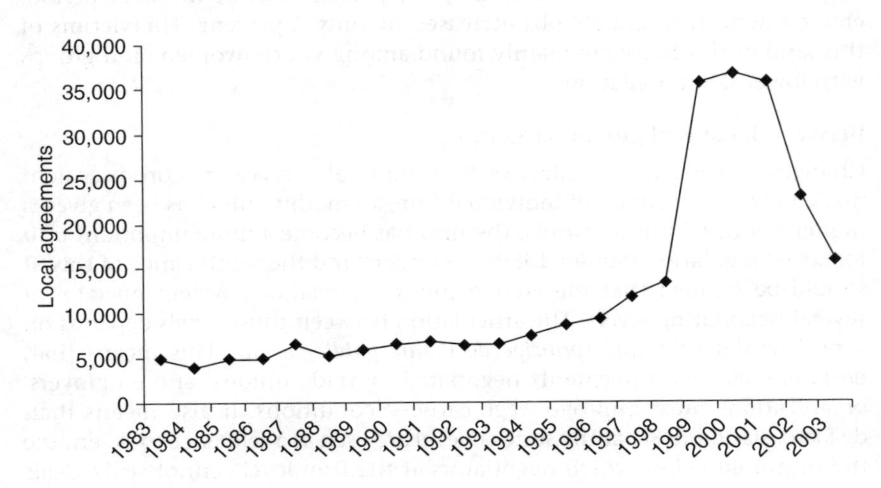

Source: Ministry of Employment.

opportunity to negotiate exceptions to the law (Morin et al. 1998; O'Reilly et al. 2000; Lallement 2003). The strong official pressure of the Aubry Acts has given an additional impetus to firm-level negotiations. In July 2001, the Ministry for Employment and Solidarity estimated that out of the 63,000 firms that have implemented the 35-hour work week, two-thirds (64.5%) did it through local agreements. It is clear that this trend has corresponded to a weakening of the tradition of sector-level regulation. Among firms that negotiated individual agreements, only a minority reproduced the sectoral bargain. In at least half of these cases, the firm's implementation of the Aubry Acts involved an agreement not only to reduce work hours but also to make hours more flexible in ways that reflected the firm's specific needs.

Despite the trend toward decentralization, the proportion of employees covered by firm-level collective agreements is generally lower than that of the sectoral contracts. This asymmentry is a product of the French Labor Ministry's "extension procedures"[6] system. This legal procedure for extending the coverage of sectoral agreements combined with the nearly 700 national or subnational levels of collective bargaining to produce a 90 percent coverage rate for sectoral agreements. Lacking such a mechanism for firm-level agreements, rates of collective bargaining coverage at that level remain much lower.[7] Despite their importance, these changes suggest neither the end of state involvement nor the breakdown of regulation at the sectoral level (Jobert 2003). It would be a mistake to think that contract has definitely replaced law in wage bargaining. Law remains an important point of reference but, with the development of procedural rules, the question has become how best to articulate standards at the national, sectoral, and local levels.

In addition to this decentralizing trend in bargaining and standard-setting, it is important to consider the influence of international factors. Globalization is an important element of the changes in Europe, especially given the construction of a "social Europe" through EU regulation. The degree of organization between European social partners (when they exist) is still very weak. The reasons for this are well known:

> As to unionization, the inhibiting effects of wide differences in national economic conditions and interests are reinforced by the absence of facilitating state capacity at the European level, which in turn reinforces the primacy of national forms of organization. Unions also lack strong interlocutors at the European level, as employers can best pursue their interests in international liberalization by holding back on supra-national organization and negotiation. (Streeck 1998: 434)

European industrial relations are also extremely complex, with levels of negotiation and intervention varying cross-nationally.

In the face of the diversity, both the means of control and the substance of a social Europe have had to evolve. European industrial relations strategy, attempting to reconcile collective goals for employment policy with various national and sectoral patterns of collective bargaining, has relied on a form of coordination based on *soft law* (Dehousse 2004; Goetschy 1999). A loose form of coordination is achieved through the adoption of procedural norms that establish a framework for local negotiations. These procedural standards deal with bargaining practices, the negotiation of different subjects, and limits not to be exceeded by the social partners. As in many other European countries, these norms are replacing the traditional logic of French industrial relations law, which placed emphasis on directives and contractual politics (Treaty of Amsterdam 1997). Despite their potential, it is not clear whether these negotiated norms have been applied effectively: "Empirical studies demonstrate a wide range between member states; rates at the interprofessional level are (at about 60%) comparatively low in countries like the Netherlands, Portugal and Spain ... Last but not least, it has to be mentioned that framework agreements may not necessarily include all member states, but only those directly affected" (Keller and Sörries 1999: 342). A similar problem has been encountered by the European Work Councils. Despite centralized communication and information procedures, the existence of these councils does not guarantee the application of homogeneous norms among members, nor does it guarantee that these institutions will respect the principles of European bargaining. In short, the globalization of industrial relations remains largely unachieved.

3. Civil society's changes

As the market reshapes labor relations within and between firms, have industrial relations actors changed their strategy? I will look at three points to address this question: first, the institutionalization of traditional social actors; secondly, the emergence of debates as to the legitimacy of these same actors; and, third, the offensive mounted by employers attempting to contractualize industrial relations.

Temptations of institutionalization

Though the topic is already old, most contemporary researchers still refer to the institutionalization of unions in France (Adam 1983; Andolfatto and Labbé 2000; Labbé 1996; Rosanvallon 1988). Work in this area tends to refer to the law adopted in 1911 by Michels. In the scientific literature, this institutionalization is described as a double process consisting of internal bureaucratization and external integration. The former suggests Labbé's expression that unions have become "clay-footed idols" characterized by bureaucratization and a decreasing membership. Internal bureaucratization can also explain the vicious circle highlighted by Tixier (1992): as militants diminish in number, they tend to accumulate responsibilities[8] and withdraw from grassroots level activities. This has led to a decline in union proselytizing and to a growing disparity between union strategies and employees' wishes.

The diverging priorities of unions and workers were clear in the results of *Reponse*, a survey conducted at the beginning and again at the end of the 1990s by the Ministry for Employment and Solidarity. In this survey, unionized and non-unionized employees viewed the most significant purpose of wage councils very differently. For example, at the beginning of the 1990s, unionized secretaries listed economic (27%) and employment (26%) concerns ahead of "social and cultural activities" (organization of pleasure trips, management of a library within the firm, organization of Christmas parties for workers' families) (19%) as their highest priorities. For the non-union secretaries, the same concerns were prioritized in the opposite order: 17 percent for economic concerns, 18 percent for employment concerns, and 27 percent for social and cultural activities. "Social and cultural activities" were listed as a priority by more than one-third of non-unionized respondents, while "working conditions" were listed as a priority by only 10 percent.

In contrast, integration means that unions have become more closely linked with other institutions. Outside the firms, unions are present in "prud'hommes" councils[9] as well as in equitable relief and various other committees. They have also taken on responsibilities for the management of different social welfare organizations such as mutual insurance companies, offices of social security and health, and other retirement and insurance organizations. Integration into this vast field of co-management bodies has provided an important means for French unions and (to lesser extent) employers' associations to maintain political influence beyond the strength of their membership and finances. Despite differences in their organizational form (administration councils, technical committees, consultative commissions, etc.) and their degree of autonomy from the state, it is clear that unions have become integrated into institutions that have a mission of representing general interests or that implement a national public service. Within this institutional framework, the representatives of particular interests administer programs that serve a broader constituency than their own membership. This forces the "social partners" to interpret and manage short-term demands arising from their rank and file in a manner consistent with broader and longer-term interests.

Union financing provides another measure of institutionalization. According to Labbé (2000), the share of total contributions that unions transfer to their confederation represents about 30 percent of the income of the Confédération Générale du Travail (CGT) and 37 percent in the case of the Confédération Générale des Cadres (CGC). For the other organizations, this rate is about one-third. If one adds subscriptions to the union press, advertisement in that press and sales of diaries and calendars to the total income, this covers less than 40 percent of the ordinary budget. The balance of union income consists of direct or indirect subsidies: allowances of the members of the Economic and Social Council, subsidies for training, research and study contracts, union checks, etc. In addition, unions still benefit from material subsidies such as personnel on secondment (e.g., permanent or technical advisers). Currently, according to Labbé, French unions benefit from some 40,000 full-time jobs arising from part-time or full-time relief from regular work duty, to the benefit of union members in administration, social security and health organizations, and big national firms.

Similar temptations of institutionalization have affected employers (Bunel 1995). Positions in the joint committees on social security or in Unedic (an organization that manages unemployment insurance) are considered important for many employers. For the heads of small companies, positions like these provide a social standing that few of them would readily surrender. In addition to social standing, there are material reasons for employers to embrace institutionalization. The various joint committees within the co-management frame administer more money than the entire budget of the French state. This is a funding source from which both employers' organizations and unions profit. Vocational training provides significant resources:

> The sums collected in the construction sector, for example, flow through a variety of employers' organizations, the usefulness of which is arguable but which collect a tax on the funds in transit. In the same way, one observes significant expenses for studies or communication, which these training organizations entrust to "friendly" survey firms, or purchases of building in which other employers' associational organizations [not dealing with training] are located. (Adam 2000: 159)

Despite official attempts since the middle of the 1990s to increase the transparency of how these funds are managed (in particular the employers' management of vocational training funds), employers' groups remain integrated in a complex and opaque institutional system from which they have little interest in being detached.

Legitimacy in debate

What are the consequences of the institutionalization we have just described? Excluding the social movement of December 1995 (*Sociologie du travail* 1997), industrial disputes have been declining since the middle of the 1970s (Figure 2.2).[10] Statistical measurement remains imperfect, but the trend is unambiguous. Moreover, these disputes have been taking new forms that reveal a trend toward contractualization. Conflicts have become more local and often feature direct discussions between employers and employees. Joint demonstrations that mobilize all the confederations occur

Figure 2.2 Strikes in France

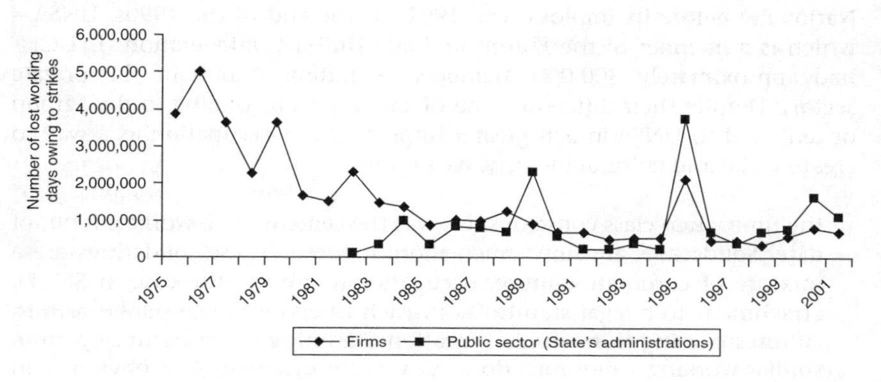

Source: Ministry of Employment.

less frequently. Industrial disputes also draw in other social actors such as consumers, unemployed people, the state, and European institutions. In many of these disputes work is no longer the central object of conflict. Industrial disputes have became a forum for conflicts over civic rights in diverse areas such as urban problems, sexual minorities or parity between men and women (Groux 1998).

One must also consider the low number of union members today.[11] The decline in membership in the largest union confederations has reduced the ability of new actors (unions and associations) to play a greater role in social disputes. These new actors, whose central goal is to help workers to benefit from more negotiated and democratic relationships with unions, are important because they illustrate the sort of issues engendered by "contractualization." SUD has been a leader in articulating these new demands. SUD-PTT (Fédération Solidaires Unitaires Démocratiques – Poste, Téléphone et Télécommunication) was born in 1989 from the dissent within the post office federation of the Confédération Française Démocratique du Travail (CFDT). It quickly gave rise to other alternative unions and became one of the major forces of the so-called "group of ten," which was founded in 1981 as a federation of autonomous unions. The "group of ten," which now comprises more than 20 unions with some 60,000 members, focuses on the same issues promoted by the CFDT during the 1970s: self-management, anti-capitalism, and feminism. Unlike the establishment unions, they explicitly address the issues of unemployment and exclusion. In an attempt to bring alternative unions into the fold, the "group of ten" meeting took place near the meeting of the UNSA (Union Nationale des Syndicats Autonomes). Their most recent gathering brought together some 15 autonomous unions in areas such as transport, national education, civil service, and agriculture. Reformist in nature, UNSA was created in 1993 under the impulse of the so-called FEN maintenue, a part of the FEN (Fédération de l'Education Nationale) before its implosion in 1992. At the end of the 1990s, UNSA – which is a member of the European Trade Union Confederation (ETUC) – had approximately 300,000 members (including 30,000 in the private sector). Despite their differences, all of the unions belonging to the "group of ten" and to UNSA attach greater importance to occupation as a way to create social and cultural identity. As a result,

> the time when class consciousness was the cement of all workers is out of date. Solidarities are now much more reduced. These solidarities are a mixture of corporate culture, occupational culture (the case of SNCF), attachment to a legal statute (as in each category in the public sector), cultures coming from similar vocational training or, more simply, from similar working conditions (lorry drivers for instance). It is obviously in the public sector that those conditions are generally met, as the components of UNSA and the Group of the Ten attest. (Adam 1997: 27)

The changes in the world of French unions found their first expression with the rise of what are known as the "coordinations" in 1980s. The "coordinations" gathered students, teachers, nurses, and railwaymen in non-unionized organizations devoted to promoting their occupational interest. They primarily mobilized people in the wage-earning middle classes and occupational groups, and they were ready to claim new advantages on the basis of restricted collective identity (Hassenteufel 1991). These alternative organizations chose to organize on democratic principles of collective action management. This explosion of "coordinations" may be explained by the increasing gap between practices and social recognition, revealing the limits imposed by institutionalization of traditional unions. The frustration caused by this gap is clear in the case of nurses, whose competencies are increasing and diversified. For example, they began to perform more technical operations and manage more patients and para-medical manpower, but without these skills being recognized by qualifications or wages. In response, new social movements with more general goals have been created. In particular, they lead the fight against unemployment, liberal free-market ideology, globalization, and housing shortages and discrimination. Examples of these include ATTAC (Association pour une Taxation des Transactions financières pour l'Aide aux Citoyens), AC! (Agir contre le chômage), DAL (Droit au logement), Aarrg! (Apprentis Agitateurs pour un Réseau de Résistance Globale). Even though they are active social movements, they are represented by only a small minority of militants. One of the smallest, Aaarg!, hardly numbered 150 members in 2001.

Although these new actors' strategies are sometimes ambiguous, they reflect the tension in the current French industrial relations system. An emblematic organization like SUD-PTT is characterized by heterogeneous aims and methods. It uses a corporatist strategy similar to the traditional confederations and legal expertise to benefit wage-earners in a very closed labor market. At the same time, the organization also comes to the defense of the unemployed and employees on short-term contracts, and advocates values such as solidarity or direct democracy (Denis 2003). This diversity of organizational forms and strategies indicates that the contractualization of social life has undermined the legitimacy of the five great union confederations, which is at least formally enshrined in their official monopoly on the representation of employees' interests.[12]

Although less well researched, similar changes have taken place among employers' associations. The 1990s were marked by conflicts within the MEDEF (Mouvement des entreprises de France), the dominant employers' confederation. These tensions illustrate the depth of structural divisions among employers. The most obvious divide is between the interests and values of "grassroots employers" who manage small firms in the provinces and employers belonging to the socio-economic elite. While the former tend to be suspicious of economic globalization, the latter tend to be made up of graduates of the most famous schools[13] who are more mobile, work for large companies, and are trained to manage the tensions between shareholder demands and the requirements of long-term economic strategy. This is one aspect of a crisis among French employers' organizations nearly as severe as that suffered by the unions. The principal symptoms are a weakening of commitment among activists, a decline in voting participation, and the growing defection of small and medium-sized firms.

Another illustration of the same movement of "de-legitimacy" (as well as contractualization) is the tendency to resort to the courts regarding conflicts. The volume of industrial disputes dealt with by the 271 "prud'hommes" councils went from 188,000 in 1984 to 213,500 in 1998. This increase is only one dimension of a more general movement to make greater use of the court that

> calls into question the French legal principle through which a function of the court is to apply the letter of the law. The profusion of specialized arbitration boards, some of which are entrusted to non-specialists (commercial courts and "Prud'hommes" councils), entails a variability of jurisprudence. Judges who are not magistrates tend to rule equitably, as friendly mediators, rather than in accordance with law or jurisprudence. (Dirn 1998: 390–1)

The fact that militants and unions have embraced this trend is a telling symptom of the "deinstitutionalization" of the industrial relations system: employees identify less with the organizations that represent their interests, so they appeal more often to the courts if disputes occur with employers.[14]

New social foundations

A few years ago the MEDEF launched different propositions for reforming labor relations in order to address these issues. What were the MEDEF's objectives when it invited workers' unions to discuss a new "social constitution" – subsequently called a "New Social Foundation" at the requested of union leaders – in November 1999 (Lallement and Mériaux 2003)? The largest French employers' association criticized the "present confusion between issues concerning social partners and those concerning the State in the areas of social protection and work relations."[15] It is indeed, the MEDEF added, "the increasing, destabilizing and unceasing State intervention that threatens the very existence of an autonomous 'social sphere' " (ibid.). The MEDEF thus employed a double-edged rhetoric. On the one hand, it refers to an "autonomous social sphere" within which social partners, through "a social dialogue and freely negotiated agreements," would define rules relating to labor relations and to social protection. On the other hand, it argues for a sphere that would fall under the state's sole jurisdiction.

The first issue debated in the New Social Foundation battle was unemployment insurance. On 14 June 2000, the first agreement arising from the New Social Foundation was signed by the CFDT and the Confédération Française des Travailleurs Chrétiens (CFTC). This agreement accepted the progressive lowering of allocations paid to the unemployed (the longer the period of unemployment, the greater the reduction in payments) and implemented a back-to-work assistance plan (PARE: Plan d'Aide au Retour à l'Emploi) that guaranteed beneficiaries more personalized follow up. Ratified by small unions, this agreement cleared up an important controversy with the government, which then forced signatory parties to revise the content of the agreement several times. The government finally accepted the agreement on 6 December 2000. The second issue involved health in the workplace, on which an agreement was signed with CGC, CFTC, and CFDT. MEDEF gave up its project of transferring industrial health care to the private sector. It also ceded to unions a greater role in watchdog organizations such as the INRS (the National Institute for Research and Security). The third issue dealt with complementary retirement plans. Started in December 2000, discussions on this theme have been conflictual. For MEDEF, the issue has been how to balance the increasing number of retirements without increasing contributions. This is why it suggested an increase in the length of time of contributions, raising the question of retirement at age 60.

Industrial vocational training was the fourth subject to be negotiated in the forum. The problems associated with this issue were the improvement of the quality–cost ratio of industrial vocational training and ways to reduce the inequalities associated with its provision. MEDEF hoped employees would undergo training outside working hours. The fifth issue was collective bargaining. This was at the heart of the "New Social Foundation" approach.

MEDEF presented a text on 18 December 2000 that aimed to revise the founding principles of the French industrial relations system, especially those dealing with the connection between law and contract. In this context, the issue of unions' financing was also raised. A common text was signed by employers and unions (except for the CGT) on 16 July 2001 stating that only collective agreements signed by organizations representing the majority of workers would be considered valid.[16] This text partially inspired the Fillon Act of 2004, which introduced the "majority principle" for the conclusion of collective agreements (see below). The sixth issue was health insurance, with MEDEF presenting a proposal to reform the social security and health system. This proposal aimed at opening health insurance management to private competition and unifying the different pension plans. It would also replace the present scheme with a point-based system based on the length of time of contributions. Other issues, about which discussions have been delayed or for which negotiations have not started, include family allowances, management's role within firms, and industrial equality.

The battle for a New Social Foundation is centered on the defense of contractual policies. But why is contractual policy so important? For MEDEF, embedding contractual autonomy in a renewal of industrial bargaining institutions has a direct and clear goal: to "optimize social expenses as they represent an exorbitant amount in France." But this optimization (i.e. the decrease of contributions in social security funds) must facilitate the restructuring of social protection along the lines of a "new risk government," the objective of which "would be less to transfer to the State the risks citizens must take than it is to allow them to rest on institutions that do not take away their responsibility" (Ewald and Kessler 2000: 71). As far as industrial relations are concerned, MEDEF proposed to "reverse the pyramid by transforming firms, and even plants, as the base of the system and to give the law its role of defining principles."[17] Subsidiarity would take up the role previously held by the law, and law would become supplementary to contracts. Contractual autonomy thus aims at reversing the hierarchy of norms, in which the law is at the top – symbolically at least – and where collective agreements at the sectoral level establish the obligations incumbent on the parties to an employment contract (Lallement and Mériaux 2003).

In 2003, the project of a New Social Foundation was far from being as advanced as MEDEF would have wished. Despite the threats made by its leaders, it would not be easy for MEDEF to withdraw from the different social institutions they co-manage with the main trade unions. Dropping these responsibilities would strip MEDEF of legitimacy, making it into a mere mouthpiece of (large) firms' interests. It is true that MEDEF disengaged itself from the health insurance and family benefits fund in 2001, but, immediately after having announced that decision, MEDEF's leader explained to the

Prime Minister what conditions had to be fulfilled so that its organization would resume its responsibilities. In other words, MEDEF's disengagement signified less a refusal on fundamentals than a pure bargaining tactic.[18] But the most ironic part of this story is that firms did not wait the New Social Foundation to change their management of human resources and to bypass unions.

> Even if practices are far from following declarations, one observes that a growing number of firms are taking into account the wage-earner's social problems. They do it at a local level, by taking into account real-life issues, unlike unions whose time is devoted to manage the social funds so that they have no influence either on the political sphere or on the social movement. (Touraine 1990: 375)

This claim has been validated by research undertaken within the *Parole* program, linking the National Center for Scientific Research (CNRS) and CFDT (Pinaud et al. 1999). This program emphasized the importance of the strong ideological and normative dimension in the participative action experiments. But, contrary to some preconceived ideas, this research also showed that employees want to be more involved in the firm's life. As Bunel and Thuderoz note,

> employees' answers show us that they believe that it is possible to be heard and satisfied via direct expression, without mediation, without resorting to collective action and without a balance in power. This direct expression, whatever its institutional forms or its privileged fields of intervention may be, generates a number of new situations where the traditional social relations (with its hierarchical leader, with the union delegate, with the engineer, etc.) are rearranged. This leads ... to the production of new requirements for employees ... However unions are always considered useful since negotiation with the direction is considered as a privileged way to make any claim progress. (Bunel and Thuderoz 1999: 124–5)

In short, the importance of unions is not contested by the employees. On the contrary, employees say that, more than ever, they need unions that can act at the local level to negotiate their claims and solve problems.

4. The state's new interventions

As previously noted, French industrial relations are decentralizing, becoming more flexible, and increasing benefits to employers, all of which can be seen as examples of contractualization. While it may seem as though this trend represents a form of "privatization" in labor relations, I will argue that the state continues to play an important role.

State and employment: a "problematic" solidarity?

Though it has taken unconventional forms, public action in the field of employment policy has increased in importance in the two last decades. During this period, policy was driven by two goals. First, the French state focused on creating jobs for youth and the long-term unemployed. The second and more innovative goal was to reduce the cost of unskilled labor through a variety of schemes organized by the RMI (Revenu Minimum d'Insertion). When created in 1988, the RMI was a benefit program that helped the unemployed reintegrate into the labor market and mitigated the consequences of financial insecurity for deprived households. Since the beginning of the 1990s, the RMI has expanded to include programs that promote part-time work, provide direct financial incentives for firms that hire the long-term unemployed, create special contracts to promote the hiring of young people, and subsidize lower-cost labor through the RMA subsidy program.[19]

All of this has taken place against a background of increased state regulation of the labor market. In the medium term, this increasing state role can be measured through expenditures such as compensation for unemployment and anticipated early retirements, assistance in job creation, and financing public services engaged in employment (Figure 2.3). In 1973, France spent 10 billion francs for employment (0.9% of its GDP). In 1995, this figure reached 300 billion (4% of GDP). A similar trend can be seen in the numbers of people participating in state employment programs. Between 1973 and 1996, approximately 30 million cases were listed by the Ministry for Employment as beneficiaries of at least one employment promotion program. If one counts the annual average volume of people

Figure 2.3 Public expenditure for employment and reduction of social contributions

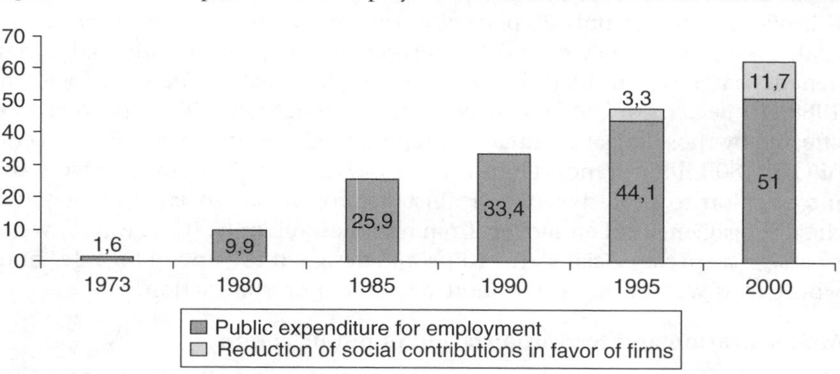

Source: Ministry of Employment.

concerned, then the figure increases almost thirtyfold, going from 100,000 in 1973 (except apprenticeship contracts) to 2.8 million in 1996. Since then the number has stabilized and even slightly decreased. At the beginning of 2001, there were 2.6 million people participating in these schemes. Significantly, more than half of them were involved in programs to promote hiring by decreasing wage costs.

This growing policy of state subsidization of employment is important because it is undermining the foundations of the social protection system built after the Second World War. This form of state intervention takes place in a period in which "social contributions" (*cotisations sociales*) are no longer perceived as a way to finance national solidarity or promote economic growth, but instead as a burden for employers and, finally, as an enemy of employment (Palier 2002). Since the 1980s, one of the most important and continuous aims of employment policy has been to decrease employers' social security contributions to the lowest rate possible. Even for the Socialist Party, this strategy seemed to be acceptable as a means of making unskilled workers more employable.

> All the Social Security reforms engaged since [Michel] Rocard's government tend to replace the social contribution by the general regime taxes (CSG and employers' exemptions for social contributions to encourage them to engage, a growing role of social minima financed with tax) and tend to give priority to financial accumulation in the complementary regimes (tax incentives to the benefit of wage savings until the development of pension funds). (Friot 1999: 108)

The replacement of one kind of employment and social protection financing (social contributions) by another (taxes) is pronounced. The "youth employment" plan (*emplois jeunes*), which was launched in 1997 and disappeared in 2002, offers an extreme illustration. An employer hiring youth labor under this plan had to pay only 20 percent of the final wage. Programs such as the RMI, disability insurance, and life insurance that provide universal social benefits based on minimal costs of living are founded on the same logic. In 1988, 10 percent of the French population (about six million people) was affected by those social minima that represented the equivalent of 1 percent of GDP (80 billion francs) (Join-Lambert 1998). This form of massive state intervention to protect people against heterogeneous social risks signaled the disengagement of employers from national solidarity. It is a way, as well, to assign a special social status to people designed as "unemployable" and whose lives are now more and more dependent on state action.

Modernization and territorialization of public action

During the two last decades, state intervention has not only increased in quantitative terms. Increasing unemployment and growing heterogeneity among those who were eligible for social benefits also provided reasons for public service "modernization" at the end of the 1980s. The ideals of this modernization involve decentralization of decision-making across levels of government, the "decompartmentalization" of functions, the differentiation of publics, and the individualization of the relationship between civil servants and beneficiaries. Given these ideals, it is not surprising that the administrative discourse should be dominated by topics such as the importance of local relationships, trust between administration and users, and recognition of the diversity of individual career paths.

One of the most concrete pieces of evidence for this change has been the territorialization of employment policies (Lallement 1999). This has led to limited initiatives promoting collective bargaining at the level of the employment field (Jobert 2000). The trend toward delegation of central authority in this area can be seen in the decentralization and the contractualization of relationships between political and administrative entities. In 1993, the state delegated the implementation of youth vocational training and placement assistance programs to the regions. In order to meet this requirement, the regions were forced to mobilize civil society, especially the unions. This granted additional legitimacy to the expertise of these organizations and contributed to their institutionalization (Besuco et al. 1998). Implementation at the regional level, however, raises a question of how diverse regional specifications for public programs can be reconciled with consistent national aims. Moreover, key interest groups are relatively weak in some regions, leading to greater regional variation in the character and effectiveness of vocational training programs (Lamanthe and Verdier 1999).

Administrative reform at the public employment agencies was a third way to promote new employment regulation and devolve greater power to the cities. For many political officials as well as researchers, the city was viewed as the place where the tensions linked to the so-called "new social question" were converging. As a consequence, it seemed to be the perfect place for experiments with unusual and innovative forms of regulation. Policies launched at the end of the 1980s in this environment were as a result less narrowly targeted than before. This meant that social policies no longer attempted to deal with social conditions as isolated and unconnected problems. Programs to improve education, housing, health, ameliorate economic insecurity, and provide employment could be coordinated with one another and target specific populations or neighborhoods. This community-based approach would overcome the old cleavages between specialized administrations and allow benefits to be tailored to local needs in the poor suburbs where vulnerable groups were concentrated. The development of "districts' and departments' projects" within some administrative areas served this goal by giving real autonomy to local officials to fight against "social exclusion" and mobilizing elected representatives, association militants, administrative executives, and social workers to work together on common problems.

Regardless of how such policies are evaluated, the most important point is that employment policy was built on the belief that contractualization and local management were more effective. We have demonstrated that this motivated changes in collective bargaining, and acceptance of this paradigm guided state action as well. New institutional forms were required to make public policy built around decentralization and contractualization effective. The creation of these institutions began in the 1980s with the creation of local employment committees. Organizational reforms at the national level included decentralization of the Ministry of Employment in 1993 and 1995 and coordination of previously separated departmental responsibilities. At the local level, institution building had involved the creation of local teams that bring together representatives of various departments. This has allowed state authorities to direct labor, employment, and vocational training to the regional and departmental level. Since the 1980s, the public employment service has also used subcontracting as a means of policy implementation.[20] As a result of this, other groups have emerged from the private sector and civil society to work alongside those of the ANPE (Agence Nationale pour l'Emploi). These new actors, including employment agencies, intermediate associations, local bodies, neighborhood service associations, training organizations, town structures for assistance with employment, and groups of employers devoted to employment and training, are playing an important role as mediators of the labor market (Bessy and Eymard-Duvernay 1997; Nivolle 1999; Chevrier-Fatôme and Simonin 2004).

Innovative as they are, these new forms of state action have begun to reach their limits. Giving more rights and initiatives to local actors has not ensured that public action is more efficient. Local groups operating autonomously often lack the financial means to implement policies. As importantly, diverse local groups working on employment policy often suffer from coordination failures that can reduce their efficiency or even make their work counterproductive. Empirical assessments have shown that it is sometimes extremely difficult to make different administrative services collaborate and to break with a strong Jacobin culture at the local level.[21] It has been observed that the greatest risk within local networks created to fight against social exclusion often involves leaving too much power to the "social engineers" who are more concerned with demonstrating their own expertise than with promoting democratic integration of the underprivileged (Laville 2005). Another unexpected result of decentralization has been the increased subordination of social workers to elected representatives. This decrease in professional autonomy nourished a collective frustration that was expressed through social workers' collective protests in the 1990s.

5. Results and prospects

Traps of contractualization

During the Fordist era, industrial relations dominated market and class relations. Unions performed both the economic task of negotiating general agreements on wages, skills, and working-time at a centralized level and the social task of channeling the anger and hope of workers. As they gained greater recognition of their social legitimacy, unions became a vital part of the process that reconciled economic rationality and social consensus. As the contractualization of French society has increased over the last two decades, disconnection between industrial relations, classes, and markets has emerged. During this period, social differentiation has displaced solidarity as the defining characteristic of French industrial relations, resulting in a weakening of the rules and patterns of influence that used to define the system. The first consequence of this is that labor relations are more influenced by forces of privatization, manifest through greater flexibility and the decentralization of collective bargaining. At the same time, this trend has not fully privatized industrial relations or moved them out of the public domain. The state has taken an even more active role in financing employment and promoting new contractual policies in the industrial relations field. The second consequence can be thought of as "glocalization" – a mixture of globalization and localization. On one side, there is stronger market pressure on working conditions and on employment regulation, new orientations for public policy (especially toward the European strategy for employment), and an extremely timid construction of a European industrial relations system (Lallement and Mias 2005). On the other side, there has been a propensity to delegate enforcement of the right to work to lower levels of government and to allow greater flexibility to adapt rules to the local situation. A final consequence is the increasing weight of autonomy and dependency. In the case of bargaining, this means that the legitimacy of the traditional social partners is contested in ways that allow new social actors to make their voices heard outside the formal institutional channels of the industrial relations system. But there is more dependency than ever in areas such as the public subsidization of unions and the exclusion of large parts of the active population (the unemployed, or people with low-level or precarious jobs) from the benefits of union representation and social protection managed by social partners.

As suggested in the introduction, the key to understanding these changes is the contractualization of French society. There are at least two changes driving this trend. First, there has been a metamorphosis of actors. As levels of education have increased, employees and employers no longer expect the same services from their representative organizations. Dissatisfied with what has been negotiated in their name, workers are refusing to delegate their power to professional unionists. Instead, workers have indicated their preference for a more democratic and negotiated means of organizing and representing their interests. At the same time, broader social changes including the evolution of the education system and greater levels of female labor force participation have reshaped the French workforce over the last three decades. The old model of labor militancy has also been eroded by demographic changes that are causing younger men to pay more attention to families and children. The time demands of being a good employee, a good unionist, a good spouse, and a good parent are such that the pool of labor activists has diminished. The metamorphosis on the side of employers has been bound up with the emergence of an entrepreneurial vision of economic action rather than the traditional patrimonial one. Marked by a growing demand for autonomy and local negotiations, these two trends have contributed to the erosion of the pillars of the industrial relations system built after the Second World War. In addition to the changes affecting the actors in the industrial relations system, the growth of contractual relationships has an economic cause. Unprotected sectors of the economy have come under pressure to increase their quality and flexibility while reacting faster to market demands and developing personal relations with clients. This is why the firm is now often thought of as a set of contractors that each has to face market-based standards of efficiency and performance. Contractualization takes different forms (such as subcontracting, the formation of economic networks, the development of profit centers within the firm, or the use of casual employment), so sometimes it is difficult to distinguish the boundaries of modern firms or to apply consistent rules to the industrial relations system.

But contractualization does not mean the death of the state. On the contrary, the French state continues to play a prominent role in the negotiation and the implementation of social and employment policies. In addition to the new functions the French state has taken on, there is a high level of continuity with its earlier responsibilities. In part this emerges from French political culture, which accepts a Rousseauian vision of the state as having a monopoly over the production of the general interest and has never encouraged the creation of a system of industrial relations independent of the political sphere (Rosanvallon 1998). This has left the confederations – unable to be the national "tribune" of interests – to become "political" entities relying on state subsidies and attempting to gain more influence in the policy-making arena. But such a strategy may be dangerous, as illustrated by the decline in membership suffered by CFDT after signing agreements on retirement[22] and artists' social protection in 2003 that led, in the name of budgetary realism, to poorer working conditions for its members. This strategy may also prove dangerous in an economic downturn, when inequality between sectors could undermine faith in the ability of the old unions to defend workers' rights either at the grassroots or the national level. Such a situation would not be completely new. Largely driven by higher rates of unionization and militancy in the public sector, the massive and unexpected political demonstrations of 1995 might be the paradigm of future social battles.

What does the future hold?

There are two reasons why the changes previously mentioned do not by themselves pave the way for change in French industrial relations. First, reform of the collective bargaining system is critical. Officially, MEDEF wishes to promote three objectives: giving priority to firms, generalizing and decentralizing collective bargaining, and guaranteeing autonomous collective bargaining (by revising, for example, the extension-based principle agreements through the state). The socio-political transformations have already proven to be more consequential than they may seem. It would be misleading to summarize conflict over the New Social Foundation as a battle between defenders of a contractual approach and defenders of a regulatory one. From a legal point of view, contracts cannot entirely replace existing law. Legal provisions and negotiated agreements have produced procedural rules allowing employers to negotiate more diversified standards for wages and working time. Moreover, the contractual approach suffers from a problem of legitimacy based on the erosion of support for the social partners. The perceived legitimacy of unions and employers' organizations as representatives of employees' and employers' interests has never been lower. Lacking the legitimacy conferred by democratic elections, how broadly accepted can contractual agreement be when made between social partners whose legitimacy is increasingly called into question? Concern over exactly this issue led to the broad acceptance by the unions of a common text committing them to accept in some cases only agreements that have been ratified by unions representing the interests of the majority of employees. The May 2004 Act (*loi Fillon*) partially modified this text by providing more room to maneuver at the local level. Except in a few areas (such as minimum wage), it allows firm agreements to depart – unless otherwise explicitly stated in the agreement negotiated at a higher level – from agreements negotiated at a higher level, even to employees' disadvantage.

If parties of the right continue to exercise power in the coming years, the trends of the recent past are likely to be strengthened. In the name of the market and flexibility, we are moving toward a social configuration where local and heterogeneous regulation will definitely supplant both general policies decreed by the state and agreements negotiated by unions and employers' federations.[23] It is not too difficult to guess what this means: more insecurity, uncertainty, inequality, and greater segmentation between social groups (a competitive professional pool of skilled workers, who are able to negotiate advantages for themselves, at one level, and the marginally employable – whose survival depends on the state – below them). Even if these developments suggest a new conception of industrial relations and union action, there are seeds for a different future outcome. The first consists of inventing new forms of solidarity, through different initiatives falling under the "plural economic" label (Laville 1999). The main purpose of such a practice is to transcend the traditional oppositions between insurance and assistance, between market regulation and state action. Even if they only are responsible for a relatively small number of jobs, the so-called "neighborhood services" have so far revealed a considerable innovative potential. At the crossroads of private, non-profit, and non-monetary relationships, they contribute to the constitution of micro-public domains. In such domains, a set of actors with multiple statutes (associations, private firms, mutual benefit societies) has already invented new ways to democratize economic relations between workers, employers, and consumers.

A second seed for change starts with the idea that labor markets could be re-regulated in order to promote mobility without the level of risks associated with contractual flexibility. Already tested in Germany, "transitional labor markets" are a way to normalize and institutionalize the various forms of labor market marginality that have increased continuously over the past two decades.[24] Such markets are not markets *stricto sensu*: they are schemes combining wages and social allowances, "classical" employment and social activities in which markets are not usually in charge. The rights of people to get such a job, the way they are paid, their social protection in training periods, etc., are either fixed by law or negotiated at the sectoral or the firm level. In other words, the "transitional labor markets" approach envisages new kinds of institutional arrangements to prevent transitions between segments of the labor market from becoming gates to social exclusion and to transform them into gates to a wider range of opportunities for the employed as well for the inactive or unemployed (Gazier 2003; Schmid 2002). In France, these "transitional labor markets" may offer unions the opportunity to stop delegating labor and employment management to the market or the state. This option not only implies an industrial relations reform but, more generally, a new link between education systems, labor markets, firms, and union responsibilities. But in order to avoid the liberal-statist scenario, the road ahead is still long.

Notes

I wish to thank P. Culpepper, P. Hall, and P. Le Galès for their relevant comments on an earlier draft of this paper. Thanks as well to M. Zuber for her invaluable help.

1 In a previous paper (Lallement 2000), I developed the idea that contractualization has to be understood in terms of the industrial society as described by A. Gouldner (1971). The game theory and the interactionist approach (Goffman) can thus be analyzed as a theoretical rationalization of structural changes of modern societies.

2 Privatization means here that more autonomy and more power are entrusted to actors in civil society, especially to firms less constrained by substantive rules, and thus more empowered to promote their own interest. That's why I will tend here to assimilate privatization with decentralization of collective bargaining.

3 The February 1950 law restored contractual freedom at the wage level and determined a new legislative framework for industrial relations. In this text, collective agreement is defined as a general contract which is applied in an imperative way to firms belonging to employer's unions which signed the agreement. This effect is called the *erga omnes* effect. Coupled with monopolistic principle (an agreement suitable to be extended must be negotiated and signed by representative organizations), this *erga omnes* principle leads to the major innovation of the law, namely "freedom to negotiate collectively to create rights, independently of a legal authorities' act" (Morin 1994: 216).

4 The so-called "Parodi salary scales" have been established after the Second World War following a statutory order ("arrêté Parodi," 11 April 1946) (Saglio 1986). The Parodi type defines a specific scale for each professional category (blue collar, employee, technician, supervisor, and manager) and it bases hierarchies on criteria such as mastery of the job (for blue collars and employees), aptitude to order (supervisors) or diploma (managers). But the most important feature is that this type of scale tries to make know-how, job and minimal wage correspond strictly.

5 In this case, French lawyers explain that collective agreement has only a "suppletive" function. This innovation is a way to weaken the "imperative effect" (Article L. 135 from the book of the Labor Code) or, in other words, to weaken the obligation for an employer to apply at the firm level new rules negotiated at the sectoral level.

6 France is peculiar in having the lowest level of union membership amongst European countries but one of the highest rates of collective bargaining coverage. This is due to the "extension" procedure, a technique whereby the Minister of Labor makes a collective agreement generally binding across a sector or territory. The conditions to which it is subject and the procedure that must be followed (consultation of the social partners through the National Collective Bargaining Commission) are specified by law in considerable detail. A high rate of coverage does not mean that all firms manage wages and working conditions in the same way. They only have to respect some rules (such as the minimum threshold) negotiated at the sectoral level, such that a high rate of coverage can coexist with the observed growth of firm-level agreements, which allows each local unit of production to adapt their regulations subject to the limits imposed by the extension procedure.

7 In 1991, 2.4 million employees were affected by such a conventional arrangement. In 1998, the number reached 3.5 million, that is to say a rate of coverage of 24%.

8 Indeed, within firms militants accumulate responsibilities. They are union delegates, union representatives, delegates to the labor council, delegates to the CHSCT (safety and health councils), representatives in the joint administrative committees, etc.

9 The "prud'hommes" councils were created in 1806. The current 271 "prud'hommes" councils are composed half of elected employers and half of elected employees. As a sort of "labor courts," these councils settle disputes on labor contracts between an employer and his employees.

10 In 1976, there were almost 5 million individual unworked days owing to strikes (except for public offices). Since then, the trend has been decreasing. In 2001, the figure was 691,000 days. These numbers place France in the middle when compared to the main industrialized countries. But the comparison is difficult to make because the definitions of strikes are not the same from one country to another, and the ways to manage conflicts are also different.

11 The slow erosion of membership is so great that only 8% of employees (approximately 2.4 million) have a union card today. When only considering the private sector, the union rate is 5.2%. This rate stopped declining in the middle of the 1990s (Amossé 2004). But the most salient fact is that the union rate is now greater among managers (*cadres*) (14.5%) than among employees (5.5%) and even among blue-collar workers (6.1%).

12 To be "representative" confers the right to present candidates at the first round of elections (election for wage council, election of the employees' delegates). But it also gives the right to designate a representative for wage councils, to constitute some inner union in the firm, and to designate some union representatives to stand in the national collective bargaining committee and in the Economic and Social Council, etc. The representation especially makes it possible for a trade union to negotiate an agreement applicable to all the employees belonging to the agreement's field of application.

13 I refer here particularly to École polytechnique and to the ENA (École nationale d'administration), two public schools that train the economic and administrative French elites.

14 In order to explain the tendency to resort to the courts to resolve conflicts, it is necessary to consider a second factor which is certainly also determinant: the changes in employment relations, and especially the changes in the management of managers (*cadres*). Between 1984 and 1994, the number of disputes dealt with by the section "Manager" of the "prud'hommes" councils went from 14,000 to 25,000. In addition to the distinction between managers' versus non-managers' statutes that often raises discussion, the majority of disputes is related to the conditions under which labor contracts are disrupted (approximately three-quarters of the examined files) (Livian 1999). This procedure often constitutes the ultimate stage of an amicable arrangement for leaving the firm or a transaction that could not succeed. This development "obliges judges to examine facts and figures and to a certain extent prevents lay-offs based solely on an employer's whim. But it undoubtedly confirms the basis of today's employment relations: loyalty and trust have largely been replaced by the assessment of achieved results" (Livian 1999: 11–12).

15 "For a new social constitution," the text adopted by MEDEF's executive council, 2 November 1999.

16 In France, indeed, a collective agreement is considered valid if at least one union belonging to a "representative" confederation has signed.

17 MEDEF's declaration at a joint meeting on the theme of "Means and ends to strengthen collective bargaining," 14 March 2000.

18 In July 2002, MEDEF met the government in order to explain once again the conditions for it to come back: no more help from social security to finance the 35-hour working week, reform and new governance of the health insurance fund.

19 Since 1 January 2004, the RMA (Revenu Minimum d'Activité) has been proposed to those who benefit by the RMI. The RMA is a part-time work contract (at least 20 hours per week). An employer who uses such a scheme gets a public subsidy corresponding to the RMI allocation (362.30 euros per person in 2004). As a consequence, he only bears the difference between the wage he pays and the RMI amount.

20 In 2002, the public service of employment spent about 700 million euros to externalize one part of its actions.

21 One area where decentralization was not carried out involved coordination with large private firms. Anticipating the danger that the political power of such firms

could overwhelm local authorities, most areas of coordination between public authority and big business were left at the ministerial level.

22 This agreement (now a law passed on 21 August 2003) forces state employees to work an extra two and a half years in order to claim a full pension.

23 The February 2005 Act, which deeply redefines the 35 hours Act (2000) by making easier the use of overtime hours, is only one step toward more flexibility and more local compromises.

24 The idea of the transitional labor market is based on the observation that nowadays people move more often between different employment statuses (between different working-time regimes, between unemployment and employment, between education and training or training and employment, or between work and retirement) and that some of these transitions are critical because they may lead to a downward spiral in the career trajectory, ending in recurrent unemployment, poverty, exiting the labor force, etc.

3
The Transformation of Corporate Governance in France

Michel Goyer

Introduction

Will the globalization of finance, trade, and investment lead to convergence across national systems of corporate governance along the lines of the American model? The topic of corporate governance – the system by which firms are controlled and operated, the rules and practices that govern the relationship between managers and shareholders, and the overall process by which investment capital is allocated – has become an important issue for policy-makers and scholars in recent years (see Gourevitch and Shinn 2005; Roe 2000 for overviews). The rise of Anglo-American institutional investors as major shareholders of blue-chip companies, the increasing importance of new information technologies, and stiffer competition have forced French managers to reconsider the process of capital allocation in the firm. The choice – or imposition – of a system of corporate governance is not a panacea. Systems of corporate governance are associated with different sources of innovation (Hall and Soskice 2001: 36–44).

This relationship between institutions of corporate governance and the innovative capabilities of firms might become a liability for the French economy as the importance of equity markets for economic development has become crucial. A growing body of research has uncovered a strong and statistically significant correlation between key features of the financial system of countries and economic growth. The results of these empirical studies established that nations with large equity markets have experienced higher rates of economic growth as compared to financial systems dominated by banks (Levine and Zeros 1998). Securities markets can stimulate economic growth in two ways. Equity markets enhance savings and perform a better job of channelling them into real investment – thereby stimulating capital accumulation. Capital-intensive sectors, moreover, tend to be financed primarily by equity markets. Nevertheless, convergence on the American model of corporate governance is by no means guaranteed as institutions of corporate governance shape the distribution of net value added of firms among employees, managers, and shareholders in different ways – thereby heightening economic inequalities across nations (DeJong 1997). Political resistance to an increased role for market forces in the form of the adoption of shareholder-friendly institutions also stands in the way of major reforms of corporate governance in continental Europe (Roe 2000).

In this chapter I investigate the divergent processes and outcomes by which large French companies have introduced shareholder value practices. A comparison with the evolution of corporate governance in Germany will serve as the analytical framework for illustrating the nationally specific transformation of France. These two systems of corporate governance have changed in the last decade – but in different ways and without any process of convergence. I present a choice-within-constraints institutional perspective to account for the divergent responses of companies (see Hall 1986 and Whittington 1988 for an overview). The construction of such a view is based on the notion that the evolution of corporate governance systems is influenced by what CEOs and top managers are pressed to do and by what the institutional structures of the political economy induce them to do. The former provides some hints about the potential direction of change since firms are facing demands from capital and product markets. The latter refers to the institutional environment that cuts down the range of strategic options. I demonstrate in this chapter the importance of the institutional arrangements of workplace organization in France and Germany in accounting for the different transformation of their systems of corporate governance. However, the actions undertaken by management are also shaped by mechanisms of strategic choices internal to the actor. Institutional frameworks also have the capacity to offer alternative adjustment paths that cannot be simply "read off": how actors operate in particular institutional frameworks, and how they learn to operate within it, matters for their effects (Hancké and Goyer 2005). Similar institutions can therefore lead to different outcomes, and institutional frameworks can offer actors new adjustment paths beyond the immediately visible ones. The perspective presented in this chapter highlights the pursuit of interests within institutional constraints combined with selection mechanisms internal to the actor him- or herself. The institutional arrangements of workplace organization restrains the range of options available, but choice remains possible since there is more than one way to develop and incorporate shareholder value strategies.

The roadmap for this chapter is the following. First, I provide an overview of the changes in the external environment in which French companies are embedded. Second, I present an empirical evaluation of the transformation of the French system of corporate governance – with a comparison with Germany. Third, I develop a theoretical framework to account for the different shareholder-value strategies adopted by French and German firms. Fourth, I proceed to a historical overview of the development of conglomerates in France – and illustrate how their foundations were ill suited to share competencies across business activities. Fifth, I present an institutional portrait of the arrangements of workplace organization in France and Germany – and discuss how diverging levels of managerial control over firm restructuring came to be associated with different types of shareholder-value strategies. Sixth, I highlight the role and limits of domestic institutional frameworks in accounting for the transformation of corporate governance in the two countries and its theoretical implications for the study of change.

1. Structural and external changes in French corporate governance

The French system of corporate governance experienced an important transformation resulting from a series of cumulatively far-reaching changes. These developments have decreased the relevance of debt finance and have heightened the importance of securities markets. Three features characterized the "old" French system of corporate governance. First, corporations had a high debt-equity ratio, that is, bank loans were more important than stock issues as a source of external finance (Zysman 1983). In addition, it is important to point out that retained earnings were low in France as compared to other continental European economies (Bertero 1994). Thus, internal financing (retained earnings) was low and external financing (bank loans, stocks) was dominated by debt finance. Second, the ownership structure of French companies was highly concentrated. The pattern of ownership concentration took three forms: cross-shareholdings among companies, large shareholder in the form of a family owner, and financial holdings with Paribas and Suez as the nominal head (Fridenson 1997: 228; Morin 1974). Third, the French State was able to exercise substantial influence over the trajectory of financial flows in the economy (Zysman 1983). The instruments at the disposal of policy-makers were capital controls, administered and subsidized interest rates for specific purposes designed by state officials, use of credit ceilings over the amount of loans banks could issue, specialized parapublic financial institutions under the influence of the Treasury, and control over the access to the bond market. The outcome was that the financing options of companies were limited.

The bank-based financially repressed French system of corporate governance crumbled under the impact of several factors. First, the financial system underwent a massive process of deregulation: the use of credit ceilings as a mean to control inflation has been replaced by the discipline of central bank independence and of high real-interest rates, capital controls have been removed under pressures from the EMS and the suspension of the dollar's convertibility into gold, and the bond market has been deregulated (Loriaux 1991).

Second, the collapse of the "old" French system of corporate governance is the result of developments that have raised the importance of equity capital.

Two key factors account for the rise in importance of the stock market capitalization of firms. In the first place, the removal of capital controls by policy-makers enabled investors to pursue a strategy of international diversification of their assets. The growth of foreign equity held by American institutional investors increased from 128.7 billion US$ in 1988 to 1,787 in 2000 (Conference Board 2002: 39). The average percentage of total assets held in international equities by the largest 25 American pension funds increased from 4.8 in 1991 to 18.0 in 1999 (ibid. 2000: 43). The resulting impact of these developments on the strategy of large companies should not be underestimated. The increase of foreign ownership has been quite remarkable in economies previously characterized by ownership concentration in the hands of large domestic banks and non-financial firms. In France, foreign investors owned 41.29 percent of the equity capital of CAC 40 firms in 2001 (*Le Monde* 15 June 2001: 22). In Germany, the similar figure for DAX 30 companies in 1999 was 28.5 percent (*Les Échos* 8/9 October 1999: 34). This percentage is higher for large European blue-chip companies as foreign ownership for members of the Euro Stoxx 50 index stood at 44.4 percent in 2002 (*Le Monde* 12 June 2002: 20). The internationalization of the shareholder structure of French firms is critical since institutional investors have expressed clear preferences for the adoption of shareholder-value practices that maximize return on equity. Moreover, the rise of foreign ownership in France came at the expense of domestic cross-shareholdings among large domestic firms as patterns of cross-shareholdings collapsed in the late 1990s (Morin and Rigamonti 2002).

Another development that has increased the importance of securities markets is the changing conditions associated with the successful completion of a takeover bid in the United States in the last decade. The importance of equity swap, whereby companies issue additional stocks to pay for the shares of the target firm, has increased dramatically. In 1988, nearly 60 percent of the total value of deals over $100 million in the United States was paid for entirely in cash. The similar figure for deals paid in stock was less than 2 percent. By contrast, about half of the value of large deals in 1998 was paid entirely in stock – and 17 percent was solely financed in cash (Rappaport and Sirower 1999: 147–51). What is the significance of the changing characteristics of takeover activity in the United States on the transformation of European systems of corporate governance? The importance of takeover activity in the United States for European corporate governance is intimately related to the process by which firms build their innovative capabilities. Large French firms are engaged in a process of institutional arbitrage (Hall and Soskice 2001: 57). They have sought to pursue radical types of innovation, thereby gaining access to new innovative capabilities, through the acquisition of companies in the United States via takeovers. Firms with higher stock market capitalization possess a substantial advantage in the global merger marketplace in using equity swap as a mean of payment

(Coffee 1999: 649). The issue of additional stocks to pay for the shares of the target company is reserved for firms with substantially higher stock market capitalization. A concern for the valuation of the value of equity capital has become a necessary condition if French companies want to be able to acquire others.

2. The transformation of French corporate governance: an empirical (and comparative) evaluation

What has been the impact of the structural changes faced by French companies? The empirical results presented in this section point to the incomplete and non-converging transformation of French corporate governance. The adoption of shareholder-value strategies by companies remains short of the full-scale adoption of American practices; and it has exhibited striking divergence in regard to the transformation of the German system of corporate governance – another former bank-based financial system.

What are the criteria to evaluate the transformation of corporate governance? Methodological developments in the financial economics literature constitute an interesting starting point. The use of event studies – which allow researchers to isolate the effect on share price of a specific event – has exploded (e.g. the effect of the adoption of non-voting shares/poison pills). These event studies provide useful indicators that can be used as proxies for good corporate governance practices (Altman 1992). This literature can also provide a guide to how companies reacted to a new financial environment in which the importance of securities markets has become important.

First, firms can address their problem of low market capitalization by tackling the conglomerate discount. The involvement in many business activities constituted a critical feature of large French and German companies for the first four and a half post-war decades (Whittington and Mayer 2000: 128–39). The diversification of business activities in many areas allowed firms to reduce risk by polling together the fortunes of unrelated businesses and contained the seeds for economies of scope as managers could transfer synergies and exploit complementary strategic assets in the portfolio of business units. However, Anglo-Saxon investors have increasingly expressed strong views against the involvement in many business activities (Markides 1995: 11–35). Conglomerates constitute an inefficient organizational form since they frequently use cross-subsidies from profitable divisions to shore up money-losing ones regardless of their long-term growth prospects. In particular, the propensity of managers to build large corporate empires proved stronger than the need to exit from business activities with declining growth prospects since job security and executive compensation correlate with firm size (Whittington and Mayer 2000: 51–5). Moreover, investors have been adamant that portfolio companies focus on a limited number of core competencies since most firms have succeeded in developing a world-leadership position in only a small number of business activities (Prahalad and Hamel 1990).

The preferences of investors for the dismantling of conglomerates are increasingly converging with managerial interests. Funds dislike the lack of transparency, cross-subsidies between corporate divisions, and the overall perceived inefficiency of conglomerates. The performance of conglomerates is particularly difficult to assess. As a result, diversified firms are penalized on financial markets. They suffer from a conglomerate discount, their stock market value being lower than the potential sum of their individual business segments (Comment and Jarrell 1995).[1] French and German managers possess strong incentives to demonstrate a strategic focus in order to avoid the discount since empirical evidence indicates that companies that are becoming focused on a limited number of activities exhibit higher stock market valuations.[2] Lower market valuations would hurt them in the global M&A market in which equity swap has become an important means of payment (Coffee 1999: 649).

The results on the evolution of the diversification strategy of large French and German companies are presented in Tables 3.1 to 3.4. The structural organization of large French firms underwent an important transition between 1994 and 2003. French companies have reduced their degree of diversification to a greater extent than their German counterparts. Radical restructuring characterizes the refocusing process in France while the corresponding trajectory in Germany is more limited.

Second, firms can also address their problem of undercapitalization via the adoption of financial transparency. From the legal perspective on financial markets, the problem of undercapitalization of continental European companies is intimately linked to the agency problem, not primarily driven by the conglomerate discount. The fundamental issue in corporate governance concerns the protection of minority shareholders (LaPorta et al. 2000; Shleifer and Vishny 1997). In particular, the underdevelopment of financial markets in continental Europe has been evidenced by the ability of a large shareholder to extract private benefits (i.e. those not shared with other owners) from the running of the company, increase using such devices as an equity stake through share issues, diversion of resources from the firm, and synergy gains and the ability to fix transfer prices between companies the controlling shareholder owns (Johnson et al. 2000). The presence of a controlling owner requires the protection of minority shareholders if equity capital is to be provided.

The central theoretical insight of this literature lies in the increase of the stock market capitalization of companies if the controlling shareholder credibly signals its willingness to stop expropriating from minority shareholders. Firms in corporate governance systems for which the size of private benefits is high suffer from a discount by investors since the incentives of controlling shareholders lie in maximizing the value of their own private benefits at the

Table 3.1 Corporate strategy of French firms[1]

Company	1986	1990	1994	1998	2003
Accor	DIV	DIV	DIV	DIV	DOM
Air Liquide	DIV	DIV	DIV	DOM	DOM
Alcatel	DIV	DIV	DIV	DIV	DIV
Aventis[2]					SIN
Bic	DIV	DIV	DIV	DIV	DIV
Bouygues	DIV	DIV	DIV	DIV	DIV
Bull	SIN	SIN	SIN	SIN	SIN
Carrefour	DIV	DIV	DIV	DIV	DOM
Danone	DIV	DIV	DIV	DOM	DOM
Elf[3]	DIV	DIV	DIV	DIV	
Lafarge	DIV	DIV	DIV	DIV	DIV
Lagardere	DIV	DIV	DIV	DIV	DIV
LVMH	DIV	DIV	DIV	DIV	DIV
Lyonnaise des Eaux[4]	DIV	DIV	DIV		
Michelin	SIN	SIN	SIN	SIN	DOM
L'Oreal	DIV	DIV	DIV	DOM	SIN
Pechiney	DIV	DIV	DIV	DOM	DIV[6]
Pernod Ricard	DIV	DIV	DIV	DIV	SIN
Peugeot	DIV	DIV	SIN	SIN	DOM
PPR	DIV	DIV	DIV	DIV	DIV
Renault	SIN	SIN	SIN	SIN	SIN
Rhone-Poulenc[2]	DIV	DIV	DIV	DOM	
St-Gobain	DIV	DIV	DIV	DIV	DIV
Sanofi[5]		DOM	DOM	SIN	
Sanofi-Synthalabo					SIN
Schneider	DIV	DIV	DIV	DIV	DOM[6]
Suez[4]	DIV	DIV	DIV		
Suez-Lyonnaise des Eaux				DOM	DOM
Synthalabo[5]		DOM	DOM	SIN	
Thales-Thomson	DIV	DIV	DIV	DOM	DOM
Total[3]	DOM	DOM	DOM	DOM	
TotalElfFina					SIN
Usinor-Sacilor	SIN	SIN	SIN	DOM	SIN[6]
Valeo	DIV	DIV	DIV	DIV	DIV
Vivendi	DIV	DIV	DIV	DIV	DIV

Abbreviations
DIV (Diversified), DOM (Dominant Business), SIN (Single Business)

Notes
[1] The definition of diversification is based on turnover rates for the largest business. A single business strategy is defined by a minimum of 95 percent of turnover for the largest business activity. A dominant business strategy is characterized by a turnover rate between 70 and 95 percent for the largest business activity. Turnover rates below 70 percent for the largest business activity are associated with a strategy of diversification. Data on turnover is recorded for the following five years unless otherwise indicated: 1986, 1990, 1994, 1998, and 2003.
[2] Data is recorded for Rhone-Poulenc in 1986, 1990, 1994, and 1998. For 2003, data is recorded for Aventis.
[3] Data is recorded for Elf-Aquitaine and Total as separate companies for 1986, 1990, 1994, and 1998. Data for 2003 is recorded for TotalElfFina.
[4] Data is recorded for Lyonnaise des Eaux and Suez as separate companies for 1986, 1990, and 1994. Data for 1998 and 2003 is recorded for Suez-Lyonnaise des Eaux.
[5] Data is recorded for Sanofi and Synthalabo as separate companies for 1990, 1994, and 1998. Data for 2003 is recorded for Sanofi-Synthalabo.
[6] Data is for 2002.

Source: Whittington and Mayer 2000: 226–32; and annual report of firms, various years.

Table 3.2 Corporate strategy of German firms[1]

Company	1986	1990	1994	1998	2003
Aventis[2]					SIN
Agiv	DIV	DIV	DIV	DIV	DIV[5]
Babcock	DIV	DIV	DIV	DIV	DIV[5]
BASF	DIV	DIV	DIV	DIV	DIV
Bayer	DIV	DIV	DIV	DIV	DIV
Beiersdorf	DIV	DIV	DIV	DIV	DIV
BMW	SIN	SIN	SIN	SIN	SIN
Continental	DIV	DIV	DIV	DIV	DIV
Daimler	SIN	DIV	DIV	SIN	SIN
Degussa	DIV	DIV	DIV	DIV	DIV
E-ON[3]					DIV
Henkel	DIV	DIV	DIV	DIV	DIV
Hoecsht[2]	DIV	DIV	DIV	DIV	
Krupp[4]	DIV	DIV	DIV		
Linde	DIV	DIV	DIV	DIV	DIV
Lufthansa	SIN	DOM	DOM	DOM	DOM
MAN	DIV	DIV	DIV	DIV	DIV
Merck	DIV	DIV	DIV	DOM	DOM
Metro			DIV	DIV	DIV
Preussag	DIV	DIV	DIV	DIV	DIV
Porsche	SIN	SIN	SIN	SIN	SIN
RWE	DIV	DIV	DIV	DIV	DIV
SAP	SIN	DOM	DOM	DOM	DOM
Schering	DIV	DIV	DOM	SIN	SIN
Siemens	DIV	DIV	DIV	DIV	DIV
Thyssen[4]	DIV	DIV	DIV		
ThyssenKrupp[4]				DIV	DIV
Veba[3]	DIV	DIV	DIV	DIV	
Viag[3]	DIV	DIV	DIV	DIV	
Volkswagen	DIV	DOM	SIN	DOM	DOM

Notes

[1] Data on turnover is recorded for the following five years unless otherwise indicated: 1986, 1990, 1994, 1998, and 2003.

[2] Data is recorded for Hoecsht as a separate company for 1986, 1990, 1994, and 1998. Data for 2003 is recorded for Aventis.

[3] Data is recorded for Veba and Viag as separate companies for 1986, 1990, 1994, and 1998. Data for 2003 is recorded for E-ON.

[4] Data is recorded for Krupp and Thyssen as separate companies for 1986, 1990, 1994. Data for 1998 and 2003 is recorded for Thyssen-Krupp.

[5] Data is for 2002.

Source: Frankfurter Allgemeine Zeitung Information Services, *Germany's Top 300: a Handbook of Germany's Largest*: various years; Whittington and Mayer 2000: 232–7; and annual reports of companies, various years.

Table 3.3 Evolution of corporate strategy, France

1986 (29 Firms)	1990 (31 Firms)	1994 (31 Firms)	1998 (30 Firms)	2003 (28 Firms)
24 DIV (82.8%)	24 DIV (77.4%)	23 DIV (74.2%)	15 DIV (50.0%)	11 DIV (39.9%)
1 DOM (3.4%)	3 DOM (9.7%)	3 DOM (9.7%)	9 DOM (30.0%)	9 DOM (32.1%)
4 SIN (13.8%)	4 SIN (12.9%)	5 SIN (16.1%)	6 SIN (20.0%)	8 SIN (28.6%)

Table 3.4 Evolution of corporate strategy, Germany

1986 (26 Firms)	1990 (26 Firms)	1994 (27 Firms)	1998 (26 Firms)	2003 (25 Firms)
21 DIV (80.7%)	21 DIV (80.7%)	21 DIV (77.8%)	18 DIV (69.2%)	16 DIV (64.0%)
0 DOM	3 DOM (11.6%)	3 DOM (11.1%)	4 DOM (15.4%)	4 DOM (16.0%)
5 SIN (19.3%)	2 SIN (7.7%)	3 SIN (11.1%)	4 SIN (15.4%)	5 SIN (20.0%)

expense of the total market capitalization of the firm (Zingales 1994). The implication is that legal rules can shape economic outcomes. The adoption of financial transparency and the elimination of unequal voting rights can substitute for the dismantling of conglomerates as a strategy to increase the market capitalization of firms (Glaeser et al. 2001). Greater financial transparency acts as a form of monitoring on management since it requires the provision of detailed information on a regular basis. Moreover, financial transparency and the elimination of deviations from the one-share-one vote principle decrease the ability of large shareholders to extract private benefits from the firm without being detected (Johnson et al. 2000). Such shareholders would find it more difficult to transfer resources from the company for their own private benefit or that of other companies they own (Zingales 1994). They would also find it more difficult to increase their equity stake through the dilution of minority holdings in the absence of unequal voting rights.

The strategies of large French and German companies are characterized by a lack of convergence in terms of financial transparency and respect for the rights of minority shareholders. The German corporate governance system has moved toward financial transparency in recent years, through the adoption of an international accounting standard (IAS or US-GAAP). In 1996, only 9 firms of Germany's largest 100 firms were using an international accounting standard. The same figure for the year 2000 is 64 (Goyer 2003: 194). Moreover, every German firm in the 2003 sample of this chapter reports according to an international accounting standard. The French corporate governance system, in contrast, has remained largely opaque. The number of companies using an international accounting standard among the country's largest 100 has risen from 35 in 1997 to 38 in 2000 (Goyer 2003: 197).[3]

Table 3.5 Firms with deviations to one-share, one-vote principle (in percentages)

Exceptions to one-share, one-vote rule	France top 40			Germany top 30			France top 120		Germany top 120	
	1996	1999	2001	1996	1999	2001	1996	1999	1996	1999
Voting caps or ownership ceilings	20	22	30	3	2	1	20	22	3	2
Unequal Voting Rights	75	68	58	25	15	13	32	68	25	15

Source: Davis Global Advisors, *Leading Corporate Governance Indicators*: various years.

Finally, German companies have eliminated most of the infringements of the rights of minority shareholders while their French counterparts still rely heavily on them in the form of unequal voting rights or ownership ceilings (see Table 3.5).

3. The choice of a shareholder-value strategy: a theoretical framework

The previous section has illustrated the different choices made by companies in regard to the strategies adopted to increase the value of their shares. These newly adopted shareholder value strategies took place in a financial environment in which equity markets have become more important. French companies have dismantled the conglomerate structure, limiting the number of core business activities; German companies have focused on financial transparency and respect for the voting rights of minority shareholders. Large companies in the two countries have introduced substantial components of shareholder value concerns in their strategies, but they have changed in different ways. The globalization of finance does not entail the convergence of European systems of corporate governance along the lines of the American model. However, the lack of convergence between the two systems of corporate governance accounts for neither the divergence in the strategies adopted by large French and German firms nor for the consequences in regard to the sustainability of their respective national model of capitalism. The central research question of this chapter deals with the different strategies adopted by large French firms to increase the value of their shares – and their consequences for the rest of the economy.

The case against the maintenance of a diversification strategy in many business activities appears strong. The conglomerate discount, the ever-present inefficiencies resulting from cross-subsidies between divisions, and the potential lack of fit between the firm's capabilities and the required competencies to succeed on world markets militate in favor of a focus on a limited number of activities. Nevertheless, conglomerates have not disappeared.

The previous section illustrates the resilience of the conglomerate form in Germany, a coordinated market economy. In the United Kingdom and the United States, the leading two liberal market economies, the breaking up of corporate empires has taken place at the same time as new diversified firms appeared (Whittington 2000). The drive toward efficiency in these two liberal market economies has been marked by two types of simultaneously occurring strategies: refocusing by poorly performing diversified firms; and the emergence of newly formed and well-performing conglomerates.

Given the above discussion, what accounts for the nationally specific transformation of corporate governance in France and Germany? I argue that the potential efficiencies (and survival) of diversified companies point to the value enhancing of conglomerates based on the use of the appropriate organizational structures and resources policies. The performance of conglomerates (or of the refocused firm) is related to the fit with their institutional context. The search for institutional fit via a focus on core competencies in France was induced, in great part, by the process of conglomerate building in the first four post-war decades – in which the influence of the state was paramount. First, the continuing viability of conglomerates is contingent on the ability to extract additional value from the mixing of different business activities – that is, on the presence of relatedness among units. The degree of relatedness of a diversified company resides in the ability of management to transfer knowledge and competencies across business units. In particular, relatedness across business activities is important if its competencies are intangible assets related to firm-specific ways of doing things that are difficult to imitate (Prahalad and Hamel 1990). However, the ability of French managers to transfer knowledge and competencies across business activities has been adversely shaped by the post-war process of conglomerate building. Economic considerations on the need to rebuild the economy in a *dirigiste* fashion led to a process of conglomerate building that was guided by considerations that often ignored the need to develop organizational capabilities. The role of the state in promoting national champions led to the emergence of a conglomerate structure that often did not provide management with the organizational capacities to transfer knowledge and competence across business units. The knowledge of the internal operations of the firm by CEOs was poor (Bauer and Cohen 1981). Instead, French *dirigisme* provided large firms with the capabilities to exchange information in a horizontal manner – that is, between CEOs of large listed companies that shared a common educational background (Fridenson 1997). I develop this argument in the next section.

Second, the gains associated with the reversal of the strategy of diversification are contingent on commensurate change in the structure of the decision-making process. The use of the internal capital market is appropriate for conglomerates, as the primary goal is to reap the financial gains of diversification (Williamson 1975). The focus on a limited number of competencies, by contrast, implies the importance of exploiting relationships among fewer but related units (Markides 1995: 135–41). The reduction of diversification invariably entails some increase in portfolio risk as more of one's eggs are put in fewer baskets. Refocused firms must exercise tighter control over their units with the head office being involved in operating decisions. The effective operation of a refocused firm also requires specific competencies, characterized notably by high levels of effective managerial control. Thus, the level of managerial control over firm restructuring accounts in great part for the advisability of a refocusing on core business activities. The process of conglomerate building in France and the process of decision-making of large firms, both shaped by their relationship to the state, led to a substantial concentration of power in the CEO and his top managers. This concentration of power and its associated institutional framework, in turn, made it attractive for French firms to dismantle the conglomerate structure in the 1990s as a strategy to promote the value of their shares. I discuss this point in section 5.

4. The historical foundations of the diversification strategy in France

An essential prerequisite for the maintenance of conglomerates resides in the managerial capacity to transfer knowledge and competencies across businesses. I demonstrate in this section that the involvement of the state in the building of diversified companies deprived French conglomerates of those capacities. The most prominent process of conglomerate building in France in the post-war period took place under the industrial policy of promoting national champions. In reaction to perceived strategic economic and military interests, state officials encouraged the formation of companies by merging together firms into one large entity that would serve as the defender of the French market and flag bearer abroad (Zysman 1977: 62). The corporate strategy of diversification, carried out by mergers and acquisitions rather than internal development and product development, was motivated by two purposes: to achieve a critical mass size to compete on European markets, and to facilitate negotiation for industrial policies (Stoleru 1969). The influence of state officials in facilitating the merger of firms into a large one was contingent on the wide range of its incentives: provision of funds in the form of loans and subsidies, guarantee of contracts, and protection of the domestic market.[4]

The pattern by which the French State encouraged the strategy of diversification of large domestic companies in many business activities contains the seeds for its own ultimate demise. In other words, the diversification strategy of French companies often ignored critical issues related to the development of the organizational capabilities needed to succeed on world markets. The concept of competitiveness inherent in the promotion of national champions associated strategic advantage with size only. In turn, these ill-designed institutional foundations provided for the rapid dismantling of the conglomerate form in the 1990s. First, the operation of French conglomerates reproduced some of the most negative practices of their Anglo-Saxon counterparts whereby money-making units subsidize the losses of others. For example, a highly profitable firm like Elf-Aquitaine was often forced to diversify in areas of activities (pharmaceutical, traditional chemistry) in which it did not have the required competencies or that were declining sectors (Cohen and Bauer 1985: 171). The preservation of employment via the rescue of firms in financial difficulty came often to be associated with the strategy of diversification of companies.

Second, the pattern of state policy in building conglomerates made it difficult for firms to develop core competencies. The concept of size was defined in absolute terms for the range of the business activities of the firm – not for a single sector of activity. For example, Thomson was unable to get rid of its medical electronics activities in the 1980s despite losses associated with this activity (ibid.: 201). Rhone-Poulenc sought to lessen its dependence on textiles and to raise the profile of its pharmaceutical branch in the late seventies. However, this strategy entailed massive firings to which state officials attached conditions. After two years of negotiation and financial losses of from 6 to10 billion francs, the Ministry of Labor finally gave its authorization for Rhone-Poulenc to reduce its textile workforce by half (~4,000 workers) (Schmidt 1996: 260–1).

Third, the state-inspired merger policy and the strategy of diversification in many business activities were poisoned gifts. The acceptance of the logic of national champions by companies lessened the problems of strategic fit and organizational capabilities development since markets for the firms' products were secured (Zysman 1977: 104). Several firms diversified in areas in which they neither possessed nor developed the required competencies. For example, CII tried to develop a presence in several niches of microprocessors at the same time that Bull was forced by its partner (GE) to specialize in niches in which IBM was absent (Cohen and Bauer 1985: 37). Pechiney suffered massive losses in dyes, electric equipment, and steel at a time when most aluminum companies had stayed clear of these activities (Bauer and Cohen 1981: 71–9; Fridenson 1997: 235). Saint-Gobain, the glass, paper, and metals group, saw its risky and profit-shy adventure in computer and electronics ultimately halted, but (ironically) only when it was a nationalized company under State control in the 1980s (Schmidt 1996: 265).

Fourth, the diversification policy of French companies served also to reinforce their problem of undercapitalization. The policy of building national champions aggravated the structural characteristics of the French capitalist system without capital. In the first place, domestic capital was the privileged solution for the ownership questions of these national champions (Cohen and Bauer 1985: 135; Zysman 1977: 85). American and Japanese firms were particularly subject to this national preference inclination. Moreover, domestic ownership also meant concentrated ownership as state officials preferred to deal with firms whose ownership structure meant continuity over time. For example, CII experienced the imposition of Alcatel as a dominant shareholder by state officials – instead of selling shares to the French public – despite the fact that these two companies were competing in similar markets and that most successful firms in this sector had a dispersed ownership structure and a managerial team highly knowledgeable of the industry (Cohen and Bauer 1985: 46–7). The outcome of these financial operations was a system of corporate governance characterized by ownership concentration in the form of cross-shareholdings, financial holdings, or investment bank control (Paribas/Suez) (Morin 1974).

However, this particular formation of ownership concentration did not resolve the financial problems of French companies. For example, the state-sponsored alliance of Pechiney and Saint-Gobain to form a national champion in the chemical industry in the 1960s collapsed since neither firm was interested in investing in that industry (Cohen and Bauer 1985: 140–2). Both firms were more interested in the core business activities than in investing in the chemical industry. Rhone-Poulenc, the largest chemical French firm, was handicapped by its financial losses in textiles as well as by the growing demands of its pharmaceutical division. Its presence in the chemical industry reflected the diversification strategy of the original founding family that sought to expand as well as preserve its control over the firm. This strategy resulted in a large industrial group that was both underfinanced and without a clear direction (Bauer and Cohen 1981: 169–73).

The post-war diversification strategy of French companies, while containing the seeds of its ultimate demise, nonetheless fits rather well with its environment. The reconstructive imperatives of the French economy, the presence of non-tariff barriers, the opacity of procurement policies, and the repression of financial capital allowed policy-makers to proceed with their strategy of national champions. Moreover, the internal operations of conglomerates and their policy of diversification in unrelated business activities also fit well with the French model of economic coordination. The pattern of recruitment and training of CEOs and top managers reveals the importance of state schools (ENA, Polytechnique) for filling the top positions in large companies. The content of training at these schools is highly generalist, thereby providing management with high degrees of polyvalence. In turn, the process of training, selection and career profiles of French managers provides them with the strategic vision and organizational capabilities to work in very different business activities and coordinate activities in a horizontal manner (Fridenson 1997: 219). Inner experience and the development of core competencies in a specific business activity were not sources of upward mobility.

5. Concentration of power and organization of the workplace

As the previous section illustrated, the foundations of the strategy of diversification in France were ill structured for economic performance. Nevertheless, it might have been possible for managers to reform their strategy of diversification with the withdrawal of the State from several areas of economic policy in the 1980s. What accounts for the focus on core competencies as the privileged strategy by which French companies have introduced principles of shareholder value? As previously mentioned, the focus on a limited number of competencies implies the importance of exploiting relationships among fewer but related units following an increase in portfolio risk, as more of one's eggs are put in fewer baskets.[5] In other words, the effective operation of a refocused firm requires specific competencies, characterized notably by high levels of managerial control. The risks associated with a focus on a limited number of business activities are lessened as top management has greater control over the direction of the firm.

The institutional framework of work organization in France strongly militates in favor of a focus on core competencies since it contributes to the concentration of power at the top. The contrast with the German case illustrates quite well the characteristics of the French case. I discuss three areas of workplace organization – segmentation of activities, skill certification and formation, and the autonomy of workers in problem-solving tasks. This discussion will illustrate the concentration of power at the top in French companies. The high level of managerial control in France, in turn, made it attractive for firms to refocus on core business activities.

First, the organization of the workplace in France is characterized by the sharp segmentation of production activities and responsibilities between blue-collar employees and managers, and the emphasis on narrow and specialized skills (Linhart 1994; Maurice et al. 1986; Sorge 1991). These institutional factors limit the ability of workers to participate in the conduct of the strategy of the firm. Employees have a limited view of its full operations. The process of problem solving is management-led with the involvement of a few highly qualified technical specialists (Linhart 1994; Hancké 2002). The French organizational system and its corresponding adjustment process entail the use of a flexible labor market for highly skilled specialists. In other words, tasks, skills, and roles are segmented and specialized. By contrast, the broad skills of German employees and the blurred organizational boundaries give them a fairly complete view of the operations of the firm (Sorge 1991). There is substantial scope for the involvement of skilled workers in problem-solving activities. The skills of employees shape their ability to solve problems that, in turn, present management with opportunities to reorganize the production process. The volatility of markets punishes firms where the skills of the workforce cannot be applied to a wide range of rapidly changing and previously unknown tasks. The possession of broad skills by employees provides German companies with the capacity for quick retooling in response to new market demands (Streeck 1991). The development of firm-specific capabilities in Germany involves employee participation in collective problem solving at the firm level and through state agencies and chambers of commerce (Culpepper 1998).

Second, the matching of jobs and worker competencies in the two countries shaped the ability of management to implement restructuring in a unilateral manner in different ways. The German economy is predicated on the presence of a majority of employees with certifiable skills. The qualification of workers determines the definition of jobs. The access to a majority of jobs in large firms is based upon the holding of a recognized diploma or qualification – most often acquired as part of a training program. Training is very often a prerequisite for employment and promotion (Maurice et al. 1986: 65–73). By contrast, French managers use their own criteria to define jobs to which employees adapt either in training programs (blue collar) or through obtaining university diplomas (white collar). The relationship between training and promotion is reversed in France. Management selects workers to be promoted and then provides them with the appropriate training (ibid.: 77). Firms provide in-house training for employees who usually have substantial experience in the firm. The various attempts by state officials to impose the recognition of state vocational training as a prerequisite for holding jobs have encountered strong opposition from employers (Marsden 1999: 98).[6]

Moreover, the vocational training system in Germany is autonomous from managerial interference. As previously mentioned, the organization of the workplace in Germany is predicated on the presence of a majority of workers with certifiable skills. It is also important to note that the importance of training in the German economy is legally based and protected from outside intervention (Culpepper 1998: 276). First, a high number of jobs requires certifiable skills that are acquired in vocational training programs. Second, industrial or regional chambers must certify the training programs of firms, and any change in the content of training certification – the modification of an existing certification or the introduction of a new one – requires the approval of a body of experts in which labor occupies half of the seats (ibid.). The veto power of employees on the board of the industrial and regional training commissions prevents significant modifications of the system and ensures a stable demand for certified employees. Third, firm-level works councils possess full veto power over hiring, thereby constraining managerial ability to rely on outside experts (Goyer 2002: 26). In other words, German managers are constrained on several fronts: skills are a prerequisite for jobs, management must provide the relevant training to employees, the content of these programs must be certified by an outside body where labor possesses a veto, and the hiring of new employees with the requisite skills is subject to the approval of works councils.[7] By contrast, the French case is characterized by the absence of a legal requirement to assign specific jobs to workers with certifiable skills. Attempts by state officials to impose the recognition of vocational training as a prerequisite for holding specific jobs have been defeated by French employers (Marsden 1999: 98). Boards of experts on training in France play only a consultative role (Culpepper 1998: 278). Firm-level works councils possess limited information rights on the hiring of new employees (Goyer 2002: 25). The content of training and the place of employees in the production process represent areas of pure managerial prerogative.

A third major difference in the organization of the workplace concerns the degree of autonomy for employees in the operation of the shop floor. The presence of extensive rules that regulate the nature of the tasks to be accomplished – rather than the functions to be performed – characterizes the organization of the workplace in France (Marsden 1999: 103–4; Maurice et al. 1986: 60–5). The implementation of the business strategy is accomplished through numerous sets of rules designed to specify the terms of exchange among parties. The organization of work is divided into fragmentary tasks whose content is predetermined. Moreover, the skills of employees tend to be narrow and highly connected to tasks. Highly qualified engineers elaborate the conception of products, and employees carry out the tasks following instructions (Linhart 1994). The organization of the workplace in France results in a high supervisor-to-worker ratio and a strict division of authority between management and employees (Maurice et al. 1986: 69–80).

The organization of work in Germany is characterized by the application of rules to broad functions, rather than by trying to predict all contingencies on the shop floor through heavy reliance on explicit instructions (Maurice et al. 1986: 65–73). The role of vocational training is also critical in this process. Employees are grouped according to the types of qualifications they possess, and tasks are organized according to their skill requirements (Marsden 1999: 38). The institutional arrangements of the workplace in Germany are characterized by blurred organizational boundaries and reduced segmentation, the delegation of control over the nature of work processes resulting in the involvement of employees in many tasks, and low reliance on formal rules in evaluating performance (Sorge 1991: 166). The degree of polyvalence of German employees is rather high since the organization of the workplace favors the acquisition of broad-based skills (Maurice et al. 1986: 69–73; Streeck 1991).

6. Discussion

What are the lessons emerging from the transformation of the French system of corporate governance? What are the implications for the French economy and society? What are the dynamics of change and the prospects for the sustainability of recent developments? The discussion in this section emphasizes the importance of institutional frameworks in the adjustment strategies of firms. The presence of institutional constraints made it extremely difficult for French (and German) managers to pursue specific shareholder value strategies. Institutions privilege some adjustment strategies at the expense of others. However, the process of institutional transformation of corporate governance cannot be read solely from the institutional matrix of incentives and constraints in which domestic companies are embedded. In the first place, the strategies of actors and the search for legitimacy among a repertoire of actions constitute critical elements in accounting for the transformation of French corporate governance (Hall 1999: 160). Moreover, the strategies of actors also matter since they often do not fully anticipate the consequences of their choices. Outcomes cannot be figured out solely from the institutional matrix since several scenarios are potentially available from even the most constraining framework (Hancké and Goyer 2005). The Cartesian bent of French policy-making is perhaps the last adjective that would be suited to capturing the nature of the transformation of corporate governance in France. I tackle four themes in this section: the importance of institutional frameworks, the role of legitimacy and strategy in institutional change, the issue of temporality associated with timing and sequence, and the unintended consequences associated with the strategies of actors with a focus on the French State.

First, the transformation of the French (and German) system of corporate governance testifies to the importance of the domestic institutional framework as a matrix of incentives and constraints that encourages some kinds of firm behavior and militates against others (Hall and Soskice 2001; Soskice 1999). Despite the presence of a range of strategies to deal with the issue of market capitalization, there are a limited number of responses available to firms and national systems of corporate governance. Some strategies are extremely difficult to pursue in a given institutional context (Hall 1999: 148). Institutions impose limited paths of adjustment upon rational actors – but these paths differ across nations because of specific domestic institutional frameworks. The process of refocusing in France and Germany took place along a trajectory shaped by the national institutional framework. The institutional arrangements of workplace organization, in this regard, constitute the key variable for the middle-range theoretical perspective of this chapter – that is, to account for the different strategies of shareholder value adopted by large French and German firms in response to changes in the external financial environment. The absence (or presence) of institutional constraints in work organization allowed (or prevented) top management to focus on core competencies (adopt financial transparency) as a strategy to raise the value of the firms' stock.

Second, institutions should not be seen as automatic mechanisms imposing a single path of adjustment upon rational actors. The drive for greater efficiency also reflects a search for strategies, operating procedures, and routines that fit well with the interpretive dimension of how companies operate (ibid.: 160). For example, the failure of French companies to adopt financial transparency is puzzling given the lack of institutional constraints in the conduct of the business strategy of the firm. However, the release of additional financial information to employees does not fit well with the mode of firm governance in France. As Hancké (2002) has demonstrated, the managerial strategy of removing skills from the shop floor in the 1980s was significantly influenced by the prior ability of craft workers to prevent the introduction of new production processes. Tight control over the production process constituted the managerial response to adversarial labor relations. The release of additional financial information in this context is likely to increase the demands of employees for a greater percentage of the gross value added of the company.[8] The institutional framework of work organization in France does not entail a single path of adjustment, but it contributes to the ranking of options according to both desirability and feasibility.

Moreover, the process of transformation of corporate governance in France cannot be understood without considering the choices and strategies of key actors involved in this process. The empirical data presented here have shown that the transformation of firm strategy in these two countries has not been system-wide but piecemeal. Each individual pattern of complementarity is characterized by some degrees of freedom (and of institutional plasticity) whereby a subset of institutional features can change without generating further demand for change in other spheres (see Berger's chapter in this volume). It is precisely during processes of transformation that the impact of institutional frameworks is more indeterminate than in normal circumstances – and that the strategies and choices of actors matter most.

Third, the timing and sequencing by which shareholder-value strategies were introduced does matter in regard to their implications for power relations in the firm. As previously mentioned in section 2, large corporations reacted differently (mid-1990s to 2003) to the new financial environment that rewards high stock market valuation: French companies have dismantled the conglomerate structure, limiting the number of core business activities; German companies have focused on financial transparency and respect for the voting rights of minority shareholders. However, this divergence has been recently lessened by a new EU directive requiring that listed firms must report according to IAS standards as of 1 January 2005. As a result, French companies are also providing extensive financial information on a regular basis. Should one conclude that the systems of corporate governance of France and Germany have converged?

I argue nonetheless that patterns of timing and sequence do matter for understanding different outcomes. A key issue is not only what types of strategies of shareholder value were adopted, but also when they were introduced. As Pierson (2000) argues, events may produce different outcomes depending on their timing. The critical issue is whether firms can translate pressures for high stock market valuation into new strategies that sustain the core complementarities of the domestic institutional framework. The focus on core competencies by large French companies – and the lack of compensation and protection for employees in peripheral units – fit within the mode of firm governance. The origins of the institutional arrangements of workplace organization in France are highly revealing in this regard. The propensity for uncertainty mitigation and avoidance of face-to-face relationships led firms to adopt mechanisms designed to both prevent the involvement of employees in the strategy of the firm as well as to protect firms from unpredictable intrusion (Crozier 1963). The relatively high percentage of supervisors, and the clear separation of planning, supervisory, and implementation tasks constituted key mechanisms designed to regulate the tensions inherent in French firms (Maurice et al. 1986: 65–120). Moreover, the withdrawal of the State from many areas of economic activities in the 1980s enabled large companies to impose firm-level flexibility unilaterally as well as being able to use the remaining state institutions for their own interests (Hancké 2002). The non-negotiated dismantling of the conglomerate structure since the mid-1990s constitutes the latest managerial-adjustment strategy that sidelines employees. The introduction of IAS standards in January 2005 – with its additional release of financial information – came "too late" as French firms have already learned to increase the valuation of their stock without relying on the involvement of employees. The potentially double-edged sword of international accounting standards for employees – pressures to adjust combined with greater knowledge of the situation of the firm – gave way to a single sledgehammer effect. Disfranchised French workers were in a precarious position and, thus, unable to seize the opportunities presented by the new EU directive.

Fourth, the strategies of actors should not be interpreted in an intentional Cartesian rationality. The strategies of actors are prone to experimentation, improvisation, and unintended consequences. The role of the State in the process of transformation of corporate governance is particularly revealing. The description of the transformation of French corporate governance in this chapter has privileged the role of management in orchestrating reforms without apparent constraints from the State. The dynamics of economic adjustment are deeply affected by the institutional arrangements of workplace organization – where the relative power of management over labor is substantial. CEOs and top managers have pursued the strategies that most appeal to them in a context where state officials ceded latitude on these issues.

Nevertheless, I argue that the role of the State has been critical in the transformation of French corporate governance – albeit best conceptualized as one of unintended consequences and of miscalculations. In many ways, the process of transformation of corporate governance in France and Germany represents instances of functional convergence as large firms in the two countries have responded, albeit in different ways, to broadly similar capital market pressures that required them to deal with the issue of stock market capitalization. But the achievement of functional convergence in one area through different means by French and German firms does not provide a basis for further functional convergence. The different strategies adopted by companies to tackle their low level of stock market capitalization actually reinforced other cross-national differences: focus on core competencies requires the continuing exclusion of French employees from the decision-making process, and the adoption of financial transparency improved the ability of German workers to act as co-managers of the firm. The greater attention paid by managers to shareholder value has left the organization of work unchanged in both countries.

The role of the State in the transformation of French corporate governance has been particularly important in this context. The key insight is that the institutions of workplace organization in France have not fundamentally changed – but the external environment in which they are embedded has. The concentration of power in top management, the non-involvement of employees in the strategy of the firm, and managerial dominance over training were previously counterbalanced by state policies under the period of economic *dirigisme*: administrative authorization for layoffs, currency devaluation, expansionist macroeconomic policies, extension of collective wage agreements, and use of the nominal rise in the minimum hourly wage as a substitute for wage bargaining. By contrast, state policies are no longer compensating employees for their lack of participation at the firm level. The implementation of shareholder value strategies in France constituted an assertion of managerial prerogatives at the expense of employees – a situation that contrasts substantially with that of Germany, where the introduction of financial transparency was a process negotiated with the workforce (Goyer 2003: 197–8). Thus, the withdrawal of the French State from many areas of economic activities cannot be interpreted simply as an attempt to behave like a neutral umpire. It has also institutionalized a set of power relations within large firms that imposed relatively few constraints on managerial autonomy – especially in contrast to the German situation.

Moreover, the sole instance where the French State intentionally tried to influence the development of the system of corporate governance – that is, cross-shareholding schemes for privatized firms – has been a complete failure. State officials employed the technique of the *noyaux durs* (a core shareholder group), in order to avoid hostile takeovers (Morin 1996). Between 15 and 30 percent of the equity of the privatized firms was reserved for a core group of shareholders, each owning between 0.5 and 5 percent of the corporation – with another 10 percent reserved for employees. These shareholders entered a pact of stability whereby they committed themselves to keep all of the shares of the privatized firm for the first year, and 80 percent for the following 18 months. The composition of the *noyaux durs* was restricted to a relatively small number of companies organized in two financial groups (ibid.). The first group was composed of BNP, ELF, Saint-Gobain, Pechiney, Suez, and UAP. The second group was composed of AGF, Alcatel, Havas, Paribas, Rhone-Poulenc, Société Générale, and Total.

The aim of these cross-shareholding schemes was not only to prevent hostile takeovers, but also to shape the preferences of firms based on a rather broad definition of mutual interests (often at the expense of shareholder value) as they became embedded in an extensive cross-shareholding network (ibid.: 1263). However, this desired feature of corporate governance collapsed by the late 1990s (see Culpepper's chapter in this volume). The percentage of shares held by fellow domestic companies fell to 3.5 percent in 2001 for the top 50 French firms – from a level of 15 percent in 1997. Foreign investors, which owned slightly over 50 percent of the equity capital of CAC 40 companies in late 1999, came in the wake of the collapse of domestic cross-shareholdings (Morin and Rigamonti 2002).

State officials did not fully grasp the implications associated with the new financial environment in which the importance of securities markets had become prominent. The network of cross-shareholding might well protect firms against hostile takeovers, but would be of little help to firms interested in proceeding to M&A via equity swaps. The critical issue is about achieving a high level of market capitalization – an objective that cross-shareholding was making harder to achieve.[9] Moreover, cross-shareholding had become a very costly scheme for companies. As of January 1996, more than 100 billion FF were immobilized in cross-shareholding (June 28 *Nouvel Economiste* 1996: 51). This figure represents three times the amount raised by all French firms on stocks markets in 1995. The system of cross-shareholding reinforced the pattern of undercapitalization, as the core shareholder group of the newly privatized firms constituted public sector corporations and other privatized companies. A limited group of relatively cash-poor firms held shares in each other.[10] The process of privatization in France aimed at protecting domestic firms from the market from corporate control through ownership concentration. The ultimate, and ironic, consequence was that the techniques of privatization significantly contributed to the low market capitalization of French companies, thereby making them attractive targets for foreign investors with the removal of restrictions on FDI in the mid-1990s.[11]

Conclusion

The transformation of corporate governance in France constitutes an exemplary case of a half-full glass. Firms have adapted quite well to the new financial environment and have become nimble players in world markets. The globalization of finance does not entail convergence along the lines of one model of corporate governance. The process of institutional change that took place in France reflects the importance of firm-level experimentation to adopt a greater shareholder-value orientation using existing institutional structures. Strategies of shareholder value have proven compatible with the institutional arrangements of workplace organization in France.

Nonetheless, the success of the transformation of corporate governance does not guarantee the sustainability of current institutional arrangements. The management-led transformation has generated a profound level of dissatisfaction. Even production-centered economic arrangements can generate political backlash if seen as illegitimate (Roe 1998). The lack of involvement of state officials and employees in the process of transformation of corporate governance took place in a context where the electorate still attached considerable importance to Republican ideals and still assigns an important role to the State in the economic sphere despite the structural transformation of the economy (Hall 2002). One should not look for a return of the State in economic affairs to resolve this tension, as the institutional apparatus that supported the *dirigiste* system has crumbled. Perhaps, the biggest missed opportunity lies in the continuing inability of French firms to develop a capacity for strategic thinking – an important attribute in a globalized economy (see Culpepper 2003). The adoption of shareholder-value practices being made on a firm-level basis – without coordination with employees and other firms – has reduced the ability of companies to coordinate adjustment. The disjunction between institutional transformation in the economic domain and malaise in the political and social spheres points to the need for further research on the nature of linkages within countries. The relative insulation of changes in the area of corporate governance from a wider impact on the rest of the system necessitates a careful analysis of how institutions operate and fit together.

Notes

Different versions of the paper were presented at the conference of Transforming France, Centre Americain, Institut D'Etudes Politiques, Paris, March 2003; and at the annual meeting of the American Political Science Association, Philadelphia, August 2003. I wish to thank Suzanne Berger, Pepper Culpepper, Peter Gourevitch, Peter Hall, Bob Hancké, Jonah Levy, and Richard Whittington for their comments on various versions of the paper. The usual disclaimers apply.

1 The conglomerate discount is calculated by comparing the stock market value of the diversified firm with that of the combined value of the different standalone businesses after the formal break-up of the conglomerate structure.

2 For example, over 72 percent of US Fortune 500 companies that voluntary dismantled their conglomerate structure in the 1980s did so precisely to increase their stock market capitalization and, thus, to avoid being targeted by hostile bidders (Markides 1995: 29).

3 This divergence in regard to the adoption of greater financial transparency also applies to the blue-chip companies. For the French CAC 40 index, the number of firms using an international accounting standard rose from 8 in 1996 to 9 in 2001. The same figures for the German DAX 30 index are respectively 2 in 1996 and 24 in 2001.

4 It is also important to note that this policy of merging firms into a larger one applies to companies in sectors in the orbit of the State (arms/Thomson-CSF, computer and microelectronics/Bull and CII, nuclear technology/Framatome, oil/Elf-Aquitaine, telecommunication/France Telecom among others) as well as to sectors in which the ability of the State to influence market outcomes was more limited (Alcatel, Danone, Pechiney, Rhone-Poulenc, Saint-Gobain, among others). It was often the managerial team of companies in the latter category that successfully used the tools provided by the State to pursue a policy of diversification (Bauer and Cohen 1981).

5 The continuing viability of the conglomerate structure, in contrast, is contingent on the ability to extract additional value from the mixing of different business activities – in other words, on the presence of relatedness among units.

6 The divergent method of coupling tasks and competencies is reflected in the role of vocational training in the two countries. The German system of occupational training is both prominent and autonomous – all in contrast to the French situation. In Germany, a substantially higher proportion of workers has received some vocational training. These cross-national differences have been long standing. In 1970, only 27.6 percent of active males had no basic vocational training compared to 79.7 percent in France (Maurice et al. 1984: 352). For the category of manual employees, 57.0 percent of German employees had completed a vocational training program compared to only 26.0 percent in France (ibid.: 354). By 1995, according to one study, the average number of trainees for large German firms (over 500 employees) was 6 per 100 workers with a retention rate of 85 percent. The corresponding figure for large French companies was 2.2 per 100 workers in 1996 with a retention rate of 35 percent (Culpepper 1998: 286, 301).

7 However, vocational training also entails some limits on the mobility of employees. German courts have regularly upheld competition clauses in labor contracts that prohibit workers from taking a job with another company with the same skill classification for up to two years. This legal restriction represents a response to the problem of poaching that is central to the issue of training – as the certifiable skills of German workers tend to be of a general nature (see Streeck 1991).

8 By contrast, employees in Germany internalize the heightened competitive requirements associated with financial transparency since they assume responsibility for the economic performance of the firm. The organization of the shopfloor in Germany ensures the participation of workers at an early stage in the decision-making process and works councils are key actors in the implementation of restructuring measures. In particular, works councils in Germany have been strong supporters of the adoption of greater financial transparency (see Hoepner 2001: 27–33).

9 For example, individual and employees equity holders who held their stocks for more than a certain period – from 18 to 24 months – were given free shares. The aim of this government measure was to stabilize the shareholding structure and prevent raiders from moving in quickly after the privatization of given firms. However, the issue of free shares without any increase in equity capital contributed to reduce the earnings per share of privatized firms that, in turn, negatively affected their share price and market capitalization.

10 For example, the core shareholders of Saint-Gobain (November 1986) were BNP, ELF, Suez, and UAP. The core shareholders of Suez (October 1987) were BNP, ELF, Saint-Gobain, and UAP. The core shareholders of BNP (October 1993) were ELF, Saint-Gobain, Suez, and UAP. And so on.

11 I wish to thank Peter Hall for mentioning this point.

Part II

4
The Long Good Bye to Bismarck? Changes in the French Welfare State

Bruno Palier

Introduction

From 1945 to the late 1970s, social policies in France expanded as one of the key features of the Keynesian compromises that underpinned the *trente glorieuses*. Social spending was perceived as favouring economic growth and employment, social insurance transfers were seen as consolidating social integration and (occupational) solidarity, and welfare-state institutions supported social peace. Since then, all the economic, social and political functions of the social protection systems have been called into question. After a long period of crisis and resistance, French social programmes are being reformed in order to become better adapted to the new economic and social environment. These reforms are supposed to increase the economic and social efficiency of social policies. Whether they are also politically legitimate and socially just remains questionable.

Besides presenting the major reforms of the French welfare system, this chapter will emphasize the changes in the dominant analyses of the problems and solutions from the 1970s to the early 2000s. Tracking the changes in ideas will show the paradigmatic shift in social policy that is underway in France, even though institutional stickiness and political protest against big changes would appear to counter the claim that the French welfare state has been radically changed. Looking at the politics of the reforms will enable the reader to see how profound changes have been introduced incrementally in France. The chapter will first recall the content of the Keynesian compromises in French social protection. It will then focus on the intellectual, political and institutional mechanisms through which the French welfare system is being reformed in three different phases. The conclusion will map out the main characteristics of the new social policy paradigm that is reflected in these changes, while at the same time underlining the social and political deficits of these reforms that seek the economic adaptation of the welfare state.

1. The Keynesian compromises in French social policy

In 1945, the French government as well as the main trade union, the CGT (Confédération générale du travail, Communist influence), chose to develop the French social security system (*Sécurité sociale*) through an ambiguous mix of Beveridgean goals (universality of coverage, unicity of the system) and Bismarckian means (social insurance). The development of the French social protection system has been based on specific Keynesian compromises, with social protection playing an important role in the shaping of the economic, social and political spheres.

The choices in 1945

In France, social insurance first emerged and developed within the realm of employment. First, the State, as an employer, provided social protection to civil servants. In the late nineteenth century, some 'social Catholic' employers began offering family allowances (*sursalaire familial*), while some workers' associations or friendly societies (*mutuelles*) offered benefits in case of redundancy, sickness or old age. These funds were managed in three different ways: directly by the workers through the trade unions (*gestion ouvrière*), directly by the employers (*gestion patronale*), or by both actors sharing the control of the funds (*paritarisme*) (Pollet and Renard 1995, 1997).

In 1945 the French Government had in mind to achieve universal and uniform coverage for the whole population (Beveridgean goals). Nevertheless, given the strength of the CGT and the strong resistance coming from those groups who already had access to specific social insurance schemes, it chose to remain within an employment-related social insurance framework instead of a universal state-run system. In 1945, the provisional government ruled by decree, and parliamentary institutions were temporarily sidelined. This political context empowered the left and the workers unions, while the employers' organizations were particularly weak because they had collaborated with the Nazis during the war (Merrien 1990). This specific climate favoured the projects put forward by the trade unions (mainly the CGT) and those among high civil servants who shared some corporatist views, such as Pierre Laroque, the so-called 'founding father' of the French *Sécurité sociale*.

Following this project, the French social welfare system was built up from 1945 to the 1970s. It is mainly based on a specific set of organizations called *la Sécurité sociale*. It covers not only income maintenance but also health care and some aspects of personal social services. The main component of the French social protection system is the social insurance system. In France, most benefits are earnings related, entitlement is conditional upon a contribution record, and financing is provided mainly by employers' and employees' contributions. The system is divided into a number of different programmes (*branches*) – health care, old age, family and unemployment insurance – and into different schemes (*régimes*) covering different occupational groups. The system is organized outside the State within social insurance funds managed by the social partners. Owing to these institutional arrangements, France is generally recognized as belonging to the Bismarckian family of welfare states.

Social policy paradigm of the *trente glorieuses*: the expansionary model

What was the role of social protection in economic, social and political life in France during the *trente glorieuses*?

Social spending and economic regulation

From 1945 to the late 1970s, social spending favoured economic growth and employment. Social policies were perceived as complementary to full employment, wage and labour-market policies. Social benefits helped to consolidate workers' earnings capacity; they guaranteed income maintenance and could be used as tools for reflation policies in order to sustain or boost demand in case of low economic growth. Governments could affect households' income through the modification of the level of social contribution (payroll taxes) and social benefits. From the late 1950s onwards, social benefits have increased. Their share in French households' income has gone from 19.3 per cent in 1960 to 32.4 per cent in 1980 and even 36.9 per cent in 1985. The French social protection system has also been conceived as directly favourable to employment, insofar as it supports the economic activity in the social and health sectors. Thanks to the social protection system, jobs have been created in hospitals, health professions, social work, etc. In 1992, 1,657,839 jobs were related to the health care sector, that is, 7.4 per cent of total employment in France (Chadelat 1995: 87–8). Social security funds employed 180,000 people in 1994 (Beau 1995).

Social protection mechanisms and social regulation

For a long time, social-protection mechanisms were perceived as improving both the living standards and the living conditions of the French population. An increase in lifelong security has occurred. Child mortality has diminished and life expectancy has increased. The elderly were much less poor in the 1970s and 1980s than in the 1940s. In all the surveys focused on these issues, public opinion finds that the French social security system is one of the major contributions of the post-war period to their well-being (Palier 2002).

With its expansion, the French social protection system also contributed to the social integration of the different components of French society. At the same time, it was establishing and legitimating the global social order of a 'wage-earner society' (Castel 1995). The main goal of the founders of the social security system in the mid-1940s was the economic and social integration of the working class, to prevent any revolutionary movement in a country where the communist party won around 25 per cent of the votes in general elections. They developed a social insurance system for the workers and their families (the *régime général de la Sécurité sociale*). In the following years, social protection expanded through the multiplication of similar, specific schemes for other occupational groups. All the different occupational groups were integrated into the same society with a common model (the wage-earner), but allowed enough room for corporatist differentiation so that each group was a member of the same society while its own identity was recognized. As in other Bismarckian welfare states, social protection is based on occupational status and acquired through the payment of social contribution, considered as a deferred wage. Social rights seem then to be obtained through work and appear to be extremely legitimate: people work for their own social security.

Institutions of social protection and political regulation

In the 1940s, there was a shared view, notably among the senior civil servants who expanded the social protection system, that corporatist organization was a good thing. In line with Durkheim's point of view on the role of intermediary institutions in society, the projects for the development of social insurance had striven since the 1920s to contribute to 'social peace through the participation of the workers in national decision-making'. The participation of workers' representatives in the management of the social protection system is called *la démocratie sociale,* with the goal of guaranteeing social and political integration of workers as well as worker/employer collaboration (Merrien 1990; Castel 1995).

The corporatist organization and management of the French social protection system has indeed contributed to 'social peace' through both the social integration of workers and collaboration between employers and employees' representatives. The development of the social protection system, in which the social partners and especially the unions play an important role, has also allowed a specific distribution of power among the major actors of the French political economy. Some commentators speak of an 'implicit Yalta':[1] as if State policies were the responsibility only of the State and its senior civil servants (with no intervention of the social partners, and no neo-corporatism for the State policies); as if the realm of production and firms was reserved for the employers (French union density being among the lowest in the developed countries); and as if social protection institutions were given (as a kind of compensation) to the trade unions. The latter could compensate for their weakness in the realm of production by the material and symbolic resources provided by their managerial role within the social protection system.

One of the most important resources that the system provides to the trade unions is the control of the staff working within the insurance funds. The legislation gives all responsibilities for employees' recruitment to the governing boards of the Funds. Therefore, belonging to the trade union that chairs the Fund becomes a criteria to be hired. Also, the Funds (mainly the national ones) provide pseudo-jobs and actual wages for people in reality working for the trade unions (Catrice-Lorey 1995; Duclos and Mériaux 1997; various reports of the Cour des Comptes, notably 1990 and 2000). The second type of resource is more symbolic: the French public's perception of trade unions as the defenders of the system and of the social advantages associated with it. In France (as in other Bismarckian countries), one of the most powerful pro-welfare coalitions is headed and represented by the trade unions. The trade unions act as the representatives and defenders of the system. They defend both the interests of the salaried population and their own interests.

During the *trente glorieuses*, the French social protection system played a positive role for economic growth and employment, social progress and social integration, political legitimization of the social order, and sustaining social peace. Step by step, all these positive connotations of the social protection system to the economy, the society and the polity would in a later period be questioned and transformed. This trend started after the mid-1970s.

2. Balancing the budget of *Sécurité sociale*

The first consequences of the economic crisis of the mid-1970s for social protection were twofold. On the one hand, the crisis meant fewer resources for the system (less social contribution due to slow economic growth, lower wage increases and higher unemployment); on the other hand, it meant more expenses: more unemployed people to protect, new social expenditure to remove workers from the labour market (through early retirement or earlier retirement age from 65 to 60). Meanwhile the system reached the acme of its maturation (universal access to family benefits, health care and pensions – laws in 1974 and 1978; more generous pensions since 1972, and more full pensions; the creation of new benefits for uninsured groups such as orphans (1970), the handicapped (1973) and single parents (1976)).

The main problem that emerged was huge deficits of the social protection budget. These deficits are no longer understood as temporary deficits that a traditional reflationary policy would eventually solve. At the beginning of the 1980s, two French governments learned the hard way that the Keynesian chain was broken. Through Jacques Chirac's failure in 1974–76 and Pierre Mauroy's in 1981–82, the Keynesian use of social benefits was emphatically delegitimized for both left and right governments. In both cases, these prime ministers had tried to increase social benefits in order to boost private consumption and economic activities. They both ended with larger public deficits, negative trade balances, inflation and increases in unemployment and taxes. Both in 1976 and in 1982, their economic policies had to be made radically more restrictive and monetarist.

After these negative experiences, every subsequent government has resolved that the social security deficits should be balanced. However, between the two solutions available to balance a social protection budget (increase of resources or cuts in the expenses), the choice was made to increase resources during the 1970s and the 1980s, for two reasons. First, social benefits were still perceived as being able to help the victims of a crisis. During the 1980s, governments used social expenditure to soften the hardest social consequences of industrial restructuring and the resulting lay offs. This was called social treatment of unemployment. These policies were designed to remove the oldest workers from the labour market, by lowering the legal age for retirement (from 65 to 60 in 1981) and encouraging early retirement: (84,000 people retired early in 1975, 159,000 in 1979, 317,000 in 1981 and 705,000 in 1983; Bichot 1997: 132). This 'welfare without work strategy' is typical of a Bismarckian welfare system, as shown by Esping-Andersen (1996).

The second reason why the government preferred to increase social contributions rather than retrench social expenditure is mainly that the trade unions contested the idea that government should cut social insurance benefits. During the 1970s and the 1980s, the social security deficit was understood in two different ways. Governments, experts and economists analysed it as a consequence of decreasing resources and rising expenses. For them, the solution was either to increase resources (social contributions) or cut expenses. However, trade unions had a different interpretation. They claimed that the deficit resulted from the State's use of the social insurance funds to finance non-contributory benefits (such as social minima for the poor, the elderly or single parents). For the defenders of the social insurance systems, the 'undue charges' (*les charges indues*) explained the deficit, which could be removed if the State paid for its own welfare policies (national solidarity benefits implying vertical redistribution). From the trade union perspective, the deficit did not justify reduction in the level of the contributory benefits for which workers had paid in their contributions. Since the unions showed on several occasions that they were able to mobilize the population in order to defend the level of social insurance benefits, and since another solution was available (increase in social contribution), governments chose the latter.

For at least 15 years, governments avoided major retrenchment and preferred to increase social contributions to balance the social security deficit. Instead of developing an accusatory rhetoric against the welfare state, which would have provoked the whole population and trade unions, they recognised the importance of the *Sécurité sociale*, but underlined the dangers of its current situation and presented measures that were aimed not at reforming the system but only at restoring its viability. Until the early 1990s, no French government, left or right, even the most neo-liberal (under Jacques Chirac as Prime Minister, from 1986 to 1988), attempted to dismantle the system.

From 1975 to 1995 (unless an election was imminent), each time a deficit of *Sécurité sociale* was announced, corrective measures were proposed in a *plan de redressement des comptes de la Sécurité sociale* (programme for balancing the social insurance system's budget). These consisted typically of increases in contributions paid by employees and some limited economizing measures, mainly in health. Between 1975 and 1992, these plans have mainly implied an increase in users' charges, through a gradual lowering of the level of reimbursement of health care expenditure.[2] However, during the same period, all contributory benefits, such as sick pay, old age pensions and unemployment insurance benefits have increased or at best been stabilized. Consequently, social expenditure continued to increase rapidly until the mid-1980s, and it has risen more slowly since then (Palier 2000). The proportion of social protection expenditure in GDP grew from 19.4 per cent in 1974 to 27.3 per cent in 1985 and 27.75 per cent in 1992.[3]

Increasing costs have always been compensated for by an increase in the resources. During the 1980s, while they were decreasing the level of direct income taxation, French governments also increased the level of contributions paid by employees. The share of contributions in taxation as well as their proportion of GDP has increased sharply: social contributions amounted to less than 20 per cent of French GDP in 1978 and almost 23 per cent by 1985. It has stabilized at this level ever since (*Comptes de la protection sociale*, various years – Palier 2002). Because of the tendency to increase social contribution to balance the social security budget (which would have been a much less attractive option if the system had been financed out of taxation), governments have long been able to maintain a high level of social protection in a period of crisis. Thus, the first responses to the financial crisis in the French welfare state resulted in changes in the level of the benefits (some new benefits, stabilization of unemployment benefits after 1984, and some reductions in benefits, especially in reimbursement for health care), an increase in the number of the beneficiaries (unemployment insurance, early retirement, pension at the age of 60) and an increase in the level of social contribution.

In order to avoid conflict with social partners and with the population, governments applied 'good old recipes'. It was politically easier to raise social contributions than to cut social benefits. Governments utilized the available social policy instruments without really creating new instruments or adopting new goals for their policies, thus implementing first-order changes (Hall 1993). Faced with social security deficits, other countries (liberal and Nordic mainly) and the mainstream literature on the welfare state expect cuts; people usually conclude that the French welfare state (like other Bismarckian ones) is frozen (Esping-Andersen 1996). In fact, it appears that the French welfare state has responded to the new situation more than the image of frozen continental welfare states would imply. As a consequence of these policies, during the late 1970s and the 1980s, both social spending and social contributions have continued to increase in France. In the 1990s, both trends became problematic in the new European environment.

3. Retrenchments in social insurance

After the early 1990s, European integration included the adoption of the single currency and imposition of the Maastricht criteria. With Maastricht, French governments were obliged to control the public deficit (including the social security deficit) as well as the inflation rate, and therefore to control the growth of social expenditure. After 1992/1993, retrenching social expenditure had to be included in the strategy of reducing public expenditure and public deficits in order to meet the Maastricht criteria. Commitment to the single currency led to the imposition of sectoral reforms in unemployment insurance in 1992, the pension system in 1993 and health care in 1995.

One could argue that these reforms would have been necessary without Maastricht (since the major problems are not linked with Europe, but with domestic developments),[4] and that Maastricht was a scapegoat to avoid blame. However, it appears that the Maastricht process helped government, at least rhetorically, to impose reforms otherwise seen as not feasible, especially in conservative corporatist welfare systems. In several continental welfare states, the timing of the reforms that have been implemented is intriguing. Reforms in the pension system, in health insurance and in unemployment insurance seem to be concentrated in the first half of the 1990s: the 1989 pension reform (called the 1992 pension reform) and the 1992 Seehofer Reform of health care in Germany in 1992, the Amato (1992) and Dini (1995) pension reforms in Italy, the 1993 Balladur pension reforms, and the 1995 Juppé plan (implemented as far as health insurance is concerned) in France. Moreover, in the early 1990s, certain European countries (Netherlands, Ireland, Denmark, Spain, Italy) have concluded social pacts which included important reforms of part of their welfare states (Rhodes 2001). It may be that the timing is purely coincidental but all the above reforms have been justified by governments as necessary in order to meet the Maastricht criteria.

If Maastricht imposed the timing, it may also have limited the range of responses to welfare state difficulties and orientated reforms. As Fritz Scharpf has demonstrated, the changes in the international environment had strong implications for policy instruments available to governments. European integration is part of these international changes. 'The Maastricht criteria for joining the Monetary Union have practically eliminated deficit spending as a policy tool; and the realization of the Monetary Union has completely removed monetary policy and exchange rate policy from the control of its member states' (Scharpf 2000). As a consequence, increases in social contributions as a solution to deficits were no longer affordable, since they could not be compensated for through an adjustment of the exchange rate in order to maintain the price competitiveness of national products. The effect seems particularly important for continental welfare states. Increasing contributions, which is politically easier than retrenchment, were not adapted in the new economic context. However, it is only under the constraints imposed by the Maastricht criteria that, in Continental Europe, a change occurred in the policies implemented: instead of increasing social contributions, governments started to try to reduce the level of social benefits through the above reforms. In this new context, social spending is viewed neither as economic investment nor as support of economic growth, but instead as a cost in need of better control.

In France, as in other countries with a Bismarckian welfare system, reforms have been implemented in order the better to control the growth of social insurance expenditure. These changes have been imposed by the choice for Europe made by all French governments, but have also been possible thanks to one trade union, the CFDT, which chose to pursue a reformist strategy and new alliances with the employers' movement in order to outmanoeuvre its two main competitors (CGT and FO).

The unemployment insurance system was reformed in 1992 through an agreement between the CFDT and the employers' association. The reform meant the replacement of all the different unemployment insurance benefits by the *Allocation Unique Dégressive* (AUD). The new unemployment insurance benefit is payable only for a limited period of time, depending on contribution record. The amount of the benefit decreases with time, and entitlement expires after 30 months. Afterwards, unemployed people must rely on tax-financed, means-tested benefits. The level and the volume of unemployment benefits started to fall after 1992, the reduction being greater for the means-tested benefits than for the insurance one. As AUD was delivering smaller benefits for a shorter period, the minimum income benefits increasingly functioned as a safety net for the long-term unemployed (Outin 1997).

In 1993, the Balladur government reformed the main basic pension scheme, which covers private-sector employees. This was made possible by a package that traded benefit cuts for the tax financing of non-contributory benefits, and by the fact that the reform was limited to the private-sector general scheme (Bonoli 1997). The indexation of benefits was based on prices and earnings, initially for a 5-year period, but it has since been extended indefinitely. The qualifying period for a full pension was extended from 37.5 to 40 years, and the period over which the reference salary is calculated moved from the best 10 years to the best 25. These reforms were introduced gradually over a 10-year transition period. In exchange for the acceptance of the reform by the trade unions, the government created a *Fonds de solidarité vieillesse* (FSV), which has the task of funding non-contributory benefits. This FSV allowed the State to pay for the non-contributory benefits, thus paying for the 'undue charges' and reassuring the social partners on the continuity of PAYG (pay as you go) old-age insurance schemes. The 1993 reform will have an impact on pension levels and retirement ages, since some employees will delay retirement in order to qualify for a full pension and others will receive a much lower pension than they expected. In 2003, the Raffarin government completed this reform with the aligning of the public sector with the private one. From 2008 onwards, civil servants will also have to work for 40 years in order to be entitled to a full pension, and public pension increases will also be indexed according to prices. This last reform also created the potential for wage-earners in the private sector to choose a personal pension plan (PERP, *plan d'épargne retraite populaire,* see Palier 2003). In 1993 as in 2003, the CFDT supported the pension reform while the other trade unions opposed it.

The numerous 'plans' implemented during the late 1970s and the 1980s (see above) were not successful in limiting the unstoppable growth in the demand for health care. After 1990, the government decided to force the medical professions, the Health Insurance Funds and the State to elaborate a *convention médicale* (medical care agreement) to help control spiraling costs. The medical care agreement is an instrument for budgetary control, as it sets a provisional target for the evolution of the health care spending, practitioners' remuneration and additional expenses. The agreement has to be negotiated and signed by the social partners, but under the 1995 Juppé plan, the State can replace the social partners when the latter are unable to reach an agreement. However, the new instruments (medical agreements, state sanction) developed in the early 1990s were still not sufficient to stem rising health spending. In the summer of 2004, a new reform for saving the health insurance system was elaborated by Philipe Douste Blazy, which further increased resources and diminished reimbursement, allowing for a greater role for private health insurance and complementary private health insurances. It has also changed the distribution of power within the health insurance schemes, at the expense of the social partners, towards a new strong man appointed by the State, the Director of all the main Health Insurance Funds.

All these reforms, as well as others implemented in other Bismarckian welfare states, share some features from the institutional settings of welfare systems based on social insurance. They introduced new instruments but remained within the traditional (historical and institutional) logic of the Bismarckian welfare system.

First, the retrenchment reforms were not presented by politicians as a means to dismantle the Bismarckian welfare state, but to preserve and consolidate it. In the political discourses justifying the reforms, one can hear that if a reform is necessary, it is not because the system is dysfunctional, but because it suffers from the current situation, where resources are decreasing (because of economic slow-down or unemployment) while spending is increasing (because of unemployment, aging or new social demands). Since it no longer appears possible to increase resources because of Europe, governments have to retrench. Since the benefits to be reduced are extremely legitimate, these reforms are not made in the spirit of criticism of welfare redistribution, but in the name of necessity to restore their viability.

Second, they are usually negotiated, often between different political parties, and almost always with social partners. This can be understood as a consequence of the participation of the social partners in the management of social insurance schemes. Since the systems are financed through social contribution levied on wages (and not through taxation), the representatives of those who pay into and benefit from the systems are central players in the political game concerning social policy reforms (Bonoli and Palier 1996). They have a say in the process of the reforms, and have the power to block them eventually if they do not agree (as illustrated in 1995). Here, the role of trade unions relates less to the general political institutions than it does to welfare state design. Indeed, France is far from being a consensual political system; however, as with its Bismarckian counterparts, no social policy reforms could be passed without (at least implicit) agreement of (at least a majority of) the social partners (e.g., in pension reforms in 1993 or 2003).

Third, the main technique used to reduce welfare benefits through these reforms is the strengthening of the link between the amount of contribution and the volume of the benefits (through a change in the calculation formula and/or stricter entitlement rules). This relies on the already existing logic of these social insurance schemes (where one receives the right to social benefits by paying social contribution), even though these reforms usually mean a shift from redistribution (horizontal and vertical) to actuarial principles.

Finally, the acceptance by social partners of these decreases in benefits is based on a quid pro quo (Bonoli 2001) based on the distinction between what should be financed through contribution and what should be financed through taxation. The retrenchment reforms in social insurance programmes are always accompanied by a clarification of responsibility, the government proposing to the social partners that they assume the financing of non-contributory benefits (the so-called *charges indues*: flat-rate social minima for the elderly, the handicapped and the long-term unemployed; credit of contribution for period out of work because of unemployment or child rearing) in exchange for the general decrease in social insurance benefits.

These changes are based on new instruments (changes in calculation rules, a shift from defined benefits to defined contribution systems, and creation of new State subsidies) but are perceived as preserving the very nature of social insurance, sometimes even as reinforcing it (social partners often think that making the State pay for non-contributory benefits helps to 'purify' and thus reinforce social insurance). They do not really challenge the principles of social insurance and can be considered second-order changes (Hall 1993).

However, since through these reforms, the coverage of social insurance is shrinking (fewer people covered, less generous benefits), more and more space is created for the development of new benefits, either complementary on top of compulsory social insurance (private pensions for instance) or, at the bottom, for those who lost (or never gained) their rights to social insurance. This development has lead to criticism of social insurance for not being able to cope with social exclusion, and to the development of a new world of welfare in France.

4. The progressive dualization of the welfare system

All the reforms presented above have had spillover effects. The plans to balance the social security budget increased the level of social contribution. Retrenchment measures meant less generous benefits, more people left out, that is, a need for new (non-contributory) benefits. All these reforms have been difficult to implement, because they inspired demonstrations, strikes and resistance from some trade unions. The accumulation of these spill-over effects led the social protection system to shift from a positive to a negative role in the economic, social and political regulation of France. In the 1990s, new diagnoses of the difficulties started to be popularized among experts, politicians and even trade unionists, which implied that the system was not a victim of the crises, but part of the cause of the social, economic and political difficulties of France.

New analyses of the crisis of the welfare state

Social insurance has been blamed for economic, social and political problems through three broad mechanisms. First, the contributory nature of most social benefits reinforces social exclusion. Second, the weight of social contribution prevents job creation. Third, joint-management of the system by social partners engenders irresponsibility and a management crisis of the system.

Since the late 1970s, France has seen a significant increase in unemployment. The social insurance system set up in 1945 was not designed to cope with mass unemployment. This predominantly contributory system is unable to deal with those who have never been involved in the labour market or who have been removed from it for a long period. Because they have never contributed to social insurance, or because they are no longer contributing, the young unemployed or long-term unemployed have no access to social insurance rights. Because of the 1992 reform of unemployment insurance, more and more unemployed can no longer rely on unemployment insurance. The number of 'excluded people' increased throughout the 1980s, so that by the late 1980s it became one of the most pressing social issues, and less-inclusive social insurance appeared unable to cope with this problem.

The system was also said to be producing unemployment. In France until 1996, 80 per cent of social protection was financed through employment-related contributions. The weight of social contributions increased during the 1980s. The high level of contributions is seen to have had an overall negative impact on the country's economic competitiveness and to be responsible for the high rate of unemployment. The argument is that social insurance contributions inhibit job creation, since they have a direct impact on the cost of low-skilled labour. Consequently, the weight of *charges sociales* has become a central issue in the French debate. Any report on the financing of the French social protection system underlines the need to lower labour costs by decreasing the level of social contributions.

The management arrangement is also criticized. In 1945, the management of the social insurance system was given to the social partners in the name of democracy (*démocratie sociale*) and in order to avoid bureaucratization and the subordination of social policy efficiency to purely budgetary considerations. As budget control became an important issue during the 1980s and 1990s, the devolution of the management of social insurance to the social partners has become problematic: the government is accusing the social partners of hijacking the social security funds, abusing their position within the system at the expense of the general good, and shirking their responsibility for containing cost increases. The strongest opposition to changes is not from political confrontation, but from trade unions and social mobilization when governments tried to implement major reforms. Within the governmental sphere, the social partners' involvement in social insurance is nowadays considered a source of inefficiency, and it is believed the State would more effectively contain expenditure increases.

In recent analysis of the problems encountered by Bismarckian welfare systems, the causes of the difficulties seem to be the very characteristics of these systems (contributory benefits, financed by social contribution, managed by the social partners). Meanwhile, all the bases of the Keynesian compromise are undermined: protecting the workers does not support social integration anymore, but leads to social exclusion; the system does not contribute to economic growth anymore, but impedes it because of its financing mechanisms; the *démocratie sociale* does not sustain social peace, but allows demonstration and blockages. The basic institutional settings of the French social protection system reinforce problems, they impede important reforms, and they cause economic and social difficulties. A change in political discourses and agenda for all governments occurred around the late 1980s–early 1990s: instead of only restoring the viability of *Sécurité sociale*, the aim of governmental intervention became to transform it. This has been done through several structural reforms that are often neglected in the analyses of welfare retrenchments. These are incremental reforms aimed at changing the politics of social protection, often marginal in the beginning (Bonoli and Palier 1998). After several years of development, their importance becomes more visible.

New benefits

In order to cope with new social problems that social insurance is unable to deal with, governments are developing new social policy instruments that make reference to new social policy goals. In light of the growing number of jobless, youth or long-term unemployed, and single parents, new benefits have been created or formerly marginal benefits have been developed. The creation of the RMI (*Revenu Minimum d'Insertion*) is the most important of these new social benefits. This new non-contributory scheme, meant for those having no or very low income, was introduced in December 1988. Its main features are the guarantee of a minimum level of resources to anyone aged 25 or over, which takes the form of a means-tested differential benefit. In addition, the RMI has a re-insertion dimension, in the form of a contract between the recipient and 'society'. Recipients must commit themselves to take part in a re-insertion programme, as stated in a contract, signed by the recipient and a social worker. Such a programme can be either job-seeking, vocational training or activities designed to enhance the recipient's social autonomy. When it was created, this new benefit was supposed to be delivered to 300,000 to 400,000 people. In 2005, almost 1.3 million people were receiving RMI. Including spouses and children of recipients, 3.5 per cent of the French population was involved. Besides the RMI, France now has seven other social minimum income programmes. More than 10 per cent of the French population is currently receiving one of these benefits. This means that through the development of new social policies and the development of minimum income benefits, part of the French social protection system is now targeting specific populations by using new instruments (means-tested benefits delivered according to needs, financed through state taxation and managed by national and local public authorities), with reference to a new logic (to combat social exclusion instead of to guarantee income and status maintenance). The use of this new repertoire of social policy has also been extended to health care. In 2000, a new scheme was created for providing free access to health care to the poorest, and, for those who could not pay for supplementary health care, free supplementary health insurance. This new scheme (called Couverture Maladie Universelle, CMU) is means-tested.

Furthermore, the development of targeted benefits aimed at poverty alleviation within the French social protection system has imported a new logic that was almost absent in France before. Traditionally in the liberal welfare states, these benefits are accused of creating a dependency culture and unemployment traps. By the late 1990s, more and more studies in France showed that people receiving social minima, especially RMI, were losing money and social advantages if they took a part-time job paid at the minimum wage level.[5] At first, people receiving RMI who found a job were allowed to collect RMI and their new wage (if very low) for a while (three then six months) so that they did not lose anything when getting a job. Moreover, in order to improve the incentive to go back to the labour market, in 2001 the Jospin government created a tax credit, the *Prime pour l'emploi*, which is a negative income tax for low-paying jobs. Both a totally new rhetoric (unemployment trap, work disincentive) and a totally new type of social policy instrument (working family tax credit) have been introduced by the development of the world of poverty alleviation in France. In the same vein, in 2003, the Raffarin government is transforming the RMI into RMA (*Revenu Minimum d'Activité*) for those having received RMI for two years, conditioning benefits to professional activities in order to increase the incentive to work.

Very recently, this trend towards activation can also be found in social insurance. In 2000, the social partners have signed a new agreement reforming the unemployment social insurance, which eliminated the degressivity of the unemployment insurance benefit while it creates a new individualized contract for each job seeker so that they are accompanied in their search for a job (The *Plan d'aide et de Retour à l'Emploi* – Pare). The social partners who signed this new convention explicitly agreed on the idea that unemployment insurance benefits should not only compensate for the loss of income, but also encourage people to find a new job. As for the pension system, the solutions that are currently promoted to solve the future crisis of the PAYG system are based on the idea that people should contribute and work longer. Increasing the employment rate has become part of the solution promoted to solve the pension problem. One can see here that welfare reform in France strives to spur the unemployed into productive activity, making a u-turn from a welfare without work strategy to employment friendly restructuring of the system. This attempt to render the system more employment friendly also reinforced the shift in financing.

New financing

During the 1980s, the employers representatives as well as many economists criticized the excessive cost of non-wage social contributions in France. We have seen that to cope with financing problems, the different French governments have often raised the level of contributions paid by the employees. However, since the late 1980s, governments of different political orientations have adopted contribution-exemptions for employers in order to encourage job creation. These measures are usually targeted on some particularly disadvantaged groups, such as the long-term and young unemployed, or on small companies, which are considered to be the most affected by the relatively high cost of unskilled labour. In order to generalize this movement of lowering labour costs by reducing the level of social contributions paid by the employers, governments have replaced some contribution with taxation.

A new tax was created in December 1990, the *Contribution Sociale Généralisée* (CSG), originally aimed at replacing the social contribution financing non-contributory benefits. Unlike insurance contributions, it is levied on all types of personal income: wages (even the lowest ones), but also capital revenues and welfare benefits. Unlike income tax in France, CSG is strictly proportional and ear-marked for non-contributory welfare programmes. In the early 1990s, the CSG appeared to play a marginal role in the system. When it was introduced, the CSG was levied at 1.1 per cent of all incomes. In 1993, the Balladur government increased the CSG to 2.4 per cent of incomes. In 1995, the Juppé plan set it at 3.4 per cent of all income, and since 1998 the rate has been at 7.5 per cent, replacing most of the health care contributions paid by employees. CSG now provides more than 20 per cent of all social protection resources and represents 35 per cent of the health care system's resources.

The introduction of this ear-marked tax has enabled a shift in the financing structure of the system towards more state taxation. This new instrument has two main general consequences that affect the logic of the system. First, since financing comes not only from the working population, the CSG breaks the link between employment and entitlement. Access to CSG-financed benefits cannot be limited to any particular section of society. The shift in financing thus creates the conditions for the establishment of citizenship-based social rights, especially in health care, where a new scheme, the CMU, was developed in 2000. Second, this shift in financing means diminished legitimacy for the social partners, participation in the management by of the provision financed through general taxation, because in France, there is a fairly strong normative perception that joint management by employers and employees is only acceptable if schemes are financed through employment-related contributions. In this respect, a shift towards taxation constitutes pressure for a transfer of control from the social partners to the State. This corresponds to more important political changes in the distribution of power within the system since the mid-1990s.

A new distribution of power

The problem of containing social expenditure is seen by French politicians and civil servants as a consequence of the lack of State control over the system. Therefore, some reforms have been implemented in order to empower the State within the system, at the expense of the social partners' influence. New instruments have been invented to reinforce the autonomy of the State within the system. These reforms were implemented after the Juppé plan of 1995. The most important reform is the vote of a constitutional amendment (in February 1996) obliging the parliament to approve the social security budget every year. For the first time in France, the parliament is taking part in the debate on the *Sécurité sociale* budget, which had never before been part of the State budget. Every year, the parliament decides the total amount of resources and expenses of the *Sécurité sociale* in a *loi de financement de la Sécurité sociale*. The use of the new parliamentary competence helps the government control the social policy agenda. Instead of always having to legitimize their intervention in a field originally belonging to the realm of labour and employers, with the institutionalization of a parliamentary vote, they are now able to plan adaptation measures, especially cost-containment ones. This new instrument also introduces a new logic of intervention. Instead of trying to find resources to finance social expenditure driven by demands of the insured, the vote of a *loi de financement* implies that a limited budget should be allocated for social expenditure. As most of the social benefits are still contributory, it is impossible to define a priori a limited budget, but governments are entering this new logic, and the parliament votes new instruments aimed at this purpose, such as limited global budgets for hospitals and ambulatory doctors, ceilings and rate of growth for social expenditure.

As a consequence, the influence of the social partners is diminishing. This is especially true in health care, where the new director, appointed by the State, is really mastering the main commands, at the expense of the trade unions and employers who have now merely an advisory role. The employers' association (MEDEF [Mouvement des Enterprises de France]) has contributed to this demise of the role of the social partners. In November 1999, in order to protest against the increasing power of the State within industrial relations (through the imposition of the 35 hours) and within social protection (through the application of the Juppé plan), the employers' association launched a project of a new social constitution, later renamed the *refondation sociale*. The *refondation sociale* consisted of a series of bilateral negotiations with trade unions on workplace and social issues, which the employers' association openly portrayed as an effort to clip the wings of the State (Levy 2001). However, these bilateral negotiations focused only on certain issues (unemployment insurance, complementary pension schemes), when others were neglected (family policy, health care). In fall 2001, the employers' association decided to leave the administrative board of all the *Sécurité sociale* funds, leaving the State coping directly with the management of health care, family benefits and basic pension. The social partners tried to reaffirm their power within the realm of social insurance (pension and unemployment) while they left others to the State.

These structural developments all contribute to change the original Bismarckian nature of the French social security system, and move towards State-run, tax-financed logic and practices, in the area of health care, family benefits and poverty alleviation. The traditional way of providing social protection in France has been fiercely criticized and destabilized, and the new instruments aimed at coping with the structural difficulties of the French social system belong to another, non-Bismarckian logic. After several years of implementation, one can see that these reforms are not marginal, but concern a large proportion of the population and a significant share of the financing, and they have given the State more avenues for intervening within the system. These changes lead to the conclusion that the system is currently being dualized.

A triple dualization is underway. First, all reforms tend to separate two worlds of welfare within the French social protection system. The first one is the remaining realm of social insurance (mainly old-age and unemployment insurance), where professional solidarity is central. In these domains, benefits are still acquired through work, but with greater reference to the level of contribution than before. The second world of welfare is called the realm of national solidarity. It entails health care, family benefits and policies aimed at fighting social exclusion. Here, the benefits can be either universal or means-tested, they are financed out of taxation, and the State plays a more important role than before. Second, since in all domains the compulsory public social protection is shrinking, new space is left open for the development of private complementary social insurance (especially in health and pensions). Each recent reform (in 2003 and 2004) has created new opportunities for the development of such private schemes. Finally, there is a third dualization going on, which separates the French population into two different groups: those who are still able to rely on social insurance (complemented by some private schemes) to provide their (still generous) social protection, and those (from 10 to 15% of the population) who only rely on targeted minimum benefits.

These trends are accommodated rather than contested by the social partners. As seen before, most of the retrenchments in social insurance benefits are negotiated on the basis of a distinction between insurance and solidarity. This lead to the separation of the two worlds that were once closely associated, when the system was supposed to reach Beveridgean goals of universality through the means of Bismarck (social insurance).

The politics of structural reforms

Contrary to the way some important policy changes have been implemented in other countries or fields (Hall 1986, 1993), these structural (third-order) changes have been implemented in a very ambiguous and incremental way in France (as in other Bismarckian countries). The analysis of the politics of such reforms shows similarities between the different political processes.

First, it is impossible to claim that one specific group of actor has been the main, unique and causal agent of all these changes. Changing a welfare system with as much political legitimacy as the French one requires that all the actors involved in social policies participate. With a coalition of senior civil servants driving the innovation, governments, employers and some trade unions have all taken part in the implementation of the reforms. Among trade unions, the CFDT (Confédération fraçaise du Travail) played an important role. During the 1980s, the CFDT changed its political and strategic position, abandoning the claim for 'autogestion' to adopt a 'responsible' and 'cooperative' approach to social policy issues. The CFDT has been out of the management of social insurance funds between 1967 and the early 1990s, when it made a change in its economic and social position. This trade union has been one of the most active proponents of re-insertion policies, and above all of the CSG (and nowadays of the 35-hour work week and activation policies engendering work). On the contrary, the FO (Force Ouvrière) and the CGT remain very defensive, opposing any kind of reform proposal. After 1995, the head of each social insurance fund changed, and the FO lost its positions of importance (especially at the head of the National Health Care Insurance Fund) to the CFDT, which made an alliance with the employers' representative. The change in at least one employees' representative position is one of the most important political conditions for policy changes in a 'corporatist-conservative' social insurance system.

Second, all these changes have been based on the collective acknowledgement of past policy failures. The development of each new measure starts with the politicization of a 'new social problem', which is seen as the result of a failure of past policies: social exclusion (social insurance is unable to deal with it or is even reinforcing it); low-skilled unemployment (because of the weight of social contribution and the passive unemployment compensation system); population aging (which the PAYG system cannot confront); the inability of the welfare state to be changed (because of the blurred assignment of responsibilities within the systems). Common agreement about why policies have failed is essential. It can take a long time before a majority of all the actors involved in social policy agree on the diagnosis of the problem. As long as the problem is not perceived in the same way, it is difficult to change the path of action. The acknowledgement of failure led to a reinterpretation of existing social and economic difficulties. In the new explanations for existing problems, the social insurance system shifted from the role of victim to cause of the problems. It took a long time before all actors shared similar diagnoses of the problems. This has been done through the proliferation of commissions and reports where the partners involved share the same approach.

Third, a large majority of the actors concerned with social-protection problems agreed with the new measures bringing about structural changes (RMI, CMU [Couverture Maldie Universelle], CSG, etc.). However, the precise analysis of the different positions that actors adopted towards the new measures shows that they agree on the same measure, but for very different reasons. Their reasons are sometimes even contradictory. All these reforms have been made in the name of the distinction between insurance and assistance (called 'national solidarity' in French). Trade unions wanted this rationalization in order to preserve their realm of social insurance whereas governments and civil servants expected more responsibilities in social protection through these changes, at the expense of social partners. The RMI was seen by the left as a means to propose money and social help (vocational training, for instance) through the contract, while the right advocated for the RMI since it was money given as a result of an effort made by the contracting beneficiary. The left support the CSG because it was a fairer tax than social contributions for the employees, whereas the right supported it as a means for lowering social charges for the employers; civil servants supported the CSG because it led to State control over the expenses financed by this new tax, whereas employers and the CFDT argued that it would allow the social partners to preserve the purity of social insurance and non-contributory benefits being financed by taxes. An important element for the acceptance of a new measure seems to be its capacity to aggregate different – and even contradictory – interests, based on different, and sometimes contrasting, interpretations of the consequences of implementing the new instrument. Structural changes in social policies are achieved through ambiguous measures rather than via a clear ideological orientation.

Finally, these types of change have been introduced at the margins of the system and gradually extended. Their expansion often leads to a change of their meaning within the system. They are first introduced to complete the system, but they gradually become the base for a new pillar in the social-protection system. The introduction at the margins allows for acceptance by the major defenders of the core system, either because they do not feel concerned by the new measure (RMI is not for the salaried workers that trade unions defend); or because it is targeted at those least able to protest (the low-skilled were the first to have their income exempted from social contribution; they were also the first to be targeted by activation policies); or because they believe that these new measures help them to defend the very nature of social insurance (tax financing of non contributory benefits). However, these types of new measures can lead to a paradigmatic change for the whole system.[6]

Conclusion

All in all, if the three types of reforms contribute to dualize the French social-protection system, they are all trying to render the system less costly and more employment friendly. The State plays a stronger and different role than it did before: it has more power within the system, which it uses to reduce or at least contain the cost of the whole system, either by retrenching social insurance benefits or by replacing contributory benefits with less generous, targeted benefits. This trend means a bigger part of the population must rely on social assistance. Shrinking social insurance also means a bigger reliance on private insurance for the rest of the population (especially in health care and the pension system). Meanwhile, all the reforms are trying to activate social spending and restructure social benefits so that they reorient people back to the labour market.

This general picture offers the opportunity to see, within concrete reforms, the emergence of a new architecture, new principles and new instruments, that is, a new paradigm, for the welfare state. Nowadays, the welfare state should become compatible with international competition. It should become 'employment friendly' in reducing its costs (especially non-wage costs) and in offering benefits that no longer function as disincentives (activation, making work pay). Targeting public expenditure on those who really need (and deserve) it is also part of the new norms, as is the fact that welfare should rely not only on public intervention but also on all the other actors contributing to the welfare mix (family, NGOs, private firms) (Daniel and Palier 2001).

The implementation of this new architecture can be identified only if one focuses on the changes both in the instruments, goals and ideas of welfare policies that the reforms have introduced (Hall 1993; Palier 2002). Then, one can see that in France, as in other Bismarckian welfare states, more and more (even if still marginal) structural changes are occurring, reflecting an overall global change in the perception of what the welfare state should look like for the twenty-first century. This new paradigm has also been observed in some research done at the European level (see Esping-Andersen et al. [eds] 2002).

This new paradigm is mainly meant to readapt social policies to new economic policies that now prevail at the European level. The Maastricht Treaty and the preparation for the single currency should not be seen as imposing only technical criteria. It also means that all the European countries accepted a profound shift in the economic policy paradigm. The main goal of macro-economic policy changed, from fighting unemployment (through reflation policy) to fighting inflation (through monetarist and strict budgetary policy). Peter Hall has shown how this shift from Keynesian to monetarist policies occurred in the late 1970s in the UK and in the early 1980s in France (Hall 1986). The Maastricht criteria reflect this kind of shift at the European level. Limitation of state deficit and debt, low inflation, these criteria correspond to a coherent (neo-classical) economic vision, based on supply-side policies, promoting free competition and budgetary restriction. If this paradigmatic shift occurred in the early 1980s in economic policies in most of the European countries, national social policies remained during the 1980s and 1990s within the same, former logic of the past. The welfare state crisis also originates in the discrepancy between its internal logic and the new global logic. In most of the welfare state reforms developed in continental Europe, the issue seems to be to readapt and realign the social policy paradigm to the new global economic paradigm.

However, this realignment process is mainly driven by economic preoccupation, more than social or political motivation. If the new paradigm is now able to define the economic role of social protection (which could be summarised as recommodification), the principle of social justice that underlines them, as well as the political processes and institutions that can legitimate them, are still uncertain.

Notes

1 Denis Kessler, quoted in Duclos and Mériaux 1997: 54.
2 In 1980, 76.5 per cent of the health expenditure paid by the insured person was reimbursed by the basic social insurance funds, 74 per cent in 1990 and 73.9 per cent in 1995.
3 SESI, *comptes de la protection sociale*, various years.
4 'The available evidence casts doubt on the claim that in the absence of growing economic integration, welfare states would be under dramatically less pressure, and national policy-makers markedly more capable of addressing new public demands' (Pierson 1998: 541).
5 See, for instance, Jean Pisani-Ferry 2000.
6 The best illustration of this kind of progressive change is given by Paul Pierson and John Myles, when they show how an initially marginal introduction of ceilings in tax benefits expanded so that Negative Income Taxes became a central social policy in the Canadian welfare system (Myles and Pierson 1997).

5
Different Nation, Same Nationhood: the Challenges of Immigrant Policy

Virginie Guiraudon

Introduction

In the fall of 1989, two girls were expelled from a junior high school in Creil for refusing to take off their Moslem headscarf in class, marking the beginning of the *affaire du foulard*. For months, while the rest of the West looked to Berlin and the fall of the wall, French politicians and intellectuals engaged in intense debates. In a secular public school system, could female minors harbor a religious signifier? How could the exercise of religious freedom be reconciled with the neutrality of the public system, known as *laïcité*? Was their expulsion compatible with their right to schooling and the State obligation to educate? The Socialists in power were divided. To put an end to internal struggles and stop the media frenzy, Minister of Education Lionel Jospin decided to refer the question to the Conseil d'état, the high administrative court. The Council wise men issued a moderate guideline: the veil should be tolerated unless proselytism and other manifestations incompatible with public order in school justified expulsion.

In the fall of 2003, two girls were expelled from a high school in Aubervilliers for refusing to take off their chadors. This new "veil affair" created an even greater controversy and, not unlike the Dreyfus affair, was the subject of heated dinner discussions in many a French household. Had nothing changed between 1989 and 2003? This time the Socialists, now in opposition, were united in favor of a law banning the veil in schools. President Chirac quickly reacted, as had done Jospin, by entrusting "wise men" with the issue, setting up a commission to reflect on *laïcité*. Yet, the ensuing bill that banned "ostentatious religious signs" stigmatized Moslems and worsened ethnic tensions. Moreover, it did not seem any clearer than the Council of State jurisprudence. The government underestimated the mobilization both within and outside France against the bill. While several thousands of people demonstrated in France in January 2004 after the French Moslem Party, a small radical anti-Semitic group, had called for the protest, there were almost as many in London and quite a few in front of the French embassy in Stockholm. Foreign governments officially denounced the French bill while foreign intellectuals expressed consternation at France's lack of tolerance.[1] Was France indeed unable to manage the diversity brought about by the settlement of new ethnic groups?

The successive veil affairs underlie the dire consequences of inaction in politics. The failure to incorporate migrant-origin populations politically both at the individual and collective level has led to the partial radicalization of these groups. The disappointment of the second-generation immigrants that participated in the 1983 "March for equality" led some to "return to Islam" instead of entering the French political system. In 1983, they voiced their desire to be recognized as full citizens and their exit option was either inward-looking or transnational (inscribing themselves within a community of Moslems at home and abroad).[2] French political elites ignored them. Many teachers in public schools also felt abandoned and have become *laïcards* hoping for a return to a strict separation of Church and State and to school uniforms. Immigrant presence in France seems to require a redefinition of the political community and its values to avoid the social exclusion of these groups and their consequences. Yet, in a polarized political climate, negotiated compromise is difficult.[3]

The veil controversy raises a number of key questions. First, could it have happened elsewhere and what is specifically "French" about the political handling of the situation? How come the same issue monopolizes public attention while over a decade has passed? In the ongoing negotiations on the place of religion in the public sphere brought about by the presence of immigrant ethnic minorities, will French public authorities adapt to the socio-demographic changes in French society?

Policies towards immigrants in France thus provide us with an opportunity to study the capacity of the French State to enact policy reform in the face of societal change and to identify the specificity of the French case in comparative perspective. Policy choices do not stem from a difference in the "objective" situation to be remedied: the United Kingdom and the Netherlands, two neighboring advanced democracies with comparable populations of post-colonials and foreign workers on their soil, have gone down a different road when developing their "race relations" and "minorities policy."[4] Policy responses depend on past institutional arrangements to the extent that they have generated "pathologies" (Favell 2001) and closed certain "paths" (Pierson 2000), empowered certain actors and legitimated particular worldviews.

The premise of French official policy has long been a form of assimilationist Republicanism. Just as peasants and, later, Belgian, Italian and Polish blue-collar workers, foreign migrants are expected to turn into Frenchmen through their equal access to the neutral institutions of the Republic (e.g., the schools), their inclusion in the labor market and related social institutions.[5] Yet, since the end of the *trente glorieuses*, when France officially stopped recruiting foreign workers and postcolonial migrants settled durably, economic restructuring and chaotic urbanization have worsened living and working conditions for migrants and their children. Hard times have also led to a rise in ethnocentric sentiment and a significant percentage of voters now supports the anti-immigration extreme right. Following these cues, middle-class citizens have started to move out of mixed neighborhoods and schools, thereby endangering the "French melting pot" (Noiriel 1996).

Far from a melting pot, France is a multicultural society where urban immigrant populations suffer from a number of socioeconomic disadvantages and are not deemed as equals by the natives. Moreover, demands for political inclusion and cultural recognition remain largely unmet. Still, the cognitive dissonance between the old model and the new situation, between the overarching "paradigm" and empirical developments that do not fit its premises, do not automatically result in policy change (Hall 1993). First, the ethnocentric sentiment of segments of French voters cannot be ignored by political parties given the electoral clout of the extreme right and the ambivalent or hostile attitude of sympathizers of mainstream parties. Reform thus often needs to take place away from the public eye. Second, policy responses must take place within the boundaries of a dominant Republican ideology that precludes certain solutions. Reform thus needs to reframe the "problems" that public policy must "solve." In this way, new participants enter the debate and change the balance of power, broadening the range of Republican, that is, "politically correct" solutions.

Analytically, we can distinguish *immigration* policy, which regulates entry and exit flows, from *immigrant* policy, which concerns foreigners' rights once they have arrived, including access to citizenship, antidiscrimination laws and policies that seek to "integrate" populations of migrant origin. This chapter focuses on immigrant policy, yet it takes place in a context of reforms that further restricted migration flows and access to asylum procedures, creating a large number of illegal residents living in precarious conditions. Ever since 1974, governments have argued that the integration of migrants requires that the flow of new arrivals is reduced. In fact, discourses against immigration discredit the presence of *immigrés*. This is compounded by the fact that official discourse draws a line between foreigners who should integrate ("ceux qui ont vocation à s'intégrer") and those who should leave.[6]

I examine how immigrant policy since the 1980s has sought to reconcile the French "model" of integration with the "reality" on the ground. In other words, we want to know how the *State* adapted to *societal* changes in this area. I focus on the recasting of immigrant policy after 1997 as antidiscrimination policy and assess the extent to which this new policy frame signals a departure from the old model.

1. Constructing immigrants as a public problem and integration as the solution

I. Problems and demands: the French "ethnic dilemma"

In this section, I briefly explain why the place of immigrants in French society has been a contentious "public problem" high on the agenda. Foreign-born individuals and their descendants – the so-called "second and third generations" – contribute to making France a much more racially and ethnically diverse society than it was 10 or 20 years ago. Yet, the expression "racial or ethnic minorities" is never pronounced in French political discourse. France celebrates its "colors" only on rare occasions: when the French soccer team wins the World Cup (12 July 1998), or when Le Pen, leader of the extreme right, gathers almost 18 per cent of the votes and features in the second round of the presidential election (21 April 2002). The most commonly used phrases are *immigrés* or "migrant-origin populations," often with only one group in mind, North Africans.[7] Oft-used expressions in political discourse include *populations des quartiers* and *jeunes des banlieues*, which in fact designate migrant-origin ethnic minorities.

The 1999 census showed that the foreign-born population has been remarkably stable for 25 years (7.4% of the total population). The number of foreigners residing in France (5.6% of the population) has declined since the 1990 census: a quarter million left the country, and the rest either died or naturalized. Forty-five per cent of *immigrés* are from Europe, the number of foreign-born from Maghreb has risen by 6 per cent (mostly Moroccans) and South-East Asians make up an important number of those who naturalize.[8] *Piano mà sano*, around a hundred thousand immigrants come to France every year and long-term foreign residents naturalize, accounting for the stability of the statistics. Still, as the head of the French Demography Institute (INED [Institut national d'études démographiques]) François Héran recently underlined (2004), with a net increase of only 65,000 migrants per year (entries minus departures), France is no longer an "immigration country" as was the case in the 1920s, the 1960s and 1970s. He also pointed out that, with 200,000 more births than deaths each year, France is the European country that least depends on migration for its population growth (Héran 2004).

When assessing how immigrants and their descendants fare in French society, their situation on the job market is an important indicator. According to the 1999 census, 24 per cent of the foreign active population and 22 per cent of foreign-born workers are unemployed, well above the national average of 13 per cent. Given their level of qualification and the fact that they are overrepresented in industrial sectors, foreign-born workers have not fared well. The percentage of unemployed men of Maghreb origin in the 16–29-year-old age group oscillates between 34 per cent and 45 per cent (20 and 25% for women) well above both the national average and that of youths of southern-European origin. Although, as a whole, children of immigrants have better career prospects than their parents owing to their access to education and training, there are important differences based on the parents' origin. Youths of Algerian descent are more likely to be unemployed and less likely to find a job again than others with the same qualifications and social background (Glaude and Borrel 2002).

The socioeconomic position of immigrant populations can be measured and constitutes an objective predicament, yet this is not enough to explain why it has become a "public problem" and a public-policy priority. Ever since France officially stopped recruiting foreign workers at the beginning of the Giscard presidency (Weil 1991), immigrants have been at the heart of long, drawn-out controversies in the public sphere.

Migrant mobilizations and counter-mobilizations by ethnocentric political forces have been numerous and more important than in other European countries, contributing to the polarization of debate and the high salience of the issue. In Europe, the French case is unique in this respect. Every decade has seen the emergence of a migrant social movement: the SONACOTRA (Société nationale de construction pour les travailleurs) and factory strikes in the 1970s, the "second generation" movement with the *marche des beurs* in 1983 and the SOS Racisme "don't touch my buddy" campaign, the post-1996 *sans papiers* movement and, since 2002, the *ni putes ni soumises* movement against the pressures and violence exerted on women living in the *cités*, France's suburban housing projects.

The media coverage of immigrant-related controversies is biased. Keen on increasing circulation or TV audience, the media also magnify the "problem" of immigration through the use of violent images, of expressions such as the *intifada des banlieues*, through the manipulation of statistics most typically on criminal aliens and asylum requests (Guiraudon 2000). Media studies on the coverage of immigration issues concur to underline that the media reproduces negative stereotypes of foreigners as victims or delinquents rather than as equals, in part because of the lack of specialized journalists and the decline of investigative journalism (Bonnafous 1991, 1999; Benson 2002).

Moreover, there has been an upsurge in anti-foreigner sentiment since the 1970s among the electorate of both the left and right as new social categories joined the ranks of those who felt threatened by immigrants, especially among the urban population (Mayer 1991; Guiraudon 2000). The French public does not favor reforms that benefit immigrants, as comparative Eurobarometer survey data show. In 1989, year of the first survey, 24 per cent of French respondents believed that rights should be restricted and 51 per cent said that they should stay the same (*Eurobarometer 30* 1989). In 2000, only 31 per cent supported legislation banning discrimination (*Eurobarometer 53* 2000). Longitudinal survey data collected annually for the Commission nationale consultative des droits de l'homme since 1989 also reveal that negative attitudes towards immigrants prevail and that the least-accepted groups are North Africans and Moslems (CNCDH 1989–2003).[9] Qualitative data based on in-depth face-to-face interview concur: Michèle Lamont's study of attitudes among French blue-collar workers also shows a greater hostility towards *Maghrébins* than Blacks (Lamont 2000).

The evolution of the attitudes of the electorate regarding immigration is also telling. As Martin Schain (2006) points out:

> In 1984, relatively few voters aside from those that supported the National Front considered either immigration or law and order to be a strong priority. By 1988, however, the importance of these issues ranked with such issues as social inequality ... After 1988, the difference on these issues between FN voters and others continued to remain large, but this difference declined over time. Therefore, in one sense the issues of immigration and *sécurité* became less important as a way of differentiating FN voters from supporters of other political parties, but only because the impact of what we can term these FN issues had been so important and so widespread.

The anti-immigrant extreme right has been an important electoral force since 1983, influencing debate on the immigration issue at the local, regional, and national levels. The electoral breakthrough of the FN at first threatened the mainstream right yet it has led to a change in the political attitudes of the working class that used to support left-wing parties. By 1997, among workers living in working-class communities, married to working-class partners, a majority identified with the right, and voted for the right or did not vote (Mayer 2002). This has exacerbated a political climate in which mainstream parties, grappling for the "swing voter" in a period of voter realignment and frustration with politics, have been incorporating part of the anti-immigration National Front policy agenda.[10] The 2002 presidential elections in which the Socialist prime minister gathered less votes than Le Pen only confirmed existing trends.

Postcolonial migrants in France are the scapegoats of parties on the extreme right. This disenfranchised minority with restricted access to policy-making centers faces hostility or indifference from public opinion, as well as negative biases in media reporting. Parties in power cannot expect electoral gains from policies that seek to better the status and living conditions of immigrants. They even risk losing voters. Immigrant policies are thus similar to the large set of policies in which one expects opponents to change to outweigh beneficiaries and supporters.[11] In these cases, decision-makers have devised a number of "blame-avoidance" strategies so that voters fail to trace the responsibility for reform, either by seeking a wide consensus or by lowering the visibility of reform (Schattschneider 1960; Weaver 1986; Pierson 1994). Reforms in favor of immigrants that are highly salient in public opinion and the media, or the subject of debates in the electoral arena, are unlikely to succeed. In the latter, important participants holding systematic negative biases against foreigners (public opinion, the media, anti-foreigner parties or politicians) can voice their opinions. In the next section, we examine how this political context limited the range of policy solutions.

II. Alternatives and solutions: the French model of integration

In the midst of a controversy over the reform of the Nationality Code, a commission of wise men set up in 1987 was the first to formalize the French doctrine of integration (Commission de la nationalité 1988).[12] Soon after, le Haut Conseil à l'Intégration, a consultative body in charge of making recommendations to the government regarding migrant integration, was born and, in 1991, gave an official definition of the goals of integration:

> Integration consists in encouraging the active social participation of all the men and women destined to live durably on our soil, fully acknowledging that differences will remain – in particular cultural ones – yet stressing resemblance and convergence when it comes to equal rights and duties so as to warrant the cohesion of our social fabric ... Integration postulates that differences can still lead to a common project while assimilation entails the suppression of differences and incorporation ensures that differences will endure. (HCI 1993: 8)

The text strikes a precarious balance between the tolerance of difference and the quest for "resemblance and convergence." In that sense, it tries to update the assimilationist model while still considering difference as a residual category. The "wise men" also seem uncertain as to whom the target public of integration policy really is since it uses the circumlocution "men and women destined to live durably on our land." In spite of its tensions, the HCI definition outlines the basic tenets of the French model:

- It is up to individuals to "integrate." This precludes the constitution of structured migrant communities that would endanger "national cohesion." Group rights and the public recognition of difference is therefore not on the agenda. The definition suggests that individuals may not shed all "cultural specificities" yet they are best expressed in the private realm.[13]
- The apex of the integration process is full citizenship which means the acquisition of French nationality. This implies that access to citizenship should be relatively open through a variety of procedures and constitutes a right for the "second generation." Conversely, reforms that de-link nationality and citizenship, such as the extension of local voting and eligibility rights for (non-EU) foreigners, are not recommended. If the "active participation" of migrants in society is encouraged, political participation can only come through citizenship acquisition.

- Integration is inextricably linked to the notion of equality as the aim to make it a social reality. Voluntarist policies should therefore aim at insuring equal chances and conditions for all members of society. To be coherent with the rest of the doctrine, "positive action" cannot be acknowledged and equalizing conditions between migrant populations and the rest of the population precludes studies that would highlight how particular groups are faring compared to others.

Long before the High Council painfully elaborated this compromise definition, its principles had been politically contested and policies had largely departed from them. As France painfully sought to "decolonize" its handling of the immigration problem, incorporating ex-colonials within general provisions (*structures de droit commun*), as opposed to special regimes, was deemed a useful step (Viet 1998). This slow and uneven process has then been reinterpreted in recent decades by political actors and scholars alike as compatible with the French revolutionary tradition, its strict division between the public and private sphere and with the concept of the "République une et indivisible" (Guiraudon 1996). In fact, as in many other European countries, "integration policy" has often been reactive and ad hoc in practice, as public authorities intervened after focus events such as episodes of interethnic tension, immigrants' strikes, and urban riots.

Moreover, one should not forget that the French Government hoped after 1973 to encourage migrants to return to their homeland by *not* integrating them and set up "language-of-origin" classes and asked national firms such as Renault to set up Moslem prayer halls (Kepel 1987). And, since the 1980s, the public agency that funds migrant associations (FASILD [Fonds d'action sociale pour l'intégration et le lutte contre les discriminations]) has financed "cultural" activities, which essentially consists in promoting ethnically specific groups or in any case actions whereby one's ethnic traditions can be valorized. The official rhetoric whereby migrants would individually be turned into Frenchmen through their participation in social institutions such as schools, the army or the workplace, just like nineteenth-century peasants (Schnapper 1991), was often contradicted in practice. One example is housing policy. When a program was set up in the 1960s to do away with shantytowns and build public housing (HLM [Habitat à layer modéré (low-cost public housing)]), Italian and Spanish migrants were given priority over other nationalities to obtain a unit in public housing (Viet 1998). Later, public housing agencies enforced informal quotas limiting the number of "other" foreigners (Weil 1991).

The reinvention of "integration" as the French policy paradigm towards the treatment of immigrant populations dates back to the 1980s. When the Socialists came to power in 1981, assimilation was under attack. Official government documents instead spoke of the *insertion* of migrants in societal institutions such as the workplace. Socialists also lent an ear to activists who called for "a right to be different" (*droit à la différence*) and "a new citizenship" for migrants (*nouvelle citoyenneté*), including the right to vote in local elections for residing foreigners, which featured in François Mitterrand's 1981 presidential platform. The alternative to assimilation was thus multiculturalism, which recognizes cultural difference in the public sphere (Kymlicka 1995), and the alternative to Republican citizenship was a variety of "post-national citizenship" (Soysal 1994), whereby political participation was decoupled from nationality. At the time, these views had informed policy change not only in North America but also in some west-European countries such as the Netherlands and Sweden, where policies targeting ethnic minorities had been developed and where foreigners could vote in local elections. They contrasted with other cases such as Germany or Switzerland that still denied that guestworkers were here to stay, and where ethnonationalist conceptions of citizenship prevailed.

After 1983, incidentally the year the National Front erupted on the French political scene, the Socialist Government shied away from adopting multiculturalism and ignored its promise to grant electoral rights to foreigners, in spite of demands expressed by the *marche des Beurs*.[14] Socialists and later the mainstream right when they returned to power in 1986 presented integration as the only solution against the ideology of the extreme right. Yet this solution also discredited the ideas of left-wing activists as "extreme." While the short-term risk-averse calculus of the Socialists partly explains their embrace of the status quo, the long-term consequences should not be neglected. (Electoral) promises were not fulfilled and migrants and *Beurs* joined the ranks of the *déçus de la gauche*.[15] The mid-1980s mark the beginning of a disaffection with mainstream politics and, in some cases, a radicalization of a segment of the second generation.

III. Policy by stealth: immigrant policy before 1997

The previous sections have made clear that policies to improve the situation of migrants and their descendants should fit with the tenets of the integration paradigm. The French case illustrates the role of administrative and judicial venues in guaranteeing equal social rights for non-nationals in spite of an adverse political context characterized by politicians' attempts to restrict these rights for electoral gains. In this section, we look at the jurisprudence of courts with respect to social rights and activist policies such as *politique de la ville* (urban policy).

The positive bias of high courts towards foreigners' rights derives from their distinct mode of functioning and reasoning. If courts treat different groups or constituencies differently, they will not be credible as neutral arbiters (Shapiro 1981). Decisions regarding foreigners are presented in the courts as a balancing of state interests and individual freedoms based on the notion of proportionality. This mode of reasoning specific to the legal world contrasts with the power relations that migrants face in the electoral sphere.

Courts apply principles such as due process and equal treatment to fill in the law when basic texts are not explicit. Moreover, there was a legal basis for courts to rule in favor of foreigners' rights. Constitutions often use expressions like "every one" or "all" when outlining rights. Therefore, once the courts were solicited, they disregarded nationality as a criterion for the attribution of rights.

In 1985, the Paris municipal council headed by Jacques Chirac, as part of its pro-fertility policy, decided to grant a new non-contributive benefit ("l'allocation municipale de congé parental d'éducation pour le troisième enfant") only to nationals. The administrative tribunal of Paris cancelled the decision on 19 March 1986 and, on appeal, the Council of State confirmed this judgement on 30 June 1989. Both jurisdictions insisted on a strict application of the universality of rights. On 22 January 1990, the Constitutional Council struck down a legislative measure that extended a non-contributive benefit (*allocation adulte handicapé*) to non-nationals but only to EU nationals. The court reaffirmed that exclusion of foreigners from welfare benefits is against "the constitutional principles of equality." Courts have increasingly been called upon to rule in cases involving access to education for foreigners (Heymann-Doat 1994: 132).

In general, it has been easier to guarantee the social rights of foreigners than foster their political participation. Neo-institutionalist studies in comparative politics argue that allocating jurisdiction over a policy issue depends on the "rules of the game" (Immergut 1992). Formal rules can circumscribe the strategies of political actors depending on the type of process that is required for a particular rights provision. In the case of immigrant policy reform, the formal rules that govern reform go a long way towards explaining why reforms extending certain types of rights are bound to spill over into the electoral arena (political rights) whereas others will not (social rights). Social rights (education and welfare benefits) do not obey the same rules as political rights. In their case, regulatory changes often suffice; or they can be extended by the passing of a bill by a simple majority. In a number of cases, legal texts are neutral as far as nationality is concerned. The issue is to render effective rights that exist only on paper or inversely to stop applying old regulations rather than to adopt new laws. Granting voting rights to foreigners entails constitutional revision and thus legislative passage by a large coalition: either a qualified majority vote by the two houses of Parliament or a majority vote in a national referendum.[16] This means that a public discussion of the issue is almost inevitable and bound to be long and divisive as all sorts of larger debates on nationhood resurface, thus hampering chances for reform.

Regarding activist policies towards immigrants, the normative consensus precluded the targeting of particular groups while ensuring equal opportunities. This was achieved in the first instance through programs that targeted socially disadvantaged migrant groups without ever including ethnic criteria to redistribute resources. Policies in the 1990s that benefited migrants and their descendants have partly "hidden" their target public and been spread among a variety of ministries and levels of governance in a way typical of "shadow politics." Urban, education, employment policies (etc.) have elaborated categories of public intervention based on age or place of residence while, in fact, they were directed at migrant-origin categories.

After 1990, with the launching of *politique de la ville* (urban policy) that was meant to fight social exclusion and "give more to those who had less," a territorial approach to redistribution was adopted. This consisted in exempting ever-smaller urban zones from taxes or using other incentives to create jobs for the young people residing there. On paper, migrants and their descendants were not targeted. Still, given their socioeconomic characteristics, they did benefit in disproportionate numbers from these spatially defined policies.

Finally, local initiatives whose objectives included social inclusion were also financed by the State through "contracts" with municipalities (known first as *contrats d'agglomération,* they have become *contrats locaux pour l'acceuil et l'intégration* since 1998 and now are also part of the *contrats de ville*). For instance, between 1994 and 2000, over a hundred contracts were signed between central state agencies and local authorities with a yearly budget of €30000 (Espinasse and Laporte 1999). The type of actions undertaken with the financial state of the central state involved a range of public, private, and associational actors in areas ranging from after-school aid for pupils, female migrant empowerment, and the prevention of juvenile delinquency. This decentralized territorial approach meant that local practices could target certain groups without the central government being accused of fomenting it.

There are other policy areas where the percentage of foreigners is used as a criterion for providing extra public funds. In education policy, for a high school to qualify as a "priority education zone" (ZEP [Zone d'éducation prioritaire (education priority zones)]) and thus obtain a better budget and smaller classes, the high number of foreigners living in the area is an argument along with the unemployment rate and the number of blue-collar workers in the area. Another example regards the sponsorship program (*parrainage*) set up in 1993 as part of employment policy. At first, the policy had no well-defined public. Yet, migrants' children benefited from the measure in large numbers. In 1997, out of the 13,500 youths who participated in the program, 35 per cent were "young immigrants" (Aubert 1999): "*by chance,* migrant-origin populations are *de facto* the (proportionally) privileged recipients of policies against social exclusion" since "the coincidence between their own characteristics and the socioeconomic criteria used allow them to benefit, without these populations being explicitly or exclusively targeted" (Calvès and Sabbagh 1999: 12).

Yet the continued inability of these policies to stem racism, guarantee social peace in the *banlieues,* or better the employment situation in these "zones" was obvious by 1997 when the newly-elected Jospin Government decided to make the reduction of discrimination a priority of French integration policy. The next section thus examines policy changes in France since 1997. The question regards the factors behind the reorientation of French policy, weighing the role of Europe and that of domestic "intermediary" variables.

2. The emergence of an anti-discrimination policy frame: how much of a change?

The change of government in 1997 offered a window of opportunity for both administrative and non-governmental actors to present policy initiatives in a domain that seemed to have exhausted possibilities and run out of steam.[17] Yet, as we have seen, if the size of the "window" can be debated, the range of possible alternatives was narrow. Since the mid-1980s, French Socialist governments had embraced the Republican paradigm of integration after a brief "multicultural moment" and, more importantly, it deemed reforms granting rights to foreigners too dangerous, given the attitude of the electorate. The Government decided to make "the fight against discrimination" a priority and claimed it was the only way to ensure equal opportunities for all and to render equality before the law effective. The Social Affairs Minister insisted that anti-discrimination policy "confirms our attachment to the Republican principle of equality."[18]

While compatible with the French attachment to *égalité*, the shift in focus from "integration" to "anti-discrimination" resulted in a very different conception of the "problem." As Didier Fassin has argued, the cause or source of the problem shifts responsibility from the migrant to the host society (2002: 407). In the integration paradigm, it is up to immigrants to integrate and their failure to do so displays some social defect. If the policy frame is antidiscrimination, it means that French society discriminates. French institutions and individuals are responsible for the migrants' situation. The old model stressed the need to socialize migrants until the logical crowning of their efforts, full citizenship. Now it was up to French societal institutions to change so as to get rid of its attitude towards people with different "origins" that suffer independent of citizenship status and regardless of their social class. No longer acting *in favour of* integration but fighting *against* discrimination, public authorities needed to develop a new policy toolbox. In brief, as Deborah Stone once put it (1989), policy reform came from a change in the "causal story" of the policy problem. This new narrative called for new policy instruments, a "second-order" policy change (Hall 1993).

I. Domestic variables behind the change

To say that the change of government provided a window for proposing a new policy orientation does not imply that partisanship is a relevant factor here. In October 1999, former Gaullist Prime Minister Alain Juppé declared in a *Le Monde* interview that, given that in some areas, 50 per cent of immigrant youths were unemployed and felt discrimination in the job market, an antidiscrimination policy would show them that they had the same rights and preserve "national cohesion." The right had realized that as populations of migrant origin became more diversified socially they were likely to be more politically diverse as well, and not only left-leaning. Juppé's statements drew from a report published in *France moderne*, the journal of his club. The report advocated the creation of an independent authority that would examine discrimination cases brought before the British CRE (Council for Racial Equality). In fact, around election time, the Haut Conseil à l'intégration (HCI), a body of wise men headed at the time by Simone Weil was preparing a report on discrimination. The *rapporteur* was none other than a RPR (Rassemblement pour la République) Juppé adviser, Frédéric Salat-Baroux. The HCI report recommended the creation of a CRE-like independent authority, proposing to disband itself or fuse with that authority (HCI 1998).

In fact, the Socialist government justified the need for anti-discrimination policy with the same arguments as Juppé, essentially as a remedy to the failings of the Republican model of integration during hard times. In the words of the Social Affairs Minister: "The firm and the work place, just as school, have contributed to making the 'integration machine' work. Notwithstanding, one should not ignore that the so-called 'French model of integration' has known difficult times, that always correspond in fact to periods of economic crises" (Aubry 1998). Antidiscrimination policy[19] generated bipartisan support. This policy orientation could generate consensus more easily than affirmative action measures, multicultural policy or proposals on foreigners' political rights that had always stirred controversy. It had other advantages compared to preceding approaches: it cost less than redistributive measures such as *politique de la ville* and other positive actions that required granting more funds for schools or providing financial incentives for employers.

Furthermore, governmental actors at first thought that they could shift responsibility for discrimination to the private sector, to the employers, nightclub owners and real estate agents that refused jobs and services to "Blacks" and "Arabs." The first studies conducted by the advisory board on antidiscrimination, the Groupe d'études et de lutte contre les discriminations (GELD) focused on public employment and public housing.[20] About seven million jobs, with the French public service or publicly-owned firms accounting for 6.2 million of these, are legally closed to non-EU nationals, making legal discrimination a serious issue (GELD 2000). Many migrants live in public housing whose rules and practices when allocating apartments have been reported to discriminate, directly and indirectly, against racial and ethnic minorities (GELD 2001).

The Social Affairs Ministry in charge of integration issues showed much prudence in setting up the anti-discrimination policy framework, establishing a hotline ("dial 114") to collect complaints. It organized colloquia and roundtables with the "social partners" (employers and trade unions); it sponsored research and ordered an official report; it created the aforementioned advisory board on antidiscrimination. Common in other European countries, the irruption of policy-relevant data-rich research into the French debate was a novelty. This has been an area defined as a normative issue requiring political and legal decisions and discussed either in juridical terms by *conseillers d'État* or philosophical ones by public intellectuals. The new policy frame has altered the participants in the debate by placing social scientists and the "social partners" at the centre of policy reform.[21] The consequence was to empower social scientists that were well versed in the international literature on ethnic minorities.

Yet Martine Aubry, the Minister of Social Affairs, did not plan legislative changes and ruled against the HCI recommendation regarding the creation of an independent authority (Aubry 1998). The delaying tactics of Martine Aubry left room for another government heavyweight: the Minister of the Interior, arch-Republican Jean-Pierre Chevènement. He set up the CODACs (Commission for Access to Citizenship) in each *département* with the help of his prefects, to hear individual complaints and advise on legal procedures. For Chevènement, whose ministry was also responsible for immigration reform, antidiscrimination could serve as a compensatory measure for his harsh discourse on migration flows and illegal migrants. The competition between Aubry and Chevènement as to who would be at the forefront to insure the Republican equal treatment of immigrants and their descendants allowed for a multiplication of initiatives. While this insured that the theme of antidiscrimination was kept alive, it did not make for coherent implementation. The dial 114 hotline set up by Social Affairs received many complaints about discrimination and then redirected callers to the CODACs under the auspices of the Interior Ministry, yet both would just listen to people.[22] In brief, neither functioned either as an equal opportunities board that examined and ruled on complaints or worked with business to improve the situation of racial and ethnic minorities, as is the case in the UK or the Netherlands.

Public speeches of government figures were still euphemistic when it came to designating the groups targeted by antidiscrimination policy. When the Ministry of the Interior announced that police officers should "look like" the inhabitants that live in the neighborhoods in which they patrol, he did not pronounce the word "race" or "minority."[23] When, on 18 March 2000, a large forum was organized so that Prime Minister Lionel Jospin could announce the measures related to the fight against discrimination, the event was called *assises de la citoyenneté,* thus resorting to the oft-used vocabulary of citizenship. He stated that *jeunes des quartiers* would occupy 20 per cent of the *emplois jeunes* (a program of temporary service jobs for young people) and described TRACE (Trajet d'accès à l'emploi) as a sponsorship program to help *jeunes en difficulté* find a job. This still corresponded to the previous approach to positive action: age and socioeconomic disadvantage rather than ethnic origin are legitimate public policy criteria, prompting Patrick Simon to rightly wonder what happens when migrant youths grow old (2000).

This was the situation at the end of 1999, when the European Commission issued an antidiscrimination package based on Article 13 of the treaty of the European communities, and consisting of a six-year Community action programme and two directives. We must now turn to EU-level developments that constituted an additional source of change in French immigrant policy.

II. The circumscribed yet crucial role of the EU

During the first months of 2000, there was an acceleration of negotiations at EU-level based on article 13. One of the directives aimed to combat racial and ethnic discrimination in a wide range of areas (employment, training and education, the provision of services including housing). On 3 February, a coalition government was formed in Austria with the FPÖ (Freiheitliche Partei Österreichs) receiving six of ten full ministerial posts, including social affairs. An informal meeting of the Ministers for Employment and Social Affairs in Lisbon had been scheduled for a week later (11–12 February). The French minister Martine Aubry was the most vocal in calling for quarantining the new Austrian government. The bottom line of the Lisbon summit was that verbal condemnation of xenophobic parties had to be followed by legislative acts. The French, Belgian, and Italian ministers soon issued a joint position paper (21 February 2001) calling for the swift adoption of the Commissions antidiscrimination proposals "to promote a diversified, multicultural Europe which espouses equal opportunities for all citizens irrespective of gender, origin, race, religion, opinions, age or disability" (Bentley 2000).

The French Government had thus become the most keen to see the directive passed yet their enthusiasm stemmed from an event, the success of a far-right leader who had praised the Waffen SS, that fitted the French conception of antiracist measures as a means of fighting ideas inspired by Nazi Germany rather than a tool primarily associated with the management of migrant visible minorities. Yet, in the end, the so-called "race directive" adopted in world record time in June 2000 greatly resembled British and Dutch approaches and required vast legal changes in France. It should be underlined that EU negotiations are largely sheltered from national electoral politics and, in this case, the decision to speed them up gave more leverage to the Social Affairs working groups and Cabinet members in the capitals, by-passing consultation with the many administrative departments that an multisector directive required (Geddes and Guiraudon 2004).

Yet, in spite of what one analyst calls "the bulldozer action of the EU" (Flauss 2001), the signing of the directive did not imply that, back in Paris, there was a full embrace of the "antidiscrimination" approach. This can be seen by intra-bureaucratic resistance to the EU Action Plan on discrimination. The directive had been adopted without the input of ministerial services that could have expressed reservations. When the Commission asked member states to provide evidence on discrimination and failing that to agree to a Eurobarometer survey asking questions about personal experience with discrimination, French official experts this time reentered the policy process. The Social Affairs Ministry expert, an INSEE (Institut national de la statistique et des études économiques [National Institute for Statistics and Economic Studies]) employee, answered that the survey idea was "stupid" and the French position was a plain "no." The Commission official in charge of the Action Plan called the French Social Affairs attaché at the Brussels Permanent delegation. The latter, as a true pedagogue, kindly explained to her national ministry that Europe was about compromise and cooperation even in domains ruled by unanimity. For researchers of the GELD, "Europe" could serve as a discursive resource in trying to convince reluctant players that, whether they wanted or not, they would have to adapt to the new agenda on antidiscrimination, once the directives and action program were adopted.

Yet the problem arose again when Parliament discussed the transposition of the directive on race discrimination in November 2001. On the one hand, MPs added grounds for discrimination not mentioned in the directive, including the person's name and residential address, thereby displaying a will to appropriate EU legislation in a way relevant to the French situation on the ground. On the other, they refused to implement the provisions on indirect discrimination fully. They introduced the concept in French labor law, but without authorizing the collection of statistics on the socioeconomic characteristics of the ethnic and racial groups that could be disadvantaged by apparently neutral laws and practices (Calvès 2002).

Binding EU rules served as a tool, both to politicians who did not want to take the responsibility for policy change and would be able to trace it to "Brussels" and to the young Turks who could use EU guidelines as a resource to respond to the resistance of agencies such as INSEE. Yet this resource on its own did not change worldviews and institutional interests.[24] Although EU policy calls for instruments that fight against indirect discrimination including so-called "ethnic monitoring" as was already the case for gender, elected officials, bureaucrats, and experts have been loath to acknowledge that groups are structurally disadvantaged, to name these groups and track their position in society. Instead, French policy after 1997 focused on individual complaints.

III. Post-4/21: the return of assimilationism

After 1997, government measures, partly drawing their legitimacy from EU developments in this area, officially acknowledged that migrants could suffer from discrimination. Yet electoral prudence and a reluctance to renounce the post-1987 bipartisan consensus on the French model of integration have made it difficult to implement antidiscrimination.

On 5 May 2002, Jacques Chirac was reelected as president for a five-year term, with Le Pen gathering about 18 per cent of the vote. On 21 April, the day of the "earthquake" when the National Front candidate came ahead of Lionel Jospin, main parties of the left had urged their supporters to vote for Chirac and denounced the racist and xenophobic ideology of Le Pen. Given this context, the words and deeds of the President as well as of the right-wing government set up after the subsequent June 2002 legislative elections on issues related to immigrants are of particular interest. In this brief section, we analyze change and continuity between the Socialist and the Union pour un Mouvement Populaire governments in this area.

This assessment exercise is not easy to the extent that policy initiatives may not be coherent and they even contradict each other. For example, the Minister of the Interior, Sarkozy, not unlike Chevènement before him, acts as both good and bad cop. The 2003 laws on entry and stay and asylum are more restrictive than the 1993 so-called Pasqua laws and they shed suspicion on migrants and asylum-seekers alike as frauds. Yet, the Minister has a softer side when he calls for "positive discrimination" and the visibility of the "deserving immigrants" in public service. In his words, "there are, among immigrants, those who are meant to integrate and those that will not be accepted."[25] There are good and bad *immigrés* and it is up to the French electorate to identify them.

President Chirac and Prime Minister Raffarin both declared that they will energetically fight against discrimination. In 2004, "an independent administrative authority for equality and the fight against all forms of discrimination" was to be set up. Bernard Stasi, who headed the Commission on *laïcité* in the fall of 2003, was put in charge of writing the blue print for the institution. This is the crucial element of the 2000 EU race directive, with which the French had not complied previously. The Prime Minister suggested that the Commission focus on "best practices" – a common word in EU-speak – and give out labels and prizes to firms and social actors that do not discriminate. For him, the problem with focusing on discrimination was that it gave "the French a bad conscience and penalizes them." He acknowledged that the children of immigrants "feel they are second-class citizens because their name is an obstacle on the job market because their address is a turn-off for employers."[26]

In the previous section, I argued that focusing on discrimination shifts the responsibility away from ethnic minorities. This is precisely what is now being questioned. The Raffarin Government nominated a new Haut Conseil à l'intégration in 2002, with a Chirac loyalist, a philosophy professor named Blandine Kriegel, as its head. Her first report entitled *Le contrat et l'intégration*, was published in 2004 before the independent authority had been inaugurated (HCI 2004). Blandine Kriegel approved the governmental stance and called for a break with "the logic of guilt and discrimination." In fact, she criticized the measures of the Socialist government: "it was a turning point when by accusing French society, considered as responsible for discriminations, we gave up on integration."[27]

One sign that the government does not intend to act vigorously against discrimination regards the creation of an independent authority to fight discrimination as required by the 2000 EU directive (the French law n° 2004–1486 of 30 December 2004). The HALDE (Haute autorité de lutte contre les discriminations et pour l'égalité) is to have a ridiculously small staff to cover all grounds of discrimination and is not likely to be independent from the State given the few number of independent experts in the consultative committee and the ways in which the 11-member college is to be nominated. It thus dilutes each issue (race, ethnicity, religion, handicap, age, sexual orientation). As of this writing, there is no sign that the government is rushing to actually set it up. In the meantime, what used to exist under the previous government has been discontinued and older institutions such as the FASILD, which funds migrant associations, have seen their budgets drastically cut.

In 2002 the Minister of Social Affairs, François Fillon, presented an initiative in the area of immigrant policy that President Chirac had announced "an integration contract." The idea of the contract, which now pervades all public policies in France and in Europe, was not a reference to Rousseau's social contract. The Dutch government coalition set up compulsory integration contracts (*inburgeringscontracten*) for foreign newcomers in 1994. The idea was that incoming migrants needed to integrate quickly in Dutch society and should receive language classes and knowledge of the host society. Welfare allowances depended on attendance at classes. The Dutch idea marked a departure from multiculturalism, which was seen in a major government report as putting too much emphasis on the cultural and religious expression of groups and not enough on the individual's responsibility in finding a place (and mostly a job) in Dutch society (WRR 1989). The French were a model that needed to be followed. Ten years later, with the *contrat d'intégration* for newcomers, the government was borrowing a policy tool inspired by the French integration paradigm. The future of immigrant policy seemed very much to rehash the past. Yet it took place in a context where the "return to assimilationism" was being heralded everywhere in Europe (Brubaker 2001).

Conclusion

French immigrant policy currently tries to reconcile the French "philosophy of integration" (Favell 2001) with its emphasis on the individual and its commitment to equality with a social reality that calls for the recognition of the mistreatment of certain ethnic groups. This balancing act is made more difficult by the fact that electoral debates and policy discourses call into question the legitimacy of the presence of immigrants on French soil: immigration is linked to crime and insecurity and, in the case of North Africans, their loyalty to France is questioned because of their adherence to Islam.

As in other areas examined in this volume where societal and policy transformations have been profound, French political leaders have tried to lower the visibility of policy change (initiatives in particular in urban, employment, and education policy in the 1990s).[28] This ambiguous discourse has so far been unable to stem in the long term the successes of populist politicians and extreme-right parties that feed on an anti-immigrant discourse.

In the 1970s and 1980s, divergence across European immigrant policies endured even in the face of similar empirical developments (Geddes 2003). Recent policy convergence in Europe and the cross-pollination of ideas across borders is also of interest since none could be an objective success story for the others: elsewhere migrant communities experience high unemployment and spatial segregation (Joppke and Morawska 2003). Today France has in part transposed the EU antidiscrimination package that echoes British policy. Antidiscrimination is an acceptable "frame" if it can be subsumed or "aligned" with wider ideologies such as equality (Zald 1996). Yet, it cohabits with initiatives such as the Dutch-inspired integration contracts. And the dominant policy discourse among experts and politicians alike refuses to identify groups and grant them preferential treatment. Societal change can be witnessed by all and policy reforms have taken place, yet French self-understanding perhaps has not.

Notes

1 Two Gulf wars later, after 9/11 and with the Israeli-Palestinian conflict widely covered in France, which hosts, according to estimates, the largest Jewish and Moslem population in Europe, the international context seemed more important than in 1989.
2 Regarding "exit" and "voice" strategies, see Hirschmann (1970).
3 The notion of "negotiated identity" in relation to immigrants and the state is developed in Kastoryano (2002).
4 Immigration policy is therefore akin to the other domains examined in this volume. The fact that many European welfare states face similar financial challenges (aging, medical progress, unemployment) does not mean that their responses converge. See chapter by Bruno Palier.
5 I paraphrase the expression "peasants into Frenchmen," which is the title of Eugen Weber's work on nationbuilding in late nineteenth-century France (1976).

6 This expression features in a speech by Nicolas Sarkozy, Minister of the Interior since 2002. See note 26. It is not new since it can be found in the official definition of integration in the report of the High Council of Integration in 1989 (HCI 1993).
7 In May 2002, when the new government headed by Jean-Pierre Raffarin was sworn in, the press described the Secretary of State Tokia Saifi as "of migrant-origin" because her parents came from North Africa; they ignored that several other government members, including Interior Minister Nicolas Sarkozy, also had migrant parents. In January 2004, when the Interior Minister called for a new *préfet musulman* and Jacques Chirac favored the nomination of a *préfet issu de l'immigration*, they both agreed on Aïssa Dermouche, an Algerian-born French man from the Berber region of Kabylie.
8 The census data is available at www.insee.fr. See also Héran (2004). Regarding "flows" rather than "stocks" of immigrants, there are around a hundred thousand new entries each year. The top two sending countries are the former French colonies of Algeria and Morocco, providing almost 20 per cent of new flows, and sub-Saharan Africa is the main geographic area of origin for new migrants. Still, there are surprising new entries, with Sri Lanka featuring in the top ten list of sending countries. In France, as elsewhere, the new flows are highly diverse, both in terms of their country of origin, qualification, and status. Chinese immigration is on the rise and more diverse than before.
9 Both the Eurobarometer and the CNCDH surveys ask the same questions over time using the same sampling methods, although there are specific questions added each year. The studies have been in part criticized for their questions on racism, yet provide consistent data on attitudes towards various immigrant groups and help also track opinions on specific issues. Opinion polls on immigration have become a growth industry. Their themes and the phrasing of the questions reflect the attitude of the media that order the polls towards immigration and the general political climate and have become a subject of study (Gaxie 1995; Gastaut 2000).
10 See the chapter by Gérard Grunberg in this volume.
11 See the chapter by Bruno Palier in this volume.
12 See Feldblum 1999 for a thorough analysis of the controversy.
13 One remembers the 1791 declaration of the duc de Clermont-Tonnerre on the citizenship of the Jews: "Il faut tout refuser aux Juifs comme nation; il faut tout leur accorder comme individus!"
14 By 2002, the Socialists had become "arch-Republicans." Their public speeches suggest that they have traded their defense of socialism with a return to the ideational roots of the French Republic. The fact that there is no longer a marked difference in the area of macroeconomics and industrial policy between left and right provides part of the explanation for the rediscovery of Republicanism by the Socialists.
15 The right not having promised anything is better positioned to attract migrant voters and has done better than the left in finding candidates from migrant families.
16 On 9 April 1992, the Constitutional Council ruled on the clause of the Maastricht Treaty that granted EU citizens voting rights in local and European elections. The magistrates stated that a government proposal to grant local voting rights for foreigners would require that a modification of Article 3 of the Constitution be approved by three-fifths of the Senate and National Assembly assembled together as well as the passing of a *loi organique* to change the electoral code.

17 This notion of an "exhausted idea" had gained prominence by 2001. Nacira Guénif-Souilamas, a sociologist working for the government, entitled her article in *Libération* (12 July 2001), "L'intégration, une idée épuisée." See also Wieviorka (2001). The notion of window of opportunity is borrowed from Kingdon (1984).
18 Martine Aubry, "Combattre le racisme au travail," *Libération*, 11 May 1999.
19 It should be underlined that antiracist policy exists since the 1972 law that established criminal penalties for discrimination, penalized hate speech and promoted the role of antiracist associations in the fight against racism. The law emerged out of the fear of a rebirth of post-Vichy anti-Semitic sentiment, yet penal procedures are few and condemnations even fewer (Bleich 2003).
20 Philippe Bataille, a sociologist from the Touraine research center CADIS (Centre d'analyse et d'interrention sociologiques), and later Patrick Simon, a sociologist specializing in urban studies and a demographer at INED, have chaired the group.
21 On the importance of the participants of policy debate, see Schattschneider (1960). For an application to immigrant policy, see Guiraudon (2000).
22 From 16 May 2000 to 31 December 2003, "dial 114" signaled 11,188 cases of discrimination to the CODACS. Source: GELD (http://www.le114.com/pres_114/statistiques.php).
23 See also Prime Minister Jospin's speech at the March 2000 Assises de la citoyenneté: 'Les services publics doivent être davantage à l'image de la population.' http://www.archives.premier-ministre.gouv.fr/jospin_version3/fr/ie4/contenu/5068.htm.
24 In the "communicative discourse" (Schmidt 2002) of policy-makers, as the analysis of the dense press coverage on antidiscrimination reveals, there are almost no references to European examples or to the EU. Source: press archives of Sciences Po Paris library.
25 Quoted in Sylvia Zappi, "Immigration: le virage à droite," *Le Monde*, 28 April 2003.
26 This quote as well as the aforementioned Prime Minister's intentions come from Raffarin (2003).
27 Interview of Blandine Kriegel with *Le Monde*. Quoted in Sylvia Zappi, "Le Haut Conseil à l'intégration fustige la discrimination positive," *Le Monde*, 26 January 2004.
28 They seek to diffuse responsibility to others, in particular to the EU, an ideal candidate for blame shifting. See the chapter by Andy Smith in this volume.

6
Social Generations, Life Chances and Welfare Regime Sustainability

Louis Chauvel

Introduction

The generational sustainability of welfare regimes is of central importance to most long-term analyses of welfare state reforms (see for example: Esping-Andersen et al. 2002). In an ideal society, individual contributions to social welfare are supposed to be counterbalanced by expected benefits, but in reality there are structural disequilibria, notably between generations. Contemporary social reforms are designed to correct such imbalances, but the rewriting of the contract between generations could cause more harm than good. Here, the analysis of the generational disequilibria in France may be useful: French society faces severe generational non-linearities and inequalities, the consequences of which could be the long-term destabilization of the contemporary welfare regime.

The aim of this chapter is to examine the concept of "social generation" as it relates to the analysis of the distribution of well-being, and to compare American and French welfare regime dynamics. The French case is not unique in its generational imbalances; the United States also faces major generational imbalances. In previous publications on the social consequences of economic fluctuations, from the *trente glorieuses* (1945–75) to the *croissance ralentie* (1975–today), I have demonstrated the existence in France of a generational cleavage (*fracture générationnelle*) between the generations born before 1955 (the early baby boom generations and the previous ones, who benefited most from the economic acceleration of the post-war period) and those born after 1955 (who are facing an economic slowdown, high youth unemployment, and the resulting social problems).[1] Thus we find an *insiderization* of previous generations and an *outsiderization* of new ones. This generational cleavage is often denied by policy-makers and in the public debate; however, the long-term implications of these generational dynamics could have major consequences for the stability of the welfare state. This cleavage may be less visible than those based on class, ethnic or gender inequalities, but it nevertheless alters the long-term sustainability of the system. After defining "social generations", and briefly discussing some theories of generational dynamics, I will analyze the consequences of macroeconomic changes in the context of strong social regulation on the opportunities of successive generations. I will first consider the different dimensions of the "generational cleavage" in France and then discuss national specificities within a French-American comparison.

1. Definitions

The use of "generations" in European social science is more permissive than in the American academic context: for American sociologists, "generation" refers to the sociology of kinship and to family issues, while "cohort" (or "birth cohort") refers to people born in the same year (Ryder 1965). Therefore, in American academic journals, the expression "social generation" is quite uncommon (except in the discussions of Karl Mannheim's theories). If some economists in the American tradition (Easterlin 1966; Auerbach et al. 1994) write about "generations" and "generational accounting," the birth cohorts they consider are also engaged in kinship relations of generational transmissions (gifts, education, legacy, etc.). The European tradition is different: we define "social generation" as specific groups of cohorts exposed to a common pattern of social change and/or sharing collective identity features such as ethnicity, gender, or class (Mentré 1920; Mannheim 1928).

Historically, four definitions of "generation" exist (Mentré 1920). The first one is less important to our argument: *genealogical generations* pertain to the sociology of family and kinship. The three others relate respectively to *demographic, social* and *historic* generations. A *demographic generation* is identical to a "birth cohort": the group of individuals born in the same year. Here is the most neutral definition that assumes no common trait. Conversely, the *historical generation* is a set of cohorts defined by a common culture, shared interests, consciousness of the generation's specificity and its historical role, and occasionally conflict with other generations. A historical generation may define itself by the time of its coming of age in history: a decisive example is the so-called *génération 1968*, which refers to the first cohorts of the baby boom (born between 1945 and 1950). The *génération 1914*, the generation of young adults of the First World War, is another dramatic example. *Social generation* is then defined as a link between these two polar definitions. In the empirical social sciences, we first look at demographic generations, and then we define historical generations from the results of sociological analysis, assessment and interpretation of the diversity or homogeneity of cohorts, as well as their objective and subjective identities and consciousness.

2. Process of generational replacement and social change

First we must look at "socialization" in general, without delving into a systematic theorization. During youth, between the end of school and the stabilization of adulthood, there is a specific period of "transitional socialization," which is a pivotal point in the formation of individuals' choices for the future: in a short period, usually some months, the potentialities offered by family and education turn into concrete positions from which people will construct their life courses. That individual process has collective consequences when a cultural or historical polarization has a "socialization effect" on most individual members of the new generation (Mannheim 1928).

For people at age 20, collective historical experiences such as May 1968 or July 1914 could form durable opportunities or scars, since they face a major transition in their lives within a dramatic social or historical context. Children cannot completely participate yet, and older people could be less affected, since they are already influenced by other experiences accumulated in other historical contexts (Ryder 1965). This "transitional socialization" is not necessarily sufficient to create or promote durable generational traits: they require a continuous process of collective recall to reinforce the social generation's identity that would progressively vanish otherwise (Becker 2000).

A major problem in generational social change analysis is the intersection of three social times: age, period and cohort. The most common time is "period" and pertains to the succession of historical epochs; the second time relates to "age" and the aging process; the third one is the *time of generations*, which consists of the continuous process of replacement of elder cohorts by new ones. These three times are organized in a two-dimensional plane (see Figure 6.1) that implies a profound indeterminacy. In any given period, different age groups coexist (defined by age thresholds, age statuses and roles), but they also represent different generations who have been socialized in different historical contexts. When we compare different age groups at a given date (period), we cannot know a priori whether their differences result from age or from generation: in year 2006, on the Lexis diagram, if the age group at age 58 (born in 1948) is at the top of income scale, we do not know whether it is an age effect (any cohort will enjoy better income at age 58) or a cohort effect (the 1948 cohort has faced the best career opportunities of the twentieth century since its entry into the labor market). Age–period–cohort models have been developed to reveal generation effects, which can be discerned when specific traits appear in the "life line" of specific cohorts (Mason et al. 1973). These methods have been developed and improved in many different fields of social science: voting, values, literacy, labor force participation, mortality, suicide, etc. (see Hastings and Berry 1979). The usual problem with cohort analysis is that we must wait for the death of a complete cohort before a complete diagnosis can be made. The major difficulty is the "right censored data problem": since the future is not known today, the coming trajectory of cohorts is only hypothetical.

To reduce the uncertainty, we could put forward two types of social hypotheses based on arguments of cohort progress and cohort socialization.

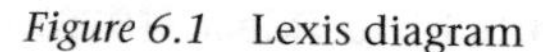
Figure 6.1 Lexis diagram

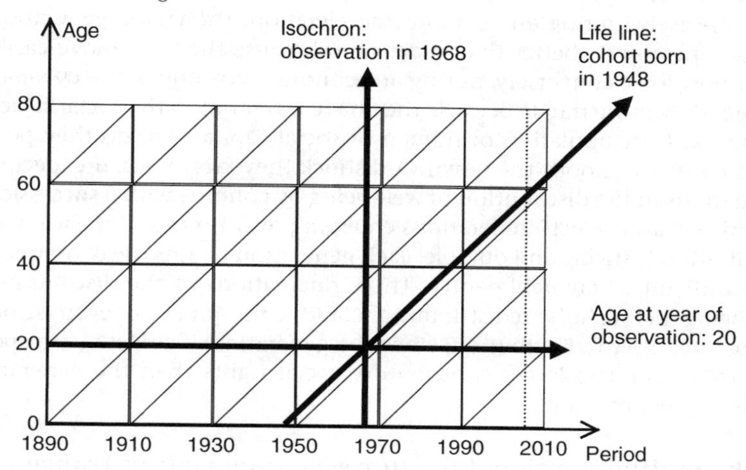

Note: the Lexis diagram offers a synthetic view of the interactions of social times: when we cross periods, horizontally, and age, vertically, the time of cohorts appears on the diagonal ($a = p - c$). In year $p = 2005$, people at age 58 are born in 1948; they were 20 in 1968. At each period, young and old age groups are also different birth cohorts for whom socialization occurred in different contexts: the 75-year-old age group of 2005 (born in 1930) is also the "welfare generation" that has had abundant access to public pensions and health systems, while the same age group in period 1968 was the remains of the "sacrificed generation" born in 1893 (21 years old in 1914).

The first one is the "long-term generational progress" (LTGP) hypothesis: later cohorts will benefit more than their predecessors from longer education, better income, improved health system, higher life expectancy, and from all the benefits resulting from technical, economic or social progress. Immanuel Kant was the first to underline this generational inequality: former cohorts are relatively deprived and later ones will receive more, and that asymmetric distribution cannot be balanced. This "long-term generational social progress" hypothesis supposes a permanent trend of improvement in economic, social and cultural terms. The *génération 1914* is certainly an exception to LTGP, but we will provide more contemporary examples.

The second hypothesis is the "short-term amplifying role" of newer generations (STAR). The LTGP conjecture suggests a long-term linear trend of progress, but the empirical dynamics are generally less stable, with cycles and non-linearities, decelerations and accelerations, breaks and ruptures. The newer generation, which has just experienced its transitional socialization, is generally reacting strongly to new trends, a fact that Mannheim and Mead observed. In periods of sudden social change, the newer cohorts are the most influenced by the discontinuities of history because they are the first to experience the new contexts of socialization that previous cohorts could not anticipate and in which they do not participate (Mead 1970). More precisely, during an economic acceleration, the young generation of adults generally do better than older ones because they can move easily to better positions; conversely, during an economic slowdown, the newcomers are generally more fragile because they have less room in the social structure and no past accumulation of human or social capital, nor do they possess social rights to smooth the downward shock they face. We can expect such fluctuations in the distribution of well-being by cohorts, with a succession of "sacrificed" and "elect" generations emerging over time; and if the effect of socialization is strong and durable, each generation retains the consequences of its difficult or favorable entry. These fluctuations in the distribution of well-being before any redistribution could correspond to even stronger inequalities after redistribution, since the generations marked by prosperity tend to accumulate larger contributory social rights than the generations marked by deprivation.

3. The multidimensional *fracture générationnelle* in France

In France, the economic slowdown has provoked a dramatic multidimensional *fracture générationnelle* since the late 1970s (Chauvel 2002, 2003). This portrait is grim, but it is founded on strong empirical bases, robust analyses of standards and alternative sets of microdata offering convergent results. Three principal topics will be highlighted here: first, the economic marginalization of new entrants into the labor market and its direct effects on social structure; second, the long-term consequences of this deprivation in terms of socialization and life chances; and, finally, the consequences for the political participation of these cohorts, and their support for the contemporary welfare regime.

The economic decline of youth

The first aspect of the dynamics of social generation in France is the change in the cohort distribution of economic means. A large redistribution of earnings and incomes occurred between the seventies and today. In 1977, the earning gap between age groups 30–5 and 50–5 was 15 per cent; the gap is now about 40 per cent. During the *trente glorieuses*, the young wage-earners generally began in the labor market with the same level of income as their own parents at the end of a complete career. For the last 20 years, we have observed the stagnation of the wages of the young while wages for older people have grown by 20 per cent or more. Here is a new compromise between age groups, whose consequences are not completely understood by contemporary social science. But it is not simply a change in the relative position of age groups: members of the elder generation (now, those at age 55, more or less) were relatively advantaged in their youth when compared to their seniors, and now, too, when these seniors are compared with their young successors. The generational gaps result from double gains and double pains.

How can we explain this increasing gap? In fact, this is a consequence of a changing collective compromise, which occurred during the mid-1970s and early 1980s. This transition in the social value of generations brought from a relative valorization of newer generations, as a positive future we had to invest in, to a relative valorization of the protection of the adults' and seniors' stability, even at the expense of the young. The main factor in the redistribution of well-being concerned unemployment. High unemployment rates were socially acceptable for young workers, provided that adult employees with dependent children could avoid these difficulties. In 1974, the unemployment rate of those who had left school during the previous two years was about 4 per cent; by 1985, those who left school recently had an unemployment rate of 35 per cent, which remained the case through 1996; in 2002, at the end of the recent wave of economic recovery, it was close to 18 per cent. The unemployment rates of recent school leavers are highly sensitive to the economic situation whereas the middle-aged and senior rates remain more stable: an economic slowdown has serious consequences for younger adults, and recovery first benefits new entrants in the labor market. Evidently, the perverse consequence of this collective compromise for the protection of adults at the expense of newcomers is the lack of socialization of the new, sacrificed generations: even if they are now adults, with dependent children of their own, their unemployment rates remain much higher, and their earnings abnormally low when compared to other age groups, because of a kind of "scarring effect." At the end of the eighties, the unemployment rate of the group at age 40 to 44 was still about 4 per cent and is now over 8 per cent. The age compromise for the protection of adults with dependent children is unclear now. This "scarring effect" is even clearer concerning earnings: the cohorts of new entrants in the labor market in a time of downturn have to accept lower wages; conversely, for young workers, a strong economy allows them to negotiate better earnings. After this entry point, the earning's gap remains because of the lack of catch up effect on earnings (Chauvel 2003: ch. 3): some generations are about 10 points above or below the long-term trend, because of the point at which they entered the workforce, and after age 30 the relative benefit or handicap remains stable.[2]

A complementary factor relates to the dynamics of occupational structure and the stratification system. In France as in the US (Mendras 1988; Bell 1973), the standard hypothesis of stratification change suggests that the long-term educational expansion of the twentieth century and the emergence of a knowledge-based society have stimulated the enlargement of the middle and upper middle classes; thus, the newer generation could have mechanically benefited from the expansion of the occupational groups of experts, managers or professionals (*cadres et professions intellectuelles supérieures*, in French),[3] to whom we often add middle management and lower professionals in the private and public sectors (such as school teachers and nurses), who exemplify the "new technical middle class," whose social hegemony was predicted in the seventies (*professions intermédiaires* in the official French nomenclature of occupations).

At the aggregate level, the expansion of these middle and higher occupational groups in France seems to be a demonstration of this idea: for the aggregated age group between 30 and 54, the rise is from 14 per cent in 1970 to 26 per cent of the total population (Figure 6.2). However, when we make a distinction between age groups, the dynamics are much more complicated: at age 30, the per centage of those in middle and higher white-collar occupational groups jumped from 14 per cent to 23 per cent between 1965 and 1975, and it reached 24.5 per cent in 1980. In the earlier period, the trend strongly accelerated for these "juniors," but stalled after 1980: it increased by 1.5 points in the two decades between 1980 and 2000, compared to a 9 point increase in the 1970s.

In the middle of the *trente glorieuses*, France experienced a dramatic expansion of the public sector and high-tech large companies (Airbus, France Télécom, civil nuclear electricity planning, health system, universities and research centers, etc.), creating strong demand for employees with higher education. The first cohorts of the baby boom (the 1945 cohort, which was

Figure 6.2 "Cadres et professions intellectuelles supérieures" plus "Professions intermédiaires"

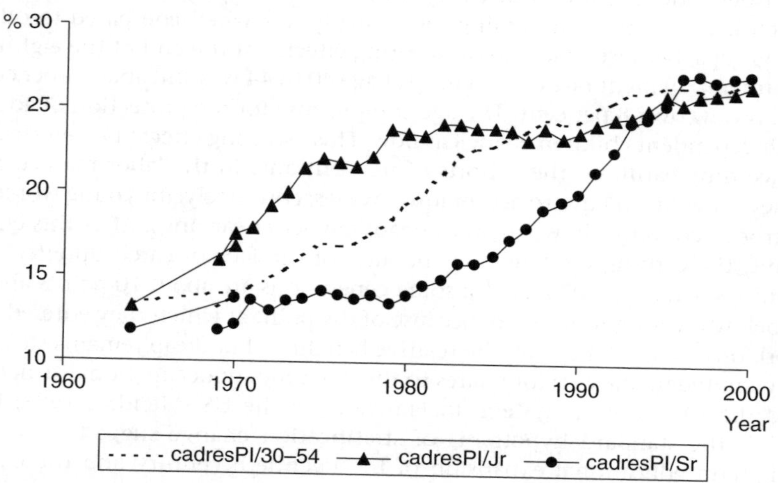

Note: In 2000, 26% of "juniors" (= age group 30 to 34) are in the middle or higher occupational groups; the figure for seniors (= 50 to 54) is 27%. The proportions were respectively 24.5% and 14% in 1980. The percentages are calculated using the total age-group population.

Source: Enquêtes *Emploi* 1969–2000 et *Formation-qualification-professionnelle* 1964 et 1977, INSEE; archives LASMAS-Quételet.

30 years old in 1975) were surely not a sacrificed generation since they enjoyed longer education in the context of a dynamic labor market, and did not face the diminishing returns to education that subsequent cohorts have faced. In 2000, 25 years later, the portion of 30-year-olds in mid-level and higher white-collar occupational groups is quite similar and stable (26%), compared to 23 per cent in 1975 and 24.5 in 1980. In this respect, the cohort born in 1970 knows no clear progress. However, during the 1990s, the expansion for "seniors" (i.e., the "juniors" of the seventies) is obvious. Thus, the expansion of mid-level and higher occupational groups across generations is not linear. The apparent linear growth results from the inappropriate aggregation of a strong expansion – for the early baby boomers – and of a strong slowdown for the succeeding generations.

Scarring effect and generational dyssocialization

These evolutions would have had no significant social impact if, for the new generations, these early difficulties had no permanent effect. If the new entrants in the labor force in a period of scarcity could catch up from their early difficulties later in their lives, the problem would be anecdotal or residual. The assessment of the long-term impact of these early difficulties is central to the interpretation; if young, deprived generations do not catch up, a kind of long-term *hysteresis* effect appears that we can call a "scar" or "scarring effect," since the handicap endures. The age–period–cohort analysis shows that cohorts that experienced a difficult (favorable) entry because of a context of recession (expansion), continue to suffer (benefit) from a relative delay (advancement) in upward mobility when they are compared to the average situation. The relative position of a collective cohort at age 30 is rapidly crystallized, and there does not appear to be a substantial catch-up effect later on (Figure 6.3).

How can we explain the lack of a generational catch-up dynamics? Those who had benefited from a period of entry marked by a strong demand for skilled jobs experienced faster career and earlier labor experience at higher levels of responsibility, with better wages; these individuals (and the cohort they constitute at an aggregated level) retain the long-term benefits of the early opportunities they enjoyed, which will positively influence their future trajectory at any later age. For those who entered the labor market under difficult economic conditions, the periods of unemployment they faced, the necessity to accept less-qualified jobs with lower wages, and the consecutive delays in career progression, imply negative *stimuli* for their own trajectories (decline in ambition, lack of valued work experiences) and could appear as a negative signal for future potential employers. The hypothesis we present here for France is that cohort-specific socialization contexts imply long-term opportunities and life chances for individuals and for their cohorts; even after difficulties disappear, the cohorts that faced these problems continue to suffer from long-term consequences of past handicaps.

Figure 6.3 Proportion of service class positions (*cadres et professions intermédiaires*) by age and cohort (cohort diagram)

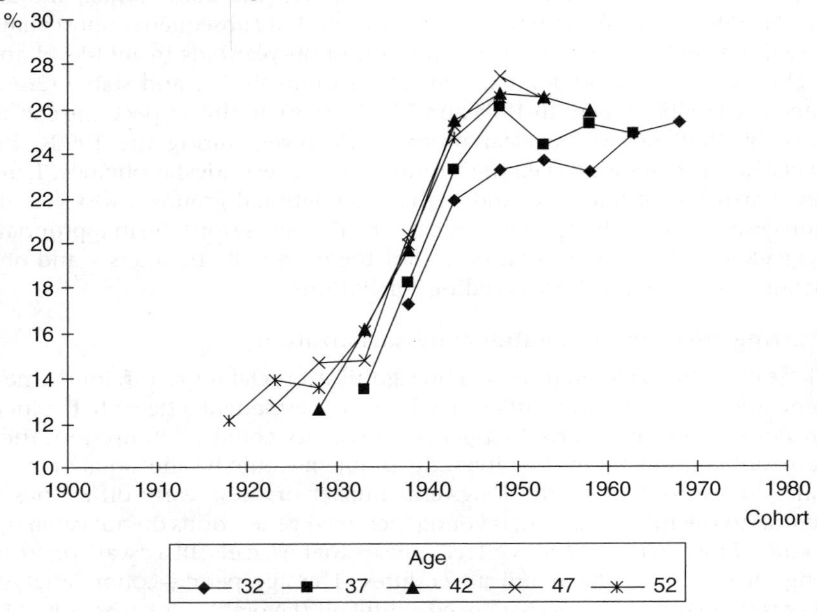

Note: The cohort diagram is a strong instrument for the analysis of cohort effects. It compares the achievement at the same age of different cohorts. If the curves are linear, we have a stable progress by cohort. If we see cohort accelerations and decelerations affecting the same cohorts, we can analyze long-term cohort effects. The 1948 cohort benefits from an acceleration of its position at age 32 (23% compared to 17% for the 1938 cohort, and less than 12% for the 1933 cohort – as we can suppose). The 1958 cohort, which at age 32 stalls relative to the 1948 one, does not catch up by age 42. At age 32, the rate for the cohort 1968 was 2 points higher than that of the 1948 one, whereas the rate for the 1948 cohort was about 13 points higher compared to that of the 1928 cohort. Since the opportunity for growth is neither similar nor linear from one cohort to another, some benefit from better careers than others. Generational history is not linear.

Source: Compilation Enquêtes FQP – Enquêtes Emploi (1964–2000).

In more concrete terms, the cohorts born during the forties, which benefited from the economic acceleration of the late sixties, were relatively privileged compared to the previous cohorts when young, and are relatively advantaged when compared to the newer ones, because of the lack of progress for the young from 1975 to the present. We can generalize this observation: the cohorts that entered the labor force after 1975 and experienced an economic slump and mass unemployment have been the early victims of the new generational dynamics, and they retain the long-term scars of their initial difficulties in the labor market.

An important point we cannot develop at length here is the consequences of educational expansion. If the level of education has increased in the cohorts born in the period from 1950 to 1975, that positive trend was accompanied by a strong social devalorization of grades (Chauvel 2000). More specifically, the first cohorts of the baby boom benefited from an expansion of education at a time when the returns to education remained stable: even if there were twice as many *Baccalauréat* recipients in the 1948 cohort as in the 1935 cohort, their likelihood of access to higher social or economic positions did not shrink. However, the generations that followed had to deal with a strong trend of devaluation in terms of the economic and social returns to education. The first consequence is a rush to the most valued and selective grades (in the *grandes écoles* of the elite such as Ecole Polytechnique, Ecole Nationale d'administration, Sciences Po Paris, etc.) whose value remains stable, but whose population becomes ever more homogeneous in terms of social origins. The second consequence is a strong devalorization of less prestigious universities, which are less exclusive but have much smaller per capita endowments in comparison to the *Grandes écoles*. In the same way, the best secondary schools become more selective, with major consequences in terms of urban segregation. In the French case, the school system was traditionally the central institution of the Republic and at the heart of its idea of progress, providing the strongest support for French-style social democracy and meritocracy. The collapse of the value of grades implies a destabilization of this myth and a pessimistic outlook on progress, developments that we can expect to have political consequences.

Now that we are nearing the end of this long-term slowdown, which began 25 years ago, we can compare two social and genealogical generations.[4] For the first time in a period of peace, the youth of the new generation are not better off than their parents at the same age. In fact, the "1968 generation," born in 1948, are the children of those born in 1918 who were young adults in the Second World War, and who worked in difficult conditions at the beginning of the *trente glorieuses*. The condition of the baby boomers was incomparably better than that of their parents. But the following genealogical generation, born around 1978 — that is now between 25 and 30 years old — faces diminished opportunities of growth, not only because of an economic slump but also because of their relatively poor outcomes in comparison to those of their own parents, who did very well.[5] We now observe rising rates of downward social mobility connected to the proliferation of middle-class children who cannot find social positions comparable to that of their parents.

These diminishing resources and opportunities imply, for the newer generation, an exceptional risk of dyssocialization. The distinction between dissocialization and dyssocialization is essential (in Latin, the prefix dis- means "lack of," whereas in Greek, dys- means "bad," "difficult," or "not appropriate"). Indeed, since Durkheim and Merton, we have known the dangers of a gap between aspirations (which result from early socialization, notably in the family) and achievements. Today's generational transmission problem comes from a lack of correspondence between the values and ideas that the new generation receives (individual freedom, self achievement, valorization of leisure, etc.) and the realities it will face (centrality of market, heteronomy, scarcity, lack of valuable jobs, boredom, etc.). All the generations of the twentieth century experienced that lack of correspondence between aspirations and achievement: the early baby-boom generations were socialized in the context of their parents' values (scarcity, abnegation, submission to a society where work remains the central issue, lack of leisure) linked to the social history of the hard times of the thirties and after, but they finally experienced the *trente glorieuses* and the period of fast growth that offered them comfort, affluence, and opportunities for emancipation and leisure. But in this sense, dyssocialization is not so problematic. The gap could be more difficult for the current young generations experiencing shrinking opportunities. Apparently, the new generation benefits from longer educational careers and higher academic qualifications than its own parents did, but the intense devaluation in social and economic terms of their improved educational assets could provoke a cruel confrontation with reality (i.e. "lost illusions"). The psychosocial difficulties of the new generation (notably, violent behavior, incivilities of any kind, suicide, etc.) could be immediately linked to the gap between what young people suppose they deserve (comparing their parents' and their own education and social position) and what they are able to achieve (Chauvel 1997).

Problems of political representation

The destabilization in the generational distribution of well-being is accompanied by profound changes in access to political power. Far-reaching changes have occurred in the access that various age groups have to political representation and power, not to mention the interest they have in political issues. Here we can apply Putnam's (2000) theory of social capital decline, regarding the replacement of the American "civic generation," born between 1920 and 1940, by the following one. In the French context, the argument is more appropriate if we switch the term "civic" with "mobilized," and the 1920–40 birth cohorts with the 1940–50 ones – in other words, the first "baby-boom generation." In terms of participation in politics, this point is very clear when we consider the last 30 years.

Even if, for the most part, people lack interest in politics and political matters, the variations in participation in political discussions with friends are strong, particularly when we collapse the results by age groups (Figure 6.4). In the late seventies, 25 per cent of those aged from 30 to 34 frequently engaged in political discussions with friends; that proportion had fallen to 12 per cent in the late nineties. The decline is severe when we compare this generation with older age groups, notably those between 50 and 55 years of age, who were significantly more likely to engage in political discussions when surveyed in the late nineties. Evidently, for people at age 30 in 1977

Figure 6.4 Frequency of political discussions with friends

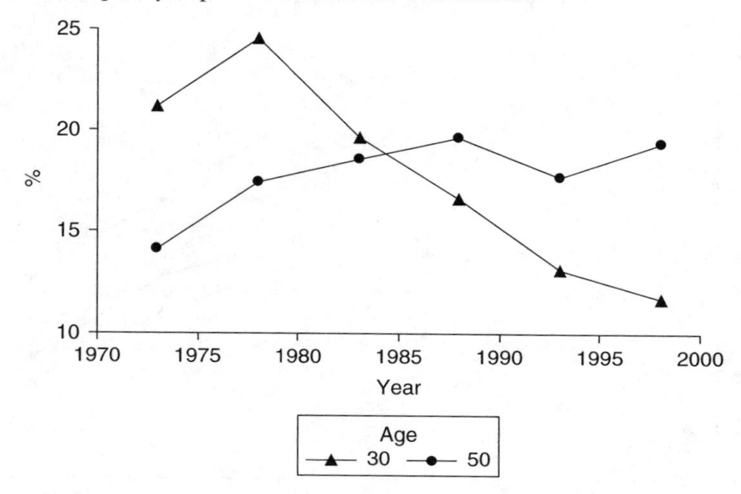

Note: the diagram tracks the percentage answering "frequently" to the question: "When you get together with friends, would you say you discuss political matters frequently, occasionally, or never?" We present periods of 5-year compilations of probabilistic samples of about 3,000 individuals per year; the statistical uncertainty on each dot is therefore about +/−2.0%.

Source: Mannheim Eurobarometer Trend File 1970–1999, MZES-ZUMA-ZEUS; Data provided by Grenoble BDSP/CIDSP Data Archive.

and age 50 in 1997 (i.e. the cohorts born near 1947), political socialization occurred during the late sixties in the context of the events of May 1968 and its aftermath.

An important characteristic of the "mobilized" generation of 1968 (the first cohorts of the baby boom, born in 1945–50) is its stronger participation in collective action in its youth, which continued in the decades that followed. However, by contrast, the specificity of the cohorts born after 1955 and particularly in the late 1960s is their political demobilization: occasional political discussions and declining political participation, notably in traditional political institutions (vote, trade-union membership, parties, and even elective bodies). Since the phenomenon is not so new now—after two decades—and since this generation's lack of participation is so clearly visible in these institutions, French political leaders have become conscious of the long-term problem implied by the difficulty in attracting young members and militants. However, the effort required to change the trend is so massive, that despite the regrets expressed for the situation, nothing is done to change it.

What is the evidence? For trade-union members, the dynamic is very strong, since the socialization effect seems to be significant (Figure 6.5): for a given cohort, the per centage of trade-union members at age 30, or even

Figure 6.5 Members of trade unions by age group from 1981 to 1999 in France

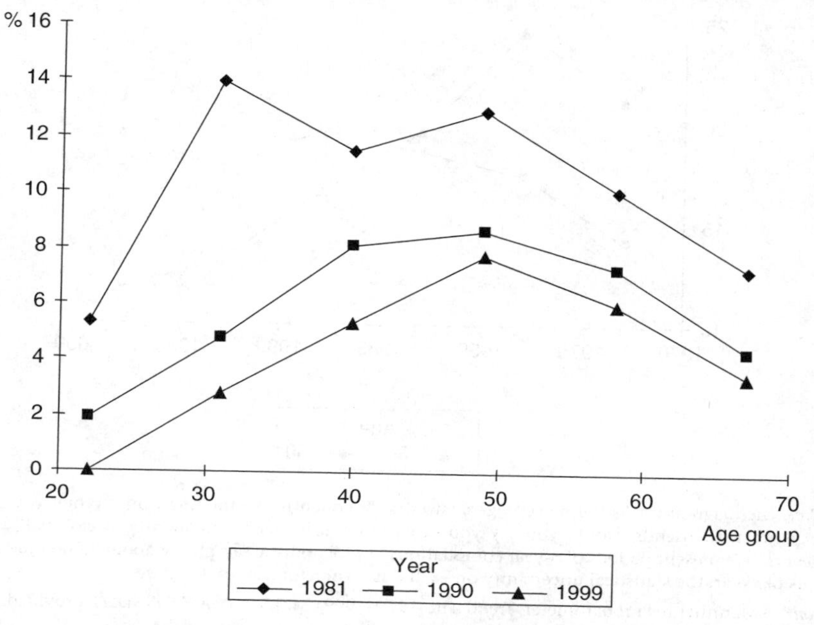

Note: the point "age 22" refers to the age group 18 to 27; people at age 22 in 1981 are 31 in 1990 and 40 in 1999; the trade-union members remain at 5% of that cohort. The dynamic here is a kind of generational extinction of trade unions.

Source: European values survey cumulative file (1981–1999).

before, is a good predictor of this percentage at later ages; since it is now about 2 per cent (and not 14% as in the early 1980s), we can expect a strong decline in union membership in the coming years. When we consider the base of trade unions and parties, the newer generation's participation is declining. What about elected officials? In 1982, the average age of trade unionists and politicians holding an elected position was 45; in 2000, it was 59. At the Assemblée Nationale (the French Congress), in 1981, 38.1 per cent of the *Deputés* were 44 years old or less, and 15.1 per cent in the new Congress of 2002. In fact, between 1997 and 2002, the most significant change is the drop in the age group between age 45 and 49, which fell from 18.5 per cent to 12.3 per cent: the political representation of those born after 1953 is clearly declining. If the French electorate is growing older (the age of the average voter jumped from 45.5 to 47.5 years old between 1982 and 2002), its representatives, and those who at the highest levels of decision-making in regards to the future of French society, are aging at a much faster rate.

The interpretation of that dynamic may be more subtle than a simple trend of aging: the political generation that had been socialized with the events of 1968 could enter very early into the highest spheres of political institutions at the end of the 1970s and 1980s; now, many of the members of this generation are still active in politics and, since there is no apparent problem, no need for dynamics for a new political generation appears to have emerged. The homogeneity in terms of the age of the French *classe politique* is now substantial, and the question of the transmission of political know-how and ideological and organizational legacy remains quite problematic for the coming decades. A consequence of this trend is the growing age gap between the bulk of French society and its political representatives. Here, in terms of generations, political power is more accessible to those who are already dominant in terms of social and economic power, and the younger generations, who lack comparable material resources, also suffer from a loss of democratic influence, and even interest, since they are not engaged in political discussions. The lack of clear collective consciousness is a remarkable trait of the democratic debate at the present time. In fact, most young employees in many economic sectors are clearly conscious, at the individual level, of the asymmetric generational play in which they are acting. The political behavior of the young, characterized by distance from institutions and by stronger instability, is somehow rational: why would they support a system where their present and future position is quite unclear?

In terms of political prospects, we should assess the consequences, notably for the sustainability of democracy, of the decline of political socialization. The first problem is the generational transmission of democracy, which supposes a strong civil society whose absence makes the socialization of newer cohorts problematic. Participation in democracy assumes shared social knowledge, political know-how and the ability to insert oneself into the collective networks of political bargaining. Since many institutions are led today by a homogeneous group of baby boomers who will retire at the end of the decade, and since almost nothing is done to socialize a new generation of successors, the sustainability of the political system is quite uncertain and the risk of generational micro-struggles is very high.

The second problem is a question of long-term decision-making. Many weighty decisions at the national level (retirement, health, debt issues, etc.) are made by a political class whose remaining life span is generally shorter than that of the average population; the new generations that will have to face (and pay for) the long-term consequences of today's choices do not participate in the decisions made about their own future, because they are supposed to be too young (even if they are 40 or older). That generational asymmetry or bias implies that many reforms are designed to have little immediate negative impact on elders, but to delay payment of the costs of reform to the point that it threatens the future well-being of newer generations. Therefore, the social contract between generations seems to be both unclear and extremely unstable.

Problems of welfare regime sustainability

It may seem that social and structural reforms affect the entire population whatever the age or generation; but in fact, social welfare, welfare state dynamics, and welfare regime[6] change with the succession of cohorts. We have to analyze this point and its consequences for social reforms and *in fine* the sustainability of our contemporary welfare regime. This crucial factor could show that the expensive but efficient public health and pension schemes of the present day could collapse with the future cohort replacement of older "welfare generations" (born between 1925 and 1950) with the generations that follow.

When France's public pay-as-you-go retirement system was created in 1946, the principle was that wage earners had to participate (and work) for at least 30 years before gaining access to a full pension. Thus, in 1946, those who were 35 or older—that is, born before 1910 – were generally excluded from the new system. Indeed, in large industries, in the public sector and in protected segments of the economy, arrangements had been developed to fulfill the contract, but most workers in smaller firms, those who had experience in agriculture or as self-employed business people, even though they were alive during the creation of this large system of welfare, were already too old to benefit from most of its outcomes: they were destined to fill the ranks of the impoverished elderly[7] during a golden age for youth. Conversely, today, the new generation leaves school at age 21, loses three years in episodes of unemployment, freelance or non-standard, non-protected activities and begins its participation in the retirement system at an average age of 24. If we add 40 years of contributions (the current requirement, which most French seniors can meet because they could start working much earlier than the youth of today) or 46.5 years (the time requirement proposed by the French employers' association), we discover that our present system of early retirement (at an average age of 58, with an average level of income close to the employed population) is simply inaccessible for the newcomers: in the most probable scenario, the generations of pensioners to come will not benefit from the generosity of the current system, even if they contribute heavily to the high level of protection that benefits today's seniors. This point is even clearer when we analyze how the lower half or third (in educational terms) of the young generation, which has to wait for years before obtaining a stable position, is socialized within the working world, and the political and welfare system: we now socialize the young within a much more unequal system than in the early seventies, and the greater inequalities within today's younger generation could (will) have consequences for their future trajectory.

Some optimistic observers of these trends argue that with a long-term annual rate of growth of about 2 per cent, the retirement system will eventually balance itself out. Moreover, when the baby-boom generation begins to retire, in 2007, new jobs will be available for the younger generation.

However, the risk is double here: on the one hand, perhaps we overestimate the number of new positions created, since productivity gains might be obtained at the expense of new entrants; on the other hand, even if new positions are available, members of even newer generations could seize these new opportunities, and an intermediate sacrificed generation, yesterday too young and tomorrow too old, could be the double victim of social change. King Lear could suggest another troubling prospect: long wars of succession among competing generations.

If the existence of such dynamics can be established for the pension system, the same kind of argument can be developed for many other aspects of the French welfare system (the health care system, social expenditures for families, education, etc.). In fact, our French equalitarian system of large homogeneous middle classes of wage earners, which reached its apogee with the generations born during the 1930s and 1940s, seems to be disappearing progressively in a cohort dynamic of dismantlement and disentitlement that the newer generations are experiencing.

4. The American way of cohort inequality and prosperity

These trends may merely demonstrate that France is an exotic country whose civil society, political culture and socioeconomic organization are quite problematic. In a more flexible country, where seniority is less systematically valued, different cohorts are competing in an open market, and the conditions of political bargaining can provoke a faster circulation of political generations and elites, we might be able to avoid these difficulties. At the first glance, the United States seems to be such a society, where mobility reduces the generational rents that we observe in France. The American dynamic partially fits that hypothesis, but is much more complex, however, since we also observe strong generational inequalities in the United States.[8]

A theoretical explanation of American-French divergence

We could attempt to systematize the link between the welfare state and cohort dynamics,[9] but we have too little space here. For an American-French comparison, it will suffice to underline the pertinent contrasts in the basic societal structures and their possible impact on cohort dynamics. Compared with France, American society is marked by a liberal-residual welfare system, characterized by the weakness of social redistribution, the submission of social policies to the efficiency of flexible markets, and the idea that the welfare system can operate only in cases of typical market failure. More generally, whereas French society is organized according to stable statuses that supposedly ensure collective security, the American one is marked by an ideal of mobility, individual progress, and the idealization of *cursus* (etymologically opposed to *status*): by achievement and not by ascription.

A central example is the valorization of inter-firm mobility: at age 40, male wage earners in France have been at the same firm for the last 11 years (on average), while in the United States they have been at the same company for the last 7.5 years (Neumark 2000; Chauvel 2003). In France, seniority offers many more protections, social rights, and implicit rents, whereas mobility implies more uncertainties than opportunities; this is a residue of the patriarchal regulation of the French labor system where the fidelity of the employee is strongly valued, as are interpersonal contacts and clienteles. In contrast, the American labor market values the accumulation of diverse experiences; the bond between firms and their employees is weaker; and the rewards of moving (higher wages, principally) surpasses the rewards of staying in place (Barbier and Gautié 1998). In the French system, if the security of a stable labor force is greatly valued by most social actors, this objective is secondary in the United States. In the case of an economic slowdown, French firms stop hiring; in the case of greater difficulties, they negotiate early retirement schemes for seniors—at the expense of public funds; if problems deepen, the last in are the first out; the dismissal of middle-aged employees is the last and most expensive course of action when companies are faced with disaster, since heavy compensation must be paid. This system advantages employees with some seniority at the expense of occasional or more casual employees, notably when high unemployment rates deepen the polarization between insiders and outsiders.

The question here is to understand the consequence of this French regime on the trajectories of different birth cohorts. Theoretically, in the case of an economic recession, the generalization of the logics of the French corporatist-conservative compromise implies an insider–outsider polarization of generations, where the new generation has to remain outside for a long time — since they do not work, they do not contribute to the social welfare system and do not participate in collective political decisions. The promise of stability for the older cohorts comes at the expense of the socialization of newer ones—who will not catch up later to the position of the older ones. Conversely, since the liberal system is less protective of the status of insiders, an economic recession will prompt negotiations on earnings and on explicit and implicit rights, with cuts affecting all workers, whatever their age. Is this theory in conformity with reality?[10]

Common patterns: a large proportion of American youth face difficulties, too

The empirical analysis is much more ambiguous, since the American case shows some aspects of cohort depression similar to those we observe in France. An analysis of United States' cohort dynamics reveals the marginalization of large segments of the young. In fact, when we apply the same methodology to the United States, evidence of strong cohort fluctuations appears in the American case, too, even if the fluctuations are smoother and somewhat blurred.

One example is the cohort evolution of American relative poverty rates,[11] which reveal that the same types of difficulties clearly confront new generations in both countries (Figure 6.6). At the national level, for the adult population between age 25 and 65, a dramatic change in the distribution of relative poverty rates by age groups has occurred since the sixties: in 1960, the older the population, the higher the poverty rates; in 2000, on the contrary, the youngest experience the highest poverty rates. Even if poverty rates are very different by region (lower in the northeast, higher in the south and west), by gender (women are at higher risk), by ethnic group (the poverty rate is lower for Whites and Asians, higher for Blacks and Hispanics), and evidently by level of education, the same right-slipping U-shaped structure of poverty rates is observed; whereas yesterday the poorest were the oldest, now it is the youngest who are poorest. A more fine-grained cohort analysis of poverty rates shows that the cohorts born before 1920 have

Figure 6.6 Poverty rates by adult age groups (census years 1960–2000) in the US

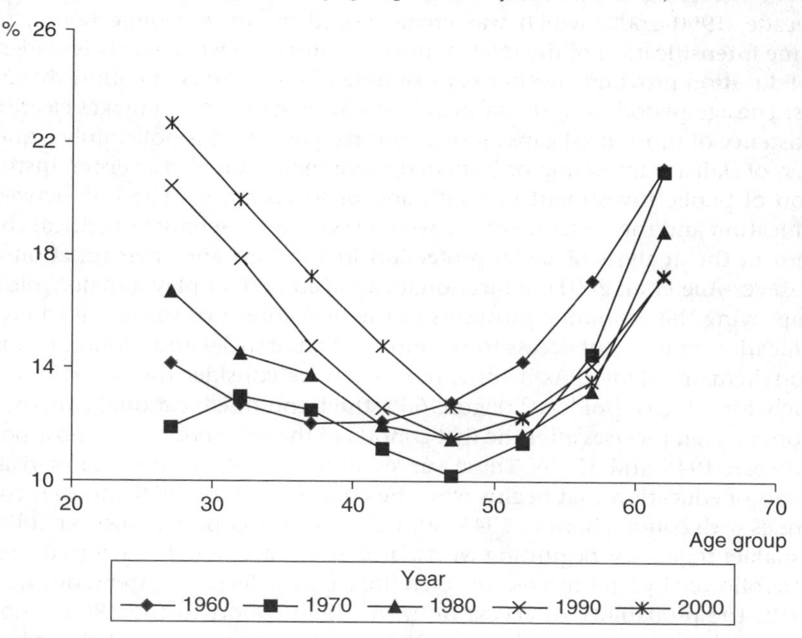

Note: the definition of poverty threshold used here is based on the European relative definition: people with standardized equivalent income adjusted for family size below 50% of the national median are poor. Since 1980, each new generation has entered the labor market with a higher poverty rate, which remains higher as the cohort ages.

Source: US Census microdata accessed at www.ipums.org.

known higher poverty rates (above 15%); those born between 1920 and 1955 have experienced poverty rates close to 12 per cent or lower (the same relative poverty rates as in Continental European countries); and cohorts born after 1955 now face poverty rates that exceed 20 per cent at their entry into the labor market. It appears that high poverty rates jumped a whole generation. Large proportions of the newer generations face difficulties that their own parents could avoid. The most important point is that newer cohorts are socialized in a context of high poverty rates, and that fact stays with them: even years after the period of socialization, poverty remains higher within cohorts that experienced higher rates at the time of their entry into the labor market.[12] A self-sustaining generational trend prepares a future of mass poverty.

Even if we exclude non-natives and members of ethnic or gender minorities (or other combinatory variants of subpopulations) and focus the analysis on the white male population born in the United States, the same pattern emerges, which is not due to higher immigration rates or to higher fertility rates within certain subgroups of the population, but is clearly a general trend occurring within American society. Even during the last observed decade, 1990–2000, which was characterized by an economic boom, the same intensification of the relative poverty rates of newer cohorts is evident.

Education provides another key example of these kinds of cohort dynamics. The age-period–cohort analysis of educational expansion makes clear the existence of substantial gaps among cohorts. Education is not simply a question of skill accumulation or human development; it is also a central institution of public investment in youth and of socialization. The link between education and the structure of the welfare system is therefore of critical concern in the analysis of social protection institutions and their functioning (Estevez-Abe et al. 2001). Educational expansion could play a major role in improving the economic prospects of the new cohort (if the social value of education in terms of access to the most valuable social and economic positions remains stable). As it turns out, when we consider the proportion of bachelor's degree holders[13] (Figure 6.7), the trend of educational expansion stops or even reverses after the first cohorts of the baby boom (i.e. those born between 1945 and 1950). These curves show a long linear trend of rising levels of education that begins with the cohorts born in 1920 and that continues with cohorts born in 1945–50. The following cohorts, however, follow a shakier trajectory, beginning with a drop in the access to bachelor's degrees and followed by a more a recent catch up: we see a decline of about one quarter in the probability of access from the 1950 cohort to the 1960 cohort. Finally, the cohort that is born in 1970 catches up the level of those born 20 years before.

This brings us to an important point for which the explanation is complex. Different complementary factors could explain the expansion of cohorts born from 1920 to 1950: mainly the 1944 GI Bill of Rights,[14] and

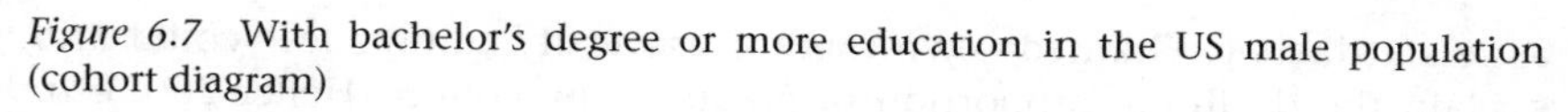

Figure 6.7 With bachelor's degree or more education in the US male population (cohort diagram)

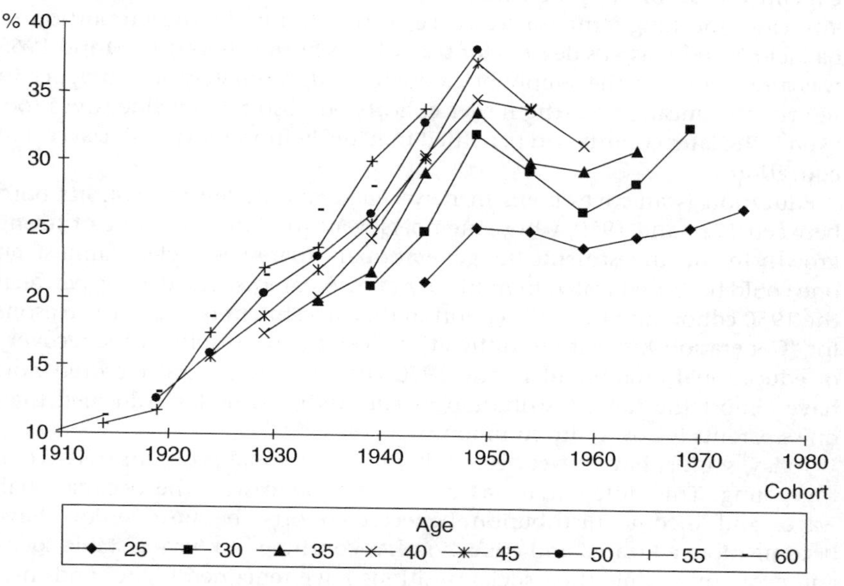

Source: US CPS 1968–1999 cumulative file; male population; N = 956, 940.

later the context of the Vietnam War—which encouraged students to remain in college (Card and Lemieux 2000). However, this is a problem with the GI Bill versus war explanation: why did women of the 1945–50 cohort enjoy longer educational carriers too? From 1945 to 1970 or 1975, other economic or historical traits could complement that explanation of the linear growth in the level of education from the cohort born in 1920 to that born in 1950: the acceleration of public investment in education, subsidies and loan supports, federal and local contracts for research, the rising inflation rates—which particularly favor loans for students – and so on. All these factors offer partial explanations.

The cohorts that followed the cohort born in 1950 experienced a reverse trend, resulting from the fiscal crisis of the seventies, and from many other factors that depressed educational attainment (Weir 2002). In fact, for these cohorts, the new context of educational investment made going to school much less attractive, because of financial and political pressures. The emergence of a phenomenon of over-education—of declining returns to education (Freeman 1976)—prompted a downward shift in public support for education and could explain the general atmosphere (*Zeitgeist*) that characterized a period of at least 15 years during which higher education was seen as less attractive. Granted, skyrocketing university tuition fees could also explain the declining proportion of graduates by cohort (Heller 2002). In any case, the long-term consequence of the decline in the proportion of bachelor's and master's degrees for the cohorts born between 1950 and 1965 was a reduction in the supply of graduates and, ultimately, a resurgence in returns to education for the newer cohorts but also for the elder ones too, even if the later cohorts had benefited previously from inexpensive access to education.

Education is an investment in newer generations. For the cohorts born between 1920 and 1950, whose members went to school at a time of strong growth in this investment, the generational progress was clear: almost no one could be less educated than his or her own parents. The decline between the 1950 cohort and the 1965 cohort in this investment is one of the reasons for "Generation X's" current difficulties. Even today, in spite of the recovery of educational attainment in the 1970 cohort, parents and children now have almost the same distribution of education: to be less educated than one's parents is now quite common.

Today, seniors have never been in better educational positions, relative to the young. This differential has clear consequences on the occupational, wage, and income distribution between cohorts: because seniors have become more educated and education has continued to have a stable social and economic value, their social positions have remained higher and their earnings better, both relatively and absolutely. Conversely, poverty rates have grown faster in the young generations. Middle- and higher-skilled occupational groups have seen slower expansion for the younger than for older cohorts. Therefore, we would have to conclude that no clear difference exists between the American and French trends. There seems to be no path dependency in the cohort dynamics, because otherwise the American "free-market" system and the rigid and statutory French system of *droits acquis* (acquired social rights) would not have produced the same kind of generational cleavage. In fact, the main difference lies somewhere else.

The American specificity: among youth, an elite benefit from exceptional growth

Despite these pessimistic trends, we can demonstrate that a small fraction of the new generation is better off at its entry into the labor market than any former one. We have difficulty assessing the size of this "privileged" population, since income polarization benefits the highest strata much more. Younger age groups provide the most vivid example of this American trend: between 1990 and 2000, for people aged 30 to 34, the median standardized income adjusted for family size grew by 1.7 per cent in real terms; for the 7th decile, it increased by 4.4 per cent; for the 9th decile, by 9.2 per cent; for the 99th centile, by 23.9 per cent. The higher the level of income, the stronger the growth. So, we could argue that 60 per cent of the population enjoyed positive growth, and 8 per cent two-digit growth. In fact, only a small minority enjoyed a very substantial increase in their income. In the United States, a young, rich and educated elite benefited from the growth of the 1990s and began its career at higher levels than previous cohorts, and it appears that this group will continue to climb the income scale in the years ahead. Those who were successful in college and obtained a bachelor's or a master's degree from a well-recognized university benefit now from the scarcity of their degree.

As a result, although the dynamics of the bottom and the top of the social pyramid are somewhat similar in France (relative to the American case), in the United States the rich, the poor, and the median classes face divergent trajectories, especially when they are analyzed in terms of cohorts. At the bottom, the downturn experienced by newer generations (from the 1950 cohort to the most recent), which face permanently higher poverty rates at the time of their entry into the labor market and later, clearly reveals declining opportunities. The median categories experience a kind of stagnation or slow growth in their opportunities (an annual trend of about +0.5 per cent in their real earnings during the two last decades, far lower than the +3.0 per cent per year of the fifties–sixties) with no major change. In contrast, the young elites continue to benefit from the "long-term generational progress" (LTGP) hypothesis. Among the young elites—notably those with a bachelor's degree or more education, and more generally for the top decile group—the life chances of the generations born after 1955 have not been reduced. In, their case, progress from generation to generation seems to be unequivocal. This segment of the American society offers a very optimistic view on the continuation and transmission of the American Dream, but its trajectory has diverged from that of other social groups for the last two decades. Therefore, the career trajectories of recent college graduates, which are quite optimistic, provide a biased point of view on American trends, since most Americans are not benefiting from such improving life chances.[15]

Synthesis: the growth of inequality by cohort in the United States

Since the early 1980s, American society has known an unequivocal polarization between two opposite social groups who face a dynamic of divergence in the newer generation. The bottom of the American social structure is subject to an economic decline and to social difficulties that are somewhat similar or even worse when compared to the French situation; at the opposite end, individuals at the top of the educational and income scale continue to improve their socioeconomic position and seem to enjoy an endless trend of prosperity. The dynamics for the median and the average classes are not so clear and greatly depend on the economic cycle.

Thus, impressive cohort inequalities characterize American society, too, and these inequalities are mechanically increasing for newer cohorts. The American cohort dynamics are not exactly similar to those in France, since they are more complex and sometimes equivocal. The French context of statutory protection of elder cohorts implies a general downturn of the status of younger generations, from the top to the bottom of the social scale; the American one, marked by stronger competition and inequalities in life chances, is characterized by greater inequality, notably for the most recent generations, who are socialized in a social structure where the gap between the top and the bottom is continuously enlarging. If Thernstrom (1973) depicted an American society where the ancient generation of young adults in 1929 (then born by 1909) never caught up after the difficulties of their youth—regardless of social class – even during the period of prosperity that emerged after 1945, the economic slowdown of 1970–92 has had a much more complex effect since the young social elite has never been subject to clear decline. In a context of economic recession or stagnation, to the point of view of the social groups at the top of the socioeconomic pyramid, the growth of inequality provides a way for increasing their income, even if the consequence is deepening difficulties for other groups.

5. France and the US: two divergent welfare systems?

The central point of my conclusion pertains to the long-term sustainability of welfare regimes. To be stable in the long term, a social system must arrange its own reproduction from one generation to the next. In France, today's seniors benefit from a large welfare state, but the vast social rights they were able to accumulate were the consequence of their relatively advantaged careers; we assert that the new generations, when they become seniors themselves, will not be able to benefit from the same rights, and the large size of the present welfare state will mechanically erode with cohort replacement, since the reproduction of the welfare regime is not assured.

In France, where the generational dynamics of the different social strata are parallel if not similar, the major problem is not generational inequalities, but the fact that newer generations heavily support a welfare system that could collapse before they benefit from it. The problem is not stagnation, but lack of preparation in the long term, at the expense of the most fragile population: the young and the recently socialized generations. Here lies the problem of sustainability for the current welfare regime: it appears large, strong, and durable, but its decline is almost certain; the security it offers to seniors is often at the expense of young cohorts facing radical uncertainty.

In the United States, the case is more complicated. For the young generations, the highest classes enjoy exceptionally better positions while the median classes see their fortunes stagnate and the poor are subjected to relative, if not absolute, deprivation. The problem there is that newer generations prefigure a future of ever-stronger inequalities: at the bottom, low wages go with a lack of social protection and, at the top, economic affluence is cumulative with unprecedented access to social and educational resources. The shortcomings of such a social structure are not so visible when the working poor are young, but when they grow older and need resources first for their children's health and education, and later for their own autonomy, health, access to facilities, service, and assistance in their elder years, problems will clearly emerge. For the last two decades, we have socialized a fragile generation (in France) and an extremely unequal one (in the United States). They were based on specific social structures and stratification systems which are fading away now, and as a result these two welfare regimes face severe destabilization in the coming years.

There are two key questions. Will the younger generation in France continue to sustain a system where their social condition is ever devalued compared to the older generations, with no clear prospects of improvement? Will the American poor (and also middle or "median" class) accept an even lower quality of life compared to the top? For the moment, these intergenerational inequalities are accepted, since they are generally unknown, their social visibility is low, and their political recognition nil. A kind of silent consensus maintains the system in spite of the strong contrast between realities and representations. In France, this situation induces a complex trend of pessimism and produces political instability characterized by stronger and shakier political U-turns. In the United States, the apparent stability comes from lower rates of participation in elections, but uncertainty is a central concern too. In both cases, as regards social structure and welfare regime dynamics, the future cannot be seen as a linear continuation of the past, since newer generations are not socialized in the continuity of previous ones. But here is my main conclusion: because today's reforms do not consider seriously the cohort dynamics, their understanding of the life chances of the generations now in play are myopic. The reforms are often very late and designed to balance previous disequilibria: thus they miss their target, give more resources to privileged generations and spoil the sacrificed ones, and ultimately undermine the sustainability of the welfare regime. Uncertainty and instability will grow apace, and given that violence is often the consequence of the tensions that inequality promotes, conflicts between generations could easily emerge in the twenty-first century.

Notes

I wish to acknowledge the helpful comments and useful questions that I received from participants at the Harvard and Paris conference, especially those from Peter Hall, Michèle Lamont and Katherine Newman, who offered several salient and patient remarks and corrections on previous drafts of this paper, and also Victor Chen for his useful comments and generous linguistic revision of this paper.

1 France and the United States both experienced a period of post-war affluence: the American "Golden Age of capitalism" (Maddison 1982) and the French

trente glorieuses (Fourastié 1979), which contrast with the subsequent period of economic slowdown and "diminished expectations" (Krugman 1992). See Chauvel (1998).

2 If in a wage panel we connect individual earnings at year t and t + 4, and are about to identify a generational parameter of relative cohort benefit/handicap (relative to the linear trend of progress) at year t, the wage growth rate $\delta\{LogW(t)\Delta LogW(t + 4)\}$ of individuals is about the same for the members of privileged or deprived generations. This means that the members of relatively deprived generations at year t cannot make up for the relative handicap they began with. In fact, more strikingly, the catch-up effect parameter is significantly negative, even if the corresponding effect is slight: the relative growth of the members of handicapped cohorts is lower, and this relative handicap increases. One interpretation could be that if the labour market is segmented by age, the relative handicap is cumulative since, in any new bargaining situation with an employer, the market value of the members of handicapped cohorts is assessed in comparison only with the members of his or her own cohort.

3 The French representation of the social stratification system in terms of occupation is different from the American one; the French tradition is very strong and contributes to a declining but still central "classist" vision of French society, shared by most social scientists, the media and social actors. In this respect, the contrast with the US is dramatic. See also Szreter (1993) who develops a comparative view of the difference in the representations of middle-class occupational groups.

4 During the twentieth century, an average age gap of about 30 years separated parents and their children.

5 These parents are about to help their children in different ways with the intensification of *solidarités familiales* (transfers and transmissions between generations, both financial, in kind, cultural, and material) that Attias-Donfut (2000) describes, but, at the collective level, the first and the most efficient *solidarité* would consist of a redistribution of social positions.

6 By welfare regime, I mean the complex system of decision, production, and distribution of social resources, where the hierarchy and the other dimensions of social differentiation are major issues; this regime includes work regulations, solidarities of family and the so-called "third sector." The shape of the class system is a consequence of the welfare regime (Esping-Andersen 1990).

7 In 1959, when a minimum income for old people was created (one-third of the minimum wage of that age), it covered more than 50 per cent of those aged 65 years and older; nowadays, this minimum income is about two-thirds of the present minimum wage, but covers 8 per cent of the same age group, since the currently generous public pay-as-you-go scheme covers almost anyone. Before, the old-age groups were poor and unequal, but now they are comparable to the active population in terms of average income and of standard deviation.

8 Most of the results presented here are systematized in my *Mémoire d'Habilitation* (Chauvel 2003), which can be downloaded at http./louis.chauvel.free.fr/HDR151003defacrobat.pdf.

9 Chauvel (2003) connects Esping-Andersen's (1990) types of welfare state and cohort dynamics of the welfare regimes.

10 The analysis of the response of the social-democrat welfare state in terms of cohorts could be interesting, but we do not address that issue here.

11 We consider here the relative poverty rates as they are calculated in Europe, where poverty is in reference to the half-median of national standardized equivalent income adjusted for family size (using the OECD equivalence scale which is the square root of household size). The Census Bureau has compiled for decades statistics on poverty in which poverty is defined in absolute terms (the same poverty threshold indexed on price is followed from one survey to the next). In Europe, we consider that if outcomes for the poor do not follow the same trend of affluence that benefits the global population, their situation is even worse; in contrast, in the American tradition of absolute poverty rates, even if the growth of the median income is much higher than the growth of incomes among the poor, if the incomes of the poor still grow even modestly, poverty is identified as declining. Relative poverty is implicitly determined in relation to the common population, which defines the standard of living of a given time period.

12 This point could be analyzed in terms of a scarring effect: the earnings increase *significantly less* for the members of relatively deprived cohorts (Chauvel 2003: 191–4).

13 The results are even stronger for master's degree holders, who experienced a decline of about 30 per cent between cohorts born in 1950 and 1965.

14 To foster the integration of young veterans back into society, free access to education was made available in 1944 to those who had served in the armed forces; the grants and loans offered became a major source of income for universities (Bennett 2000). The economic acceleration absorbed this new graduated population and this successful experiment was later extended to Korean and Vietnam veterans.

15 I have not analyzed here the changes in political participation and representation that I have indicated occurred in France. However, we may find a strong cohort decline in trade unions, political participation, and comparable changes in the age distribution of the US Congress. Chauvel (2003: 152–8) develops these points.

Part III

7

The Government of the European Union and a Changing France

Andy Smith

Introduction

Empirical research has conclusively shown that the task of negotiating and implementing European Union (EU) laws and policies now permeates contemporary relations among the French State, markets and civil society. Notwithstanding this empirical evidence, the analytical consequences of European integration's impact upon France have yet to be directly addressed. The principal reason for this failing is that the social sciences obdurately persist in examining the EU through the blurred lens of "international bargaining". Despite clear signs of its obsolescence, this perspective on contemporary politics continues to encourage researchers to study "levels" of government upon which "European" and "national" actors neatly align themselves to do battle. Whilst producing a great deal of important data and insights, such research inevitably produces highly predictable and over-general interpretations of the EU's impacts upon individual member states such as "states still matter" or "in some sectors the state matters more than in others".

This chapter proposes a different way out of this scientific cul de sac by claiming it is analytically beneficial to consider that a single government of the European Union actually exists and should be studied as such. European integration is both a cause, and has been caused by, a major reorganization of politics in Western Europe. Consequently, it is only by looking at the processes, relationships, coherencies and contradictions that mark the EU's form of government that one can begin to unpack change within state–market–civil society relations in any member state. Indeed, without wishing to overstate the importance of one national experience, given the distinctive history of such relations in France presented elsewhere in this volume, but also because of the involvement of this country's elites in the government of the EU, paying specific attention to the French case provides a challenging test of the chapter's central claim.[1]

1. A government in all but name

Of course, an enormous gap exists between what empirical research can identify as the government of the European Union and constitutional or popular images of what government is or should be. In this chapter, "the government of the EU" denotes the law and policy-making institutions and institutionalized processes that today structure the ways through which a significant number of collective choices are made within the frontiers of the 25 member states, decisions that go to the heart of the state–market–civil society trilogy. It follows that "*Government* here is not the particular body that in contemporary polities is supposed to take decisions, implement laws and run public policies; instead government encompasses the range of acts which together contribute to the way social life is organized and orientated" (Lagroye 1997: 25).

The first consequence of such a definition is that these institutions and processes of government cannot simply be reduced to those that exist or occur "in Brussels". Instead, the "Europeanization"[2] of numerous sectors of public life has lead to a situation where the government of the EU encompasses a series of public actors ranging from nominally "European" politicians and bureaucrats to their national and regional counterparts. Conceptualizing these actors as part of a single government enables one to go beyond the static category of "levels" or "tiers" in order to investigate the emergence and evolution of the EU's *intragovernmental* processes and relationships.

The second consequence of this approach to the EU's government is that one does not presuppose that it is, or ever will be, unified and coherent. Rather, as Orren and Skowronek have effectively underlined with reference to the polity of the United States (1993: 317), from an analytical point of view, it is more useful to consider any institutional arrangement to be a "patterned disorder". From this standpoint, some of the consequences of the EU government's fragmentation will be dealt with in later sections. Nevertheless, a wide range of consistent patterns of public action have emerged over the last 50 years, patterns that have extremely powerful effects upon what politicians and bureaucrats in Europe now consider they are able to lawfully and practically do. In a word, for these actors the government of the EU is not some abstract constraint, but a constant set of rules, processes, relationships and expectations that have to be engaged with whenever they develop and pursue their respective goals and strategies.

Before applying this perspective more directly to analysis of how France has changed, a little more needs to be said about how it can enable research to go beyond some implicit and explicit assumptions that continue to dominate interpretations of how the EU is governed.

Beyond visions of European integration as a "three-speed bicycle"

An initial, and particularly powerful, assumption about the contemporary politics of Western Europe stems from positivist accounts of the EU as a treaty-based international organization featuring three distinct and enduring degrees of European integration: "common" policies where member states pool their sovereignty; "shared" policies where both EU and national institutions can intervene; and national policies where the EU can do little more than develop "accompanying measures". At least in France, this vision of the EU has become a largely unchallenged element of political discourse. It obviously suits national politicians and civil servants who are anxious to assert that sovereignty is still alive and kicking. In many ways, it also provides European parliamentarians and Commission officials with a convenient explanation with which to downplay and dedramatize Europeanization. Less understandably, this discourse has also penetrated the social sciences and permeates much of what is written and taught about the EU (Marks et al. 1996). Challenging this three-speed vision of the EU has three principal advantages.

- First, it shows that Europeanization is a process that now covers a vast range of governmental activity and that treaty provisions are only one of several possible causes of this trend.
- Second, it allows one to grasp how even supposedly "common" policies can unravel over time and, particularly during their implementation, lead to decidedly uncommon practices.
- Third, it sets the scene for reflection upon the recurrent features and consequences of the government of the EU, in particular on the empirically identifiable interfaces between representatives of public authorities, industry and civil society.

The two most frequently cited examples of "common" EU policies are the Common Agricultural Policy (CAP) and policies that aim at "completing the Single Market". Both these sets of policies undoubtedly do provide excellent illustrations of sectors within which decision-making arenas and procedures have become "Europeanized". Farm prices and animal hygiene norms are set by the Council of Ministers, aided and abetted by the Commission and the European Parliament (Fouilleux 2003). Similarly, competition in sectors such as telecommunications is regulated by the European Commission, a body also responsible for creating and enforcing a series of norms on what telephone operators can and cannot legally do (Rivaud 2001). However, it is illusory to consider that in these sectors decisions are simply "taken" in Brussels and that therefore this means they belong to a distinct category of "EU-only" public action. First, decisions are only taken on the basis of negotiations that begin the moment different configurations of actors throughout the EU set out to define or redefine "a European problem". A wealth of public-policy literature indicates that European problems are almost invariably defined through conflicts and compromises which involve a wide range of Brussels-based, national, subnational and private-sector actors. Second, even in the case of so-called "common" policies, it is analytically dangerous to distinguish too clearly between decision-making and implementation. For example, the EU's agricultural policy may be common in name, but much of it is translated into action in quite different ways within different parts of France (Le Pape and Smith 1999), let alone between member states. Indeed, recent developments within the CAP which introduce more regional variation serve as a strong reminder that the deepening of even "common" policies is not inexorable. It follows that only longitudinal studies are able to capture the importance of time in the often paradoxical institutionalization of the EU's government.

Looking at the reality of policy areas that are ostensibly "shared" between the EU and national governments provides a second means of questioning the idea that there are three speeds of European integration. Regional development and policies concerning the environment are generally thought about and studied from this perspective. In both cases, and despite the fact that a wide range of regulations and financial inducements are now formally set "in Brussels", specialists agree that local authorities in particular have a great deal of leeway when interpreting these norms and distributing subsidies (Nay 2001). Nevertheless, other actors, such as transnational environmentalist groups and some national Ministries of the Environment, are just as active in seeking to ensure that policies in their sector are formulated on a European-wide basis (McCormick 2001). Again, the question of time is essential. Throughout the member states, the politics of both regional development and environmental policy-making have indeed been reorganized by the introduction of EU laws and policy instruments. Nevertheless, in both sectors a reduction in Commission influence since the beginning of the 1990s (Faure and Smith 1998; Golub 1996) highlights the intense interinstitutional competition that takes place on a daily basis at the heart of the government of the EU.

Finally, proponents of a three-speed image of the EU point to policy areas such as internal security and defense as examples of national government bastions where Europeanization simply has not taken place. Whilst it is certainly true that formal EU legislation in these two sectors is relatively small, it is nevertheless misleading to conclude that they have been immune to changes caused, at least in part, by the intensification of debate and negotiation involving actors from different member states. An increasing quantity of French policing and "internal security" policies provide an initial example that shows how French doctrine and law has evolved and opened itself up to external influences (Bigo 1996). Without positing that a common European defense policy now exists, empirical studies of how France's foreign (Buchet de Neuilly 2001)[3] and military (Irondelle 2002)[4] policies are now made, also show that the actors involved in shaping and making decisions in this sector today treat the European Union as an institutionalized constraint on, and/or an opportunity for, their goals, strategies and working practices.

Of course, at least four massive swathes of governmental activity in Europe – social security, health, education and taxation – appear to remain dominated by national and subnational actors. Monetary Union nonetheless places many constraints on what can now be done in these fields. Moreover, as Bruno Palier argues in his chapter in this book, the French welfare state is now heavily influenced by a variety of Europeanizing influences. More research is needed upon these issue areas and their relationship with different dimensions of the government of the EU. But it must be stressed that the validity of studying the government of Europe simply does not hinge upon being able to show either that Europeanization affects all sectors or that it has given rise to an all-powerful European superstate. Instead, the principal justification for this research perspective is to focus more directly upon the divisions of institutional power that have developed over time, as well as the institutionalized processes and interdependencies that impact upon the type of intervention now favoured within each member state.

Beyond standard and static images of European governance

Indeed, the choice to examine the government of the EU can and must also be justified as a means of developing sharper analytical questions and tools than those produced, and constantly reproduced, by the three approaches to European integration that currently dominate political science.

Two of these approaches – intergovernmentalism and neo-institutionalism – are essentially inspired by the same quest: to determine whether sets of national or supranational actors dominate EU decision-making. Intergovernmentalists (Moravscik 1998; Milward 1992) assert that the former nearly always win by knocking out their opponents using the weight of treaty-based resources and the sheer power of "national interests". More precisely, proponents of this approach argue that the EU has only deepened because representatives of national states have agreed to participate in setting joint policies whilst carefully preserving their autonomy to take many other decisions on the basis of the interests of their respective countries. The definition of these interests is considered to be a process that still takes place within the frontiers of each nation.

In contrast to the intergovernmentalist vision of an EU dominated by actors who represent the member states, a range of researchers inspired by neo-institutionalist concepts and theory (Pierson 1996; Sandholtz and Stone Sweet 1998) claim that, through using more subtle forms of powering, the Commission and the European Court of Justice often scrape through "on points". Such authors place particular emphasis upon the constraining and cumulative effects of EU law and upon the specific resources enjoyed by EU institutions. For these reasons, it is argued that, although national representatives may consider that they have not ceded any significant amount of their own authority, the sedimentation of Community law and their combined and unattended consequences have resulted over time in a distinct shift in the locus of authority towards supranational bodies and arenas.

Both these approaches to studying the EU are clearly more sophisticated than the above sketches can describe. For the purposes of this piece, however, they do highlight how neither approach is actually driven by the question of *how* this political space is governed and *who* governs it. Notwithstanding the degree and nature of political and economic interdependence that lies at the heart of EU decision-making, the question of how and who continues to be overlooked or treated in disincarnated forms. Put bluntly, both intergovernmentalism and neo-institutionalism (as applied to the EU) structure research which is stuck in a "scientific time warp" where one can blithely pretend that neat "levels" of authority, complete with national or European flags, continue to constitute pertinent categories for analysis.

A third major approach to studying the causes and effects of European integration, multilevel governance, partly avoids the national-supranational trap by concentrating more upon the "variable geometry" of European integration. Starting from the premiss that power distribution between European, national and regional institutions varies by sector, researchers animated by this approach seek to trace and compare the trajectories of EU public policies and policy-making (Hooghe 1996: 18; Marks 1993; Marks et al. 1996). Notwithstanding the many insights generated by this approach, three of its features result in its ultimately discarding the question of how the EU is governed and by whom.[5]

The first difficulty with the concept of multilevel governance is its tendency to generate studies that are highly sectorized. Given that one of the objectives of this concept was to compare degrees of multilevel governance across sectors and countries, this tendency is logical and has of course produced useful data. However, the price for concentrating research efforts on sectoral dynamics has been to underresearch the arenas within the government of the European Union where intersectoral political exchange takes place.

The second problem with the multilevel governance approach is the way it defines and operationalizes the term "level". Despite their interest in institutional interdependence, proponents of this research perspective do not actually study the networks of actors who constantly cross national frontiers, public/private distinctions and scales of government in order to influence the setting and "solving" of European problems. Policy networks are examined from a distance, institutions are not disaggregated and enquiry into relationships that cross national boundaries is sacrificed in favour of the question as to *which level of governance wins*. This question is limited because it discourages one from even reflecting upon, let alone studying, the dynamics of the relationship between public authority, markets and civil society in contemporary Western Europe.

Finally, the third problem with studying the EU from a perspective of multilevel governance, one it shares with intergovernmentalists and supranationalists, is that it reduces government to the taking of decisions and the setting of policies. If the construction of public problems and the development of policy responses do indeed constitute a major dimension of government, governing also entails legitimation and competing for political office. Actors are considered legitimate, or fail to be, not only because of judgments on the efficiency of their actions, but on the way their public discourse and symbolic acts are perceived and interpreted. This component of "the work of politics" takes place within political and public spaces where actors, such as national ministers or European commissioners, compete not only in the name of their respective institutional posts, but also to enhance their individual careers.

2. Three recurrent features of Europeanized French politics

Focusing specifically upon the case of France, and building upon a conceptualization of the government of the EU, this section proposes analytical "solutions" to each of the three problems that have just been identified with a multilevel approach to EU-member state relations: its neglect of intersectoral mediation; its cursory examination of the relationship between public authority, markets and civil society; and its disregard for legitimation and political competition. Put more directly, the claim made here is that the way the EU is governed

- transforms and often dilutes intersectoral political exchange;
- reflects and encourages a shift in the balance between public authority, markets and societal influences towards proponents of market-based forms of regulation;
- has created a form of public discourse and symbolic action that obscures political competition while rendering attempts to legitimate the EU largely unintelligible to the general public.

More generally, the "added value" of conceptualizing the EU as one fragmented and conflict-racked government is that it allows one to build a bridge between studies of Europeanization, analysis of the distribution of power within the EU and the challenges of governing without a public sphere.

A government short on intersectoral mediation

The point of departure here is a paradox: although discrete and public forms of intersectoral deliberation and decision-making are generally recognized by political science as being vital parts of any polity, they are very rarely the direct subject of indepth research and analysis. As a potentially potent producer of "the general interest", at least in theory, organized coordination across sectors could logically be expected to mitigate the externalities of many problem-specific policies, encourage more efficient use of resources and heighten democratic responsibility by encouraging more public debate about the wider consequences of sectoral objectives and choices (Peters 2005). If in practice such lofty aims are rarely attained, analysis of how and why this is so is particularly revealing of the underlying dynamics and relationships that underpin any polity.

This is certainly the case in France, where a number of detailed studies of this country's public authorities has repeatedly underlined three traits of intersectoral governance *à la française*. The first of these characteristics is the absence of societal level or "macro-corporatist" fora which regularly bring together representatives of capital, labour and the state. Instead, and despite the rhetoric and practices of state planning, confrontation between these three sets of actors has tended strongly to take shape and place at the sectoral, or meso-corporatist, level (Jobert and Muller 1987; Hall 1986). In the absence of an executive resembling what the British call cabinet government, intersectoral negotiation therefore depends heavily upon the intervention of the prime minister and his or her personal staff.

The second recurrent trait of intersectoral politics in France is the weak involvement of the National Assembly and the Senate. Although these two bodies repeatedly produce reports on cross-sectoral issues, they have little means of direct influence upon policy-makers and implementers. The weakness of these parliamentary institutions is one of the causes of a third feature of intersectoral negotiation in this country: the omnipresence of state civil servants whose primary allegiance is to their respective administrative corps (Suleiman 1974: ch. 10). Indeed, although steeped in the rhetoric of "the general interest", the preferred career paths of these administrators thus provide yet another explanation of sectoral fragmentation and meso-corporatist bargaining arrangements.

Before setting out analysis of how this form of intersectoral politics has evolved and to what extent European integration is its cause, it is useful to add into the equation a distinction between two ideal-types:

- "intersectoral coordination" is essentially of a tactical nature where different national ministries thrash out interbureaucratic compromises in the name of policy and administrative efficiency;[6]
- "intersectoral mediation" is a much "thicker", and usually longer, process involving a wider range of actors from both inside (ministers, ministries, MPs) and outside (business associations, trades unions, the media) the state.[7] Modes of expression are less controlled and controllable as the

different protagonists attempt to define problems meriting public intervention and ways of treating them.

On the basis of this distinction, two claims will be made. First, that intersectoral negotiations within the government of the EU are weighted heavily in favour of diplomatic coordination and against substance-centred mediation. This trend is partly attributable to recurrent characteristics of the EU's institutional arrangements wherein the Council of Ministers and the European Parliament clearly exacerbate sectoral fragmentation (Smith 2005). However, the behaviour of national politicians, administrations and interest groups also contributes heavily to this institutionalized form of sectoral bias.

The second claim concerns the particular impact of this trend towards technicized coordination upon the French polity. Although the Fifth Republic has never encouraged highly participative styles of intersectoral debate (Kessler 1982), its involvement in the EU has accelerated a shift even further away from mediation and towards coordination.

Before proposing explanations of this change, two brief examples of the nature of intersectoral negotiation that have taken place within the government of the EU will be used to illustrate the general argument made here. The first concerns the making and implementing of policies designed to protect the environment. Although over 200 directives now exist in this field and have had considerable effects upon national and local polities, the government of the EU is largely incapable of generating intersectoral negotiations where sectors such as transport or agriculture are forced to engage genuinely with advocates of stricter environmental law. More accurately, since the 1970s the EU has had relatively little difficulty in devising six-yearly "Environmental Action Programmes", each of which contains commitments to transform environmental protection into a transversal objective applying to all sectors.

However, when it comes to translating this discourse into legislation, the strength of established sectoral-policy communities almost invariably ensures that ambitious draft directives are diluted into lowest-common-denominator obligations (Jordan et al. 2005). The intersectoral dimension of the way the EU governs the environment can also been seen from the "bottom", for example, in the French region of Aquitaine. Regional actors are currently attempting to induce industry and hauliers to transport more of their goods by sea or by rail. Despite the range and cost of the "carrots" they can offer, their action is hamstrung by the fact that under EU freedom-of-movement laws, no legal "stick" can be put into place in order to penalize producers who continue to transport their goods by road.[8] More exactly, EU and local negotiating arenas complement each other in ensuring that no genuine mediation has taken place where proponents of "the internal market at all costs" and "defenders of the environment" would have confronted each other in a public setting.

A second example concerns the replacement of the concept of "public service" in the telecommunications sector by the notion of "universal service" (Rivaud 2001). With the exception of the UK, until the mid-1990s telecommunications in Europe had been dominated by national monopolistic operators financed and regulated through highly institutionalized neo-corporatist arrangements involving ministries of industry and, in most cases, the trade unions. At least in France, this organizational form was legitimized by linking it to the concept of "public service". Between 1987 and 1997, a steady stream of EU legislation led to the deregulation of these national models and their reregulation on a European-wide basis. In order to do so, proponents of a liberal form of reregulation demanded that the concept of "public service" be abandoned in favour of a market-based approach to competition between telecommunications operators. This proposal provoked considerable resistance in France, in particular from the trade union movement and certain MPs, although the government of the day adopted a more ambivalent stance. In any case, resistance in other member states was difficult to orchestrate and coordinate, thus leaving the Belgian Presidency of the Council of ministers with the relatively easy task of developing a compromise concept ("universal service") as a means of placating the French delegation without significantly changing the substance of the draft legislation under discussion.

What is striking here is first that the momentum of the Council negotiation tended strongly to limit the character of public debate over this issue even in a society such as France's, which had previously seen the guardianship of "public service" as a central role of the state. Secondly, the concept of universal service has subsequently been elevated to the status of a legal precedent which acts as the handmaiden for institutionalizing and legitimating liberalization as a method of government in a number of other sectors such as electricity and postal services. Despite resistance by the trade unions, liberalization of such services has not engendered a high and sustained level of politicized intersectoral debate.

In both the case of the environment and of telecommunications, change in the nature of French intersectoral governance has certainly been facilitated by the structural weaknesses of the protagonists contesting the sectorization of public policy-making (essentially environmentalists and trade unions). Nevertheless, the key explanatory variable here is more the institutionalized processes through which French actors develop their country's position before and during negotiations over EU directives and policies.

At first sight, it would appear erroneous, even absurd, to claim that the deepening of European integration has led to less contact between sectors of governmental activity. In the French case, European policy-making has systematized interministerial contact in and around the Secrétariat Général du comité interministeriel pour les questions de coopération économique européenne (SGCI). Attached directly to the prime minister and his or her cabinet, this body ostensibly provides one national voice during negotiations in Brussels within the European Council, ministerial meetings, COREPER[9] and Council Working Groups (Lequesne 1993; Eymeri 2002).[10] Without denying the extent and importance of this activity, it is important to examine more carefully what actually happens in and around the SGCI. Over and above the essentially short-term tactical reasoning that dominates this body, it is important to realize that its officials only have quite limited control over how agents within various line ministries behave during the myriad of consultations that precede or run parallel to Council negotiations. Just as importantly, coordination within the SGCI is invariably carried out with great urgency and under conditions of considerable secrecy, thus largely precluding either any direct involvement by "social partners" or publicity through the media.

National parliaments make up the second type of institution that is formally involved in intersectoral mediation but in reality is not. Consulted in most cases after EU negotiations rather than beforehand, national parliaments have rarely redefined their procedures in such a way as to articulate themselves effectively within the government of the EU (*Politique européenne* 2003). In the case of a French National Assembly and Senate already out of sync with the characteristics of contemporary national policy-making (Muller 2000), the demands of participating in the politics of the EU have left most representatives of these bodies struggling with the challenge of anachronism.

Ultimately, most intersectoral coordination within the government of the EU is actually dealt with in and around the college of European commissioners (Joana and Smith 2002). In order for a draft EU directive to become an official Commission proposal to Council, coalitions must be built between commissioners by their respective *cabinets*. These processes usually begin weeks or months before formal meetings of the college through a range of inter- and intra-DG (Directorate General) meetings that first shape the issue in hand (usually in the form of draft legislation). This interlocking process of coordination, internal to the Commission, spills over into a second point that needs highlighting: the degree of imbrication between the Commission, its college, national administrations and interest groups. Contact with actors in the member states is constant and takes place through a variety of channels and arenas ranging from highly political networks to European-wide policy communities. Consequently, the intersectoral exchanges that occur in and around the Commission are frequently highly complex, because they are simultaneously intersectoral and international. Although rarely secret, neither are these interfaces genuinely public.

To sum up this brief explanation of intersectoral governance in the EU, it is important to recall that it does actually exist. However, this form of intersectoral governance is quite different from national traditions in general, and that of France in particular. The most striking difference common to many member states is the degree to which traditional social partners, in particular the trade unions, are largely excluded. In the French case, this has further accentuated a pre-existing development of the interface between political, administrative and societal actors. More specifically, it has further weakened the role of parliamentary institutions in intersectoral politics and encouraged members of administrative corps to intensify their efforts to protect their right to make policy in a highly sectorized manner.

A government with institutionalized neo-liberal bias

In more substantive terms, change in the modes of intersectoral mediation have also reduced the possibility of government's introducing coherent programmes of action in order to tackle issues that many actors consider to be inherently trans-sectoral. In further "sectorizing" the government of Europe, it then becomes easier for proponents of competition-based regulation to press their case for markets as coordinating mechanisms and to disqualify alternatives as "impracticable". In explaining this development, authors such as Elie Cohen (2001) are certainly right to underline that the EU has often been used as an alibi by national and private-sector actors with pre-existing neo-liberal preferences. Over and above the strategies of such actors, however, it is essential to grasp that certain intrinsic properties of the government of the EU structurally encourage policy-makers throughout Europe to produce "regulative" rather than "interventionist" policies (Majone 1995). As the following two examples highlight, in the French case, this structural constraint now influences how the State itself distributes resources to a more pervasive degree than is commonly recognized.

A first example of how the government of Europe has rendered itself unable to adopt high degrees of interventionism concerns the issue area of regional development. From 1944 to the 1980s, many European governments, and that of France in particular, sought to redistribute industry and other economic activities throughout their territory rather than let the market decide over patterns of spatial wealth and opportunity. Since 1988, the EU appears to have given additional encouragement to this approach by increasing the budget of its structural funds in the name of "economic and social cohesion". Notwithstanding some important institutional and cognitive effects of this policy (Smith 1995), it is seriously misleading to consider that these funds have led to a significant redistribution of wealth and life chances between rich and poor areas of Europe. When explaining the weakness of EU regional development policy, most commentators focus exclusively upon the relatively low budget attributed to the structural funds. A few others quite rightly point out that by focusing essentially upon regional disparities, EU policy does very little to ameliorate the condition of social categories within the member states (Pierson 1996). However, this critique can be taken a stage further by analyzing more fully three features of the policy instruments that currently do exist.

The first of these features is the sectorization of regional development programmes cofinanced by the EU through the structural funds. Whilst the 1988 reform of the structural funds sought to encourage more transversal approaches to spatial development by chanelling aid through regional "partnerships" and "programmes", in reality sectoral cleavages are still omnipresent. In the French case this trait is particularly evident, largely because EU funding has become a constant bone of contention among competing regional and *départemental* elected councils and what remains of the field services of the State (Nay 2001). The very least one can say on this issue is that the French State now has much less power over the substance of regional development programmes than it did in the mid-1980s.

The second major characteristic of the EU's government of regional development is that no genuine arenas exist for structuring interterritorial hierarchies or trade-offs. In Brussels the Committee of the Regions, like the European Parliament, is singularly ill-equipped to involve itself in any negotiation involving choices between regions. The Commission's services do occasionally call for more selectivity but are constantly defeated by national governments seeking to retain the right to cut up their part of the structural funds "cake" as they wish. In the French case, such governments have rarely taken the risk of establishing any firmer criteria for organizing financial redistribution. Indeed there is little debate, let alone action, about the merits or problems of encouraging growth in areas such as Ile de France or safeguarding jobs and incomes in areas such as the Massif Central. In short, the EU's policy concept of "Economic and social cohesion" provides a convenient "fig leaf" behind which the ugly consequences of interregional competition can be hidden.

The third and final trait of regional development policy in the EU is the way it is linked into trends towards decentralization. Indeed, many practitioners justify the relative inefficiency of the structural funds by underlining that, in the medium or longer term, this form of financing development is progressively consolidating the relationship between the EU, national and subnational governments under the flag of "subsidiarity". However, in reality this notion synthesizes less a political theory than it does a series of a posteriori, and rather unconvincing, justifications for the incoherent state of the government of interterritorial relations in Western Europe. As Adrian Hyde-Price and Charlie Jeffrey (2001) have shown, far from bringing order to the question "what decides who decides?", subsidiarity continues to be used as a fatalistic rationalization of a state of affairs where the response to this question is constantly the result of multiple meso- and micro-negotiations. More precisely, from once being thought of as the basis for a European political theory, subsidiarity is now a political resource claimed by a variety of national, subnational and sectoral interests ranging from German regional banking to anti-Federalist British Conservatives. In short, as the French case serves to highlight, subsidiarity here means "every region for themselves" in a competition for scarce EU resources which continues to favour those who are already relatively strong (Faure 1997). Viewed from the long-term perspective of regime-building, some practitioners connect the subsidiarity principle to the progressive construction of institutional arrangements and relationships which make up the government of the European Union. However, many political scientists are excessively indulgent with the outcome of this institutional order and its "constitutive politics" (Duran and Thoenig 1996) or "governance" (Scharpf 2000). Whilst these effects are not the results of a deliberate conspiracy, neither are they purely accidental or merely temporary.

A second example of bias towards market type regulation in EU policy concerns the relationship between agriculture and public health in general, and wine and alcohol policies in particular. The "mad cow" crisis of the mid- to late 1990s led to a certain opening up of the agricultural policy community, symbolized in 1999 by the Commission creating a DG for Health and Consumer affaires (DG Sanco [Directorate général "Santé et consommateurs"]). However, research has already shown that the logic of this administration is centred principally upon the objective of improving food safety in the name of the powerful myth of the European consumer, rather than on a wider issue of public health, which would involve appeals to a more tendentious myth, that of the European citizen (Guignier 2004). The weakness of treaty provisions on health provide one explanation of this trend. More fundamentally, Commission initiatives in favour of public health policies are severely hamstrung by organized resistance from the food and drink industry on the one hand and resistance from some of its own DGs on the other. Ongoing research into the politics of wine provides a striking illustration of the unequal competition between supporters of the market as a vehicle for policy and partisans of a more interventionist approach (Costa et al. 2005). Since 2000, a unit within DG Sanco has set up an "Alcohol Working Group" as an arena within which proposals for limiting "irresponsible" alcohol consumption can be debated. More particularly, attempts have been made to impose stricter controls upon the content of alcohol advertising. However, officials from DG Sanco can only count upon a weak public health Eurogroup (EUROCARE) for sustained support. Their efforts to introduce tougher legislation are constantly opposed by a coalition from the beverage industry ("The Amsterdam Group") as well as colleagues from other DGs (in particular Market, Enterprise and Competition). Representatives of French industry and government have been deeply involved in activating this coalition, as they have for the promotion of a more transversal enthusiasm for "self-regulation". Within the government of the EU, the invocation of this term consistently places industry's representatives in an advantageous position from which they can oblige proponents of interventionist policy to "prove" the inefficiency of market-based law.

This example brings me to a final, more general point regarding the involvement of interest groups in the government of the EU. Parts of the Commission do attempt to favour the consultation of social movements and groups, rather than simply listen to the representatives of multinational companies. Some Directorates General, such as Environment, have even tried to go beyond the lip-service of Internet hotlines by consciously avoiding fora where big business dominates. Nevertheless, the dominant trend of interest representation at the level of the EU favours actors advocating low-budget, market regulation-type policy solutions. These solutions not only possess the advantage of costing very little for the European budget (Majone 1995). They also often mean that "troublesome interference" from a range of actors who may want to introduce values into the equation (pressure groups, European Commissioners, national politicians) can be defused and disqualified as inappropriate to "the Community Method" of making law and policy.

Technicized political representation

Both the nature of intersectoral governance and neo-liberal bias in the EU's government are reflected in its third and final recurrent feature: a relationship between technocracy and politics that persistently discourages public forms of politicized debate. In analyzing this question, it is important to discard the commonly held idea that European integration is, and has always been, an essentially "economic" and "apolitical" process. Not only has Europe's economy been governed by a range of actors working within and between EU and national institutions, but politicians from all the member states have been intensively involved in this process. The puzzle is therefore not who has been involved in governing Europe or even how they have gone about it; it concerns instead how these actors have presented their activity to the general public. More precisely, the question is not only how have such actors represented themselves, but also how they have been represented by their principal link with the public: the media. In presenting briefly three reasons why EU politics continues to be presented as "technocratic" by the vast majority of Frenchmen and women, this section therefore seeks to shed additional light upon the theme of popular perceptions of government that is treated more directly in other contributions to this volume.

The first reason EU policies and policy-makers are depicted as apolitical is that political socialization in Western Europe continues to be dominated by the naturalization of the nation-state (Billig 1995). Despite the emergence of public programmes designed to encourage exchanges between students from different countries, education policies in particular continue to perpetuate the idea that the French State is not only sovereign but also rendered even more powerful by its unerring commitment to European integration (Baeyens 2000). Given the importance of the European Council and Council of Ministers within the government of the EU it is particularly difficult for representatives of the Commission and the European Parliament to even begin to challenge the myth of state sovereignty, let alone to request that national education administrations treat the EU as something other than an international organization.

The second source of the depolititicization of the government of the EU concerns the structure and interests of the media in Western Europe. Despite the fact that the Commission regularly boasts of giving the biggest daily press conferences in the world, journalists based in Brussels have to struggle constantly to attract the interest of their respective editors "back home" in the member states (Baisnée 2003). Convinced that their readers, viewers or listeners are only interested in EU policies to the extent that they impact upon national political life, these editors therefore act as powerful gatekeepers on the way contemporary decision-making is presented to the general public. For this reason, many articles on the EU in France end up in the "economy" section of newspapers, thus reinforcing the pre-existing stereotype of European integration as an "economic" process.

The third source of a depoliticized EU is the dominant mode of behaviour of the very actors who make up its government: ministers, European Commissioners, national or European civil servants. More precisely, what is at issue here are the forms of argumentation such actors use in order to stand a chance of winning, or at least not losing, during the negotiation of EU policies. In order to position oneself effectively within the sectoral fora that dominate these exchanges, many if not most actors consider it essential to "technicize" their arguments in order both to attract the support of other actors and to avoid blocking the negotiation process as a whole (Robert 2004). For agents from both the European Commission and national administrations, an essential part of technicization concerns the use of EU law as a means of rendering their policy proposals "inevitable", "pragmatic" and "European". But technicization more generally involves a refusal to argue from the point of view of explicit values or an openly admitted political ideology. Instead, policy is presented as the logical consequence of politically neutral expertise. Little wonder then that French ministers in particular are adept both at acting technocratically in order to participate in EU decision-making, while stigmatizing this very process as "technocratic" whenever the final result goes against the interests of their compatriots.

A great deal more research needs to be undertaken into the role of politicization and depoliticization in the government of the EU. For the purposes of this essay, however, it is above all important to underline how the technicization of European "problems" and policies so frequently accompanies the weakness of EU intersectoral mediation and the strength of actors motivated by neo-liberal policy preferences.

Conclusion

In concluding an essay that probably covers too much ground in too little space, each of the three recurrent features of the government of the EU—weak intersectoral governance, neo-liberal bias, depoliticization—needs brief revisiting in order to answer two questions: how has European integration changed France over the last fifty years; what is the analytical pay-off of thinking about the EU as a single, fragmented, incoherent, that is "normal" government?

As regards the claims made about intersectoral governance, it is important to stress that sectoral fragmentation is not a new feature of government in Europe and certainly not in France. European integration has exacerbated a pre-existing characteristic of French politics by weakening certain actors and strengthening others. Institutions, in particular the National Assembly and the Senate, have not been redesigned to attenuate the negative effects of sectoral overspecialization. Instead, administrative corps have been given a free rein to adapt their traditional modes of behavior in order to develop influence over the position the official French delegations and spokespersons defend within the context of EU negotiations. Short-term, reactive and tactical reflection about policy alternatives is the cumulative result of this trend, and general-interest driven strategic planning the principal victim.

The weakness of intersectoral mediation, both within France and the EU as a whole, provides one of the key reasons why policies based on neo-liberal economic theory and market-linked policy principles have come to dominate the way the EU is governed. For proponents of such policies, it is particularly helpful that advocates of interventionism or of exceptions to free-market principles are largely excluded from both sectoral policy communities and intersectoral fora. The weakened position of French trade unions, but also of civil servants seeking to plan the economy, exemplify this trend. Built upon an *acquis communautaire* of law that is heavily skewed towards neo-liberal priorities by an overriding commitment to a single, protectionist-free market, actors in favor of limiting the role of civil society in policy-making begin each and every individual negotiation with a considerable head start upon their opponents. In short, neo-liberal bias is not only institutionalized, it is largely locked in by the institutional "pattern of disorder" (Orren and Skowronek 1993) that is the EU.

Finally, this pattern of disorder has had clear implications for the way the EU is represented through the discourse and acts of national politicians on the one hand, and through the content of media coverage of European politics on the other. Partly because the government of the EU has no explicit underlying political theory, but also because the French press, radio and television remain nation centred, French ministers in particular have been able to continue to perpetuate the myth of national sovereignty. This practice clearly hampers attempts to legitimate both EU policies and the very institutions through which these are, at least ostensibly, formulated and implemented. The end result is not a polity without politics but rather a configuration of institutions within which depoliticization is a political resource that most actors are constantly tempted to use in order to obtain short-term gains. However, the indirect impact of this practice upon the legitimacy of both the EU and the contemporary nation-state cannot be overstated.

In unpacking the political features and policy outcomes of the government of Europe, it is all too easy to become nostalgic for a golden age of ordered institutions that (even in the early years of Fifth Republic France) probably never existed. Nevertheless, by examining the relationships and the processes that attempt to deal with the resulting conflicts and contradictions, one is better able to understand the way the government of Europe has been institutionalized. Moreover, this analytical perspective provides a means of grasping the concrete challenges faced by representatives of the government of the EU when attempting to legitimize this institutional order. As integral and central parts of the government of the EU, contemporary national polities in Western Europe also need to be examined from the angle of disorder, conflict and negotiated compromise. Given that such terms clash so directly with traditional principles at the heart of French Republicanism, the challenge for its actors (not to mention political scientists interested in the French case) is perhaps even more stark than in most other EU member states.

Notes

1 Developed more fully in a recent book (Smith 2004), the arguments put forward in this chapter are essentially based on a series of studies conducted by the author over the last ten years. They include research into the invention and implementation of the EU's rural development policy (Smith 1995), regionalized dimensions of the Common Agricultural Policy (Le Pape and Smith 1999), the activity of European Commissioners (Joana and Smith 2002), the inner-workings of the EU's Council of Ministers (Fouilleux et al. 2002), a comparison between French and British military policy-making (Genieys et al. 2000) and ongoing studies of EU wine, food quality and internal security policies.

2 Claudio Radaelli both reviews a stream of research on Europeanization and comes up with his own definition: "Processes of (a) construction, (b) diffusion and (c) institutionalization of formal and informal rules, procedures, policy paradigms, styles, 'ways of doing things' and shared beliefs and norms" which have become incorporated in the logic of "domestic discourse, identities, political structures and public policies" (Radaelli 2001: 110).

3 In particular, Y. Buchet de Neuilly (2001) underlines the gap that separates diplomats and diplomatic "institutional games" within the French Foreign Ministry, and counterparts within the same ministry which are more directly involved in European Union policy-making.

4 B. Irondelle (2002) presents a compelling argument for considering that decisions such as the end of conscription in France, are in fact the result of "Europeanization without European policies".

5 For a more developed critique of multi-level governance, see Smith (2003).
6 Throughout Kassim et al. (2001) books on the coordination of national government positions on Europe, emphasis is constantly placed on "administrative efficiency" both by the practitioners studied and the authors themselves.
7 Pierre Muller goes so far as to define a public policy as "a process of social mediation given that the object of each public policy is to deal with the disarticulation that can occur between a sector and other sectors, or between a sector and society as a whole" (1990: 24).
8 Between April 2002 and March 2003, the author served as a participating observer in the commissioning, guidance and restitution of an evaluation of regional policy on this issue.
9 Le Comité des représentants permanents des pays membres is a forum which brings together the ambassadors and the assistant ambassador to the EU of each member state. The COREPER essentially deliberates and negotiates over draft legislation prepared previously by sectoral specialists and thus constitutes the last "filter" before issues are put to ministerial meetings.
10 Similar analyses conducted on the British approach to European policy-making also underline the importance of the European Secretariat of the Cabinet Office as an effective co-coordinating mechanism (Wallace 1995).

8
The Ongoing March of Decentralisation within the Post-Jacobin State

Patrick Le Galès

Introduction

The unification of French society by political elites took many centuries. Despite the continuous efforts of the Jacobin elites, the *Code civil*, the single currency, the accord between Church and State, wars, the influence of trade unions, parties and the Church, not to mention railways, municipalities and schools, unification remained elusive. Local and regional diversity in France only really became blurred in the 1960s, with the advent of a large welfare state, industrialisation and urbanisation, mass consumption and television. Modernists of the 1960s regarded the preservation of regional peculiarities as an archaic pursuit of traditions on the verge of extinction. The political nationalisation of local elections and the modernisation of the Fifth Republic were perceived as the continuation of State-led modernisation and direction of French society.

Four decades later – the appropriate timescale to assess change here – a complex mosaic pattern now emerges from any analysis of the French local and regional systems in France. The 'before' picture of the Jacobin state still works until the late 1960s. New trends gained prominence in the 1970s and profoundly restructured public policy, conflicts over redistribution, and the quality of local democracy, leading to the internal differentiation process and the coexistence of heterogeneous structures, which have also become the norm in all the large EU countries. Similarly to what is observed in the UK, Italy, or Spain, the restructuring process is not over: it is ongoing, and so estimations of the impact of these changes remains speculative.

The changing territorialisation pattern of economy and society in France modifies the parameters under which wealth is produced and distributed. It frames the debate and the organisation of interests about inequalities and makes more salient the spatial dimension of redistributive issues. Indirectly it also provides increasing resources and legitimacy to urban political elites. Local and regional government is enshrined within a world of conflicting norms, competitive politics, mosaics of local and regional governments, and a restructuring State which, although less present in day-to-day politics and policies, is also distancing itself from the immediate demands and needs (including financial) of local government.

This chapter first provides evidence of the slow but wide-scale decentralisation dynamics within the French Republic and assesses its impact in terms of the pluralisation and territorialisation of politics and policies. Secondly, it argues that this ongoing change is best explained by political competition between political elites. Thirdly, it assesses the impact on the role of the State and French democracy.

1. 'Jacobinism tamed' and economic centralisation within the French Republic

The Jacobin centralised state inherited from the Revolution constituted the core of the unique French Republican model. For a long time, France was a centralized state, characterised by mistrust of local institutions, since the Revolution suppressed municipal corporations and *Provinces*. The Napoleonic consolidation provided for uniform municipal institutions and *départements*, but it was not until the Third Republic (1870–1939) that major laws granted municipal freedoms – notably in 1884. Yet the *commune*, preserved by the Revolution, has remained a frequently mythologised foundation of French democracy (Joana 2001), with the exception of the city, which appeared as a threat to the Jacobin Republic (Ascher 1998). Local elected political representatives have long been powerful and legitimate, notably through their access to the centre due to either political parties or the practice of holding multiple offices (Grémion 1976). Local government was organised around a pair of administrative structures inherited from the Revolution – over 36,000 *communes* and about 100 *départements* – which survived the call for rationalisation in the 1960s, unlike other European systems.

Despite being a major source of political innovation at the turn of the twentieth century, local government became more integrated within the State (Pollet 1995; Renard 1995). Within that system, the State, with its different ministries and services both in Paris and within each *département*, increasingly monopolised resources and the production of public goods until the 1970s. Public expenditure, investments and the power to raise taxes were under the strict control of the prefect and the Ministry of Finance/ Caisse des depôts and Consignations. Local authorities had little money and not much room to manoeuvre. Expertise was mainly within the hands of ministries' external services and their various agencies. Since the clear defeat of municipal socialism against the Council of the state in the 1920s, the legal powers of the prefect and state ministries and their capacity of control far exceeded those of local councils. Last but not least, although local authorities and local mayors in particular enjoyed a high level of political legitimacy, state-led modernisation was far more legitimate. 'Hands-on' style of territorial management from the State translated into powerful organisations all over the country. State external services for each major ministry were put in place within each *département*. The prefect was in charge of coordinating State policies and was the symbol of the authority of the Republican State, and the *Grands Corps* ran the major ministries of the State. This political centralisation was reinforced by cultural and economic centralisation.

The post-war decades saw the unification of the French economy under Parisian command (Veltz 1996), with industrial policy driving the change. This resulted in the demise of the primacy of small and medium-sized enterprises (SMEs) in organising and integrating local and regional economies. Bigger was better, and Parisian was better still. French industrialisation took place on the eastern side of the imaginary line from Le Havre to Geneva that is mainly in the Parisian region; the steel/coal/textile area of the northeast or St-Etienne Le Creusot; the harbours of Marseille and Le Havre; the automobile industry in the Seine valley; and Rhône Alpes (Lyon Grenoble). In particular, economic centralisation within the Paris region included the centralisation of capital, firms, elites and the transport system.

However, the formal centralisation of this system was somewhat diluted in practice, as local elites embedded in the dense network of state representatives and local politicians – including multiple office holders who integrated the system through their interaction with the prefect – adapted the system to the demands of their roles on the ground. This led to the system identified by Gremion (1976) as 'tamed Jacobinism'.

2. From the Jacobin state to the *République décentralisée*: decentralisation dynamics within a more urban society

France became an urban society in the 1960s. *La fin des paysans* identified by Mendras (1967) was accompanied not only by the continuous growth of Paris and its surrounding region but also, more surprisingly, by the rapid expansion of regional, medium-sized cities all over the country. Supported by large-scale public investments in the 1960s, those cities took full advantage of the metropolisation process in the 1980s and 1990s. These cities – that is, Nantes, Rennes, Bordeaux, Toulouse, Montpellier, Nice, Grenoble and Strasbourg – became the major centres of demographic and economic growth at the expense of rural areas and small, isolated towns.

This more urbanised French republic, influenced also by a closer connection to Europe, has seen three key developments. The first is the ongoing process of decentralisation reforms. The second is the institutional strengthening of the 22 regions. The third, and most significant, is the creation of interterritorial bodies with their own tax system, including a new range of compulsory tasks. These include the intercommunal revolution, the reorganisation of the policy process along new territorial lines, and the changing scale of the polity.

2.1 The silent revolution: never-ending reforms of the legal and financial setting mark the slow road towards decentralisation and local autonomy

The dynamics of decentralisation gradually began in the late 1960s (Mény 1974). The pace of reforms started to accelerate in the late 1970s and has continued unabated, despite the major decentralisation Acts (1982–84) and the attempt to create a new framework to stabilise the territorial organisation of the French State. New power configurations have emerged, leading to new conflicts that fuel the dynamics of decentralisation. Decentralisation reforms tell the story of the emergence of a new territorial system based upon dynamic cities, intercommunal governments and slowly emerging regions. However, the old system remains in place, demonstrating its strong capacity to resist and adapt. The interface of these two systems is uneven because of the restructuring of the State territorial apparatus within a context of growing legal and fiscal autonomy of those different levels of government (Balme et al. 1999). What emerges is a more pluralist, fragmented and differentiated polity, within which urban and regional politicians have accumulated even more resources to play a role at the national and European level.[1]

2.2 Many successive laws to destabilise the old system

The dynamics of decentralisation in France constitute a continuous process that a succession of laws and referenda has regularly reshaped, legitimised or reoriented. At first, the attempt to decentralise through the Gaullist referendum in 1969 failed. This prevented the creation of regions, blocked the reform of the Senate (due to entrenched rural interests and right-wing parties), and led to the creation of pseudo-regions in 1972[2] with no power, but which nevertheless gave rise to regional elites. Decentralisation became a flagship proposal for the new generation of urban and regional socialist leaders. Once in power in 1981, the left passed the laws of 1982–84, which gave wider resources, powers and legitimacy to all levels of local government, without any hierarchy between them, from the municipalities (and the larger ones were able to use it best), to the *départements*, up to the creation of a new tier, the region. Together with the retreat of local state external services, the suppression of prior administrative control symbolised the new legal autonomy of local government in France. Beyond formal powers, local and regional councils started to deal with nearly every item they felt they had political legitimacy to act upon, as they had always done, despite the fact that the prefect had always sought to limit their initiatives. Different laws were then passed, in particular, the law about the territorial administration of the Republic in 1992, which marked an attempt to adapt State services to decentralisation (i.e., to reinforce deconcentration) and a new period of intercommunal cooperation.

Under the Jospin government (a Socialist-Communist-Green coalition 1997–2002) a series of three laws was passed that reinforced cooperation between municipal governments, created a more competitive conception of territorial development, and legitimised the formulation and delivery of policy along new territorial lines.[3] They also indicated the extent to which the search for new instruments to manage the national territory has become a major concern for state ministries, in competition with each other. Together, often in contradictory terms, they organise the territorialisation of State priorities, the making of collective strategies for different types of territories, the institutionalisation of intercommunal bodies (*communautés*), and the redistribution of social and spatial responsibilities and powers on a different scale. Lastly, a constitutional reform, or Act II of decentralisation, was pushed forward by the Raffarin government (2003) to include the rights of local authorities to organise the transfer of 150,000 civil servants to local and regional authorities, to oversee the transfer of powers to different levels of government (i.e., roads, social aids and waste disposal to the *départements*; and aid to firms, training, regional strategic planning and public equipment to the regions), and to grant the right to experimentation in terms of organisation and public policy. The French State is no longer a uniform state; it is a unitary state with regions and local authorities. France is now officially defined as such in the first article of the Constitution: 'L'organisation de la République est décentralisée.'

Those legislative moves paved the way for a profound restructuring of the structures of government at the subnational level. Three contradictory images emerge from three decades of reforms: (1) the slow erosion, adaptation and firm resistance of the old system: communes/*départements*/Senate; (2) but, at the same time, the coming of age of metropolitan and regional governments; and (3) a reshaping of state organisation, with a progressive retreat from day-to-day management to a more strategic role at the regional level. Slowly, cities and regions are becoming a more important locus of organisation of interests, decisions and implementation of public policy, and creation of collective strategies. A more complex picture of local government has emerged, a mosaic-like pattern resembling the situation in other countries throughout Europe and very different from the previous well-organised State-view of local government: uniform, controlled by civil servants, and enshrined within financial and legal constraints set by the State.

Regions mainly deal with economic development, training, the building of secondary schools, culture, environment, and now, increasingly, railways. *Départements* have particular power and resources to manage social services, transport and roads. Communes mainly deal with social services, their own roads and primary schools, basic services, environment, sports and culture. Intercommunal *communautés* mainly work on utilities, waste management, transport, economic development and water. However, each level of government feels free to intervene in any domain: all have policies for the environment, culture or economic development, for instance, hence there is a considerable amount of overlap. The world of local and regional government includes 500,000 elected members and 1.6 million (soon to be 1.8) public-sector employees, which constitutes about 30 per cent of the French public service.

The domain of local government also comprises myriad other organisations. Non-governmental bodies, such as associations acting as quasi-services for local government, run festive or social services. Public-private bodies, such as *sociétés d'économie mixte* (private agencies with majority public ownership), often act as subsidiaries or manage services for local government. Public agencies run social housing. Quasi-public or public-private agencies provide services operated by private firms (Caillosse et al. 1997). Finally, a number of these organisations are clearly privately-run utilities (e.g., environment, transport and social housing). The 'municipal public sector' (Lorrain 1991) thus comprises a variety of organizations, many of which do not have public status (even though they may well operate on public funding), and whose integration is highly problematic, if only because they do not always operate on the same geographic scale.

The 1999 Chevènement Act was intended to reduce once and for all the inconsistency in the different forms of municipal cooperation. In order to do so, the government went for a more voluntary approach, mixing direct constraints with strong financial incentives. Quickly (at least by French standards) 14 urban communities (the largest urban areas, in general), 120 *communautés d'agglomération* (large-size communities) and 2,033 *communautés de communes* were created. Altogether, this amounts to about 2,200 groupings with a specific and distinct tax base, coordinating 26,748 cities and towns with over 45 million inhabitants (75% of the total population). Participation is now more consistent, with a large majority of towns participating in some form or other of cooperative community. In years to come, it is expected that all municipalities will belong to one of these communities.

Financial autonomy and the control of public investment

Last but not least, the rise of local control of finance and public investments indicates the increasing autonomy of local and regional government, along with increased interdependence between the different levels of government.

The Administrations publiques locales, APUL, represent public finance spending at the local level. This category comprises elected local and regional authorities, intercommunal bodies, and a range of other less-important local public or semi-public organisations such as the Chamber of Commerce and certain industries, including some under the direct control of the central state (DGCL [Direction Générale des Collectivités Locales] 2005) (Table 8.1).

Table 8.1 Role of the State and APUL in expenditure and public local investment

	Expenditure	FBCF
State	354,99	8,03
APUL	162,98	34,84

Note: Figures in billion 2003 euros. FBCF (Formation Brute de capital fixe) represents spending on local investment.

APUL represent just less than 45 per cent of state expenditure, but 71.3 per cent of public FBCF, which is more than 70 per cent of public investment, a percentage that has continued to increase over the past two decades.[4]

Public investment in France is now firmly under the control of local and regional authorities, with intercommunal urban communities gaining the most significant influence in the investment process. State public investment remains central in transport (trains, motorways), hospitals, defence, police and justice administration. However in a number of cases, for instance universities or railways, local and regional authorities are gradually participating in the investment and claiming a say in the decision-making process.[5]

One of the classic pillars of local autonomy in France remains the high level of direct fiscal finance within local authorities' budgets: taxes represented 52.6 per cent of local authorities' budgets in 2002. In many ways, the 1980s were the golden years (Gilbert 1999). Although local and regional authorities have smaller budgets than the state, they had a relatively high degree of autonomy both in terms of tax revenue they received and in terms of spending. Within the mosaics of local finance and State transfers, local and regional authorities are gradually gaining more autonomy and capacity to spend in accordance with their own goals.

2.3 Territorialisation of public policies: strategic local and regional government within a more pluralist, competitive and negotiated polity

Faced with increasing pressure towards fragmentation, groups of actors most often within French cities, but sometimes within regions or in dynamic rural areas too, are trying to mobilise in different ways, to organise cities or regions as collective actors (Balme 1998; Le Galès 2002). They want to elaborate collective spatial strategies, institutionalise collective action to mobilise groups, and extract resources from the EU, the State, other local authorities, and firms. Although it is premature to measure the impact of these mobilisations on the ground, economically and socially France already appears as a more differentiated society, less Jacobin and uniform, in line with what has happened in many other countries. This change is fueled by the way public policies are designed and implemented.

The rise of local government in political and legal terms went together with increasing expertise and resources. 'Shooting where the ducks are', interest groups and associations have reacted accordingly and reorganised to take those changes into account, more rapidly for associations, more slowly for business and trade unions used to negotiating only at the national level. Within a context where political legitimacy seems more related to public-policy outcomes and the capacity to implement programmes (Duran 1998), French local and regional governments have played an increasing role in terms of public policy when classic, vertical State-led policies collapsed (Muller 1992).

Since the 1980s new types of public policies have been initiated by the State (urban policy, new social policies, environment and health), which gave the subnational level of government and its associated social and political groups and actors new responsibilities to integrate different programmes, to give a territorial logic and coherence to a whole range of programmes and policies, and to compensate for the decline of the old vertical integration through interest groups and State administrative elites (Lascoumes 1995; Warin 2004). In fact, this integration and coherence supposedly given by territorial politics was more often a myth (a myth that became, in some ways, a self-fulfilling prophecy). In fact, fragmentation and the multiplication of intergovernmental/private-public networks prevailed (Palier 1998; Le Galès 2001; Borraz and Loncle 2000). However, urban elites were also very busy building new alliances, networks and partnerships, with the appearance of being at the forefront of new forms of governance (Cole and John 2001; Jouve and Lefèvre 1999).

Among new policy instruments, the practice of contractualisation stands out as it relates both to local authorities and other levels of government; indeed, local authorities play an essential role in linking the latter together. Contractualisation has become a central instrument of cooperation between actors, whether between actors at different levels (Marcou et al. 1997; Gaudin 1999) or between public and private actors. They frequently act against the momentum towards institutionalising collective activity within the public sector to coordinate different elements of the State with local authorities in France (Le Galès and Mawson 1995). The same argument applies to partnership approaches. Because of the rules governing public accounts in particular, it is difficult to envisage partnerships without the development of a complex bureaucratic structure: this represents an additional barrier to the mobilisation of local residents and small associations. Local governments are keen to develop partnership as long as it does not run against the political interests and the legitimacy of political elites (Loncle 2000).

Mobilisation and consultation of different groups has become essential for local officials in order to increase their political capacity and extract resources from the State or the EU. Obviously fragmentation prevails in many places, but groups, actors and elites often mobilise within cities and rural intercommunal bodies, and sometimes in the regions, to produce strategies; stabilise contexts for interactions, norms and collective choices (Faure 1997; Douillet 2003); and obtain specific outcomes in terms of public policies. The revival of strategic urban planning probably represents one of the developments most symptomatic of this change (Pinson 2005). Urban elites of French cities – politicians, cultural leaders, economic interests, representatives of myriad associations, state external services representatives – by direction of elected politicians, organise to develop strategies, create reciprocity and institutionalise dynamics in the form of a city strategy. They aim to strengthen horizontal interactions within the city among all the city actors, so as to facilitate shared representation, and to regulate complex, enmeshed systems of action. Yet they must address concerns of efficiency, management of the territory, the building of consensus between urban elites, development of an urban common good, creation of capacities for action and renewal of power relations. Because they are developed collectively, they give a stronger legitimacy to elites imposing specific projects such as public transport or major public investments and overcoming resistance (Bardet and Jouve 1999).

Those mechanisms that integrate actors within cities, rural intercommunal bodies and, sometimes, regions should not be reified, but issues such as infrastructural investments, dealing with different populations, and combating water pollution are now mainly dealt with and negotiated at the local or regional level within the parameters set by the State. Conflict-solving mechanisms are structured at that level, for instance, for the construction of a mosque, to fight against poverty or to develop initiatives to deal with drug dealers and sustainable development issues.

However, the multiplication of these schemes has created new incoherence in the system. Each of them is supposed to be empowered to embrace a global approach encompassing diverse interests and actors. Yet State attempts to provide more coherence and strategic capacity to local government often lead to chaos. Local government and their bureaucracies spend their time designing new strategies and new schemes in order to coordinate fragmented public policies. Political rivalries between local governments and between ministries produce different parameters for each contract and each development strategy, although each of them presumes to provide coherence to the whole urban or rural area. Political entrepreneurs are able to instrumentalise those different schemes.

Spatial differentiation leads to increased interterritorial conflicts for welfare redistribution and increased competition for what remains of State investments. The question of geographical inequalities remains central to the political debate and evolution of the French Republic.

Interestingly, the structure of territorial inequalities has followed a particular path. By all accounts, the dual structure of the rich Paris region on the one hand and the rest of the country on the other remains the central feature. However, two contradictory points are crucial. In terms of GDP per inhabitant, and in terms of productivity, the gap has increased between the Ile de France region and the rest of the country since the 1980s. Ile de France comprises about 23 per cent of the population and produces about 30 per cent of the GDP. In similar measure, the same gap is increasing between cities and the rest of France.

But GDP per capita measures only the raw economic production of the region, not income after transfers. Regional inequalities measured in terms of post-transfer income have by contrast declined, as shown by Davezies (2001).

Figure 8.1 from Davezies (2001) sheds some light on one of the main redistributive stakes related to decentralisation. The Ile de France region is dynamic, getting younger, and producing the highest level of wealth and inequalities. It is the filtering pump attracting the most qualified labour force and firms in dynamic economic sectors. Other regions such as Limousin or Languedoc Roussillon are getting older, with their economies relying upon tourism, state redistribution (pensions, social security) and what Davezies calls the residential economy. There are therefore large groups of organised interests within those regions that oppose any regionalisation of welfare or social issues that would threaten the large-scale redistributive mechanisms. However, it is important to stress the interdependence of those regions: busy Parisian middle classes need rural countryside, the seaside, or the mountains to escape the pressure of metropolitan life, and they need smaller cities for living with their families or retiring.

Figure 8.1 Per capita GDP and after-transfer incomes in Ile de France

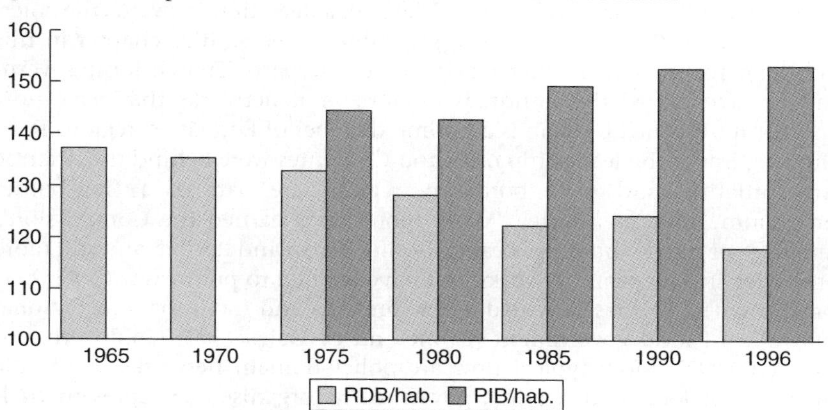

Note: the vertical axis compares to the corresponding French average, scaled at 100.
Source: Laurent Davezies's own calculation using INSEE figures.

2.4 Changing scale: Europeanisation and transnational utility firms

Communes, cities, *départements* and regions are now part of the EU. Together with the strategy of transnational utility firms, they create limited exit strategies for metropolitan actors who have access to private goods that are not produced within the borders of the nation-state.

The Europeanisation of local government

The opening of the European polity beyond center–periphery relations automatically modifies hierarchical relations between levels, reinforces overlapping policy networks (Smith 1995), and offers new potential for local government (Hooghe and Marks 2001). Appeals are lodged against state decisions through the European Court of Justice. Lobbying is organised in Brussels to influence decisions and policies, utilising resources from EU programmes – most notably the structural funds. Expertise is acquired independently from the state, fostering the development of horizontal, transnational relationships (sometimes beyond Europe) with other local authorities who claim to represent and defend the interests of their citizens and question the state's formulation of the common interest.

EU programmes and funds are only one of the elements of European public policy that have had a direct impact on local government. Although initially seduced by the new political horizons of the European Union, local government has for instance gradually learned that EU institutionalisation is accompanied by a new set of constraints: implementing environmental norms, getting used to the 'partnership norm' to obtain structural funds, limiting public aids to firms, and feeling financial pressure exerted by the state in the name of EU fiscal criteria. Beyond top-down programmes and rules, the increased density of transnational relations and networks among social and political actors is a key indicator of a deep trend towards the emergence of more Europeanised local government (see Smith's chapter in this volume). Together with their European counterparts, French local governments have joined the hundreds of horizontal networks that have now spread all over the EU: Lyon is a leading member of Eurocities, regions from the west under the leadership of Poitou-Charentes were behind the Atlantic Arc initiative, and most bordering regions are part of a transborder programme such as Interreg. Many more have learned the Commission's language of the programmes Leader, Recife, Urban and Rechar, and still more are active in European networks and have learned to put forward their best practices. The EU has provided a new impetus and focus for transnational networks of local government (Balme and Le Galès 1997; Goldsmith and Klausen 1997). More typical now are policy-domain networks or specific networks of local and regional governments organised to represent their own collective interests. These transnational networks are privileged sites for obtaining information, exchanging experiences and ideas, knowledge of various kinds, and challenging European programmes or states; therefore, they are also places for learning policy norms and styles.

Increased market pressure: utilities and finance

Decentralisation reforms in the 1980s were mainly seen in terms of transfer of powers, legitimacy and resources from the central to the local, and to a lesser extent the regional level of government. However, it also led to a greater role for the market and its pressures, and a growing role for large utility firms.

French water management and construction firms (Suez and Veolia,[6] Bouygues and Vinci) have become worldwide utility groups with markets of global size, diversifying through increasingly varied activities: funeral directing, urban transport, motorways, major projects, waste collection and treatment, energy, transport, construction, private developments, moving on into new information and communication technologies, and even Hollywood studios. French public enterprises, such as Electricité de France, now facing increasing competition under EU law, have also undertaken to gain a foothold in new markets. These groups have become major actors, offering technical and financial solutions to cities' elites, whether to solve their technical problems or to carry out major facilities projects. The move towards privatisation of services and utilities in the 1980s was rightly analysed as a silent revolution for local government that gave prominence and power to large utilities firms, which in turn gained a whole set of new urban markets. They also provided funds for political parties and leaders, ran various utilities (from water to new metro and tramway lines), and built new neighbourhood and flagship projects (Lorrain 1993, 1997).

Firms still play an important role in running urban utilities in France, but they now maintain some distance from local government, restructuring their activities on a regional level and dropping out altogether from construction activities. First, large utility firms became world leaders, and consequently had less interest in running local utilities (Lorrain 2001). Secondly, after political corruption scandals (whereby some mayors and firm managers were sent to jail), firms decided to disengage somewhat from local politics. Thirdly, a reaction against privatisation occurred, and pressure increased from state officials, the Green party and local government to have stricter control on contracts and their implementation, along with the quality of services offered. The gravity of the conflicts put in front of courts worried business leaders. The intermunicipal revolution also marks a decisive change that is supported by leading utility firms. The making of intermunicipal government is an opportunity to rationalise their organisation and to concentrate on markets of a reasonable size.

Nonetheless, city councils are not without resources and capacity to make choices. Private firms need public spaces, access to refuse collection, and coordination for carrying out works: in short, if there were open conflict with a city council, network operators might find themselves in a difficult position (Lorrain 2000; Coutard 2001). Local government remains a major player in running urban utilities and faces more and more political pressure from citizen groups to make sure fair prices and environmental and sanitary norms are respected.

Increased market pressure on local government also takes different forms, for instance, access to financial markets to borrow money. The financial branch of the state-owned Caisse des Dépôts et Consignations has become autonomous as Crédit Local de France, and, after mergers with a Belgian financial organisation, it became the leading European bank to finance local governments' projects under the name of Dexia. Although Dexia does not have a monopoly in this matter, it exerts very strong influence on local-government borrowing and sets norms for good practices. More generally speaking, local and regional authorities are under more financial scrutiny from financial institutions which assess and rate their financial management and their risk. This does not completely change the way they behave, but it does create an institutional environment in which they have to respect different rules of the game.

In terms of market pressure, the combined effect of EU deregulation and strategies of national firms is also creating a different environment for local authorities. Small towns can no longer expect France Telecom, Air France, possibly SNCF (Société nationale des chemins de fer français [French railways]), and others to deliver services on a classic logic of public service. There is increasing pressure from the market for cooperation between local authorities and the development of strategies to deal with those groups. Competition does not always mean marginalisation of the small towns. In some cases, deregulation is an opportunity. The development of airports in Carcassonne or St Etienne is directly related to the rise of low-cost air companies.

3. Long-term radical change without revolution: the combined dynamics of political competition and state restructuring

3.1 Political competition feeds the dynamics of decentralisation

In France, political competition between different groups of elected representatives and between political parties is the main factor behind both the rise of local and regional government and the territorialisation of public policies.

Local and regional elected leaders, whether holding a national mandate or not, sometimes in cooperation with economic and cultural interests, have been the driving force behind decentralisation reforms from their inception. In the 1960s and 1970s when decentralisation became a theme supported by the left (PSU [Parti Socialiste Unifié] in particular) and later by the Socialists and the Greens, local mayors and chairs of *départements* and quasi-regions worked consistently to develop bottom-up initiatives and policies and to advocate more powers and resources for themselves. They have not ceased to argue, to organise politically and, as a result of the *cumul des mandats*, to enforce change when they were in power. Progressively, they colonised political parties, which were always relatively weak. Even the neo-Gaullist party or the Communist Party, historically the most centralised, became controlled by mayors and presidents of departmental and regional authorities (Knapp and Le Galès 1993). Major reforms were always related to powerful groups, for instance, urban mayors within the Socialist Party elected in 1981 (Pierre Mauroy and Gaston Defferre in 1981), and right-wing chairs of regions in the current Raffarin government (Jean Pierre Raffarin or François Fillon). The left tends to emphasise the role of cities, urban areas and regions to a lesser extent, without arguing for the suppression of *départements* whose representatives still hold strong position within the party. The right tends to support *départements* and regions at the expense of cities, but has now made important electoral gains in such cities as Strasbourg, Marseille, Bordeaux and Toulouse. Regionalist groups from the 1960s onwards and Green activists tied to social movements are a second group of actors that has consistently argued for more decentralisation. They do not represent a major force, and their political weight is limited, but they play a role in raising those issues in the public debate and bringing in new ideas.

Strong political battles take place both in Parliament and between national associations of local government (Le Lidec 2002).[7] These groups are engaged in a ceaseless struggle to develop transfers of power from the State and to prevent other levels of government from benefiting at their expense. This competition between groups of politicians from different levels of government is an important competitive dynamic over time, even within political parties.

The collision between the former system (communes/*départements*/Senate) versus the urban/regional system reinforces the dynamics of decentralisation. The success of the 1999 Act reforming local intercommunal organisations has much to do with local patterns of leadership, stabilised forms of political exchange and organisational learning through previous or pre-existing forms of cooperation (Michel 1999; Le Saout 2000; Baraize and Négrier 2001). Intermunicipal governments offer new opportunities for local leaders willing to establish local strongholds on a wider scale: a large majority of *communautés* are chaired by mayors, often the mayor of the central city around which the *communauté* was built. Mayors are reinforcing their authority on a larger territorial basis at the expense of *départements*.

Lately, the Raffarin decentralisation reform also reflected the power relations in the new right-wing party, the UMP (Union pour la majorité présidentielle). Although the prime minister managed to strengthen the role of the regions in the Constitution, he could only do so by giving more resources and powers to the *départements* and by increasing the role of the Senate in local matters.

In political terms, French local and regional government is rooted within a complex system of representation. At times the mayor or chair has been misrepresented and oversimplified as the sole locus of power, in describing a municipal presidential system or denouncing quasi-monarchist behaviour

(Mény 1992; Mabileau 1995). In fact, political chairs of *départements*, regions and mayors have strong legitimacy and are elected by different systems. Representation is at the core of French municipal government, both in the way mayoral authority is established and maintained, and in the legitimacy and efficiency of an institution that has always established strong links with its environment through cooptation (Borraz 1998). But the dynamics of decentralisation give a new role to political leaders, and change the way these leaders operate, in particular in mobilising fragmented interests groups while implementing policies. The question of political leadership, and competition for it, is central to analysing the particular political and social dynamics of any given territory (Sorbets and Smith 2003).

The turnout for local elections is slowly declining (Hoffman-Martinot 1999) although it remains robust for municipal elections (61% participation in 2001 against 78% in 1983). The question of local democracy was not an issue during the main decentralisation reforms, hence the characterisation of decentralisation as 'par les notables, pour les notables' (Rondin 1985). This tension, along with the growing importance of intermunicipal government and the weakening participation in local elections, prompted the government to pass a new law on 'democracy and proximity' in February 2002. Among other things, the Act makes the creation of neighbourhood councils compulsory in cities over 80,000, along with consultative committees on local utilities in cities over 10,000 (and intermunicipal structures over 50,000). The law also makes it easier for citizens to participate in the decision-making process on major infrastructure projects (through public enquiries and consultations, for example). Finally, the minority in the communal assembly has seen its powers enlarged. All in all, the aim is to promote new forms of participation and greater means for debate inside what remains formally a representative system of government.[8]

This characterisation of change helps explain what could be seen at first as a French paradox. In the US and the UK, decentralisation dynamics go hand in hand with decentralisation of the responsibility to implement cuts in public spending (social services, for instance) and implementation of cuts in public expenditure. Central governments delegate more authority to local government but do not allocate commensurate taxing powers or resources transfer. Although those pressures exist in the French case, and may increase in the near future – see above – this has not been the dominant pattern so far. Increased power has been matched by increased resources for local and regional governments, either in terms of increased taxes or increased transfers from the State, usually both. This makes sense because of the power and mobilisation of local and regional politicians both as local politicians, as represented by local-government associations, and as national politicians, either minister or *députés/sénateurs*. In terms of the remaining prestige and resources controlled by urban mayors, let us just mention that it has become common for former prime ministers to become mayors of Lyon or Bordeaux, but the current mayors of Toulouse and Lille are aspiring prime ministers.

Most national politicians in France are mayors or chair a region, and most MPs and senators still hold a local mandate. Leading representatives of the interests of local and regional government are in Parliament, often powerful former ministers, for instance, finance ministers, and they possess a very high degree of expertise and political leverage to defend the interests of local and regional governments.

3.2 What about the state?

The rise of local and regional governments in Europe has been classically analysed as the dynamic combination of two forces: bottom-up and top-down. Bottom-up pressure comes from regionalist movements, democratic demands, local elites' demands, social movements against the state, and hierarchies, while top-down pressure comes from decentralisation of welfare cuts, mobilisation of the periphery for modernisation and economic development, rationalisation of public investments, declining requirement to prepare a war against a neighbour, and the end of colonialism (Keating 1998). The former is central to the French case.

However, the state has also been peripherally involved and is slowly coping with the consequences of the political dynamics analysed so far. At first, the rise of local and regional government – with their resources, power, expertise – signalled the decline of the state external services organised at the level of the *départements*, such as infrastructure, social services, and even the prefect to some extent. Prefects and their services had to cope with the absence of state strategies in many areas, while, by contrast, political entrepreneurs tried to increase their leadership and to strategise, enrolling different actors, including state services. Slowly, the state apparatus is being reorganised at the regional level with a less hands-on and a more strategic and regulatory role. The case of the Agences Régional Hospitalières, which are restructuring the maps of French hospitals despite powerful local and professional interests, is an interesting example.

Civil servants of the central government have usually not been key supporters of decentralisation reforms, and that remains true today. However, rivalries between *grands corps* (notably the Ministry of Finance and Trésoriers Payeurs généraux, the Ministry of infrastructures and Directions départementales de l'Équipement, the Ministry of the Interior, and prefects) and within ministries themselves have led some sections of the state to support decentralisation in some specific ways.

On the financial side, the French state increasingly appears impoverished in the eyes of local and regional elected politicians because of its decreasing capacity to finance public investments. The role of the Ministry of Finance is pivotal. Instead of increasing the tax-spending powers of local authorities, the ministry has agreed to foster the role of state transfers. Those transfers have two main purposes: either the state grants exemption to some groups without wanting to reform the local tax system and provides financial compensation to the local authorities, or financial transfers go together with transfers of competence. All in all, those financial transfers increased by 50 per cent between 1997 and 2002 (DGCL 2003). However, this development allows state elites to negotiate objectives of local expenditure increases – in other words, to stabilise the macroeconomic framework within which local and regional expenditure takes place, even if that means a gradual erosion of the financial transfers to them, for instance, with the goal of limiting the deficit. The Ministry of Finance is progressively increasing its capacity of control on local authorities and is setting the parameters under which local leaders are freer to act, providing they respect the rules of the games set by them. Also increasingly powerful Chambres Régionales des Comptes have developed a real expertise in the financial control of local authorities' actions in cooperation with local government (Benoit 2003).

Other sections of the French central State and the large State civil service are strongholds of resistance against decentralisation in the ministry of education, the ministry of infrastructures or the ministry of social affairs. Civil servants' unions often see decentralisation as a means to reduce staff, above all when reforms are elaborated by centre-right governments, hence the demonstration against the Raffarin decentralisation, which, for the first time, linked transfer of power and restructuring (i.e. cuts) of the State.

Although impoverished and fragmented, the French State still has significant capacities to act. Its influence, though, resides more in constitutive than in substantive policy actions. In other words, the State defines rules, procedures, roles and settings, but it does not go into details as to how exactly these should contribute to a particular purpose: that task is left to local officials. The central government defines priorities and procedures to achieve these goals, while local actors are left to adopt the necessary means and concrete measures within that defined framework (Duran and Thoenig 1996), but with a weaker grasp on what exactly goes on inside those defined procedures.

What is striking in public-policy terms is not just the dynamics of territorialisation but the search for new instruments of the state to exert control, bring coherence, and adjust. In a speculative way, those changes are signs that the French State is moving away from the classic model of 'hands-on policy', with direct intervention, resources and expertise in every *département*. A more 'hands-off' role entails a more strategic and regulatory role, and possibly an enabling role. This leads to serious internal conflicts, because it tends to strengthen the Ministry of Finance and the regional level of the state (i.e. the prefects), and perhaps it forces a change in the role for the *grands corps*, as seen by the Cour des Comptes playing with the idea of becoming more clearly a National Audit Office. This is at the expense of traditional State external services, which are facing ongoing decline. Within the EU polity, the French core of the State is also becoming more independent from powerful local and regional interests, hence a view which emphasises decentralisation in order to on the one hand implement cuts and reforms and on the other hand to accentuate capacities of control. This constitutes a move towards a French version of a more regulatory state. The French State is not leading the movement to decentralisation and the territorialisation of public policies, but it is adapting to it and is now trying to invent a framework, instruments and a new role to control it.

Conclusion

This chapter has argued that dynamics of decentralisation and the rise of local and regional governments have led to wide-scale restructuring of the French polity within a context of EU institutionalisation and market pressure. This chapter provides elements to support the thesis of the erosion of national norms, of decreasing hierarchies, of interdependence between levels of government within the EU governance, and of contestation of the classic general interest of the French state articulated by the *grands corps*.

Although the changes discussed took place over three decades, the impact is nonetheless massive in terms of public policies; hence the idea of a silent revolution. Competition between local and regional political elites within the national political system was presented as the main factor to explain change. This raises questions for interpreting change that echo the theme of the volume and lead us to interpret the consequences for French democracy.

Classically, massive changes in France were seen as either state led, derived from the heroic figure of the enlightened, entrepreneurial state, or the result of upheavals, massive protests and revolutions. Those two factors of change do not apply in our case. The State did not lead the process (see above), and no social movements organised large-scale protests to initiate decentralisation. By contrast, the case of changing local and regional government provides fertile ground to think about changes within the French polity. In line with most chapters of this volume, the role of market forces – accelerated or imposed by the EU – is the obvious suspect to explain or interpret changes as well as to explain the fall of State economic *dirigisme* or welfare state reforms. Similarly, in Europe or in the US, the spectacular rise of diverse, market-led globalisation processes have given rise to a literature explaining local governments and state restructuring (Jessop 1995; Brenner 1999). In the French case, this chapter has identified insights about the dynamics of changes in relations, for instance, with Europeanisation (i.e., the availability of public goods beyond the frontiers of the nation-state, and a new set of rules) or market dynamics (utility firms, access to international funding, and the importance of economic development priorities).

However, the key argument here is that France, as most European nation-states, is a deeply institutionalised and territorialised polity, hence the importance of political and social factors that do not just vanish under the pressure of more globalised capitalism. The dynamics of decentralisation in France came from the localities and the regions, first from Alsace and

Brittany in the late 1950s and then from innovative urban mayors in the 1960s, and then from local, urban and regional elites since the 1970s. Competition between those, and then within and between political parties, has fed and enhanced the decentralisation process.

This raises a more general point about the broader character of political change in France. At first glance, it is easy to conclude that the French State has given way to the market, and there is a good deal of evidence to sustain that claim in several areas, as shown in different chapters of this volume. However, one may first challenge the view about the category 'French State': at the very least, it is crucial to analyse the welfare state separately (see the chapter by Bruno Palier). Also, this chapter has shown that resources that used to be under the strict control of the State are now controlled by local and regional government. They are part of the State, but in an increasingly differentiated way.

In other words, it does not suffice to limit the explanation of changes in France to the classic view of the state and to the role of markets. As Michel Lallement shows in his chapter, changes in industrial relations are better explained by interactions between organised actors and interests at different levels within a context of market pressure and state restructuring. The picture emerging from Lallement's chapter or this one is not just fragmentation, mosaics or more markets, but a more pluralist and negotiated polity within which processes of changes are not the same in different sectors. In those cases, the usual suspect of market forces contributes to set a different scene and shapes a different set of constraints and opportunities. However, the main dynamics of change rely upon organised actors and interests both at national, local and regional level. A post-Jacobin polity emerges, more differentiated, more negotiated and more pluralist, requiring different intellectual tools to explain changes, and focusing on the governance of different sectors and territories, the institutionalisation of collective actors, and politics (Lallement 1999; Le Galès 2002).

A second running theme of this volume deals with the quality of French democracy. Is a post-Jacobin France a better democracy? At least two difficulties arise: first, French democracy is being transformed by other forces such as educational change, individualism, inequalities, the labour market, the institutionalisation of the EU, and the fragmentation of the party system; secondly, it would not make any sense to make a causal link between decentralisation and a better democracy. On the negative side, the decentralisation reforms did not give high priority to democratic issues, nor did they reinforce the leadership teams in local government. They created confusion, fragmentation and overlapping governments, and thus a strong decline of accountability. Local political leaders have often opposed the demands of various groups to join the policy process or ignored the needs to hear the voice of minorities. Foreigners and long-term, established immigrants in particular have no say in local elections. Political parties have played a limited role in relaying demands towards the political sphere at the local and regional level, but they are often well connected to the local society (Sawicki 1997). Competition between local and regional political elites leads to lack of coordination, closure and fragmentation of the policy process, while the risk of clientelism, corruption and conservatism is always present. There is now an increasing variety of political parties competing during elections (Chiche, Haegel and Tiberj 2002). From two to three on average in the 1970s, their number has risen to almost four recently, and even five in major cities, subsequently producing a higher volatility in voting patterns (Hoffmann-Martinot 1999). Some of these parties are strictly local but most of them tend to adopt nationwide labels (either the various extreme-left parties, the far-right parties or the Green movement). There is a problem of representation for these groups, individuals and areas, along with a lesser understanding by political officials of their needs and demands. But low turnout at the polls does not mean an absence of mobilisation and political activity: it simply means that voting is not always regarded as the best mode of formulating and promoting interests and demands (Grunberg et al. 2002). Nonetheless, in a political system based on representation, this can be a source of legitimacy crisis. Also, a more competitive political system has strengthened the powers and capacity of the most important cities, at the expense of the urban periphery in crisis or small town in decline. The remaining urban crises in large neighbourhoods located in the periphery of these cities – Paris, Lyon, Marseille and the northeast in particular – has something to do with both the absence of political rights given to immigrants and the marginalisation of their political representatives (Garbaye 2002; Body-Gendrot 2000; Oberti 1999; Beaud and Pialoux 2003). Urban violence in those areas reveals the strength of the social question as an urban question and the limits of the representative model of local government (Masclet 2003).

On the positive side, the strengths of local and regional government have successfully prevented a neo-liberal reshaping of the state so far. In many cases, local and regional elites are trying to use their powers and resources to foster change and adaptation of local societies, to mobilise for local economic development, together with providing social assistance to the poorest population. In the most dynamic cases, such as in cities, there is a considerable amount of policy innovation to solve social problems, to deal with different social groups, and to bring coherence to a fragmented policy process.

New forms of participation are emerging through local mobilisation, consultations and referenda, and procedures promoting dialogue. This marks a shift from representative democracy towards a more participatory or procedural type of democracy. Some of these forms derive from laws and regulations, such as consultative committees, referenda and popular initiatives on planning issues, provided by two laws in 1992 and 1995. A public space for political discussion is emerging in many cities, including Paris, although not without difficulty (Blondiaux 1999). Other forms stem from local-government initiatives, and still others from direct collective action. A great number of actors are part of the policy process, from the professionals to the policy users on issues such as environmental protection, planning, transportation infrastructures, social housing, work promotion, health, industrial pollution and risks (Barthe et al. 2001; Lolive 1999). The way demands are formulated, priorities drawn, resources distributed, information produced, and decisions taken reveals elements of democratization.[9]

Associations have in particular played an increasing role in the policy-making process over the past two decades (Worms 2002; Barthélémy 2000), using different tools such as the law and the courts. Clearly, some or even most of these actions exert strong pressures on local elected officials, both in terms of conflicting legitimacies (between representative and participatory modes) and as a test of their capacity to take demands into consideration, provide answers and arbitrate between contradictory pressures. In this sense, the mix between representative and more participatory procedures (i.e., for the consultation of individuals and groups, but also organised interests, alongside public officials) still holds a number of imperfections.

This is a difficult and messy process, with many failures. Still, the mix of dynamic associational life, more open policy process in some domains (at least in comparison to the domination of *grands corps*), more local and regional decision-making, political entrepreneurs building on these trends and associating organised interest, and organised groups contesting policies, together with a relatively robust local representative democracy, is an opportunity to develop a more democratic post-Jacobin polity, less structured by hierarchies and the domination of leading state and economic interests. Within a decade, there should be less confusion and fragmentation in both the policy process and the organisation of local and regional government.

However, this more differentiated French polity has already become more competitive, and may lead to increased spatial inequalities in the future. Local political elites sometimes get close to economic groups to create new forms of oligarchies within some localities (Padioleau 1991).

It may also be the case that the rise of cities and regions, and the rise of the governance capacity of local public spaces, goes hand in hand with the sidelining of traditional national institutions of representative democracy within a polity increasingly dominated by global firms, powerful economic groups, EU norms and transnational voluntary sector organisations. More democratisation in dynamic cities and rural areas and the making of modes of governance and strategic projects fostered by state elites allows for the marginalisation of poor rural areas and *quartiers en crise*, with less support from the state.

If French policy is more decentralised, pluralistic, more negotiated, more territorialised, and less dominated by a Parisian elite, it remains to be seen what the long-term impact will be in terms of inequality, integration and democracy.

Notes

1 The brief and non-exhaustive review of the main legislation does not include the debates and changes in relation to overseas territories and Corsica, which have special legislative status and an influence on the debates.
2 Établissements publics régionaux, created in 1972, were non-elected administrative bodies.
3 The 1999 Voynet Act on regional planning and sustainable development (Ministry of the Environment and Regional Policy), 1999 Chevènement Act on intermunicipal cooperation (Ministry of the Interior), and the law Solidarité et Renouvellement Urbain (Ministry of Planning, Housing, Infrastructures), 2000.
4 Provisional figures for 2002 suggest that 100 *départements* were planning to spend 44.10 billion euros, compared to 17.25 for 22 regions, about 80 billion for 36,000 communes and over 30 billion for intercommunal bodies. Over the past two decades, local authority expenditure has grown more quickly than state expenditure.
5 A good example of this is the Plan Université 2000 under the Rocard government where local and regional governments co-financed new buildings or the contract between SNCF and regions to regionalise railways.
6 Veolia was for several decades the old 'Générale des eaux' before being part of the rise and fall of Vivendi.
7 Associations des Maires de France, Association des presidents de Conseils Généraux, and lately not very effectively the Association des Présidents de Conseils Régionaux and the Association des Maires des Grandes villes de France, the only one chaired by a Socialist.
8 A similar analysis could be developed at the other level. Both the *département* and the region (Nay 1997, 2001) are characterised by the dominance of leadership teams. At the *département* level, elections take place within an old constituency, *cantons*. In rural areas, there are several communes in one *canton* and the elected representative, *conseiller général*, defends the local interest to obtain more roads and equipment within the Conseil Général, which runs the *départéments*. In cities, however, there are several *cantons* in one city, and the boundaries are meaningless. In many *départéments*, the main urban area organised within a community could represent between 40 per cent and 60 per cent of the population of the whole *département* when there is a regional capital. Two-thirds of the *départéements* are firmly in the hand of the right, and one-third is run by the left. Rural interests and population are massively overrepresented. Because of their role in the elections of senators (and most *présidents de conseil général* are 'natural candidates' for the Senate), the majority of the Senate has always remained rightwing during the Fifth Republic. Because of its constitutional power, the Senate is the key guardian of the interests of communes and *départéments*.
9 In France, where the 1901 legislation makes it easy to form an association that can engage in local issues and the promotion of interests, it is estimated that there are about 700,000 associations or groups, of which from 15 per cent to 20 per cent are inactive (Barthélémy 2000), but the rest are active at a local level for most of the time.

Part IV

9

The French Party System and the Crisis of Representation

Gérard Grunberg

Introduction

The crisis of representation has been a recurrent theme in recent discussions of the state of the French political system. The rise in voter abstention and the obvious weakening of the link between voters and political parties have led observers to blame Fifth Republic institutions as well as the parties, seen as responsible for not having been able to adapt to citizens' demands. The French political system, which in the seventies and eighties was a well-oiled machine, is said to have slowly frozen up, putting democracy in France in a critical situation.

The present chapter aims to put this viewpoint in proper perspective and considerably qualify it. The point here is not to deny voter dissatisfaction and the electorate's increasing wariness of the political class, nor to claim that the successive governments have conducted the best-suited and most effective policies, nor even to dismiss the tensions that have fraught the bipolar party system which gradually took shape in the 1970s. By focusing on the functioning and evolution of the French party system, I instead intend to show how it has adapted since the early days of the Fifth Republic to the various constraints weighing on its performance and to what extent the crisis it seems currently to be undergoing is largely due to the very real contradictions facing it. Contrary to a widely entertained idea, the French party system has not remained either inert or unresponsive to the citizenry.

To demonstrate this, it should first be recalled that representing voters is not the sole task of a party system. Its purpose is also to make institutions function and contribute to the exercise of power. An overall assessment of its performance must therefore take into account the way it executes these various functions.

To understand the new tensions and transformations that have affected the French party system since the mid-eighties, it is important to examine first how a new relationship was established between the parties and Fifth Republic institutions in the preceding period.

1. Establishment of the bipolar multiparty system with two dominant parties

The system that gradually took shape during the 1960s and 1970s resulted from the failure of two conflicting conceptions of institutions that clashed in the early years of the Fifth Republic. The Fourth Republic succumbed to ministerial instability and an inability to settle the issue of the constitution and the Algerian question. The real power lay in Parliament. The President did not govern and council of minister presidents changed with every new political alliance that was made and undone in Parliament, as had been the case under the Third Republic. Political parties dominated the political system.

In 1958, and especially in 1962 with the constitutional revision instituting the election of the French President by universal suffrage, the new constitution, in the mind of General de Gaulle, its principal author, primarily intended to restore most of the power to the executive and, by subjugating the Prime Minister to the President, diminish the power of the Parliament and destroy the "rule of the parties." Now elected by popular suffrage and wielding the power to hold referendums, the President established a direct relationship with the voters and owed his power to them alone.

Suffice it to say here that, from 1958 to 1969, two conflicting interpretations of the constitution pitted De Gaulle against the parties born of the former republics and attached to the power of Parliament and the political parties' role in the system's functioning. The President, elected by the people, could dissolve the National Assembly, but the latter could censure and therefore dismiss the government. The parties' efforts to prevent the presidentialization of the regime and the President's symmetrical attempts to destroy the parties' influence both failed. The parties were smashed at the polls in 1962, and General de Gaulle, having lost the referendum in 1969, resigned. The two differing conceptions, one plebiscitary, the other parliamentarist, proved inapplicable. The political forces were thus obliged to redefine their conceptions and use of institutions.

The constitutional provisions (Duhamel and Parodi 1988), the electoral laws in effect and the way in which the first presidential election by universal suffrage took place in 1965 fostered a bipolarization of political forces (Schlesinger and Schlesinger 2000). The two main political actors in the period following De Gaulle's departure, Georges Pompidou and François Mitterrand, grasped this. Both of them worked within their party to deeply transform the system to adapt it to all of the institutional and political constraints it faced. The battle between partisans and opponents of the new regime changed into a combat between two opposing political camps within this new system. Paradoxically, this sea change, which ran counter to the hopes of the regime's founder, would ensure the viability of a system that could thus survive its founder without perpetual battles over its very nature.

Georges Pompidou, the new President elected in 1969, who from 1962 to 1968 had been General de Gaulle's Prime Minister, and François Mitterrand, the sole candidate on the left to run in the 1965 presidential election, and who had forced General de Gaulle to go a second ballot and garnered against him 45 percent of the votes cast in the second round of voting, partly shared De Gaulle's views about how the institutions should function. But each of them were up against different situations. Both believed that the primacy of the presidential office would be – or should be – upheld and that the presidential election therefore remained the most important election in the French political system, but they also believed that the plebiscitary Fifth Republic could not – or should not – survive its founder. The institutional constraint was a determining factor: presidential power should be able to rely on a parliamentary majority. This meant that for the President, building such a majority should be, despite what General de Gaulle claimed, a focal objective of his policy.

Pompidou and Mitterrand also both felt that political parties necessarily played a major role in forming parliamentary majorities. They each intended to build a system of party alliances hinging on a central cleavage between left and right, the only configuration capable in their minds of ensuring victory at the polls. If their respective plans were to come to fruition, it would entail the disappearance of an autonomous center.

Aside from their personal political qualities, it is because these two leaders best understood at once the constraints and opportunities provided by the new institutional system that they were able to play a flagship role in transforming the party system and that each won in turn. They fulfilled the three prerequisites for gradually setting up a new political system: priority given to the presidential election, bipolarization of the party system and creation of two major parties, each heading up a broad and solid alliance. Between 1965 and François Mitterrand's election in 1981, a left–right bipolar multiparty system with two dominant parties, the Gaullist party and the Socialist Party, took shape (Duhamel and Grunberg 2001).

Though these two leaders' conceptions of Fifth Republic political institutions were largely in agreement, the difficulties they each had to face in order to make them prevail differed. The transformation of the political system required the parties to become more "presidentialized" and the regime to become more "partisan." The first condition was easier to fulfill for the right than for the left since the Gaullist party had been created as a presidential party from the start, whereas the leftist parties had never come to terms with the constitutional revision of 1962. In contrast, the second condition was easier for the left to fulfill than the right, since the left was partisan by nature whereas General de Gaulle's hostility toward political parties had inspired the new institutional design.

With the 1973 legislative elections, the right began to gather around the Gaullist party UDR (Union pour la Défense de la République) both from an electoral and parliamentary standpoint. These elections also marked the defeat of the center, which was opposed to bipolarization and had already suffered a loss in the second ballot of the 1969 presidential election when its candidate, Alain Poher, was beaten by Georges Pompidou. These elections were the center's last attempt to thwart the establishment of bipolarization on the basis of a left–right cleavage. With the death of Georges Pompidou in 1974, support of a segment of the Gaullists for a moderate candidate in favor of the Fifth Republic, Valéry Giscard d'Estaing, and his rallying to the center enabled the right-wing parties to join forces.

On the left, the bipolarization rationale necessitated reintroducing the Communist Party onto the mainstream political game board. The non-communist left also had to unite to ensure its ascendancy over the left on the whole, a precondition for it to win. It took François Mitterrand 16 years to impose his views and win the presidential election. Without reviewing this period in detail, let us mention here only the major political issues facing the left and François Mitterrand's achievements.

In order to govern, the socialists and the communists first had to agree to join forces, which was not a foregone conclusion on either side. By rallying the left under his name in 1965, François Mitterrand made a serious wager that he would take control of his camp. But, as his undertaking gained credibility, he had to face both the socialists and radicals, who did not want to leave him the leadership of the non-communist left, and the communists, who did not want to leave the leadership of the left to the socialists. Despite repeated failures, François Mitterrand scored four decisive points during this period, one of them, in 1969, by default.

In 1969, prevented by the communists as well as his rivals in the non-communist left from being the left's presidential candidate again, he took advantage of the electoral rout of the candidate fielded by the SFIO (Section Française de l'Internationale Ouvrière) socialists and the radicals in the first round of voting (5 percent) and the failure of the centrist candidate backed by the socialists in the second ballot. These failures showed that a union of the left, which François Mitterrand had been calling for, was the only credible electoral alternative to the Gaullists in power.

In 1971, François Mitterrand took control of the Socialist Party and rebuilt it with the central aim of making it a genuine party of government. This decisive move meant that the socialists, by choosing as their leader a man who drew his legitimacy from the election battle of 1965, recognized at least tacitly that the presidential election was the major election date. In 1972, the signature of a common government program between the socialists and the communists sealed the Union of the Left and reintroduced the Communist Party into the political game. Finally, the 1974 presidential election, held after the death of President Pompidou, in which Giscard d'Estaing beat Mitterrand in the second ballot with 51 percent of the votes cast, clearly marked the establishment of bipolarization based on an alliance on the left and one on the right.

The formation of right and left electoral and parliamentary alliances did not prevent intense competition within each camp. Presidential elections have provided particular opportunities for this competition to come to the fore. The first phase of competition for domination on both the left and the right was played out in the period ranging from 1974 to 1981.

As of 1974, the communists, rightly fearing that the Socialist Party, whose candidate they had backed already in the first round of the presidential election, would become the most powerful group in the National Assembly although it had only lost the presidential election by a slim margin, and decided to combat their former ally. On the right, Jacques Chirac, in 1976, after having contributed to Valéry Giscard d'Estaing's victory against his own party and being named Prime Minister by him, decided to take control of the Gaullist party and retake the leadership of the right for the Gaullists. He thus had to stand against the President and therefore resigned as Prime Minister.

The only possible way for the communists and the Gaullists to prevent each of their ally-opponents from gaining the leadership of their camp was to make them lose the elections. On the left, the communists deliberately provoked the defeat of the left in the 1978 legislative elections when it had a strong chance of winning. On the right, in 1978, Valéry Giscard d'Estaing had brought the centrists, moderates and liberals, rallied to the Fifth Republic together, under a new party banner – or rather a federation of parties – the UDF (Union for French democracy) so as to be in the best possible position to compete with the Gaullist party recreated by Jacques Chirac and now named the RPR (Rally for the Republic). Chirac wanted to prevent Valéry Giscard d'Estaing from being reelected in the 1981 elections by running against him in the first round and actually campaigning against him in the second. The incumbent President was beaten by François Mitterrand in the second ballot. Once he had dissolved the National Assembly, Mitterrand enjoyed an absolute majority in the new legislature, having been way ahead of the communist candidate in the first round. The communist defeat was such that the Communist Party, crushed by its score, officially called its electorate to vote for the socialist candidate in the second ballot.

Thus in the aftermath of the 1981 presidential election, the party system was bipolarized with four major parties, two on the left and two on the right. In each camp one party managed to hold sway. On the left, the socialists definitively took the lead over the communists, who agreed to participate in a subordinate position in the new government headed by the socialist Pierre Mauroy. On the right, although the Gaullist leadership was not yet clearly established, the incumbent President's defeat and the slightly more favorable parliamentary position of the Gaullists over the moderates should logically have allowed the former to recover leadership on the right. At the start of a new seven-year term, the party system could be described as a left–right bipolar multiparty system with two dominant parties that allowed changeovers in power between the two political blocs. From an institutional standpoint these transfers did not constitute a break. The legislative victory won by François Mitterrand following his election as President allowed him to pursue the Gaullist institutional practice that he had so ardently fought against: to hold the greatest power in his hands, that of appointing and dismissing his Prime Minister at will. Political changeover in no way modified the primacy of the president's power or the importance of the presidential election. The institutions of the Fifth Republic endured in the face of power transfers. The institutions and electoral laws thus largely contributed to transforming the party system, which had to adapt to the new institutions. The parties became more presidentialist, all the more to make the political system more partisan. It was up to them to back a credible candidate in the presidential election and then leave the candidate and would-be future French President considerable leeway. In exchange, they regained importance as actors in French politics. Thus, the party system ensured both the representation of the French citizens, since the near totality of voters had cast their ballot for one of the two major coalitions. It also ensured the working of institutions. Presidents with a parliamentary majority governed in stable conditions and were able to make decisions. The political system functioned effectively, whatever one might feel about its strong presidentialism, and the French seemed generally satisfied with their institutions. The system, unlike those under the previous republics, had managed to withstand the serious crises it had to face: the Algerian war, the constitutional revision of 1962, the events of 1968 and General de Gaulle's resignation.

2. Forces destabilizing the system (1981–2002)

Between 1981 and 2002, a number of different types of forces threatened to destabilize the system gradually built up between 1969 and 1981. They operated on three different levels: the institutional level, with challenges to the primacy of the presidency during the three periods of cohabitation (power-sharing) between a president from one political camp and a prime minister from the other; the level of left–right bipolarization, with the fragmentation of the party system; and the level of the two dominant parties, each facing new difficulties in forming broad and solid coalitions. What looks like a crisis of representation is the product of these three elements, which should be kept distinct.

The institutional level

The way the regime had evolved since 1969 made it into a truly mixed presidential/parliamentary system, and the successive presidents after General de Gaulle's departure knew that the primacy of the presidency relied on the existence of a majority favorable to the President in the National Assembly.

In 1986, President Mitterrand's legislative defeat prompted him to make two major decisions for the system's future. In the rationale of a parliamentary regime he appointed as Prime Minister the leader of the new majority, Jacques Chirac, but in a presidential rationale he decided to remain as head of state, his office having been awarded to him via the direct vote of the French citizens. Did these decisions help provoke a crisis of representation and/or a crisis of power?

From the representation standpoint, the answer must be put in perspective. On one hand, François Mitterrand's decision was in keeping with the rationale of representation. The French did not want a regime crisis and accepted power-sharing up until midway through the third period of cohabitation, around the year 2000. On the other hand, the necessary compromises that power-sharing required of both the two main opponents and the parties that backed them probably helped to blur the dividing lines between the two camps. The consequential absence of outright opposition may have promoted the electoral boom of anti-system parties, the National Front in particular. The head-on opposition between socialist Prime Minister Lionel Jospin and President Jacques Chirac during the presidential campaign of 2002, despite their having co-governed for five years, probably disturbed a share of the electorate. The Prime Minister's violent stand against cohabitation also contributed to the increasingly negative response to it by the French. But in the end, the fact that the two major political forces agreed to play the game of power-sharing does not seem to have betrayed the logic of representation, given the constraints of the institutional system and the French opinions toward it over the course of the 1986–2002 period.

From the standpoint of continuity and effective exercise of power, the periods of cohabitation do not seem to have significantly affected the functioning of the system despite the ongoing rivalry between the two heads of the executive. The Prime Minister conducted domestic policy. As for foreign policy and defense, although the President's role was substantial, the two saw eye to eye on the main issues. The President and the Prime Minister on the whole jointly ensured policy continuity.

Thus the periods of cohabitation, despite their usual disadvantages, did not prevent the regime from continuing to represent its citizens – honoring the voters' choice at both the legislative and presidential level – nor from ensuring the continuity and effective functioning of the executive. The institutional reform of 2002 – reducing the presidential term from seven years to five, ratified by referendum, and later the inversion of the election calendar called for and implemented by Lionel Jospin, which placed the 2002 presidential election before the legislative elections – combined with Jacques Chirac's reelection followed by his party's triumph in the legislative elections, have dismissed the prospect of cohabitation for some time in the near future. The 2002 election sequence reestablished the functioning of the Fifth Republic regime as it originally existed. The primacy of the executive was completely restored. The President appointed a Prime Minister of his choice from his own camp and enjoyed an absolute majority in the National Assembly. As Pierre Avril (2003) explains, the new cabinet "is a presidential government as attested in the communiqué published after the Council of Ministers on May 10, which set the 'main orientations decided by the President,' as well as Raffarin's statement on radio station RTL on the 12th: 'I am here to implement the President's declarations.' " The likelihood that legislative elections will no longer be held during a presidential term further increases the presidential nature of the government. This new era inaugurates the "five-year Fifth," in other words "a parliamentary democracy conducted by the President" (Duhamel and Grunberg 2002). The institutions have finally reached the logical conclusion of the 1958 compromise and the 1962 revision. Whatever their drawbacks in this configuration (diminished role of the Parliament and the Prime Minister, excessive power to the President, central importance of legislative elections but only better to establish the power of the President), the current advocates in favor of founding a Sixth Republic in such conditions seem highly optimistic. It is the Fifth Republic, at once restored, strengthened and partly modified, that has yet again prevailed. The institutions set up in 1958–62 may have changed, as can be seen in their capacity to adapt, but in accordance with the dynamic that grew out of the contradictory rationales that presided over their foundation.

If there is still a crisis of representation today, then cohabitation cannot be said to be the root of it. Jacques Chirac, reelected with a voter turnout of 80 percent and 82 percent of the votes cast, whatever the particular political circumstances that held sway over his election, has both the legitimacy and the means to fully exercise power and ensure its continuity.

The level of left–right bipolarization

The dual objective that can be assigned to an effective party system – to represent the people and ensure the continuity of government – was greatly facilitated in the period prior to the 1981 change of power by the bipolarization of this system, a bipolarization that was tightly bound by the logic of majority rule governing the legislative and presidential elections. During this period, nearly all the votes cast were shared among four parties (the Socialist Party, Communist Party, Rally for the Republic and Union for French Democracy), which formed two competing alliances, one on the left, the other on the right. In 1984, the situation changed considerably. A certain number of new or previously marginal political groupings, on the strength of their success at the polls, attempted to loosen the grip of bipolarization and pose a challenge to the domination of the left–right cleavage. Bipolarization was then in jeopardy.

The main reason for this crisis in bipolarization should first be sought in the effects of this first power transfer. It should first be pointed out that this power change, painstakingly prepared by François Mitterrand, was itself proof of the capacity of institutions and the party system to ensure voter representation. In fact, since 1958, the right had been in power without interruption. A slim half of the electorate had thus never been represented in government, except in the National Assembly. The power change proved not only that the institutions allowed the opposition to rise to power but also that the party system had been organized in such a way that the opposition could acquire enough strength and credibility for the electorate to vote in a new team if they were dissatisfied with the authorities in power.

But in rising to power the left lost a good deal of the legitimacy it had acquired in its opposition to right-wing rule. The Communist Party in particular, already on the decline, was in serious danger of not being able to exercise its usual *fonction tribunitienne*, which according to Georges Lavau had given it its strength, identity and usefulness.

The constraints of governing, and in particular economic constraints, which first forced the socialist government to abandon its policy of "breaking" with capitalism in 1983, and then to adopt stringent economic and social measures not unlike those of the previous government, transformed the image of left-wing parties from opposition parties into management parties in the context of a market economy. The left thus fell into step with mainstream parties.

On the right, the vanquished parties did not adopt a radically opposite stance, familiar with the constraints of governing and hoping to return swiftly to office. The ousted president Giscard d'Estaing had given his previous cabinet a centrist image despite the more conservative evolution of the final years of his seven-year term, and his doctrine was to govern in the center with the middle classes. Despite their numerous differences, some of them major, left and right were no longer at loggerheads on the economy, the direction society should take, the central values of republican humanism, or the building of the European Community. The many changeovers that have occurred since then have convinced a large segment of the electorate that the policies of the left and right do not differ significantly. This has opened a gap for outsider parties.

But does that mean the rapprochement of the two major parties and two major alliances can be considered to have fueled the crisis of representation and has it jeopardized the left–right bipolarization of the system that allows changeovers in power? Was this rapprochement at odds with the voters' wishes? How did the party system react, particularly as regards the development of new parties? Have the changes in this system provoked a crisis of bipolarization and fragmented the system, putting in jeopardy the exercise of power and continuity of government?

Party and electoral fragmentation

Beginning in 1983–84, party and electoral fragmentation seemed to have challenged the control the two major coalitions had managed to exercise over the electorate. Five types of parties or movements developed. They are the extreme right, the ecologists, the hunting movement, *souverainiste* parties and the extreme left. Each of them attempted to weaken the ascendancy of the left–right cleavage over French politics. Each was trying to expand its influence by exploiting one or more themes likely to mobilize significant segments of public opinion from an electoral standpoint. These themes are, respectively, immigration and across-the-board criticism of the political class, nuclear power and environmental protection, defense of regional identities and lifestyles in the face of "orders from Brussels," the fight against a federal Europe and the relinquishment of sovereignty, and lastly the struggle against the market economy and economic liberalism. It is true that on each of these themes, at least as far as the policies implemented are concerned, the two major coalitions were closer to one another, whatever their disagreements may have been, than the peripheral forces attacking them. Both the moderate left and the moderate right accepted the market economy, combated xenophobic tendencies, took part in the European integration process and defended nuclear power production.

The development of these various peripheral parties and movements, ending in a dramatic increase in party fragmentation, at least shows that the system did not prevent the representation of voters who did not identify with the policies conducted by the two major coalitions.

The main factor destabilizing the bipolar system came from the Front National (FN). By capturing 11 percent of the votes cast in the 1984 European elections, it gradually imposed itself as the "anti-establishment," nationalist, xenophobic and authoritarian party. It attacked all "system parties," called the "gang of four." On the eve of the 1986 legislative elections, which polls gave up for lost for the left, François Mitterrand, to rescue the socialist parliamentary group from a defeat that the vote on a majority basis would have produced, reinstated voting by proportional representation at the risk – some say with the aim – of giving the FN a larger parliamentary representation than it would have gained had the proportional voting system been maintained. This fundamental change in election procedure could have produced a new, ungovernable National Assembly, thereby giving the President some leeway. But the moderate right still managed to secure a slim majority in the National Assembly. It immediately learned its lesson from the situation by reinstating the vote on a majority basis in the next legislative elections. This would prevent the FN from having any deputies in Parliament, or only a handful. But throughout the entire period it remained an electoral force to be reckoned with. Twice it threatened to destabilize the system, first during the early legislative elections in 1997 and then in the 1998 regional elections. In fact, though it no longer managed to have any elected representatives, the FN was still able to inflict considerable harm on the right by depriving it of victories at the polls. In the 1997 elections, despite the high threshold required to remain in the second ballot (12.5 percent of registered voters), its new high score of 15 percent allowed it to stay in the run-off ballot in 132 legislative constituencies, thus contributing to the defeat of the Chiraquian right. The following year, the regional elections, held by the proportional representation system, triggered serious political crises in several regions, since the right needed the extreme-right elected officials' vote to hold on to the presidency of the regional council. The moderate right was torn apart by this conflict over whether or not it was legitimate for it to strike up alliances, at least at the regional level, with the extreme right.

Jacques Chirac took a strong stand against any alliance with the FN. The moderate right was to remain threatened for a long time by a powerful and hostile extreme-right party.

On the left, the socialists had to face competition from the ecologist movement, which was hostile to the left–right cleavage. As with the FN, it was also an election held under the proportional representation system, the 1989 European elections, that handed the ecologists their first major success: 11 percent of the votes cast. The 1992 regional elections saw a repeat performance, bringing several ecologist representatives into regional councils. The socialists, weakened and in disarray, were thus confronted with a new force that intended to hold to its strategy of "neither left nor right."

Luckily for the socialists, this success was short-lived, for reasons having partly to do with internal divisions in the ecologist movement, the weakness of its leadership and doubts regarding its aims and its strategy. During the 1993 legislative elections, the socialist defeat was not counterbalanced by further progress on the part of the ecologists. On the contrary, the ecologists won a mere 7 percent of the vote and only 7 deputies in Parliament, then only 5 percent for the two lists fielded in the 1994 European elections. During the 1995 presidential election, Green candidate Dominique Voynet garnered only 3.5 percent of the vote and subtly urged her electorate to vote for Lionel Jospin in the second ballot. The Greens, which now represented most of the ecologist movement as an organized political group, moved closer to the socialists and abandoned its "neither left nor right" party line. Ecologist hopes of breaking the mold of bipolarization were shattered.

Symmetrically, the Socialist Party was soon convinced of the need to reach an agreement with the ecologist movement and incorporate a considerable share of its platform into its program. In 1997, the Greens were part of a socialist-centered alliance that included the communists, the center left "radical" and Jean-Pierre Chevènement's supporters. After the victory of what was henceforth labeled the "plural majority," the Greens entered the cabinet headed by Lionel Jospin. The left-wing pole was thus for the most part reconstructed. From 1997 to 2002, the Greens took part in government. Hence, during this period, the socialists did not remain inactive, and the formation of the plural majority attests to the priority the socialists gave to achieving unity among the left wing.

It should still be pointed out that as of the 1995 presidential election, the Trotskyite extreme left achieved much higher scores than before, taking advantage of the PCF's weakness and its entrance into mainstream politics, and later its participation in government: 5 percent in 1995 and 5 percent again in the 1999 European elections as well as significant scores in several municipal elections that same year. Although the extreme left is not – or not yet – a real force in the legislative elections, its advances in other elections show that in time it may present a danger to the governmental left and also threaten bipolarization.

The last real threat to bipolarization in this period is represented by the birth of *souverainiste* movements that cropped up during the campaign to ratify the Maastricht Treaty in 1992. The leaders of the two main right-wing parties, the RPR and the UDF, both in favor of ratifying the European Union Treaty, had to face opposition from within, culminating in splits in both parties. In 1994, Philippe de Villiers, UDF deputy, left his party to found the MPF (Mouvement pour la France). In the 1994 European elections, he presented a list that garnered 12 percent of the votes cast. In the 1999 European elections, Charles Pasqua, who had left the RPR, struck up an alliance with Philippe de Villiers to present a *souverainiste* list that won 13 percent of the vote, beating the RPR–UDF. In November of the same year, these two leaders founded a new, forthrightly *souverainiste* party called the RPF (Rassemblement Pour la France).

On the left, Jean-Pierre Chevéenement, who had also called for a "no" vote in the 1992 referendum and had left the Socialist Party to found the Mouvement des Citoyens but still belonged to the left-wing coalition, resigned in 2000 and broke with Lionel Jospin, then with the left entirely. On the eve of the 2002 presidential election, he created a new movement, the Pôle réepublicain, a *souverainiste* group that rejects both the left- and right-wing labels.

On the eve of the 2002 presidential election, bipolarization seemed in jeopardy. On the left, the plural majority survived, although it lost all offensive capacity and its future seemed doubtful. The rise of the extreme left added to the incumbent majority's difficulties. On the right, the National Front and the *souverainistes* also constituted a threat to bipolarization. Moreover, relations between the UDF and the RPR grew tense. The 2002 elections thus represented a moment of truth for the party system.

Party fragmentation increased with the first ballot of the 2002 presidential election. Sixteen candidates were in the running, the highest figure in the history of the Fifth Republic. The two major coalitions together won their lowest score ever, 61 percent, compared to 30 percent for candidates from the extreme parties and nearly 10 percent for "neither left nor right" candidates. But mainly, Le Pen came in second, and Lionel Jospin was eliminated (Table 9.1). The second ballot was to pit a right-wing candidate against an extreme-right candidate.

Table 9.1 Party system, presidential candidacies and results of the first ballot

Party system	Party	Candidates	Votes
Extreme Left	LO	Laguiller	5.7
	LCR	Besancenot	4.3
	PT	Gluckstein	0.5
Moderate Left	PS	Jospin	16.2
	PC	Hue	3.4
	Green	Mamère	5.3
	Radical	Taubira	2.3
Former Moderate Left (pro-sovereignty)	Mouvement des Citoyens	Chevènement	5.3
Moderate Right	RPR	Chirac	19.9
	UDF	Bayrou	6.8
	DL	Madelin	3.9
		Lepage	1.9
		Boutin	1.2
Former Moderate	MPF		
Right (pro-sovereignty)	RPF		
Anti-European regionalist	CPNT	Saint-Josse	4.1
Extreme Right	FN	Le Pen	16.9
	MEN	Mégret	2.3

Bipolarization: preserved but weakened

Despite the earth-shattering result of Lionel Jospin's elimination, close scrutiny of the overall electoral sequence in 2002 and the political fallout show that bipolarization was preserved, even if it is weakened today.

Two factors combine to ensure its preservation: voter behavior and the effects of the voting system used in the legislative elections.

The second ballot of the presidential election showed that a tally of the votes of the extreme parties on the left and the right, and more generally those that were not part of either major coalition, yielded no political implication. In fact, all voters except for those of the extreme right came out in strength against the National Front candidate (Table 9.2).

The very clear rejection of the extreme right registered in the second ballot of the presidential election proves that the extreme-right/non-extreme-right cleavage cannot be said to replace the left–right cleavage. The moderate right candidate, for whom the left-wing electorate voted en masse, garnered over 80 percent of the votes, with a noticeable rise in voter turnout from the first ballot to the second (from 72 percent to 80 percent).

Already in the first ballot, the inability of the right-wing *souverainistes* to field a candidate and Jean-Pierre Chevènement's disappointing score did

Table 9.2 Vote transfers between the two ballots of the 2002 presidential election

	Vote in the second ballot			
Vote in the first ballot	**Abstention, blank or void ballot, NA**	**Chirac**	**Le Pen**	**Total**
Laguiller	33	63	4	100
Besancenot	18	77	5	100
Hue	14	79	7	100
Jospin	21	76	3	100
Mamère	10	86	4	100
Chevènement	27	70	3	100
Bayrou	10	88	2	100
Chirac	4	94	2	100
Madelin	2	94	4	100
Saint Josse	7	77	16	100
Le Pen	8	16	76	100
Abstention, blank and void	48	46	6	100
Total electorate	23	63	14	100

Source: CEVIPOF-CIDSP Survey May 2002

much to ward off the danger this current posed for the survival of bipolarization.

In the June 2002 legislative elections (Table 9.3), the moderate left and the moderate right together scored more votes than in the 1995 and 1997 elections, 80 percent, thus increasing their combined score in the presidential election by more than 20 points. The extreme left and the "neither left nor rights" were wiped out and the extreme right only captured 12.5 percent (Table 9.3).

In the second ballot of the legislative elections, the voting system allowed the two major coalitions to convert their scores in the first ballot into a triumph as far as seats were concerned. In the second ballot, out of the 516 constituencies where at least two candidates were in the running, there was a battle between moderate left and moderate right in 469 of them. Out of the 577 candidates elected, absolutely all of them were backed in the second ballot by one of the two major coalitions on the left or the moderate right (Table 9.4). The moderate right, with 399 seats, once again came to power, thus allowing for a new political changeover, and the moderate left, with the remainder of the seats, formed the new opposition, thus preserving political bipolarization at the parliamentary level.

The level of the dominant parties

For bipolarization to function effectively in a mixed parliamentary and presidential system, the parties in each of the two camps must be able both

Table 9.3 Results of the presidential and the parliamentary elections 1995–2002 (percentages)

	Presidential Election 1995 First Round	**Parliamentary Elections 1997 First Round**	**Presidential Elections 2002 First Round**	**Parliamentary Elections 2002 First Round**
Extreme Left	5.3	2.1	10.4	2.8
Moderate Left	35.2	41.5	27.2	37.1
Moderate Right	39.4	36.5	33.7	42.3
Extreme Right	15.3	15.1	19.2	12.6
Neither Left nor Right and Pro-sovereignty	4.7	4.8	9.5	5.2
Moderate Left + Moderate Right	74.6	78.0	60.9	80.6

to form broad and solid alliances and have at least one credible presidential candidate who is capable of making it to the second ballot of this election. Both camps made great efforts to adapt in this regard, but huge difficulties remained that laid their future on the line. In each of the two camps, the domination of one party enabled them to adapt during the previous period.

In the period from 1981 to 2001, the two main parties, the Gaullist party and the Socialist Party, managed to dominate their camps and form electoral and parliamentary alliances, but not without major difficulties and periods of crisis (1992–95 for the left, 1994–99 for the right). Their domination was not totally guaranteed. On the left, the Communist Party walked out on the government in 1984 and half-heartedly opposed the socialists. It wasn't until 1997 that it once again took part in a socialist government. In the course of the last two years of the socialist legislature, it showed less and less respect for governmental cohesion, sometimes calling for protests against the government of which it was part. As for the Greens, even if they participated in the Jospin cabinet, they also did not hesitate to take a hostile attitude toward the socialists on a number of occasions.

The electoral system nevertheless greatly facilitated socialist domination. The communists' decline forced them to form electoral alliances with the socialists to keep some of their positions. As for the Greens, without an alliance with the socialists, they could not win seats in the National Assembly. But, as the 2002 elections drew closer, it appeared clearly that the plural left recipe had run its course politically, even if it had survived from an electoral standpoint. The socialists' allies increasingly resented the Socialist Party's increasingly evident domination. The Socialist Party was confronted with the dashed hopes of the ecologists, the swift decline of the communists and the Mouvement des Citoyens' growing assertion of its difference. Its ability to rally the left to it seemed doubtful.

The right did not experience the same type of difficulties. The RPR–UDF alliance was fairly solid, but the issue of the moderate right's leadership had not yet been definitely settled. The Gaullists may well have been the dominant party, but this domination had an Achilles' heel: the lack of a procedure for nominating a joint candidate for the presidential election (Haegel 2002). The Gaullists at first took advantage of this drawback, which had enabled them to help defeat incumbent President Giscard d'Estaing in the 1981 elections and regain the leadership of the right. But later, in 1988, Jacques Chirac had to face competition from UDF candidate Raymond Barre, which contributed to his defeat against Françcois Mitterrand. Then, in 1995, Edouard Balladur, the RPR candidate backed by the UDF, nearly cost Chirac defeat a second time. The 1998–2001 period is contradictory from the standpoint of RPR dominance. On the one hand this dominance was strengthened by the breakup of its rival, the UDF, shattered by the departure of Alain Madelin (Démocratie Libérale) and Charles Million who formed "La Droite." But on the other hand, a smaller but more homogenous UDF united behind a true centrist leader, François Bayrou, was intent on reinforcing its autonomy with respect to the RPR. On the eve of the 2002 election, the incumbent President was politically weakened and his leadership called into question.

As they went into the 2002 presidential election, each of the two major parties faced mounting difficulties both from the standpoint of forming alliances and control over the process of nominating candidates.

The 2002 presidential election heightened these difficulties considerably, although from this dual perspective the right seemed in a better position than the left. Neither the Gaullist party nor the Socialist Party was capable of controlling the nomination of candidates in its own camp. On the left five candidates from the plural left and three from the Trotskyite parties all ran. On the right, there were five candidates in the parliamentary opposition running along with two from the extreme right. The two main leaders of the two major parties, Chirac and Jospin, consequently won only 36 percent of the votes cast in the first ballot, compared with 43 percent in 1995. The elimination of Lionel Jospin further reinforced the impression that the two major political groupings were weakened. Chirac's 82-percent score in the second ballot did not entirely wipe out his poor score in the first ballot. More generally speaking, in the future the two major parties will clearly have to try to shield themselves from being eliminated in the first ballot, a lingering threat as long as the National Front remains in the running.

The moderate right was determined to react quickly to this situation and managed to. The reinforcement of the RPR's dominance through the creation of the UMP is one of the most significant changes that have occurred in the party system in recent years. For this reason it warrants particular attention (Haegel 2002).

Several vain attempts had been launched over the past years within the moderate right to federate its various currents within a major right-wing party. But the situation has changed since 2002. The precedent set by the 1995 presidential election in which Jacques Chirac had to run against Edouard Balladur, then the UDF's assertion of its independence, convinced Jacques Chirac and Alain Juppé that legislative and parliamentary accords no longer sufficed. Right-wing parties needed to go a step further in adapting to the presidential logic of the regime. To reduce the risks of a profusion of candidacies in the first ballot of the presidential election and to better ensure coherent and continuous support from the right's elected officials for a future right-wing government the idea was to create a big party bringing together the various right-wing currents. The plan, put forward and defended by Alain Juppé, had as little chance of succeeding as previous attempts, since the party apparatuses were, understandably, not in favor of engineering their own disappearance. But the unique set of circumstances that prevailed in the 2002 presidential election finally offered a serious opportunity to put this plan into action.

The profusion of candidacies within the moderate right in the first ballot prevented Jacques Chirac from garnering more than 20 percent of the votes cast, and if the right-wing *souverainiste* movement had been able to field a good candidate, the incumbent President may well have met a similar fate to that of the Prime Minister. The downward trend of scores of the two primary candidates in the presidential election presented the serious disadvantage of diminishing the legitimacy of the elected president. It was time for the right to organize better so that its candidate would enjoy a margin of safety and a high enough score already in the first ballot. The obvious unsuitability of party politics to the presidential election weighed in favor of the advocates for reform. But it was above all the division and the weak scores of the two other main moderate right candidates (Bayrou 6.8 percent, Madelin 3.9 percent) that enabled Alain Juppé to get things moving. For the first time, the RPR was clearly ahead of the UDF. Finally, the very evening of the first ballot, it was clear that Jacques Chirac would be reelected President with a very ample majority. He thus had all the cards in hand to put his plan into action immediately.

On 23 April 2002, two days after the first ballot of the presidential election, the UMP (Union pour la Majoritée Présidentielle) was officially created. On 11 May a preliminary list of candidates was published, 52 percent of them from the RPR, 20 percent from the UDF and 16 percent from DL. Only about one hundred UDF candidates refused to don the UMP label. On 16 June, the UMP won 33 percent of the votes cast and 369 deputies, compared to 5 percent for the UDF and only 22 seats, or 92 percent of the seats totaled by the moderate right, whereas in 1993 and 1997 it had won a little more than half. With an absolute majority of deputies all by itself, the UMP did not need any help from the UDF.

Things moved swiftly after that. On 18 June, Alain Juppé was appointed president of the new party, which held its founding conference on 17 November once the DL and the RPR had merged on 21 September. The big right-wing party finally existed. Its dominance over the moderate right was unquestionable. The UDF was no longer a dangerous competitor. To finish the job, in other words to bring the UDF to submission, Alain Juppé, with the agreement of Jacques Chirac and Jean-Pierre Raffarin, drafted an election law for the regional elections that delivered yet another severe blow to the UDF. It required a total of 10 percent of registered voters in order to qualify for the second ballot of the regional elections. This in fact obliged the dominated UDF to strike alliances with the UMP as early as the first ballot. François Bayrou, incensed at this maneuver but deprived of any leeway since the UDF was part of the government, could not vote in favor of the motion of censorship the left filed against this project in February 2003.

Thus, on the right, the domination of the Gaullist party – transformed and expanded into the UMP – over the moderate right was reinforced considerably (Tables 9.4 and 9.5). But, especially, it should be remembered here that once again changes that occurred in the party system were brought about by institutional constraints. The primacy of the presidential office fosters the creation of genuine presidential parties bringing together most of the trends and parties of a single political camp.

The right's attempt to adapt the party system to the rationales and constraints of the presidential election demonstrates the reactive capacity of political organizations. It will probably have positive consequences in the future for the new UMP Party, but at the same time it raises certain difficulties for it, at least in the short term. In fact, the strategy that led to the creation of the UMP sidelined the two other major moderate right parties. Démocratie Libérale was absorbed by the UMP, and the UDF severely weakened. In this rationale, Alain Juppé's strategy to weaken the UDF further by changing the voting system for the regional elections, which had been by proportional representation and is now on a majority basis, and by setting a very high threshold for a list to stay in the running in the second ballot, was coherent. This attempt was only partly successful, because the threshold first chosen was finally lowered. But mainly, François Bayrou, the UDF party leader, justifiably feeling attacked and his party threatened, chose a tactic of direct and open confrontation with the UMP that may cause problems for the latter in the future. As a result, the UMP/UDF alliance is currently on the rocks. For the moment, the absolute majority it enjoys in the National Assembly protects Chirac's party. But, in the event of political and electoral difficulties, the end of the right-wing alliance could seriously weaken the right. This situation suggests that in a mixed parliamentary and presidential regime, the dual constraint for the dominant party to impose its domination over its camp while forming solid and lasting alliances within it is difficult to meet, all the more so since a segment of the right, the extreme right, remains on the outside but represents a considerable electoral force. In other countries, the moderate right has chosen to govern in collaboration with the extreme right. In France, for historic reasons and because of the voting systems, the right can discard this option. But it consequently lays bare a certain electoral vulnerability.

The Socialist Party is faced with a similar challenge, but it is not in a position to meet it using similar methods. Like the UMP, it is clearly the primary force in its camp (Tables 9.4 and 9.5).

Table 9.4 Results of the presidential and the parliamentary elections 1995–2002 (percentages)

	Presidential Election 1995 First Round	**Parliamentary Election 1997 First round**	**Presidential Election 2002 First round**	**Parliamentary Elections 2002 First round**
PS	23.3	23.5	16.2	24.1
PC	8.6	9.9	3.4	4.8
Greens	3.3	3.6	5.3	4.5
RPR (UMP Parliamentary Elections 2002)	20.5	15.7	19.9	33.3
UDF	18.5	14.2	6.8	4.9

Table 9.5 Deputies elected in 1993, 1997 and 2002

	Parliamentary elections		
	1993	**1997**	**2002**
PC	24	37	21
PS	56	246	141
Radical	5	13	7
Other Left	10	9	6
Greens	0	8	3
Mouvement des Citoyens	4	7	
UDF	206	109	22
RPR (UMP en 2002)	259	139	369
Other Right	13	9	8
Total	577	577	577

In the 2002 legislative elections, the socialists further increased their percentage in the total of the moderate left (including the Greens), reaching 75 percent. And the share of socialist and radical seats out of all the seats won by the moderate left reached 79 percent, compared to 57 percent in 1993 and 77 percent in 1997. Socialist domination over the left has thus not at all suffered from the serious presidential defeat; indeed, the party has strengthened its position within the left. This does not mean the disenchantment of the first ballot can be analyzed as a mere accident. Under the two-round voting system, the first round now had the effect of weakening the main candidates in the second round. Party organization on the left is no longer adapted to the increasing profusion of candidacies and the rise of the protest vote (see Berger's chapter in this volume).

But the Socialist Party today is not in a position to transform leftist party politics in a way that Jacques Chirac is currently managing on the right. The socialists' political partners are severely weakened and extremely divided. Their strategies are uncertain and even their alliance with the PS is unsure. The project of a big unified left-wing governmental party is thus infeasible for the moment. And the rise of an extreme left that is trying to unify and occupy the place once occupied by the Communist Party by rejecting any alliance with the socialists poses an additional challenge. As things stand today, the PS on its own is structurally too weak to face the right with any hope of success. The evolution of the French party system towards even greater domination by the two major parties that could lead to bipartisanism thus seems rather unlikely in the foreseeable future, even if it fits within the institutional logic that prevailed in 2002. And even without considering the creation of a single moderate left party, the weakness of its potential partners and their concerns as to the exercise of power compromise the formation of a new, solid and lasting left alliance that would also be able to cover a broad political space. This current lack of symmetry in the respective evolution of the right and the left may also work against the left, and primarily against the Socialist Party, in the years to come. Some observers have hypothesized that the new political system will be characterized in the future by the existence of a single dominant party, the UMP. The bipolar multiparty system with two dominant parties alternating in power would thus be called into question. Such a hypothesis should not be ruled out, given the left's, and particularly the PS's, extremely difficult position and their lack of horizon. Several factors, though, argue to the contrary: increasing electoral volatility (recalling the socialist rout in 1993 and Chirac's party's defeat in 1997), the facts that since 1978 no incumbent government has won an election, that Jean-Pierre Raffarin's government is currently highly unpopular and, lastly, that the PS, despite its relative weakness and vulnerability, remains the only alternative government party besides the UMP.

Still, the Socialist Party has to demonstrate a capacity in the upcoming period to restore unity and give impetus to the left. Otherwise, the persistence of a strong National Front could recreate the situation that occurred with the second ballot of the 2002 presidential election, in which the moderate right, whatever its relative weakness, would be the only political force capable of winning the elections. This would be a reversion to the situation that prevailed in the 1960s before bipolarization came about.

In conclusion, and whatever the uncertainties about the future, it seems that throughout the entire period following the Gaullist victory in 1962 and especially the 1969 referendum, the party system has been anything but inert. Despite their difficulties, weaknesses and inadequacies, several parties have attempted at once to adapt to the new institutional rules, put themselves in a position to govern over time and represent their voters. A fair judgment must take into account both their achievements and their failures in all of these areas. By becoming bipolar, the system has allowed the political regime to function in a way that is closer to the requirements of representative government while at the same time preserving central elements of the regime that ensured the proper functioning of public bodies and a capacity to govern over the long term. It is still too early to say whether bipolarization is truly in crisis and what the consequences of such a crisis would be on the functioning of the French political system. Its resilience must not, however, be underestimated.

10
Convergence, Fragmentation and Majority-Cycling in French Public Opinion

Richard Balme

Introduction

The shock of Sunday, 21 April 2002, when Front National (FN) leader Jean-Marie le Pen qualified for the second round of the presidential election, eliminating the Socialist candidate and incumbent Prime Minister Lionel Jospin, raised doubts about the quality of the democratic process in France. Since the foundation of the Fifth Republic, the presidential election has been the cornerstone of the regime, forming the basis for executive power and grounding its legitimacy upon a direct majoritarian election. For the second time, the left would not participate in the final round of the elections.[1] For the first time, a conservative candidate faced an extreme-right candidate in the final stage of the competition for State leadership. A large part of the French public (some 43% of votes for the left in the first round) faced the dilemma of supporting Jacques Chirac to stop Jean-Marie Le Pen or abstaining in the second round. After two weeks of massive demonstrations against the National Front leader, Jacques Chirac was elected by 82 per cent of the vote compared to 18 per cent for Le Pen. Abstention remained at 20 per cent, revealing large numbers of crossover votes from the left to Chirac. The emotional shock soon calmed down.

These events marked a tremendous failure for parties of the left participating in the governing coalition and for Lionel Jospin as a candidate, leading to his retreat from public life on the night of his defeat. The leftist government nevertheless had a very honourable record. It had remained in power for five consecutive years, enjoyed overall positive economic performance, and passed important legislation regarding nationality, working-time, universal access to health benefits, and women's rights in public life. It was the first government since the 1970s to be able to take credit for a decrease in unemployment, and it remained popular until a few months before the election. Moreover, Le Pen is one of the most radical far-right leaders of Western Europe, stridently populist in contesting the leadership of political elites, openly xenophobic, activating racist and sometimes revisionist trends in public opinion, and opposed to fiscal policies, taxes and European integration. Le Pen defines himself as "nationalist", "patriotic" and a defender against threats to national identity. After the results of 21 April 2002, Le Pen committed himself to withdraw from the "Europe of Maastricht" if he won the election. But the main issue on which he had campaigned for many years was immigration, advocating a "national preference" principle, which would give priority for jobs and social services to French citizens over foreign residents, and a drastic policy to send immigrants back to their home countries. Clearly, such perspectives would have meant a major shift in French public policy, both at the domestic and international level, which would have threatened the core identity of the French political system, the "Republican model". Thus Le Pen's strong showing produced this political shock. But in leaving the final choice between the right and the far right, April 2002 was also an electoral breakdown of the left–right cleavage structuring French politics. The ability of the regime to perform its representative functions is at stake, and a lasting crisis may therefore be the result of these events.

This chapter attempts to explain the electoral breakdown of 2002 by focusing on citizens' values, political identifications and policy preferences. We aim to qualify changes in public opinion in recent years, and to understand how public opinion has responded to changes in the French political economy and political representation.

There are three different lines of inquiry to consider. Looking at the literature on electoral change (Dalton et al. 1984; Martin 2000), we first need to understand if 2002 was an accident, a provisional collapse in electoral mobilisation, or instead the result of deeper, ongoing trends in French society. The local collapse hypothesis stresses erratic movements and short-term determinants in electoral alignments, often counter-cyclical. The selection of Jean-Marie Le Pen for the second round was a political shock because it was largely unexpected. It has been largely interpreted as an anomaly of French democracy, mostly due to the volatility of voters, and unlikely to recur. Contrariwise, the structural hypothesis suggests that the electoral outcome of April 2002 is consistent with public opinion shifts observed over the long term, which are likely to persist in the future. To explore the contrast between long-term structure and emerging fluctuations in the present situation, we first analyse electoral change in presidential elections over the last 20 years.

A second line of questioning lies in neo-conservatism. Although dramatic, the rise of the far right in France is by no means unique. Austria, Belgium, Denmark, Italy, the Netherlands and the United States all witnessed the electoral gains of radical right-wing populist, nationalist and most often xenophobic leaders (Betz and Immerfall 1998; Hainsworth 2000; Hermet 2001; Mény and Surel 2000; Perrineau 2001). The issue then is to evaluate how much these partisan changes match public opinion. We here expand from works by Ronald Inglehart (1997), Herbert Kitschelt (1995), and Gérard Grunberg and Etienne Schweisguth (1990). In different settings, these works stress the role of social change on the formation of values and preferences, and their impact on political attitudes. The rise of postmaterialism and cultural liberalism in Western democracies introduced a new line of political cleavages, which has progressively gained in relevance since the seventies. In this respect, the current crisis could be interpreted as a backlash against cultural liberalism and the openness of society, and as the development of an "anti-cultural change" movement in public opinion. This would mean the rise of a neo-conservatism, one possibly more authoritarian than the traditional right. According to the neo-conservatism hypothesis, the rise of the far right is a result of changing attitudes that value more authority, more liberal economic policies, and more aggressive attitudes towards migrants. We try to estimate the scope and trend in support for neo-conservative values in French public opinion through key policy issues such as the State and the economy, moral conservatism, and openness of society to immigration, European integration and globalisation.

Finally, the democratic capacity of the regime and its ability to fulfil citizens' expectations may also be at stake here. The idea of institutional performance has been introduced in political analysis to study the relationship between political cultures and public policy outcomes. Social trust is a key intermediary variable in this perspective (Putnam 1993; Nye et al. 1997). We borrow from this perspective in conceptualising the democratic performance of the regime as the capacity of the partisan system to motivate political identifications, and as the ability of public policies to sustain some level of confidence and loyalty towards political leaders. From this perspective, the electoral breakdown of 2002 would mainly be the result of a growing distance between citizens and politics in two different aspects. First, citizens lose their identification with the main political cleavages, such as socioeconomic status, that structure the partisan system; in the French case, this cleavage is mainly between the left and right. And second, citizens may withdraw the confidence they invest in political leaders and lose their trust in politicians' capacity to act as representatives. Perception of poor policy performances and corruption would lead to scepticism and suspicion towards political organisations and governing elites. To assess the political and institutional aspects of the crisis, we therefore look more carefully at political cleavages and alignments, and at the level of trust in leaders by citizens.

Our different hypotheses can be depicted in Figure 10.1.

These interpretations are not necessarily exclusive. The variables may interact with cumulative or counterbalancing effects. They are used to qualify the present state of French democracy as revealed in April 2002, and help to identify the main processes underlying its critical trends. To try to disentangle these issues, we use election results, descriptive data from mass

Figure 10.1 Competing explanations of the electoral breakdown of 21 April 2002

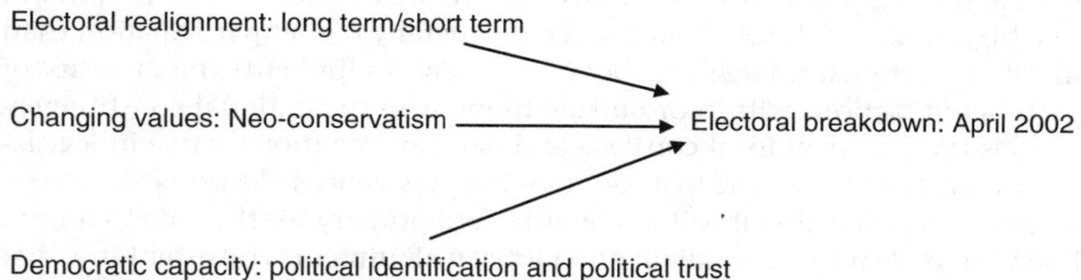

surveys, and some insights brought from our own qualitative studies "Political Trust and Public Policy" and "Reasons to Vote", based on focus group analysis since 1999 and during the 2002 electoral campaign.[2]

1. Electoral change since 1981: political fragmentation and depression

The first issue relates to the nature of electoral change in 2002. The presidential election may in some respects appear as an example of stability and continuity in politics, as Jacques Chirac was, after all, soundly re-elected to his position as President. But the first round of the election dramatically expressed that cleavages structuring French politics, organised around two major parties on the left (the Parti Socialiste) and on the right of the political spectrum (the Gaullist party RPR), could no longer be taken for granted. The exclusion of the left from the presidential race clearly indicates that major electoral realignments have been taking place. But for how long? Obviously, the meaning of this event differs if electoral realignment occurred during the five years of the last legislature, or even during the last weeks of the campaign, or if it followed a continuous trend over several decades. In the first case, short-term fluctuations in political mood mainly explain the selection of Jean-Marie Le Pen for the second round. The second case suggests more structural changes within the French partisan system. We therefore need a clear picture of electoral change over a long period.

To analyse the state of electoral alignments in French politics, we focus on presidential elections since 1981, which is a good reference point in time, not because opinions were necessarily stable in the previous period, but because this was the first time a change from right to left occurred at this level of government since the founding of the Fifth Republic in 1958, and because such a change was the peak of left–right partisan alignments in French politics. François Mitterrand, first elected in 1981, was re-elected in 1988 against Jacques Chirac. The latter beat Lionel Jospin in 1995 and qualified for the second round in 2002 with Jean-Marie Le Pen, leaving the socialist leader out of the race. We concentrate on the first round of the election, as it offers a unique opportunity to estimate the state of public opinion. The high stakes of the election results in generally higher participation than in other elections. A large number of candidates represents the diversity of parties and factions within or outside them. And the national constituency cancels the effects of local contexts and partisan coalitions active in legislative or local elections. The first round of the presidential election can be considered as a proportional ballot operating as a primary for the second round. If left–right cleavages are salient and partisan alignments consistent, the first round of the election naturally selects one candidate from the left and one from the right.[3] If this is not the case, two candidates from the same side can be selected, as was the case in 2002.

Declining electoral mobilisation and political fragmentation

The unexpected result of 21 April 2002 has been largely attributed to two main factors: the low level of turnout in the election, and the scattering of votes among multiple candidates. Were these new developments?

Let us first consider electoral mobilisation, with the evolution of turnout and valid votes (*suffrages exprimés*) for the four points in time corresponding to presidential elections in the last two decades. Both decreased sharply in the 1990s, from 81 per cent in 1988 to 72 per cent in 2002 for turnout, and from 80 per cent in 1988 to 69 per cent in 2002 for valid votes. The percentage of abstentions (*bulletins blancs*)[4] regularly increased over the period, reaching 3 per cent in 2002.

The trend is common to all Western democracies, although it was somewhat delayed in the case of France, probably because of the late experience of political swing in 1981, after 23 years of rightist domination over executive and legislative powers since 1958. This decline in electoral mobilisation is especially noticeable as it is coupled with the increase in the number of candidates (from 9 in 1981 and 1988, to 10 in 1995, and 16 in 2002). Put differently, the diversification of political supply did not counter the decline in political participation in the election.

A second significant trend pictured in Figure 10.2 is political fragmentation. Fragmentation refers here to the dispersion of votes among candidates. In a purely fragmented political space, all candidates would attract the same number of votes, making the selection of one of them with a majoritarian rule impossible. In a purely concentrated political space, all votes would spontaneously converge upon one candidate immediately elected. We constructed two simple measures to estimate political fragmentation: the share of valid votes captured in the first round by candidates selected for the second round, and the share of valid votes attracted by candidates running for parties belonging to government coalitions before or after the election.[5]

Again, both trends are sharply declining. Candidates in the second round fall from 54 per cent in 1981 and 1988 to only 37 per cent in 2002.

Figure 10.2 Political fragmentation in presidential elections (first round)

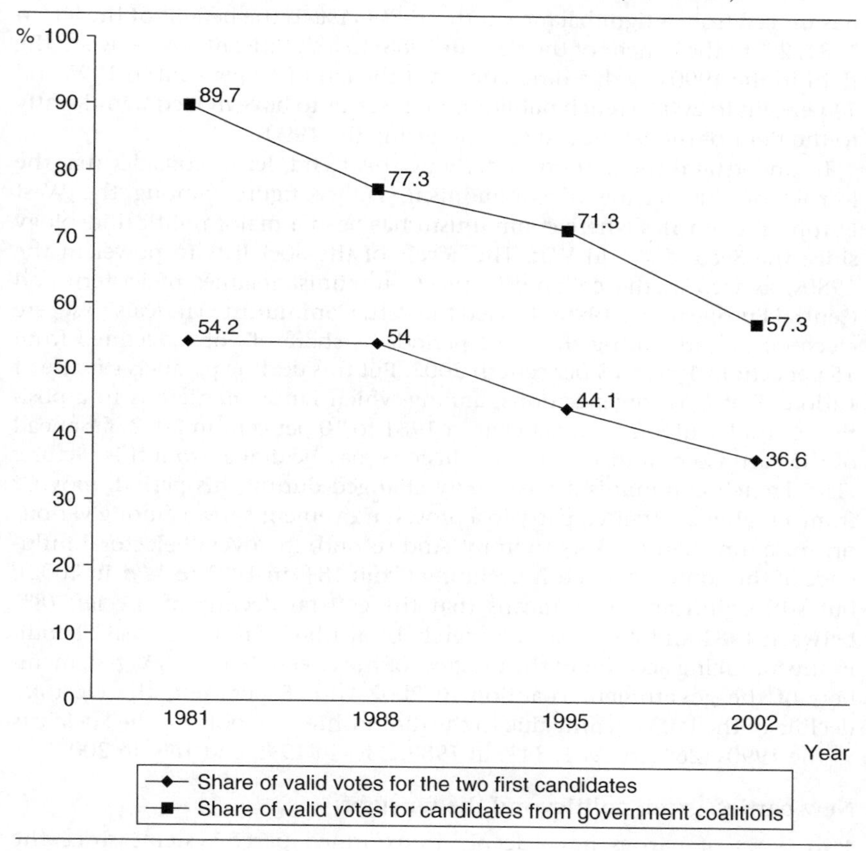

Source: Electoral results from Ministère de l'Intérieur. Indexes and figures computed by author.

Government parties follow the same pattern from 90 per cent in 1981 to 57 per cent in 2002.

Both the retreat in electoral mobilisation and the increase in political fragmentation display the decline in political legitimacy of the French presidency. In 2002, roughly speaking, one potential voter in three did not vote or did not support a candidate in the main election, one in three voted for a candidate running for a government party, and one in three cast a vote of protest. But those factors by no means came out of the blue. They reflect continuous trends over the last two decades.

The left–right balance and the decline of communism

We now turn to changes in political forces, starting with the balance between left and right. We consider the difference between total votes for the left and total votes for the right in the same elections. Clearly, the period has moved from a tight balance in the 1980s (1% to the benefit of the left in 1981, 2% to the benefit of the right in 1988) to a significant advantage to the right in the 1990s, with a difference over the left of 19 per cent in 1995 and 14 per cent in 2002. French public opinion seems to have moved significantly to the right of the political spectrum during the 1990s.

To understand the pattern underlying this trend, let us consider first the impact of the decline of communism. France figures among the West European countries where communism has been a major political ideology since the Second World War. The access of the Socialists to power in the 1980s, as well as the collapse of the Communist regimes of Eastern and Central Europe in the 1990s, has led the Parti Communiste Français to severe electoral defeats during this time period. Its share of votes declined from 15 per cent in 1981 to 3 per cent in 2002. But this decline parallels the rise of various Trotskyist organisations, among which Lutte Ouvrière is in a position of leadership, from 2 per cent in 1981 to 10 per cent in 2002, far ahead of the Parti Communiste. Two conclusions may be drawn from this picture. First, French communism has deeply changed during this period, moving from a highly centralised party to a protest movement spread among various organisations hardly likely to unify. And second, the overall electoral influence of the communist left is declining (from 18% in 1981 to 14% in 2002), but still significant. This means that the general decline of the left (8% between 1981 and 2002) cannot merely be attributed to the retreat of communism. Taking account of the progress of the Green Party (Les Verts), members of the government coalition in 2002 with 5 per cent, the electoral decline of the left is mainly due to the diminishing support for the Socialists in the 1990s (26% in 1981, 34% in 1988, 23% in 1995 and 16% in 2002).

New parties: green politics and the far right

Two types of parties have deeply transformed party systems since the 1980s: ecologist and populist or far-rightist parties. France is rather unique with regard to these two sorts of parties. For different reasons, including the statist dimension of political culture, the strength of the communist left, the late political swing of 1981, and the competitive relations between social movement organisations, ecology has been late to become a salient political issue and to give rise to a significant political party (Boy et al. 1995). This was only accomplished with the unifying of the main movements in Les Verts, and their participation in government in 1997.[6] Accordingly, the impact of candidates running on environmental issues in presidential elections is mainly important over the last period (from 3% to 7% between 1995 to 2002). Nevertheless, if green movements epitomise changes towards "new politics" and postmaterialism, these scores do not suggest any watershed in French politics. They instead indicate a growing, moderate concern in public opinion for environmental issues as such, but certainly a lack of broad-based support for green leaders, their organisations and their campaigns.

The level of influence of green movements contrasts sharply with the impact of extreme-right and populist candidates. Jean-Marie Le Pen and the FN have deeply influenced French politics since the early 1980s, first with the local election in Dreux in 1983, where the FN won the municipalité in coalition with the right, then in 1986 when several seats for deputies were won by FN candidates,[7] and in 1988 when Jean-Marie Le Pen won 14 per cent of the votes in the presidential election. Subsequent electoral gains followed in European, local and regional elections, leading to a political crisis in 1998, when the proportional representation system used in the regional elections led to the formation of governing coalitions between the right and the FN. President Jacques Chirac firmly opposed these coalitions, and several regional leaders were excluded from the RPR or from the UDF, but without preventing such agreements from being implemented in three regions. The subsequent internal crisis within the FN led to its division into FN and MNR (Mouvement National Republicain), led by Bruno Mégret, and the duplication of candidacies in European elections in 1999 and local elections in 2001 yielded weaker results for the far right, partly explaining the surprise effect of 2002.

Nevertheless, from 1981 to 2002, the rise of the extreme right in France is dramatic (Mayer 2002). Le Pen debued at 14 per cent of the vote in 1988, and since then he has never won any less of the vote. He rose to 17 per cent in 2002, to which we need to add the score of Bruno Mégret (2%). Moreover, more moderate candidates (at least on racial issues) have emerged in the political arena. In 1995, Philippe de Villiers and Jacques Cheminade both obtained 5 per cent of the votes, while in 2002, Jean Saint-Josse (CPNT [Chasse Peche Nature Tradition]) and Christine Boutin, respectively campaigning for hunters and against liberal legislation regarding the family,[8] received 5 per cent of the votes.

Besides the transformation of communism, the rise of the far right and of a more diffuse populist right is clearly the major trend in French politics during recent years. The partisan system has been stretched and polarised to the extremes, while the strength of the centre has diminished.

If presidential elections give a fair picture of public opinion, they still do not capture all its short-term fluctuations, nor do they necessarily express all of its substantive transformations. Concerning short-term changes, the stability of presidential leadership (Mitterrand 1981–95, Chirac 1995–2007) contrasts with the systematic swing in legislative elections. Parliamentary majorities have switched from left to right or vice versa in every legislative election.[9] The duration of these governments is rather long, and the executive branch is not unstable. But every possible presidential and parliamentary combination has been experienced during this time period.[10] Overall, the left has been in government for 15 years and the right for 6 years.

Through *cohabitation,* executive power has been shared for 9 of the past 20 years. The consequences of this situation are momentous. Voters have experienced multiple swings from left to right and from right to left at all levels of government. In 2002 they also faced a situation where major candidates from the left and the right were both incumbents in the executive, which allowed the parties or candidates out of parliament to portray themselves as the true opposition.

Most of the trends depicted above began in the 1980s and accelerated in the 1990s. Overall, French politics has moved from a binary left/right structure to a political space broadly divided into three camps – radical left/governmental left – governmental right/extreme right – while public opinion seems to be drifting to the right. These changes did not suddenly appear under the government of Lionel Jospin, but result instead from a long-term trend, consistent across different types of elections and issues, despite short-term fluctuations.

The declining electoral mobilisation, increasing political fragmentation, rise of the far right and retreat of the left are all structural features that contributed to 21 April 2002. But they did not lead inevitably to such a political crisis. They had to be combined with short-term factors to yield this outcome. We will return to this issue when trying to explain how Lionel Jospin lost the support of many leftist voters. As security appeared as the major issue in the campaign, one of the possible explanations lies in the shift in public opinion towards neo-conservative ideology.

2. Changing values: liberalism, neo-conservatism and polarisation

The rise of the extreme right, as well as the defeat of the left after five years in government, seems to suggest a turn in public opinion towards more conservative politics. The saliency of the security issue before and during the campaign, the importance of immigration in the media and in public-policy agendas over the last two decades, and the convergence of economic policies of both leftist (since 1983) and rightist (since 1986) governments on the monetarist paradigm of European integration seem to support this view. However, this idea of a conversion to a radical right-wing ideology of French public opinion is misleading, and it hides much more subtle changes. We conceptualise neo-conservatism as the conjunction between economic liberalism, moral conservatism and a revival of nationalism in the context of globalisation. The National Front ideology epitomises these traits in radical features. Did French public opinion move closer to its positions on these issues? Using surveys from the SOFRES, we look in this section at some key issues to better depict these transformations, starting with the economy.[11]

The economy: more liberal than statist, more regulationist than liberal

Traditionally, both the French style of public policy-making and the French variety of capitalism have been analysed as "statist", giving a large role to the State over civil society, especially over the private sector to regulate the economy. This view is grounded in the importance of the nationalisation policies of Gaullist governments after the Second World War and of the first years of the Mitterrand presidency, in the size of the public sector, and in the role of the State in innovative industrial policies (aircraft building, nuclear plants, high-speed trains, and telecommunications). The changing policy of the leftist government in 1983, renouncing the devaluation of the franc to stay in the European Monetary System and the contribution of France to the launching of the Single European Act are usually interpreted as a "neo-liberal turn", then confirmed by the political swing in 1986 (Jobert and Théret 1994; Hall 1986). Does this evolution match public opinion trends? Have French citizens become significantly more liberal on economic issues over this period of time?

Consider Figure 10.3. Citizens were asked by SOFRES surveys to estimate what should be done to meet economic challenges: either trust companies

Figure 10.3 State regulation versus freedom for firms

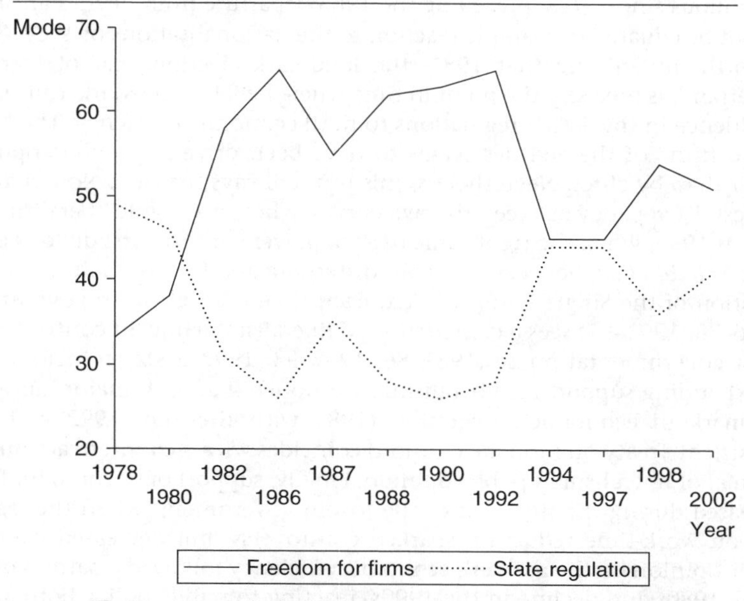

Source: SOFRES Survey 2002.

and give them more freedom for initiative or, instead, use more severe controls and regulations over firms.

In 1978, a majority (49%) favoured State regulation over freedom for firms (33%). But the ratio changed in 1981 with the election of François Mitterrand, when public opinion became clearly economically liberal, around or above 60 per cent throughout the 1980s. Nevertheless, this support for supply-side policies declined after 1992 (after the Maastricht Treaty) and public opinion remained divided on the issue. It rose again in the late nineties, to decline again, under the Jospin government. In 2002, 51 per cent favoured freedom for firms, while 41 per cent favoured State regulation.

The picture is very telling. First, a significant shift occurred in the early eighties with the majority reversal, and public opinion remained largely liberal on the issue later on. The side of favouring regulation more than freedom for firms never again gained a majority. Second, this enthusiasm for the market significantly and suddenly cooled in the early nineties, with the foundation of the European Union, the launching of the Monetary Union, the new round of the GATT negotiations, and the return of the right to the government in 1993. Overall there is a clear gap in the level of economic liberalism between the eighties and the nineties. And third, public opinion interacts with public policy in complex patterns. Note that the early trend is continuous since 1978, preceding the 1983 departure from Keynesianism. It cannot be equated to a simple reaction to the nationalisations of 1981–83. It is worth underlining that 1981, the landmark election year of François Mitterrand, is precisely the point in time where belief in the Market surpasses confidence in the State's regulations to fulfil economic efficiency. The "neo-liberal turn" of the eighties seems to have been driven by public opinion rather than by elites. Nevertheless, this is not always the case. Note that the highest discrepancy between the two curves, where economic liberalism is at peak, is 1986, when the right came back to power with the first divided executive (*cohabitation*) between François Mitterrand and Jacques Chirac, and the adoption of the Single European Act. Each time the right is in government (1986–88, 1993–97) sees a constriction of liberalism, while, in contrast, each leftist governmental phase (1981–86, 1988–93, 1997–2002) coincides with an expanding support for liberalism. Also notice that each major European landmark in economic integration (1986 with the SEA, 1992 with the Maastricht Treaty on Monetary Union) coincides with a counterreaction and a retreat of liberalism in public opinion. Finally, support of freedom for firms increased during the first year of the Jospin government, when the legislation on work-time reduction sparked controversy, but decreased later on. Public opinion on the market's economic efficiency followed a pattern of rise in the 1980s and decline in the 1990s, reacting to public policy both at the domestic and European levels.

On the same liberal side, a large majority supports State retrenchment through reduction of public spending (in 2003, 79% thought that cutbacks in public spending were necessary) and taxation (in 2000, 86% thought that the level of taxes was excessive or unbearable). Nothing in these data suggests any radical liberal view. They nevertheless show that there is no consensus for a traditional Keynesian approach to economic policy. Given the high level of State regulation, they also show that public opinion has moved to more market-oriented positions over time, in accordance with changing ideologies among the elites.

French citizens increasingly share a belief in freedom for firms and in the market over the State to achieve economic efficiency. Does this mean that they trust the market to fulfil their expectations and to yield an optimal social welfare? This idea is at the core of economic liberalism and neo-conservatism. Data and evidence on this issue are more difficult to produce. Nevertheless, when asked about the appropriate level of the State's intervention in the economy, more people think that the State does not intervene enough, rather than too much (in 2002, 47% over 15%). This preference for more public intervention holds both for supporters of the left and of the right, albeit smaller in the latter case. Significantly, the gap between the two opinions mostly increased between 1985 and 1994, following the same decline in liberalism as above. It then moderately declined in 1997, when the socialists came back to government.

How should we interpret the apparent contradiction between the belief in freedom for firms and the demand for more State intervention? Obviously, and we borrow here from our own qualitative studies, economic efficiency does not equal social efficiency for public opinion. People both recognise the burden of taxes and bureaucratic rules for the activity of firms and their impact on jobs, *and* ask for stronger regulation concerning job protection, conditions at work and status of employees. They also demand public services to compensate for market failures and complain about the decline of services over the last years. Attachment to welfare and to the social security system is also very strong. In December 1995, a few months after the election of Jacques Chirac, a massive movement of protest raised against the "Plan Juppé" to reform the financing of social security. In particular, the project planned to expand the duration of subscriptions for retirement pensions in the private sector from 37.5 to 40 years, and to change the basis for calculation of pension amounts, as had been decided for the private sector a few years before (see Palier's chapter in this volume). Some of the unions (CFDT) supported the project, while most of them vigorously fought against it. Leftist intellectuals were equally divided about the project and about the movement, understood as the *arrière-garde* of corporatism, or as the forefront of anti-liberalism. Strikes, in public transportation systems in particular, were so long and so effective that the government had to withdraw the project. Jacques Chirac chose later on to call the legislative election one year in advance, but the right lost the majority in parliament to the benefit of the left. Cleavages occurred within the left and the right in taking sides with regard to these events. The most significant fact is that public opinion supported the movement against the "Plan Juppé", with 58 per cent supporting or feeling sympathy towards the strikes and demonstrations. Since 1995, 25 out of 26 social movements in civil service, private firms, agriculture, transportation, education, health, regarding retirement schemes, employment and revenues received more approval than opposition from public opinion, showing a strong attachment to social rights and employment (Rozes 2001).

In a way, the French seem to want to "have their cake and eat it too", and to display inconsistent or partial preferences, probably due to bias in survey questioning. But this holds only on the "classical" left/right cleavage, roughly opposing liberalism to Statism in the economic dimension. In qualitative studies, people prove to be consistent. When faced with the possible contradiction between the two arguments, they maintain their point of view. They acknowledge it might be hard to accomplish, but they want both economic freedom and social regulation of the economy, to the moderate left and to the moderate right of the political spectrum.

Overall, the change in public opinion regarding the economy does not fit with the neo-conservative view, as expectations about the State still remain high. But neither does it match the traditional statist French political economy. A rather large consensus favouring economic freedom, lower taxes and public spending, and State intervention on market failures, seems now to exist. Public opinion appears both more liberal than statist, and more regulationist than liberal. The State is expected to keep "hands off" economic management and initiatives, and to provide a high level of social welfare and protection. State intervention no longer means imposing rules on firms, but offering guarantees for employment and standards of living. Current public policies do not seem to match either of these expectations expressed by public opinion.

Moral conservatism

Another key aspect of neo-conservatism lies in relation to authority and to moral issues. The postmaterialism theory of Ronald Inglehart states that economic development and increased level of education since the mid-twentieth century deeply transformed the needs and values of citizens. Their concerns would have moved from material issues, such as income, defence and security to "postmaterial" ones, such as self-realization, quality of life, respect for individual rights, and environmental protection. Affluence and education would generally orient societies towards more individualistic and tolerant values, favouring cultural liberalism. According to the theory, the relation to authority has profoundly evolved, with citizens nowadays more critical towards traditional forms of authority, more tolerant of different ideas and different lifestyles, and generally favouring self-determination over general principles in everyday life. Nevertheless, the success of populist and far-rightist leaders in Western Europe seems to challenge the view. How can we understand the rise of the FN in this context? Does this mean that France does not fit with the theory, and that public opinion has generally turned more conservative on moral issues? Or that cultural liberalism has reached a peak and generated a backlash? We address the issue looking at four different attitudes to authority regarding the death penalty, homosexuality, education and juvenile delinquency.

Consider first the death penalty. The guillotine is a major political symbol of the French Revolution and has long been linked to French political specificity. Its abolition was also one of the major and most symbolic decisions of François Mitterrand after his election in 1981, after the long campaign of his then Minister of Justice, Robert Badinter. Public opinion favoured the death penalty at that time, and the President took his decision, although people, as in most Western democracies, were very sensitive about the issue. The FN has campaigned since the 1980s to restore the death penalty.

Figure 10.4 displays the evolution of public opinion regarding this issue. In the early eighties, support for the restoration of death penalty increased to a peak of 65 per cent in 1985. It then regularly declined, until it crossed the curve of opinion opposed to the restoration in 1999, then becoming

Figure 10.4 Restoration of death penalty

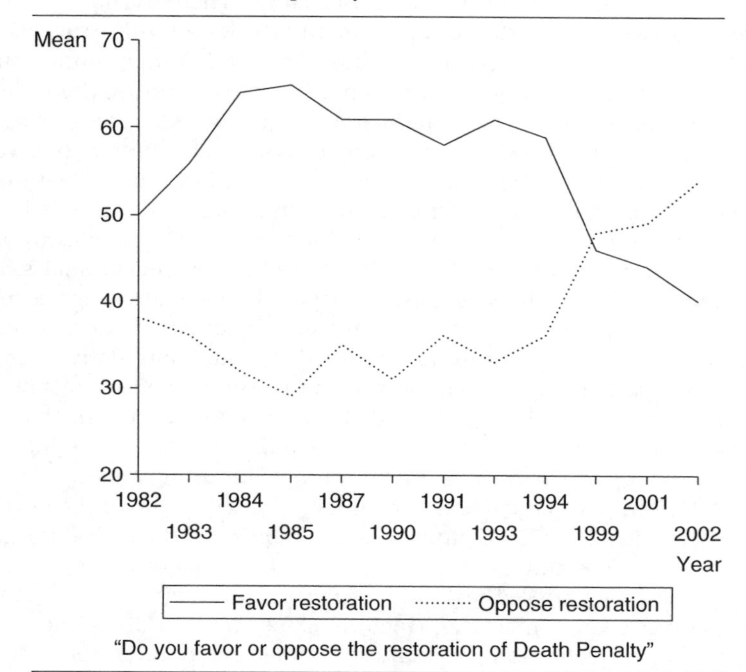

Source: SOFRES Survey 2002.

majoritarian. In 2002, 54 per cent opposed the death penalty, while 40 per cent favoured it. Clearly, although still divided, public opinion has become more progressive on the issue. This is remarkable, as insecurity and crime also became important issues in recent years, when the inversion in the pattern of opinion occurred.

Let us now turn to homosexuality. Attitudes towards homosexuality are a clear indicator of tolerance towards different lifestyles. The survey asked people "If you learned that your son was homosexual, what would your attitude be? I would not be upset/I would be hurt, but I would let him live the way he wants/If possible I would try to make him change/I would be deeply shocked and do everything to make him change."

The data show a clear trend towards greater tolerance with regard to homosexuality, sharply increasing in the nineties. People "not upset" rose from 5 per cent in 1981 to 22 per cent in 2002, and people "hurt but tolerant" from 28 per cent in 1981 to 56 per cent in 2002; people "deeply shocked" declined from 32 per cent in 1981 to 11 per cent in 2002; and people "trying to make him change" from 28 per cent in 1981 to 9 per cent in 2002. Public opinion still displays some ambivalence about homosexuality in light of these data, as a majority would feel some pain in such a situation. Nevertheless, the trend over the last two decades is clear. Public opinion has become more tolerant towards homosexuality. There is no significant difference between supporters of the right and the left on this issue.

On the two previous issues, cultural liberalism, rather than moral conservatism, has clearly taken hold, with dramatic changes during the nineties. But the picture is different for other issues. Education is a salient issue, not only because people are generally concerned about their children, or because the quality of education has a strong impact on families and on the satisfaction parents can draw from their own lives. In France, education is largely assumed by the public sector, and its performance directly relates to opinions assessing the government. Regular strikes in the educational system since 1968, led by teachers, pupils and students, have also been a major aspect of protest politics and an important site for contesting existing forms of authority. Education reforms have resulted in various alternative forms of teaching and participation at school and in universities, while dissatisfaction has increased with regard to social and ethnic exclusion and, more recently, with violence. Do people favour more discipline or the development of critical thinking in their expectations from the education system?

Figure 10.5 shows that citizens overall favour discipline over the development of the critical minds of pupils. But the trend over the period is significant. Between 1978 and 1997, discipline, although majoritarian, seems to decline to the benefit of self-realisation. After 1997, though, the gap between the two curves sharply increases, reaching 65 per cent for discipline and 32 per cent for self-realisation in 2002. This time period corresponds to the Socialist government of Lionel Jospin, and to the failure of his Minister

Figure 10.5 Attitudes towards education

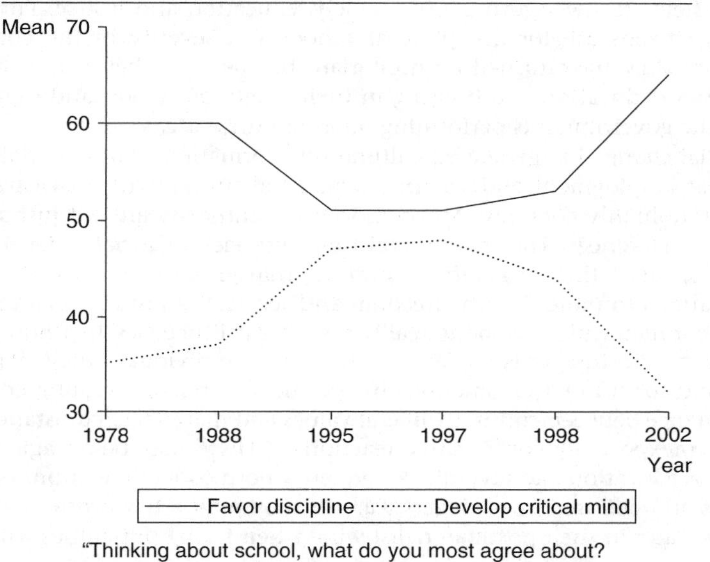

Source: SOFRES Survey 2002.

Claude Allègre to reform the system, while insecurity and violence at school, at least as reported by the media, significantly increased.

Let us now look at justice, one of the main institutions exerting authority upon society. We collected opinions about the severity of judges regarding juvenile delinquency. The question asked people if they thought judges were "too severe, too indulgent, or neither too severe nor too indulgent" with regard to juvenile delinquency. The data demonstrate a dramatic shift in public opinion on the issue. While in 1980 the three opinions are almost equally shared, tolerant opinions (too severe) regularly decline, to the point of almost disappearing in 2002 (2%). In contrast, opinions asking for more severity from judges regularly increase, with a sudden boom between 1997 and 2002, reaching the peak of 72 per cent. Opinion has evolved dramatically, especially in the last five years, in relation to the rise of insecurity on the public agenda. A clear majority favours more severe justice, and opinion is no longer divided on the issue.

What conclusions can be drawn from these data regarding authority? First, there is no evidence that there is consistent support for moral conservatism, as cultural liberalism has progressed on a number of issues, as witnessed by the data on the death penalty or homosexuality presented here, but also regarding women's rights, abortion, or sexuality. Generally speaking, people favour personal choice and individual rights. But those trends are also issue specific and sensitive to context and can nourish demands for authority in some fields (Schweisguth 2000), namely, education and justice. Put differently, citizens ask for discipline at school and severity in the court not because they have turned authoritarian, but because they care about the quality of education and housing in their neighbourhoods, and they think that the government is performing poorly in these areas.

Social change has generated cultural transformations, but material issues, such as employment and security, remain salient. Patterns of cleavage are therefore highly complex. Attitudes towards authority are not just abstract moral preferences. They also reveal the legitimacy of social order for individuals, and their tolerance towards transgression of social norms. Aspirations to more fluidity, freedom and self-realisation in social relations may conflict with dissonant realities such as difficulties in finding jobs, exclusion or insecurity. Therefore the same individuals may express a demand for normative sanctions in specific situations, revealing cognitive dissonance between culturally liberal values and material circumstances that elicit unexpectedly conservative reactions.[12] There may be an aging effect here, as education and juvenile delinquency both concern relations between adults and children or teenagers. Parents may pour a few drops of authoritarian water in their postmaterialist wine when facing difficulties with their children.

We therefore conclude that there is no consistent moral conservatism shared by a majority or a growing minority of citizens. Attitudes towards immigration support the same view. But cultural liberalism, more than a value as such, is rather a set of preferences associated with social situations, and consequently subject to variations across issues and across time.

The open society and its enemies

Finally, neo-conservatism is deeply associated with a revival of nationalism. Jean-Marie Le Pen rejects the far-right label, but claims to represent the *Droite nationale*. The present situation in France in many aspects epitomises the conflicting trends active in European politics, where domestic politics is largely affected by the colonial past, by European integration, and more recently by globalisation.

Like many other European societies, France has been significantly shaped by the heritage of its colonial past. This means the presence of foreign populations, noticeably from North and West Africa, and a significant part of the French population of foreign origin over two or three generations. Naturally, foreign populations from previous colonies are not in the best social position once in metropolitan France. They suffer most from economic recession, urban segregation and social discrimination. Teenagers facing moral, cultural and economic disadvantages tend to drop out of school, have difficulty finding jobs and sometimes commit criminal acts. In contrast, the memory of the colonial past is still vivid for the French population. It is worth noting that

Jean-Marie Le Pen fought against independence in Vietnam and Algeria, was an activist of the anti-independent movement during the Algerian war, and is challenged for his alleged participation in war crimes in Algeria. The development of new poverty in European cities and ethnic tensions inherited from the colonial age interact to foster current xenophobic and racist attitudes.

Alternatively, France is often depicted as the ideal-type of the absolutist and Jacobin State. Obviously, European integration transforms the context and the reality of State power, by reducing the magnitude and instruments of governmental policies. The tension between national sovereignty and European integration, because France is both an active player at the European level and the archetype of the Jacobin State, may be here at its highest.

And finally, European countries are also more or less sensitive and reactive to globalisation. The importance of the anti-globalisation movement in France, with the activism of the Confédération Paysanne of José Bové and the ATTAC movement led by Bernard Cassen since 1998, suggest strong reactions in public opinion about this issue.

On these three issues – immigrants in France, European integration and globalisation – what are the main attitudes of French citizens? Do they want a society more open to the world, or do they prefer to stay among themselves?

SOFRES surveys asked the following question regarding immigration, about the integration or the repatriation of immigrants. "In the coming years, what do you favour? Integration into our society of immigrants currently living in France? Or the return of a large number of immigrants living in France to their home countries?"

Figure 10.6 shows that during the 1990s, public opinion, although divided, favoured return over the integration of immigrants. But the trend shifted in 1998, and people favouring integration became the majority (53% in 2002). Between 1992 and 2002, the balance of opinion is reversed but perfectly symmetrical. This means that public opinion generally became more tolerant towards migrants in the last years. The progress of the far right in the last presidential election cannot be equated with larger support for more exclusive policies regarding migrants. Although a majority (59%) thinks that there are too many immigrants in France, the policy stands of Jean-Marie Le Pen are indeed in decline. The FN has long been campaigning for the "National Preference" principle, aimed at favouring French citizens over foreigners for employment and social benefits. Opposition to both measures has clearly progressed over the nineties (from 51% in 1991 to 73% in 2003 for employment, and from 52% to 71% for social benefits [SOFRES 2003]). Still, around 25 per cent of French citizens support the National Preference principle, and this is consistent with the electoral scores of the far right. But what is significant here is that this position is declining in popularity.

Figure 10.6 Attitudes towards migrants

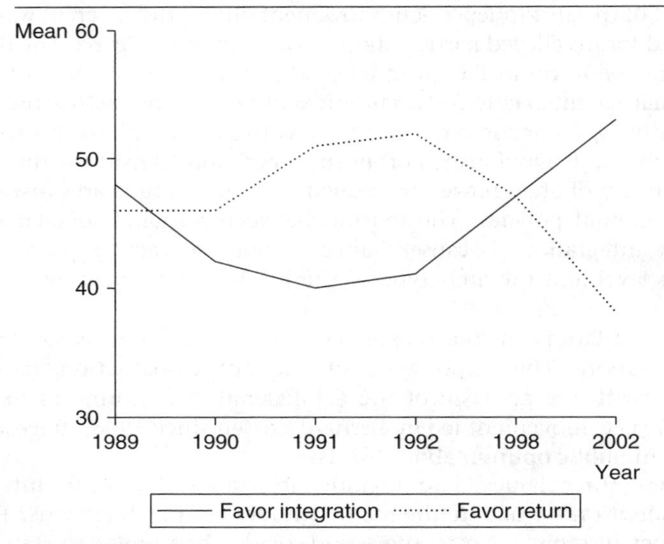

Source: SOFRES Survey 2002.

Let us now turn to European integration. In 1992, the referendum for the ratification of the Maastricht Treaty appeared much more difficult than expected, and revealed deep cleavages between and within political parties. Major parties from the left and from the right had to campaign on the same positions, while dissidents at the extremes of the partisan spectrum or minorities within large parties expressed opposing views. The treaty was barely ratified by a slim majority. Did this put an end to the "permissive consensus" softly supporting European integration in French public opinion?

Figure 10.7 shows the evolution in attitudes about the impact of European integration on national identity and values. The question asked, "Which opinion do you most agree with? European integration will in the end destroy French identity and our values/French identity and our values are not threatened by European integration."

Trust in European integration ("no threat") largely outweighs fears for national identity throughout this period. The gap between the two curves significantly increased in the last year, to reach 58 per cent of trust over 36 per cent of distrust just before the arrival of the Euro in January 2002, showing more support for European integration with rather than

Figure 10.7 Attitudes towards Europe

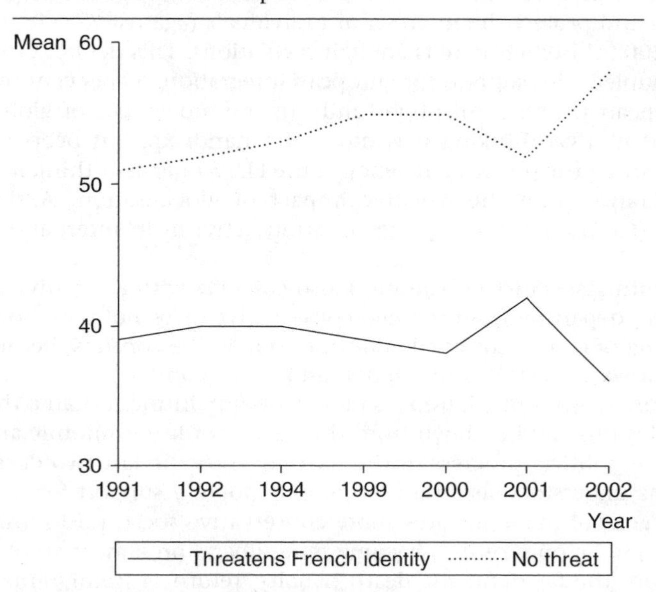

Source: SOFRES Survey 2002.

without the Euro. The Maastricht Treaty in 1992 does not seem to have affected the confidence citizens invest in Europe. Other data confirm the trend: in December 2001, 60 per cent thought that France benefits from its membership of the European Union, while only 26 per cent thought the opposite.[13] In 2004, 85 per cent agreed that the European Union must adopt a Constitution, above the mean for EU 25 (79%).[14] As the referendum of May 2005 would demonstrate, however, this popular sentiment would not automatically translate into support for the Constitutional Treaty at the ballot box.

Finally, attitudes towards globalisation also need to be considered here. We have found no longitudinal data on the topic, as the issue has only recently been on the public agenda. Some recent data are nevertheless available.[15] They show that a majority (55%) think that globalisation will be a threat to French jobs and firms, while 37 per cent think it will be an opportunity. Multinational companies, financial markets and the US are perceived as benefiting most from globalisation, far ahead of Europe and consumers in general. Most significantly, a large and increasing majority (from 60% in

2000 to 76% in 2002) thinks that there are not enough rules to regulate the economy and protect the interests of individuals (against 22% in 2000 and 19% in 2002 thinking there is enough regulation). This demand for regulation is coupled with support for European integration: 69 per cent think that the European Union is an opportunity in the movement of globalisation compared to 18% thinking it is more of a handicap. But people are also sceptical about the present efficiency of the EU: 54 per cent think it does not protect France from the negative impact of globalisation. A significant majority (63%) approves anti-globalisation activism in international summits.

Fears with respect to globalisation also coincide with a negative image of capitalism, departing from the neo-conservative view. But they do not lead to a closing of French society. Public opinion, on the contrary, became more positive towards immigrants' rights, and more confident about European integration. If anything, Europe is more a disappointment than a threat.

Many lessons can be drawn from this review of key economic and social issues. The political progress of the far right over the last two decades can neither be understood as a sign of growing popular support for its agenda, nor as a general move towards more conservative social positions. On the contrary, public opinion has become more liberal on almost all of the proposals from the far right: the death penalty, return of immigrants to their home countries, the national preference principal, conservatism on sexual and gender issues, and European integration. Overall, we face here a large diffusion of cultural liberalism in public opinion and a process of polarisation and radicalisation of moral conservatism to the extreme right, for roughly 25 per cent of the opinion. A rather broad consensus is established around freedom for firms in the market, welfare and public services provision from the State, and progressivism on moral issues.

It is also noticeable that the FN has been successful in presenting issues such as immigration and security in the national discourse. But it failed in convincing a majority to support its major policy proposals, such as restoring the death penalty, implementing a national preference principal, and exiting the EU. It can be argued that governments were quite successful in mainstreaming issues such as membership in the EU, moral issues and immigration. As shown above, the Jospin government, with a growing consensus after 1997, displayed strong records on all of these issues. It also benefited from good economic performance, as it was actually the first government to register a decline in unemployment since 1981. It failed nevertheless to meet public expectations regarding social welfare, education and juvenile delinquency. As a result, Lionel Jospin could not win the confidence of voters as a candidate.

Overall, there is little support for the neo-conservative hypothesis, and it does not contribute to understanding the electoral breakdown of 2002. Let us now turn to the institutional explanation.

3. Democratic capacity: the quality of political representation

We now consider the institutional dimension of the electoral breakdown of 2002. We already mentioned the long-term trends of decline in turnout and political fragmentation. In September 2000, a referendum was launched to reform the duration of the presidential term from seven to five years. The idea was included in the legislative platform of Lionel Jospin in 1997, and later on pushed in Parliament by the former president Valéry Giscard d'Estaing, and imposed on President Jacques Chirac. The rationale for the reform was to shorten the duration of the presidency (one of the longest in the world, especially when the president is re-elected), and to avoid situations of a divided executive by coupling presidential and legislative elections. The project was mutually agreeable among parties and deputies, but the turnout for the referendum was only 37 per cent. This was a major signal of the low interest of citizens in institutional issues, and of the distance they feel from their representatives, including the president. We therefore examine the democratic performance of the regime as the capacity for political representation of the partisan system and political leaders, considering political alignment on the left–right spectrum and trust in political leaders.

The convergence and declining relevance of the left–right dimension

The left–right cleavage structures electoral politics by defining the identities and relations between political parties. Left–right alignments can be considered the main cognitive device ordering political perceptions and structuring unidimensional choices. In the social-choice approach, they are fundamental to allow for democratic decision-making and avoid cyclical majorities (Arrow 1951; Mueller 1979). The left–right dimension is therefore necessary for the cognitive operation and the social legitimacy of electoral choice. Nevertheless, all indicators show the declining relevance of this cleavage in public opinion. Consider first self-positioning of citizens on a left–right scale. This indicator has been used by French political scientists as a substitute for party identification used in bipartisan systems. Self-placement on the left is always higher than self-placement on the right, as more people think of themselves as apolitical or non-ideological on the right than on the left. There was no significant increase to the extreme left, nor to the extreme right between 1981 and 2002; indeed, there was a slight decline. The most dramatic change revealed by these data is the rise in the percentage of people refusing to take a position on the axis, from 19 per cent in 1981 to 31 per cent in 2002. Polarisation and stretching in the partisan system as reviewed above do not match movements in self-position of citizens on the major dimension of the political spectrum. They rather interact with an increasing distance between citizens and the structure of political supply, and with a decreasing capacity for identification.

This is confirmed by the attitudes towards the relevance of left and right categories in forming political judgements. Wording of the question was, "Which opinion do you most agree with? The ideas of left and right are obsolete: they no longer help to assess political stands/the ideas of left and right are still valid to understand political stands of political leaders and parties." The data show a clear reversal in the early eighties where the "obsolete" answer progressively became majoritarian, stabilising over 55 per cent in the nineties. In 2002, 60 per cent of respondents thought that left and right have become obsolete for political judgements, with 33 per cent thinking they are still valid.

Such a change not only indicates an increasing distance between citizens and the structure of political supply. It also reflects the convergence of policy positions of supporters of the left and the right. SOFRES surveys show that the difference in attitudes between leftist and rightist supporters has lessened over the last decade on all social issues reviewed above, except for the issue of State regulation versus freedom for firms. For a set of 13 different political or social issues, the average difference in scores between supporters on the left and on the right declined from 17 per cent in the early nineties to 12 per cent in 2002. This discrepancy declined significantly regarding homosexuality (−11%), education (−8%) and immigration (−8%). It remains relatively high regarding the role of firms in the economy (31%), immigration (21%), justice and juvenile delinquency (17%), the death penalty (17%) and education (15%). But attitudes towards homosexuality, women at work, self-perception of belonging to a social class, the need to reform society, and political leaders (see below), display no significant left–right difference.

Our qualitative approach based on focus groups documents this view (Balme et al. 2004). Participants were selected with a homogeneous level of income and education and a low level of interest in politics. Most of them were nevertheless able to express a preference between left and right. But this preference was not necessarily a good predictor of their position on policy issues. Moreover, individuals argued vigorously about objectives and effectiveness of policy instruments. But it was difficult – and indeed nearly impossible – to have groups arguing along clear-cut left–right lines of cleavages on policy issues. Take security, the main policy issue framing the 2002 campaign. From previous meetings, we hypothesised two different kinds of reasoning about the issue: the leftist line of reasoning, interpreting juvenile delinquency as a social problem and connecting insecurity to economic liberalism, unemployment and poverty, the lack of social services and education; and the rightist line, referring to individual responsibility, the crisis of authority and moral values, immigration and failures in parenting. We wanted to test our idea using the "blackboard experiment". The experiment asks the group to list issues related to insecurity, then to locate and connect them using a "post-it" on a board. All factors (and more) were indeed listed and progressively ordered. But, to our surprise, the group was not divided on the topic. Instead of two clusters of issues dividing participants, we observed a continuous multicausal schema, ranking growing social inequalities to ineffectiveness in judicial implementation, and forming a consensus among individuals. The demonstration was particularly dramatic on this issue, but most of the time it was impossible to observe a left–right divide within the group.

The declining significance of French class voting

The reduction in policy distance between left and right in public opinion coincides with a decline in class voting over the period. Class voting is most commonly assessed by measuring the difference in support for the left between workers and other social groups. Here we use data collected by the CEVIPOF (Centre d'Étude de la Vie Politique Française) (Platone 1995) and analysed by Pierre Martin (2000), and a Libération-Louis Harris AOL survey conducted after the first round of the election in 2002.[16] We computed an index measuring the ratio between the percentage of workers' votes for the left and average votes for the left. This index declines from 1.3 per cent in 1981 and 1988, to 1.1 per cent in 1995 and 0.9 per cent in 2002. The graph (Figure 10.8) clearly displays the trend along which worker support for the left has dropped below the average support for the left in the electorate.

In 2002, the largest number of votes from workers went to Jean-Marie Le Pen (26%), far ahead of Lionel Jospin (12%), the communist candidate Robert Hue (5%), the extreme left candidate Arlette Laguiller (10%), and Jacques Chirac (14%). Employees followed the same pattern, although they were spread more equally among candidates (20% for Le Pen, 19% for Jospin, 3% for Hue, 10% for Laguiller, and 16% for Chirac). Le Pen also scored remarkably high among craftsmen, shopkeepers and businessmen (32%), and independents (28%). His electorate was clearly working class and petty bourgeois, while Jospin found a better audience with the middle and upper classes, and Chirac among independents.

Overall, three major trends should be underlined concerning class voting. First, these data show the dealignment of social classes with the left–right cleavage. Lionel Jospin and Jacques Chirac capture a roughly similar and rather low proportion of votes from workers and employees. Secondly, workers and employees' behaviour reflects the tendency towards the dispersion of votes of social groups over multiple candidates and parties. Working-class votes tend to go to candidates from non-governmental parties contesting the political system. And, finally, these protest votes more easily go to the extreme right than to the extreme left (Le Pen attracts significantly more votes from workers than Laguiller). Currently, thinking of electoral behaviour as the mobilisation of social groups constituting a relatively stable electorate is misleading. Our qualitative data show the extreme diversity of voting trajectories, with rarely stabilised loyalties to one party or leader, but

Figure 10.8 Trends in class voting (presidential elections, first round)

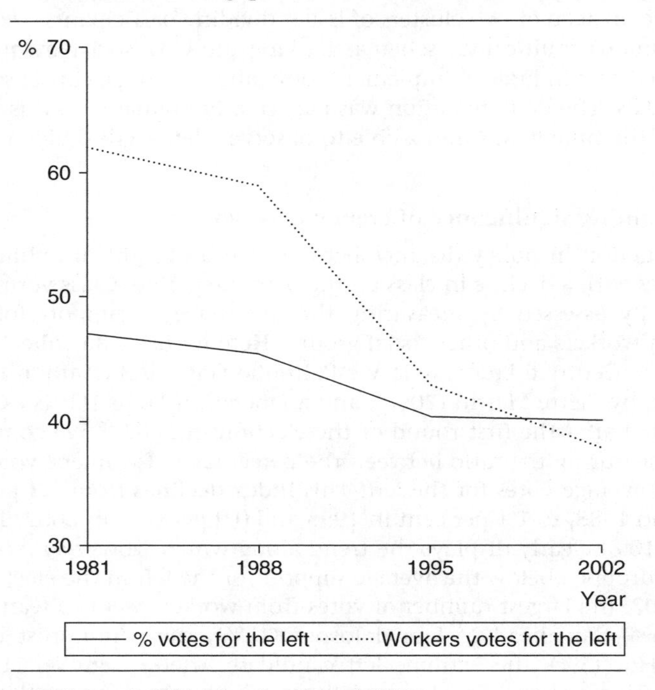

Source: Platone 1995; Martin 2000; *Liberation* 23 April 2002.

rather regular swings from abstention to participation, frequent shifts in support for candidates, sometimes from left to right or vice versa, and with occasional support for extreme right or extreme left (Balme et al. 2004).

The picture drawn so far from these data shows that the convergence in values analysed above is logically associated with a decline in the left–right cleavage as the main axis of French politics. This does not mean that French politics has simply turned to a form of consensus democracy. The events of April 2002 were conflictual enough to show the opposite. But general convergence on the main left–right dimension tends to exacerbate secondary cleavages, left against left or right against right. To the left, there is a clear cleavage between governmental parties and the radical communist left. To the right, a similar cleavage opposes the FN to the RPR–UDF coalition. These secondary cleavages were more salient in the 2002 election than the classical left–right opposition embodied by their champions, Jospin and Chirac. Moreover, within each pole, and sometimes within each party, there are also cleavages defined by environmental issues and attitudes towards European integration (each camp has environmentalists and *souverainistes*).[17] And finally, one last "republican" cleavage opposes the FN to every other position of the political space. Although Europe and the environment were not really raised as issues in the campaigns, we clearly face here a situation of multiplication of cleavages coupled with electoral dealignment (Chiche et al. 2000).

In public-choice literature, Arrow's impossibility theorem generated a considerable amount of comment. One of the issues of these discussions concerned the empirical relevance of the theory. Does majoritarian decision-making as used in democratic institutions indeed produce unstable outcomes? Empiricists could reject the normative speculations of social choice, arguing that Arrow's condition of "unrestricted domain of preferences" was most often not seen in real life, mainly because politics tends to be reduced to unidimensionality with the left–right axis, and because voters' preferences are not randomly distributed, but rather socially shaped and clustered. Such features are crucial to democracy in allowing for majority rule to yield a stable decision, consistent with the preferences of voters.[18] Under the conditions of multiple cleavages and dealignment of electorates depicted above, the election is more likely to produce an outcome not suitable to a majority of voters in one or several dimensions, and to generate political discontent and instability. Arguments presented above converge to suggest that this is what happened on 21 April 2002.

If this is true, then dissatisfaction with political leaders should display cyclical declining trends, each election bringing new disappointments and further distance between voters and party leaders competing for government offices. This is what we examine in the next section.

The political distrust cycle

Consider first trust in individual leaders in executive offices. SOFRES surveys regularly measure the level of citizens' confidence in presidents and prime ministers to solve the problems of French society. Looking at these data for prime ministers since 1981 is quite instructive. Once in office, all leaders face the same pattern of deterioration of power (*usure du pouvoir*). Public opinion initially grants them a positive image and political trust, both of which then quickly decline. This deterioration can be either fast and dramatic (for Edith Cresson or Alain Juppé) or more gradual (Michel Rocard or Edouard Balladur). Six out of nine prime ministers since 1981 sooner or later faced a prevalent distrust in public opinion. This was noticeably true with Pierre Mauroy in 1982 and Jacques Chirac in 1987, showing the incapacity to establish a sustainable consensus on classical Keynesian or openly neo-liberal policies. In itself, the fact that all governments progressively lose the confidence of voters, and that most of them inspire distrust, supports the interpretation suggested here. A new, opposing majority rejects each policy, from the left or the right, once implemented. Such majority cycling nourishes the convergence of policy positions among governmental parties.

Distrust is not assured, however. Three governments have been able to motivate and sustain trust in public opinion while they were in office: Michel Rocard (1988–91), Edouard Balladur (1993–95) and Lionel Jospin (1997–2002). However, none of them was able to win a subsequent national election. Edouard Balladur in 1995 and Lionel Jospin in 2002, although granted with a positive image, both lost the confidence of voters during the presidential campaign. The campaign itself probably matters, and a good prime minister is not *ipso facto* a good candidate (Jaffré 2003). This common view regarding French politics, according to which it is impossible for an outgoing prime minister to win the presidential election, should nevertheless be questioned. This is quite different from the deterioration of power reviewed above, as it holds true even when citizens trust leaders in government. Public opinion reacts as if good governmental performances were not enough to secure electoral support. But this means two different things, in our admittedly speculative view. First, it refers to the instability of political cleavages already mentioned and to the permanent formation of opposing majorities. And second, it suggests that the rise of citizens' expectations matters more than the decline in governments' performance in explaining political distrust.

Finally, we will examine the general level of trust in political leadership. SOFRES regularly asked citizens, "Do political leaders care about the opinion of people like you?" Figure 10.9 clearly shows the reversal of the early eighties, when distrust became majoritarian in public opinion, and the sharp increase in the discrepancy between the two curves after 1997. In January 2002, 74 per cent said political leaders care about "very few" or "almost none" of their opinions, compared to 25 per cent responding that they care "a lot" or "somewhat". This institutional divide between leaders and citizens is equally valid for supporters from the left and from the right.

It is noticeable that general trust in political leaders largely declined after 1997, while public opinion was remarkably confident in Lionel Jospin's capacities in government. This picture may seem somewhat puzzling. But it clearly shows, in our view, that the deterioration of political trust has more structural than short-term determinants. The experience of multiple political swings and policy convergence of governmental parties has disillusioned voters about outcomes to be expected from governmental change. In reducing the alternative for democratic choice, it has also increased the distance between citizens and political leadership. Political distrust has become a systemic property of French politics. Whatever government performances might be, general trust in political leaders is declining. In return, the general loss of confidence in ruling elites affects the credibility of leaders in office, and a "good" prime minister in the eyes of public opinion hardly makes a good candidate. The long period of the trend (two decades) suggests an elitist transformation of French society, where politics and government are

Figure 10.9 Trust in political leaders

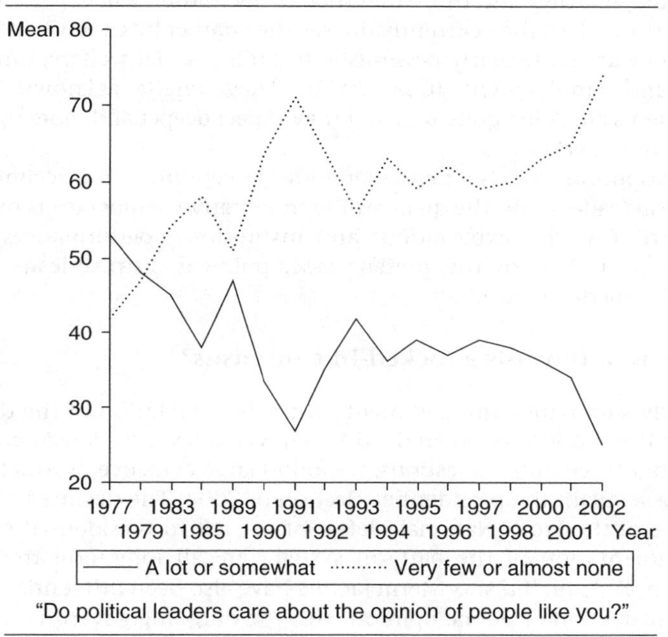

Source: SOFRES 2002.

increasingly distant from citizens, and perceived as the activity of an elite motivated by perks of personal privileges and sometimes corrupt.

Corruption does not help political trust, but is probably not the main source of democratic disaffection. Surprisingly, political scandals are considered in our qualitative surveys as inherent to power and political competition. Citizens are not indifferent about corruption, but they are not surprised either. Jacques Chirac for instance, largely disliked by a majority of participants in our survey, was not challenged because of political scandals, but because he did not keep his promises once elected. Some voters supported François Mitterrand in 1981, and were disappointed by his policies, and then for Jacques Chirac in 1995, and once again felt deceived by the President. Citizens clearly feel a gap between candidates' promises and policies implemented by governments, and, more profoundly, a wide distance between public policy and the ability to change their own lives effectively. In our view, the key of political distrust lies in the pessimism of citizens. They generally think that the situation of the country and their own situation has declined in recent years and the possibility for improvement in the near future to be low. They believe that they have better opportunities than their parents did, but they also think that their own children will experience more difficult times than they currently do (see the chapter by Chauvel in this volume). They are particularly pessimistic regarding social welfare, purchasing power and employment (CSA 2003). They might acknowledge that governments are doing quite well, but they expect deeper and more significant changes in society.

Public opinion reflects a particularly low perception of the accountability of political leaders, and the quality of representative democracy is directly at stake here. Citizens' expectations and institutional performances ground political trust. But, in the present case, political distrust leads to poor democratic performance.

Conclusion: towards a locked-in consensus?

We briefly summarise and comment on the interpretation of the data, and consider the relations between the different variables considered here. Going back to our three initial questions, we found large evidence of structural features that explain the presidential election of 2002. The decline in turnout, influence of the Front National, defeat of the left in presidential elections, and fragmentation of the partisan system, are all long-term trends confirmed on 21 April. But short-term factors have also been influential, notably the dissatisfaction of public opinion with the outgoing government regarding social welfare and insecurity and the poor campaign of Lionel Jospin. In contrast, there is virtually no support for the neo-conservatism hypothesis. Public opinion has generally evolved towards more progressive positions on social and moral issues and towards a tempered economic liberalism, while remaining strongly supportive of social welfare. The data we reviewed draw a triangular space for political consensus, limited by cultural liberalism, economic liberalism (freedom for firms, lower taxes and public spending) and social protection (welfare, employment and revenues). The National Front definitely stands outside this consensus, opposing moral conservatism to cultural liberalism, and polarising the political space. As shown by the issue of the election and confirmed by the data, it has succeeded so far in gaining support from 20 to 25 per cent of public opinion and influencing public controversies and agendas, although without countering the wide support for cultural liberalism.

Finally, the analysis of the election of 2002 showed that the democratic capacity of the political regime has substantially deteriorated over the last two decades. Its capacity for political representation declined with identification with the left–right axis, class-voting, and trust in political leaders. This situation has two major consequences. First, dealignment from the left–right dimension favours the multiplication of cleavages, increases the saliency of secondary cleavages and issue-voting, and makes majority cycling more likely. And, secondly, the long-term decline of trust in political elites combined with short-term confidence in executive leaders favours turnover in elections and political instability.

It seems somewhat puzzling to observe both convergence in public opinion and governmental parties on policy issues and the declining democratic capacity of the regime with the rise of political distrust. The data we examined can be interpreted in three complementary ways to solve this apparent contradiction. First, the increase in people's expectations has exceeded governmental performance during this time period. Citizens not only prefer individual choice on moral issues, freedom for firms and lower taxes in the economy, *and* social welfare from the State; they also want much more of everything. Put differently, the rise of citizens' expectations seems to matter more than effectiveness of policy output, even when the latter is positive, in explaining political distrust. This explanation might not always be true, and it is subject to short-term conditions. But it seems valid to explain the contrast between the positive image of the Jospin government and the failure of its leader in the presidential race.

Why did citizens' expectations towards governments rise so significantly during this time? A common view is that public policies moved away from citizens' preferences, and that governments increasingly ruled against public opinion. Dissatisfaction over unemployment, social security reforms, insecurity, or the level of taxes supports this view. This question is not easy to disentangle, but analysing these data leads to a more complex understanding. Indeed, there is no clear disparity between governments' policies and public-opinion trends. Liberal legislation has been passed on many social issues, economic policy has become more liberal, and the welfare system has been globally maintained and somewhat expanded with new rights such as the creation of the RMI and a universal health benefit. We understand that this last point about the maintenance of the welfare system is debatable, as many reforms limiting benefits have also been introduced. We suggest nevertheless that the neo-liberal turn in France was not a radical turn as in the British case, welfare spending continuously increased and remained at a high level in comparative perspective.

Rather than dissensus between public opinion and governments, we explain distrust in governments as the result of a lock-in effect of convergence in citizens' preferences. Indeed, as strong majorities support both lower taxes *and* the provision of public services and social benefits, the room for manoeuvre of public policy is largely limited. A rightist government aiming at substantially lower taxes will have to cut public services and social benefits, and will soon face an opposing leftist majority. On the other side, given changes in the occupational and demographic structure, a leftist government would have to increase taxes significantly to expand, or even maintain, the level of social benefits without changing the criteria for allocation, and would then nourish the making of a rightist coalition. Room for manoeuvre does exist, but is too limited to produce clear policy changes as perceived by public opinion. The level of taxes remains high, while welfare benefits are progressively reduced. The feeling that politics does not matter and that changes in leadership do not affect public policy largely explains political distrust. If they cannot expect real changes about a situation they are worried about, why would citizens support political leaders, and why should they trust them? The declining support for political leadership is grounded on a loss of policy effectiveness. But the reduction in space for policy change is based on the structure of political consensus as reflected in public opinion.

The third explanation is more institutional. Policy convergence does not simply produce consensus. Rather, it reduces the alternatives offered to political choice, in terms of policy positions and personal profiles of leaders. In doing so, it also generates disappointment with regard to governmental change, electoral disinterest and partisan dealignment, and multiplication of secondary cleavages. In turn, political fragmentation favours majority cycling. This is probably true in many countries. But policy convergence has been doubled in the French case by the institutional feature of the divided executive (*cohabitation*). In particular, both the President and Prime Minister are associated with a shared responsibility for a common state of public policy and public affairs. This makes it difficult for public opinion to give credit to distinctive policy platforms, and to expect a real change from partisan change in the executive.

All three factors – the rise of citizens' expectations, reduction of space for policy choice, and divided executive government – contributed to establish a locked-in consensus, leading to a cycle of political distrust. The features of public opinion described here are consistent with the conventional image of French political culture, joining a strong sense of individual freedom to attachment to the State to guarantee social equality. We argued that their dynamics of convergence over time help to explain the electoral breakdown of 2002 and more durable characteristics of the regime. In a way, French politics seems to have gained in pluralism. Society became more liberal on economic and moral issues, more tolerant of different groups and behaviours, while still attached to welfare. Politics became more diversified with the rise of new parties, and less conflictual with policy convergence between governmental parties. But this increase in pluralism is coupled with a growing divide between popular classes and political elites, caused by a set of mechanisms related by systemic relations. These are distinct but interdependent and cumulative processes, generated by the combination of long-term and short-term trends. As such, they are likely to persist, continuing to affect French politics in the coming years.

Notes

1 In 1969, there were two Gaullist candidates, Georges Pompidou and Alain Poher, in the final round of the election. Nevertheless, François Mitterrand was not a candidate in the first round, as opposed to Lionel Jospin in 2002.

2 The "Political Trust and Public Policy" project is conducted in partnership with Paul Snidernam, Jean-Louis Marie and Olivier Rozenberg. The "Reasons to Vote" project was conducted with Olivier Rozenberg and Céline Bélot. These projects have been funded by the Fondation Jean Jaurès, the National Science Foundation, the CEVIPOF (Paris) and the CIDSP (Centre d'informatisation des donnees socio-politiques) (Grenoble). For methodology and a more extensive presentation of results, see Balme et al. (2003) and Balme et al. (2004).

3 Only the two candidates with the highest scores in the first round can compete in the second one.

4 French electoral Law distinguishes among *suffrages exprimés* (valid votes), *votes nuls* (spoiled ballots, or votes discounted because ballots were damaged, or two ballots were included in the envelope, or voters wrote something on the ballot) and *votes blancs* (voters insert a white peace of paper in the envelope). The latter are quite distinct from spoiled ballots as voters actually do vote without choosing a candidate. They offer a measure of positive civic participation without political choice. There is a whole debate in France about this, as election results are counted as percentages of valid votes, while some civic groups claim for the inclusion of these white ballots in the total before calculation of share of votes for candidates.

5 For both measures, a higher score indicates a lower level of fragmentation.

6 Brice Lalonde, leader of Generation Ecologie, was Minister in the Jacques Chirac government of 1986. His electoral audience was nevertheless weaker than the one for the Greens in different elections.

7 A proportional rule was temporally introduced at the time for the legislative elections.

8 In 2001, the Parliament adopted a law creating the *Pacte civil de solidarité*, introducing the possibility for lesbian and gays to contract a union with similar benefits to marriage. Christine Boutin, a rank-and-file deputy from the right, was the main opponent to the project.

9 1981, 1986, 1988, 1993, 1997.

10 Coinciding presidential and parliamentarian majorities to the left (1981–86 and 1988–93); coinciding presidential and parliamentarian majorities to the right (1995–97); divided executive power (referred to as *cohabitation*) between a leftist president and a rightist government (1986–88 and 1993–95); divided executive power between a rightist president and a leftist government (1997–2002).

11 Most data in the following section are results from SOFRES surveys as reported in TNS-Sofres 2002.

12 The most demonstrative case being probably anti-authoritarian teachers facing violence at school.

13 SOFRES 2002b.

14 TNS Sofres/EOS Gallup Europe 2004.

15 SOFRES/*Le Monde* 2001.

16 *Libération*, 23 April 2002.

17 Promoters of national sovereignty, such as the socialist Jean-Pierre Chevènement or the Gaullist Philippe Séguin.

18 Other features in the institutional design of decision-making are also able to reduce majority cycling (Riker 1986; Ordeshook 1986).

11
Representation in Trouble

Suzanne Berger

Introduction

Over the period 2002–2004 France experienced two electoral earthquakes. For political scientists who believe that the forces shaping the electorate mainly change gradually, with the entry of new generations of electors, new issues, and new contenders for power, and only infrequently change radically, in elections of critical realignment, this is one earthquake more than the usual accounts can manage. The puzzle this chapter hopes to unravel is how the same underlying factors could produce such contradictory results as those of the 2002 presidential elections and the 2004 regional elections. More generally, it explores the stalled reform of French politics which lies at the origin of this apparent fickleness of the electorate. In the case of each of the elections, there were a host of contingent events like school holidays, misleading polls, and multiple candidacies that might explain outcomes. That these accidents could produce such wide variance in the results, however, reflects the underlying weaknesses of the structures linking society to politics in France today. With the disappearance of the old anchors of religion and class, the preferences of the electors now swing along with the tides of political discontent and distrust. This chapter starts, then, from the two elections; it goes on to propose, not an electoral analysis, but some ways of understanding the break-down in the system of representation. It is this break-down that makes the support of citizens for their elected representatives so tenuous and fragile.

In the first of the two elections, the 21 April 2002 presidential balloting, against all expectations, Lionel Jospin, the Socialist Prime Minister, was eliminated and Jean-Marie Le Pen, the historic leader of the National Front, a xenophobic far-right party, emerged as the run-off candidate against Jacques Chirac. This shock wiped out a general expectation that the transformation of French society and economy that had been underway for the past 30 years was slowly but inevitably producing a transformation of politics and the disappearance of French exceptionalism. A third of the electorate did not vote, and another third voted for parties of the extremist right and left. The repudiation of the parties of government spread far beyond its previous level in the 1997 legislative elections, when already almost half of the registered voters had either abstained or voted for an anti-system party (Chiche and Reynié 2002: 82). With 19.2 percent of the votes cast, the far right (Le Pen and Bruno Mégret) achieved its best-ever score in national elections. With 10.4 percent of the vote the three Trotskyite parties far outdistanced their old enemy, the Communist Party, with 3.4 percent of the votes, their worst-ever score.

This election took place in a period of relative prosperity and growth, with unemployment levels substantially lower than in the recent past. The electoral collapse of the parties of government did not derive from an inability to produce satisfactory outcomes in the economy. In fact, in polls carried out before the election, concerns about the economy took second place to concerns about security, an amalgam of fears about crime, immigration, and long-term economic decline. However unexpected, the 21 April election results came rapidly to be understood as a marker of the radical disaffection of the French from their representatives in government and of the unreformed state of French political organizations and ideas. Interpretations of the election emphasized that the structural factors—abstention, loss of support for parties of government, strength of the far right, the disappearance of working-class attachment to the left—were ones that had been in the making for a long time and finally by a kind of "tipping effect" culminated in this dramatic outcome.

The results of the 21–8 March 2004 regional elections were equally unexpected and resembled, as one defeated center-right candidate, the Minister for Social Affairs François Fillon, put it, "a kind of upside down April 21." The Socialists won a crushing victory over the candidates of the governmental majority parties and captured 24 out of 26 regions. The Socialists' score (50.2% of the votes cast, as against the UMP–UDF 37%) was their best ever in the Fifth Republic (aside from the 1981 legislative elections following Mitterrand's election as president). The electorate of the three small parties of the extreme left, whose votes had deprived Jospin of a place on the second ballot of the presidential election, shrank and many of these voters apparently returned to traditional left parties. The trend towards growing levels of abstention was reversed, and even more people voted on the second ballot than the first.

Times had changed over the two years, and the voters' concerns about unemployment and the state of the economy had once again risen to the top of their priorities, displacing security (Perraudeau and Timbeau 2004). But it would be difficult to argue that this shift in the economy could explain the massive turnabout of the electors. Rather what seems to have been at work, in the 2004 elections as in the 2002 elections, was a sanctioning of the parties in government—in 2002, the Socialists, in 2004, the center-right.

As Dominique Goux and Eric Maurin argued in an analysis of the results, the basic forces at work in 2002 and 2004 were the same. "In both cases, the variations in the vote from one district to another reflect a more or less strong rejection of the government in power and a greater or lesser sense of distance from the political system. The difference is that in 2004, the rejection of the government played out against the Right alone, whereas in 2002, because of cohabitation, both Right and Left parties shared the blame" (Goux and Maurin 2004).

Even more important than a shift in attitudes on particular issues, the returns demonstrated in successive elections the inability of candidates in the parties of government to convince many of the voters that politicians see a horizon beyond the politics of personal and party gain. Citizens still believe that politics can and should regulate social and economic life, but since 1983 one government after another has failed, in the eyes of the voters, to deliver on its commitments to do so (see Teinturier 2004). Even as the old meanings of left and right have shifted and blurred, no new vision of social order and justice in French society or of France's role in the world has taken their place. There has been a failure by the parties and politicians to articulate convincing new understandings of the public interest and of what can and should be undertaken by the State. On the side of the public, what has emerged is a mixture of fear and anger. On issues perceived as major threats to wellbeing—whether physical security in 2002 or economic, in 2004—the parties of government appear to citizens to be rudderless and incapable of steering a course that promises a more secure future.

1. Representing civil society

Broadly speaking, a system of representation encompasses both the organizations that link citizens to government and the political ideas and programs that structure citizens' conceptions of how the world works and, consequently, their expectations about what can and should be achieved through politics. To assess the organizational dimension of representation, we need to focus on the creation, reproduction, and renewal of capabilities that allow parties and civil-society associations to express and structure the demands of broad segments of society and to mobilize citizens as members, supporters, or electors. Organizational capabilities depend in the first instance on some degree of fit between given socioeconomic environments and party institutions. It was obvious, for example, that the sharp decline of heavy industry in the old territorial bases of the left and the expansion of a service economy in those constituencies would undermine institutions that the Communist Party had deployed in the 1950s and 1960s to mobilize workers in mass production industries and to link voters, supporters, party members, party leaders, and elected representatives. Even party members and electors employed in parts of the economy that did not undergo such drastic shrinkage over the past 20 years have nonetheless experienced major changes: in employment contracts and the content of jobs, in female labor force participation, rising average levels of education, new forms of sociability, and with exposure to new media and internet technologies. These transformations in society all made it highly unlikely that the old party institutions could carry on without major restructuring.

Even as the socioeconomic terrain on which the parties had to operate was shifting, there were also far-reaching changes in the public's desires and expectations about the kinds of individual experience that participation in a civic association or in a political party should provide. Without subscribing to any particular theory of the transformation of individual preferences in post-industrial societies, one can still observe that over the past 20 years new recruits into political organizations have had different aspirations for individual expression and participation than those who joined political movements in the past. As Boy et al. have shown for members of the various parties of the left, degrees of satisfaction with their organizations were closely linked to perceptions of openness and democratic practice within the group (2003). The rejection of the kinds of hierarchy, subordination, and discipline that were integral features of political party membership in the sixties and seventies created another and autonomous source of pressure on the parties to reform their internal systems of governance. Yet there is not much evidence of adaptation on this dimension. The decline in party membership and the rise in participation in civic associations suggest that militants are voting with their feet for organizations within which they can have more voice and closer, less-hierarchical relations with others.

As Herbert Kitschelt's work on the transformation of the organizations and strategies of social democratic parties in Europe has emphasized, there is no simple correspondence between structural changes in society and the economy and the responses, successful or otherwise, of political parties (1994). Kitschelt identifies two key dimensions of party internal structure that condition the party's ability to respond to changes in the environment: organizational entrenchment and the autonomy of party leaders (1994: 212–15). In this analysis the central interaction is between these internal institutional properties and the characteristics of an external competitive environment in which the party strives against others for influence and voters. From this perspective, party organizational configurations appear quite resilient and ordinarily likely to change in only limited and incremental fashion. In the case of massive party defeat or the entry of a wave of new members, such organizational changes may be accelerated, but in normal times these structures are relatively stable.

On this grid of analysis, Kitschelt identified France as one of the countries in the 1980s (along with Belgium, the Netherlands, and Spain) where Socialist parties had organizational forms that matched up well with the challenges they faced in the competitive party environment in contrast to the communist parties in the same systems (1994: 230–1). In retrospect, it is hard to know what happened to the capabilities of French parties that Kitschelt saw in the eighties as providing flexibility and responsiveness to changes in social demands and to the opportunity structure in the competitive political arena. Was the problem that organizational supply adapted too slowly, or was it that social demand accelerated and diversified too rapidly for any party to have been able to capture? The organizational supply explanation would point to the failure of political entrepreneurship and emphasize the progressive atrophy and rigidification of party organizations that made them undesirable vehicles for citizens looking for new forms of political participation. Alternatively, a political-demand story would focus on the complexity and heterogeneity of demand in a society that by the end of the century was very different from the one in which the party organizations and strategies had been born. Both of these explanations of the decay of the links between the parties and society seem plausible. In any event, because of the feedback between problems arising from inflexibility of organizational supply and those arising from the diversification of social demand it would be difficult to choose between these two accounts or even to weigh their relative importance.

Beyond some minimal fit between a changed society and the party organizational infrastructure there is also the issue of how the parties identify concerns of the population and how they express these new anxieties and demands in political ideas and programs. The challenge for a political party is to build programs that accommodate increasingly diverse societal interests and the range of views of a more heterogeneous party membership. It is also to structure the demands of its members and electorate. The parties need organizational capabilities that, minimally, allow them to lay out new cognitive maps of how the problems experienced in daily life are linked to political choices and to articulate new visions of what is possible through political action. Representation in this sense is not only capacity for transmission but also a capacity for shaping and reshaping the preferences of voters and party members. Without attempting an exhaustive account of the failures of representation on these dimensions in France over the past 20 years, this chapter focuses on two aspects of the dilemma which seem especially important today: (1) the atrophy of the organizations of political representation; and (2) the failure of the main political actors to convince the French public of the legitimacy of the new relations between France and the outside world.

2. Parties in decline, participation on the rise

Despite the enormous changes over the past two decades in French society, economy and in the policies of the State, the organizations that articulate, aggregate and represent French society have reproduced themselves as quite faithful copies of the old models. They have changed mainly by subtraction: by a sharp decline in the numbers of French who participate, by a withering away of the core ideological issues that used to animate them, and by a shrinking of the social terrain over which the parties today exercise their authority. As Serge July in *Libération* concluded after the 21 April election:

> All the intermediary bodies have entered into an advanced state of decomposition over the past 20 years. The decay has been continuous, and the effects of this disaggregation are becoming more and more serious. Political parties, unions, social forces, bureaucracies, the school are all weakened. None of them can organize society, that is, organize its voice and expression, provide accountability, or make a bridge between government and social actors, the citizens, employees or the unemployed. (2002: 3)

Well before the election, political analysts had been signaling the multiple signs of weakness and fatigue in the system of partisan representation (Chiche et al. 2002). The first symptom was a dramatic increase in the hostility of the electorate to politicians. Support for the idea that "politicians do not care about what's worrying people like us" rose from 42 percent in 1977 to 72 percent in 1995 to 83 percent of the voters polled before the 21 April election, and 58 percent of the respondents in that survey believed that political leaders are more or less corrupt (Mayer 2002: 359). In the wake of the 2002 election, as journalists fanned out into the areas that had high rates of abstention and high rates of shift to Le Pen, the stories they reported were of a kind of revolt against the political elite, with strong echoes of the old Poujadist battle cry, "throw them out!" (*sortir les sortants*!). Dominique Goux and Eric Maurin have developed an analysis of the election results as a rejection of the political class (Goux and Maurin 2002). They found that rather than a left–right divide, the real cleavage lay between an electorate that supports the current political system in departments that voted relatively heavily for Jospin or for Chirac and relatively less for Le Pen; and an anti-system electorate in departments that voted heavily for Le Pen, Laguiller, and Hué. This divide appeared again in the results of the second ballot, which showed Chirac making gains in departments that had voted for Jospin on the first round, but not in those areas in which Hué or Laguiller had done especially well in the first round.

The sense of distance and distrust between voters and their representatives in power has undoubtedly been fed by multiple sources. In part it may reflect a more general phenomenon of falling confidence in elites, since over the past 15 years polls show a huge increase in those who lack confidence in private corporate leaders as well (from 25% in 1985 to 54% in August 2002) (TNS SOFRES 2005). There were also specifically political drivers of these sentiments. Over the past decade a long run of scandals involving politicians under investigation for abuse of office for private financial gain or for party coffers dragged on interminably through the courts. The politicians implicated in these scandals came from all the major parties, and inevitably the public came to feel that there was rot all the way through the system.

Even where there was no criminal betrayal of faith, the gap between the views expressed in the electorate and those defended by political parties has been widening. Within parties, as Daniel Boy et al. (2003) show for the militants in the parties of the left, there has been increasing fragmentation in the views held by members of the same party. This widening of the gap between the range of views within the electorate and within the militant base of the parties, on the one side, and the positions proposed by the political elites may fall short of a "radical disconnection between ideological 'demand' and partisan 'supply,' " as Chiche, Haegel, and Tiberj conclude (2002: 235). But across the board, in the polls of public attitudes over the past 20 years one finds evidence of the erosion of the links of trust and identity between electors and their representatives.

The elections of the past 15 years present a similar picture. Chiche and Reynié (2002) point to the continuous decline since 1988 in the votes cast in legislative elections for left and right parties of government. In other European countries as well, the traditional governmental parties of left and right face new challengers within their own ideological camps. Chiche and Reynié emphasize, however, that despite the growth of protest parties and a certain fragmentation of the electorate in Italy, the Netherlands, and elsewhere, the French case stands out as exceptional for the sharpness of the decline of the governmental parties. They conclude: "The fragility of the French parties of government shows up in any European comparison. The weakness of the parties of government is a French problem" (2002: 52).

Other indicators of the disaffection of the electorate are the growth of abstention, the increase in the numbers of blank ballots cast, and the rise in the number and success of candidates not associated with a national party in local and regional elections. The weakness of the parties is manifested as well in their inability to hang on to supporters who gravitate to other parties without necessarily crossing the left–right divide. The old cleavages of religion, class, and union membership matter less today than they did in the past for shaping the party preferences of the voters.[1] But even when these sociological variables structure the likelihood of a voter's choice of left or right, they do not account for which of the parties of left or right the voters choose. Rather, there has been an increasingly loose association between the ideological predispositions of the voter and the *particular* party of left or of right that he or she chooses. The dispersion and volatility of the electorate within the camps of left and right is yet another demonstration of the parties' inability to stabilize their relations with even those electors who are, so to speak, ideologically and sociologically their closest of kin.[2]

Even as the French express more negative attitudes towards the parties and retreat from party membership, there has been a significant increase in support for other forms of political action. The French are increasingly willing on a case-by-case basis to participate in political protest. Pierre Bréchon points out that today over three-quarters of all French have joined in some protest activity—whether signing a petition, demonstrating, or striking—whereas 20 years ago, only half of the population had done so (Bréchon 2000: 112–15). Over the past 10 years public opinion has approved virtually all protest movements in favor of protecting the rights, jobs, or benefits of established social groups. During the December 1986–January 1987 public-sector strikes, a large majority (67%) of those polled criticized the strikers; by the December 1995 strikes there were majorities who endorsed the strikers, and that has been true across a wide range of social conflicts through the past decade (Rozes 2001). Public support for these protests is higher in France today than elsewhere in Europe (Jaffré 2001) and it seems to be a kind of counterweight to the growing discrediting of the parties.

Jacques Capdevielle has argued that the new wave of corporatist mobilizations of the nineties rushed in to fill a vacuum left by traditional political organizations, and he concluded: "These narrow group identities and demands are not remnants of backwardness: they are part of French modernity. They reveal its political deficiencies and will only be changed by fixing these political problems." The growing support for forms of civic participation that substitute for party militancy does not, however, only flow into these corporatist movements. There has been a boom in the participation in new social protest groups, some of them focused on single issues, like the illegal immigrants (*sans-papiers*) or the unemployed (*chomeurs*) committees, some with broader agendas, like SUD-PTT, a break-away from more traditional trade unionism (with 15,000 members), or the regional ethnic movements, or the NGOs focused on development.[3] Martine Barthélémy has identified a major surge in the creation of new associations in the late 1970s and early 1980s.[4] In 1973 about 28 percent of all French over the age of 15 belonged to some civic association (including parties and unions); by the end of the 1990s, the figure had risen to about 40 percent. But this general increase obscures very different trajectories of evolution, with participation in parties and unions on the decline and participation in cultural and sports activities on the rise. The vitality of these diverse forms of association suggest a widespread interest in participation, but a potential that has not translated into a new reservoir of recruits for political organizations.

3. Open borders = vulnerability

In the diversity of problems troubling the French electorate, one common element recurs. Many of the matters on which the French feel that their representatives have failed to hear them and to respond are perceived as having their origins outside of France. Foremost among these issues is crime and violence, which are widely perceived to be on the rise and widely believed to be the doing of North-African immigrant youth. While there has been an increase in crime, with growth in the numbers of reported violations of 5.7 percent in 2000 and 7.7 percent in 2001, certain categories of serious crime, like homicide have declined over the same period.[5] So the question of why the French suddenly feel so vulnerable and unprotected cannot be answered by any simple reference to crime statistics. The sense of insecurity may have been amplified, rather, by the fact that the issue lies along a political fault line that identifies openness to the outside world and the removal of the State from its traditional functions on the frontiers as the source of new dangers and menaces to French society. The dangers that threaten to pour in over the unprotected borders of the State are of three kinds: first, there are the immigrants, both those already in and asylum seekers and others trying to get into France by all means legal and illegal. The principal danger they pose is felt today as one of security, since people believe that foreigners are responsible for a disproportionate share of crimes. Beyond the issue of crime, there lurks the threat the immigrants present for the racial, cultural, and religious composition of the country.

The second manifestation of high levels of concern about France's openness to the outside world and the shrinking of the protective functions of the State is the growth of the anti-globalization movement. Various public opinion polls provide rather different readings of French perceptions of the impact of globalization.[6] Over the past few years, however, the proportions of those expressing anxiety about globalization seem to be on the rise. In a SOFRES 12–13 July 2001 survey 55 percent of the respondents described globalization as a threat for French jobs and companies (Spitz 2002: 117). Three-quarters of them agreed that there was not enough regulation in the international economy and that government (39%), unions (48%), or citizen movements (67%) should play a larger role. By the fall of 2002, those polled who expressed "worry" about globalization rose to 63 percent, and only 10 percent expressed "confidence in globalization," half the number who had been confident about globalization three years earlier.[7] The election results of 2002 also reflected a shift in the weight of candidates hostile to globalization (the three Trotskyites, the Communist, Chevènement, the Green, Le Pen, Mégret, and Saint-Josse) who won close to half the votes, a rise over the success of candidates opposed to globalization in previous elections (Fougier 2002: 32).

This division of public opinion appears again in polls on French feelings about France's membership in the European Union. Here again, there are significant fluctuations from year to year even over the near past and variations depending on the question posed. In early 2001, 43 percent expressed reservations about the effect of the EU on France (in contrast to 53% who were confident); asked about whether they were committed to Europe,

49 percent said yes; 50 percent, no.[8] Although European political leaders, French among them, often approvingly describe the EU's institutional capacity to regulate globalization, their message has apparently been received with considerable skepticism by the French public. In a July 2001 poll, asked whether Europe could provide some kind of protection against the negative effects of globalization, 54 percent answered no; 40 percent, yes.[9]

What the questions both on globalization and on Europe appear to tap is a set of concerns about the consequences of openness. At least as many see it, globalization and Europe mean an end to national borders, hence to the possibilities of national regulation within society. Widely shared perceptions of the impact of change in the international economic arena on domestic politics have led to a growing fear of globalization in virtually all advanced countries. Even after years of economic growth and prosperity in the United States, various opinion polls find the public roughly evenly divided over whether free trade is bad for the US. However sophisticated or ignorant citizens' beliefs may be about the relationships between trade, growth, and employment, they do tend to focus on the issue of open borders and on the implications for security and national policies. There is a growing sense of the loss of control over the basic foundations of societal well-being and the belief that globalization means that no one can be held accountable for basic choices about society's use of resources and allocations of reward and risk.

Concerns about globalization are hardly uniquely French. But there are specific features to the French response. First, the attacks on globalization fall along a political fault line that traverses the left–right divide. The emergence in the debates over the 1992 Maastricht referendum of a "sovereignty" camp has operated over the past 10 years to reformulate and revivify the old categories of French nationalism and to give them new content and targets (Alliès 2000). The arguments of the sovereignty group cut not only against transfers of authority to the European Community but also against reducing the role of the State in regulating all transactions—capital mobility, migration, trade in goods and services—across France's borders. For these left and right nationalists, what is at stake in Europe and in globalization goes far beyond material issues. The nation itself is jeopardized not only by the explicit transfers of sovereignty to other bodies, but by the renunciation, as in the Uruguay Round, of the instruments through which the State's intervention might be implemented.

For the *souverainistes*, the foundations of the national exercise of control and choice are borders. As Philippe Séguin expressed it in the debates over Maastricht: "The idea of frontiers as outdated! There's a dogma to attack. Bringing back the frontiers today is the condition of any policy ..." (1993: 42). By giving up the powers that allow it to implement social solidarity, justice, and equality, the State is seen to be destroying its own foundations. And on this, whatever their other differences, Jean-Pierre Chevènement and Séguin or Philippe de Villiers or Charles Pasqua would agree. The result has been that within both left and right, the emergence of the nationalist fissure has pulled voters away from the parties of government and into the minor parties of the camp.

Even more significant than the sovereignty camp in providing political expression of popular anxieties about globalization have been the new anti-globalization movements. As Marcos Ancelovici explains, out of the political battles and strike wave of December 1995 a novel formulation of the contradictions between social democracy and capitalism emerged. Ancelovici calls the new vision a "politics against global markets" frame. It expresses the opposition between social solidarity and justice and markets in terms that both borrow from old anti-capitalist left ideology and also innovate in identifying the enemy as the global character of markets.[10] Ancelovici points out that where in the past the anti-capitalist left saw the units of political confrontation as social classes—workers against capitalists—the new perspective sees citizens within a national community struggling against global markets in which multinational corporations and financial interests are the strongest forces. Far from identifying the State as the instrument of powerful economic interests as in the old left, the anti-globalization militants regard the State as the basic instrument that citizens can use to defend their rights, and, above all, the right to shape their own lives. State intervention and regulation are understood as the ultimate resort against the commodification of human social relations and the destruction of democratic politics by market forces.

The main political actor in France in advancing this new view of the world has been ATTAC (Association for the Taxation of Financial Transactions for the Aid of Citizens), an organization founded in 1998 by a coalition of left-wing intellectuals, trade unions, newspapers, and civic action associations. Today, the organization has 230 local groups throughout France and about 30,000 members (probably equal to half the membership of the Socialist Party) (Fougier 2002: 62). It has played a highly visible role in international demonstrations against the IMF and at the G8 summit meetings; and it was the leading organizer of the Porto Alegre World Social Forum meetings. ATTAC's relations with the political parties of the left have been at arms length; it has neither presented candidates for election, nor supported any. As Bernard Cassen, ATTAC's first president put it, the organization wants to be a "democratic pacemaker to force [parties and institutions] to do their jobs properly."[11] A break-away faction of ATTAC members who in 2004 proposed to run "100% altermondialistes" electoral lists was beaten down by the leadership. ATTAC describes its objective with respect to the left parties as one of forcing the parties to recognize that the new basic cleavage in politics is between liberals (on domestic issues, like privatizations, and on the international economy) and the defenders of the social democratic welfare state (Monnot 2002). Its advances on the Socialist Party look more like efforts to split the party than to join it or replace it.

Viewed from the parties' perspective, the rapid growth of this new movement with its call for radical change in policies at the national, European, and international levels is a mixed blessing. The anti-system parties of left and right have embraced the anti-globalization themes, albeit with different perspectives, the left supporting alternative forms of internationalization (*altermondialisation*), the right identifying the continuities between its old anti-immigration programs with the newer antiglobalization ideas. For the left and right parties of government, however, to endorse fully the new "politics against global markets" frame of ATTAC would mean drastic renunciation of the European and international commitments of past governments. It would involve major innovation in party programs. Though the new streams of activists entering politics through local organizations centered on globalization would appear to be potential candidates to be drawn into party politics, the parties have not been recruiting these activists—in part, at least, because the parties have not been willing to address the globalization issue in ways that connect with the new associational mobilization.[12]

Even the Socialist Party—which in principle had perhaps the best chance of recruiting the militants from associations like ATTAC—has been unable to articulate a stand on globalization that goes beyond half-hearted steps for regulating and moderating globalization in mostly unspecified ways.[13] The Socialists did officially accept the idea of a "Tobin-like" tax on international financial flows. But to go further than this on the new issue would have required revising the old templates of left politics for a "politics-against-markets" frame and thus risking the support of old members and electors. However reduced the salience of categories linked to *laïcité* or class conflict for interpreting contemporary society, still the parties believe (or believed, until 21 April) that a stable component of their electorate relies on those old touchstones of partisan identification. So there was deep reluctance both in the Socialist Party and in the Communist Party to jettisoning their old themes and to bringing the new issue fully on board.

There was, moreover, another risk in taking on the globalization issue: that it would reinforce internal strains within the party between reformers and radicals. After the 2002 elections, globalization did in fact become one of the issues on which the cleavages within the Socialist Party crystallized. While the party leadership and more moderate factions called for "new rules to organize a world order based on rights, solidarity and citizenship" (François Hollande) or for "inventing new and more effective regulatory institutions" (Dominique Strauss-Kahn), the rebels against the party leadership called for "an all-out struggle against liberal globalization in alliance with others who are battling against liberalism in the world" (le Nouveau Monde de Henri Emmanuelli et Jean-Luc Mélenchon) or for fighting against "the savagery of the new capitalism and its risky deregulation" (Noblecourt 2002). Far from operating to build links between the Socialist Party and new generations of militants within the civic associations and to channel these activists into party politics, the antiglobalization issue has been pulled into the old divisions of the party and functions to revitalize them.

4. The public-private divide

Finally, the French anxiety over the disappearance of national border-level regulations under the combined impact of European construction and international trade and financial market liberalization has refocused attention on a sensitive internal boundary: that between the public and private sectors. Over the past 15 years, the scope of state ownership and control has shrunk dramatically, as both right- and left-wing governments have reprivatized most of the nationalized industries and utilities. The issue of the extent of state control of the national economy has basically lost its partisan colors: the Jospin government privatized more than any right-wing government. Despite these profound changes in the dimensions of the private and public sectors, the issue of where the boundary should lie, far from fading, seems to remain as divisive as ever. The battles no longer focus on ownership of corporations producing tradable goods, but on services, whether those provided by public utilities, like EDF (Electricité de France), or social services, like those provided by schools, hospitals, municipalities.

There is generally much greater support in Europe than in the United States for a social model with public provision of services, but the French stand out even in European comparisons for the intensity of their preferences in this respect. Even in a period (1990–2000) of strong pressures to contain public expenditures in order to respect the EMU limits on public deficits, the French have increased the proportion of GDP paid in wages to government employees, while this item in the budget fell in Germany, the UK, and the US (Fleming 2002). Government employees as a percentage of the workforce grew in France from 1990 to 2000, while this figure declined in Germany, the UK, and the US. Proposals to "reform" the public service or to align the compensation and social security treatment of public employees with those in the private sector trigger strikes and massive demonstrations, as the ill-fated proposals of the Juppé government, or the Sautter plan to reform the tax services, or the Allègre reforms all demonstrated.

With the issue of the future of the public-private divide, the question of France's relationship to the outside world has now become embedded in domestic debates over the "democratic balance." What the French perceive as most menacing in globalization are the forces at work to move France towards an Anglo-Saxon model, in which public services are transferred to the market. These pressures may derive from the European Commission, or from the WTO, or from the competitive strength of foreign multinationals. Resisting these pressures and defending the dimensions of the State and its regulatory controls at the borders has become synonymous with protecting the public sector. Because public services are seen as the guarantee of social solidarity and justice, their vulnerability to external pressures appears to many French as an unavoidable and unacceptable consequence of globalization. Thus, antiglobalization associations like ATTAC are on the front lines of the battle to protect the public services. The new president of ATTAC, Jacques Nikonoff, linked the never-paid-back Russian loans, the emblematic disaster of the first globalization (1870–1914), to the dangers of France's current liberal regime in a phrase that said all, when he charged that "the pension fund issue is today's version of the Russian loans."[14]

5. Reforming representation?

This picture of the failing relays between civil society and government suggests that whatever transformations may have taken place in French society and political economy, there is no "natural" carry-over into political organizations. If there are to be real alternatives to more of the same, they would require deliberate political engineering and leadership. As the dust of the 2002 elections began to settle, it did indeed appear that new projects were in the works. The shock of public recognition at the consequences and costs of the disaster provoked by 21 April appeared to provide new legitimacy and resources for political reformers within the old parties of government. The first impulses on both left and right were to promote a set of solutions to reduce the fragmentation of the party system and to restore and reinforce bipolarization, which had been a strong tendency of the system since de Gaulle's introduction of the popular election of the president (see Grunberg's chapter in this volume). The dispersion of votes over a large number of parties was indeed one of the factors responsible for Jospin's failure to make it into the second round and for Chirac's poor showing on the first ballot.

After the election, Chirac and Alain Juppé were able to pursue a long-cherished ambition and turn an electoral coalition, the Union pour une majorité présidentielle, which had come into being to support Chirac's re-election bid, into encompassing a new party of the right, the Union pour un mouvement populaire (UMP). Within a year, however, infighting within the new UMP had seriously undermined the project of creating a single party of the center-right, and the devastating defeat of 2004 may well prove fatal to the grand unifying ambition.

The formation of a broad party of the right immediately provoked debates on the left about the possibilities of a merger within this camp. But the conflicts that continued to rage within the Socialist Party over who was responsible for the electoral defeat, over leadership succession, and over rebuilding the party quashed any real effort to explore the terrain of creating a new party out of various components of the left. The providential victory in the 2004 regional elections—as startling to the Socialists as their defeat had been two years before—may offer the opportunity for a new start.

The second response to 21 April was a classic move, familiar from all French parliamentary history, to change the electoral system in order to weaken the smaller parties. The Sarkozy proposal to change the voting system in regional and European elections would raise the bar for candidates remaining in the second balloting from 10 percent of the votes cast in the first round to 10 percent of the voters registered as of the first round of the election.

The history of such re-engineering of the electoral system in France does not give grounds for optimism about the prospects of reducing anti-system voting or revitalizing the major parties in this way. If there is an effect, one likely outcome would be to transform anti-system voters and the electorate now voting for smaller parties into non-voters, thus accelerating the growth of abstention. Should abstention continue to rise, the system would become more fragile and vulnerable to shocks, even if there were simultaneously a certain reconcentration of the electorate around the UMP on the right and the Socialists on the left. If those voters who now cast votes for the small parties withdraw from the voting booths, they need not withdraw from the streets. Pushed out of the electoral system, they might well seek other channels for expression. Even in the Raffarin government's first months in office it faced major demonstrations over some of its new policies; it is clear that this political arena still functions well in France.

After the electoral shocks of 2002 and 2004, many of the basic questions about the connections between the French and their political representatives remain open. Why are the linking institutions between French society and French politics so resistant to change? What kinds of change would party organizations have to undertake in order to reach out to a population that is increasingly participating in a wide variety of cultural, sports, civic, and single-issue associations, but also, apparently, increasingly allergic to party membership? Which political entrepreneurs might emerge as reformers? How could they win a mandate for the organizational and programmatic innovations needed to rebuild the connective tissue of French democracy? These questions echo old debates about the relationships between society and political institutions in France. Particularly in troubled times, the most challenging arguments about French democracy have always turned on whether the real problems lie in the divided, complex, and changing nature of French society or in the institutions that the French have built to govern themselves. At least with respect to the representative role of parties, the case for institutional dysfunctions seems the more convincing one today.

Postscriptum

As this volume was going to press, yet another electoral earthquake shook French political terrain. In the 19 May 2005 referendum on the European constitution, after an intense and bitter campaign involving many people beyond the usual political militants, 55 percent of the electors voted "no." The rejection was massive among younger voters, and encompassed public as well as private-sector employees, and more educated as well as less-educated groups in the population. In retrospect, this turn against the European project that elites of both left and right have been promoting since 1983 looks like a virtually inevitable one after the Maastricht referendum—an event waiting to happen, given the growing anxieties of the electorate over the loss of control over the borders (of Europe as well as of France) and over the liberal character of European economic rules. High employment, hostility to the enlargement of the European Union (and the possible entry of Turkey), and fears about globalization and off-shoring were all important factors in the election—themes that had not loomed large in the two other elections analyzed in this chapter. But the one great continuity was the massive rejection of the parties of the government—both center-right and left. In 2002, this rejection took the form of abstentionism and votes for parties on the fringe; in 2004, it showed up in the vote against the center-right. In the 29 May referendum, the electors could vote against them all together. This time, it would seem, surely something will have to change in the parties. And yet after the first shockwaves, nothing was less certain.

Notes

1 See Balme's chapter in this volume and Martin (2000).
2 This summary draws on Chiche et al. (2002).
3 For descriptions of these movements, see Crettiez and Sommier (2002) and Fougier (2002).
4 This discussion draws on the research presented by Barthélémy (2000: 60–6).
5 *Le Monde*, 10–11 March 2002: 16. See also the interviews on this issue with Emmanuel Todd and Robert Rochefort, p. 20.
6 For a view that emphasizes the acceptance of globalization by the French, see Gordon and Meunier (2001). For an account that lays out the contradictions in French responses across a number of different polls and questions, see Ancelovici (2002).
7 CSA survey, 24–5 September 2002. Cited in Weill (2002).
8 SOFRESa.
9 *Le Monde*/SOFRES 12–13 July 2001 survey (SOFRES/*Le Monde* 2001).
10 The description and analysis of ATTAC here draws on Ancelovici (2002).
11 In a speech at Maison Française, Oxford, 20 February 2002.
12 The wave of new members that the Socialist Party gained after the 21 April shock did show a significant number of recruits who already belonged to some association—mainly cultural or athletic. Only 13 percent of the incoming members belonged to unions, in contrast with 65 percent in 1998. *Le Monde*, 20–1 October 2002: 7.
13 See for example, Jospin (2001).
14 *Le Monde*, 3 December 2002.

Bibliography

Adam, Gérard. 1983. *Le Pouvoir syndical*. Paris: Dunod.

Adam, Gérard. 1997. "Les Confédérations syndicales en mouvement." *Management et conjoncture sociale* 508 (May): 22–7.

Adam, Gérard. 2000. *Les Relations sociales, année zéro*. Paris: Bayard.

Albert, Michel. 1991. *Capitalisme contre capitalisme*. Paris: Seuil.

Alliès, Paul. 2000. "Souverainistes versus fédéralistes." *Les Temps Modernes* 55 (September–November): 120–55.

Altman, Richard. 1992. *Investor Response to Management Decisions*. New York: Quorum Books.

Amable, Bruno. 2004. *The Diversity of Modern Capitalism*. New York: Oxford University Press.

Amossé, Thomas. 2004. "Mythes et réalités de la syndicalisation en France." *Premières Synthèses – Premières Informations* 44 (2) (October).

Ancelovici, Marcos. 2002. "Organizing against Globalization: the Case of ATTAC in France." *Politics and Society* 30 (3): 427–63.

Anderson, Benedict. 1983. *Imagined Communities*. London: Verso.

Andolfatto, Dominique, and Dominique Labbé. 2000. *Sociologie des syndicats*. Paris: La découverte.

Arrow, Kenneth. 1951. *Social Choice and Individual Values*. New York: John Wiley and Sons.

Arthus, Patrick. 2002. "Le Déclin de la France, mythe ou réalité?" *Cahiers Français* 3111 (Novembre–Decembre): 11–19.

Ascher, F. 1998. *La République contre la ville: essai sur l'avenir de la France urbaine*. La Tour d' Aigues: Editions de l' Aube.

Attias-Donfut, C. 2000. "Rapports de générations: transferts intrafamiliaux et dynamique macrosociale." *Revue française de sociologie* 41 (4): 643–84.

Aubert, Patrick. 1999. *Politiques pour faciliter l'accès à l'emploi des populations immigrées*. Notes et Documents 45. Paris: Direction de la Population et des Migrations.

Aubry, Martine. 1998. *Communication en conseil des ministres de Mme Martine Aubry, ministre de l'emploi et de la solidarité sur la politique d'intégration, mercredi 21 octobre 1998*. Paris: Ministère des Affaires sociales (http://www.social.gouv.fr/htm/actu/34_981021_2.htm).

Auerbach, A. J., J. Gokhale, and L. J. Kotlikoff. 1994. "Generational Accounting: a Meaningful Way to Evaluate Fiscal Policy (in Symposia: Generational Accounting)." *The Journal of Economic Perspectives* 8 (1): 73–94.

Avril, Pierre. 2003. "Les Conséquences des résultats des élections sur la nature du régime. L'improbable Phénix." In *Le Vote de tous les refus, les élections de 2002*, eds. Pascal Perrineau and Colette Ysmal. Paris: Presses de Sciences Po, 371.

Baeyens, H. 2000. "Les Stratégies de socialisation scolaire à l'Unification Européenne." PhD. dissertation: Université de Grenoble 2.

Baisnée, O. 2003. "La Production de l'actualité communautaire: Eléments d'une sociologie comparée du corps de presse accrédité auprès de l'Union européenne." PhD. dissertation: Université de Rennes.

Balme, Richard. 1998. "The French Region as a Space for Public Policy." In *Regions in Europe: the Paradox of Power*, eds. P. Le Galès and C. Lequesne. London: Routledge, 181–98.

Balme, Richard, Celine Bélot, and Olivier Rozenberg. 2004. "A quoi jouent les mobiles? Approche qualitative de la subjectivité des trajectoire électorales." In *Le Nouveau Désordre electoral*, eds. B. Cautrès and N. Mayer. Paris: Presses de Sciences Po, 325–50.

Balme, R., A. Faure, and A. Mabileau. 1999. *Politiques locales et transformations de l'action publique locale en Europe*. Paris: Presse de Sciences Po.

Balme, R., and P. Le Galès. 1997. "Stars and Black Holes, French Regions and Cities in the European Galaxy." In *European Integration and Local Government*, eds. M. Goldsmith and K. Klausen. Cheltenham: Edward Elgar, 146–71.

Balme, Richard, Jean-Louis Marie, and Olivier Rozenberg. 2003. "Les Motifs de la confiance (et de la défiance) politique: Intérêt, connaissance et conviction dans les formes du raisonnement politique." *Revue Internationale de Politique Comparée* 10 (3): 433–62.

Baraize, F., and E. Négrier, eds. 2001. *L'Invention Politique de l'agglomération*. Paris: L'Harmattan.

Barbier, J. C., and J. Gautié, eds. 1998. *Les Politiques de l'emploi en Europe et aux Etats Unis, Cahiers du CEE*. Paris: PUF.

Bardet, F., and B. Jouve. 1999. "Entreprise politique et territoire à Lyon." *Sociologie du Travail* 41 (1): 41–61.

Barthe, Y., M. Callon, and P. Lascoumes. 2001. *Agir dans un monde incertain*. Paris: Seuil.

Barthélémy, Martine. 2000. *Associations: un Nouvel Age de la Participation*. Paris: Presses de Sciences Po.

Bauer, M., and B. Bertin-Mourot. 1997. *L'ENA: Est-elle une business school?* Paris: L'Harmattan.

Bauer, Michel, and Elie Cohen. 1981. *Qui gouverne les groupes industriels?* Paris: Le Seuil.

Baverez, Nicolas. 2003. *La France qui tombe*. Paris: Editions Perrin.

Beau, Pascal, ed. 1995. *L'œuvre collective, 50 ans de sécurité sociale*. Paris: Espace social européen.

Beaud, Stéphane, and Michel Pialoux. 2003. *Violences urbaines, violence sociale: Genèse des nouvelles classes dangereuses*. Paris: Fayard.

Becker, H. A. 2000. "Discontinuous Change and Generational Contracts." In *The Myth of Generational Conflict: the Family and State in Ageing Societies*, eds. S. Arber and C. Attias-Donfut. London/New York: Routledge, 114–32.

Bell D. 1973. *Coming of Post-Industrial Society: a Venture in Social Forecasting*. New York: Basic Books.

Bennett, M. J. 2000. *When Dreams Came True: the GI Bill and the Making of Modern America*. Washington, D.C.: Brassey's.

Benoit, O. 2003. "Les Chambres régionales des comptes face aux élus locaux: les effets inattendus d'une institution." *Revue française de science politique* 53 (4): 535–58.

Benson, Rodney. 2002. "The Political/Literary Model of French Journalism: Change and Continuity in Immigration Coverage, 1973–1991." *Journal of European Area Studies* 10 (1): 49–70.

Bentley, Neil. 2000. *Belgium, France and Italy Present Joint Priorities for Lisbon Summit."* European industrial relations observatory on-line, 28 March 2000. http://www.eiro.eurofound.ie/2000/03/InBrief/EU0003232N.html.

Béret, P., A.-M. Daune-Richard, A. Dupray, and E. Verdier. 1997. *Valorisation de l'investissement formation sur les marchés du travail Français et Allemand: Distinction entre valeur productive et valeur de signalement*. Aix-en-Provence: Commissariat Général du Plan.

Berger, Suzanne. 1981. "Lame Ducks and National Champions: Industrial Policy in the Fifth Republic." In *The Fifth Republic at Twenty*, eds. Stanley Hoffmann and William Andrews. Brockport: SUNY Press, 292–310.

Berger, Suzanne. 1985. "The Socialists and the Patronat: the Dilemmas of Coexistence in a Mixed Economy." In *Economic Policy and Policy-Making under the Mitterrand Presidency*, eds. Howard Machin and Vincent Wright. London: Frances Pinter, 225–44.

Berger, Suzanne. 1995. "Trade and Identity: the Coming Protectionism?" In *Remaking the Hexagon*, ed. Gregory Flynn. Boulder: Westview, 195–212.

Bertero, Elisabetta. 1994. "The Banking System, Financial Markets, and Capital Structure: New Evidence from France." *Oxford Review of Economic Policy* 10: 68–78.

Bessy, Christian, and François Eymard-Duvernay, eds. 1997. *Les Intermédiaires du marché du travail*. Paris: PUF.

Besuco, Nathalie, Michèle Tallard, and Françoise Lozier. 1998. *Politique contractuelle de formation et négociation collective de branche*. Paris: La documentation française.

Betz, H. G., S. Immerfall, eds. 1998. *The New Politics of the Right: Neo-populist Parties and Movements in Established Democracies*. New York: St. Martin's Press.

Bichot, Jacques. 1997. *Les politiques sociales en France au 20ème siècle*. Paris: Armand Colin.

Bigo, D. 1996. *Polices en réseaux*. Paris: Presses de Sciences Po.

Billig, M. 1995. *Banal Nationalism*. London: Sage.

Blanchard, O., and P. A. Muet. 1993. "Competitiveness through Disinflation: an Assessment of the French Macroeconomic Strategy." *Economic Policy* 16: 11–56.

Blanchard, Olivier, and Justin Wolfers. 2000. "The Role of Shocks and Institutions in the Rise of European Unemployment: the Aggregate Evidence." *Economic Journal* 110 (March): 1–33.

Bleich, Erik. 2003. *Race Politics in Britain and France: Ideas and Policymaking since the 1960s*. New York: Cambridge University Press.

Blondiaux, L., ed. 1999. *La Démocratie locale: Représentation, participation et espace public*. Paris: PUF.

Body-Gendrot, S. 2000. *The Social Control of Cities*. Oxford: Blackwell.

Bonnafous, Simone. 1991. *L'Immigration prise aux mots: les immigrés dans la presse au tournant des années 80*. Paris: Kimé.

Bonnafous, Simone. 1999. "Les Immigrés sont-ils 'in/égaux': Etude des usages lexicaux dans la presse depuis 1950," *Les termes de l'égalité et de l'inégalité, flux et reflux: Variations, déplacements, substitutions (18e–20e siècles)*. Paris: L'Harmattan, coll. Sémantiques, 223–38.

Bonoli, Giuliano. 1997. "Pension Politics in France: Patterns of Co-operation and Conflict in Two Recent Reforms." *West European Politics* 20 (4): 160–81.

Bonoli, Giuliano. 2001. "Political Institutions, Veto Points, and the Process of Welfare State Adaptation." In *The New Politics of the Welfare State*, ed. P. Pierson. Oxford: Oxford University Press, forthcoming, 314–37.

Bonoli, Giuliano, and Bruno Palier. 1996. "Reclaiming Welfare: the Politics of Social Protection Reform in France." In *Southern European Society and Politics*, Special edited by Martin Rhodes intitulé "Southern European Welfare States: Between Crisis and Reform" 11 (3): 240–59.

Bonoli, Giuliano, and Bruno Palier. 1998. "Changing the Politics of Social Programmes: Innovative Change in British and French Welfare Reforms." *Journal of European Social Policy* 8 (4): 317–30.

Borraz, O. 1998. *Gouverner une ville: Besançon 1959–1989*. Rennes: Presses Universitaires de Rennes.

Borraz, O., and P. Loncle. 2000. "Action publique et matrices institutionnelles, les politiques locales en lutte contre le SIDA." *Revue Française de Sociologie* 141 (1): 37–60.

Bouffartigue, Paul, ed. 2001. *Les Cadres: Fin d'une figure sociale*. Paris: La Dispute.

Boy, D., François Platone, Henri Rey, Françoise Subileau, and Colette Ysmal. 2003. *C'était la gauche plurielle*. Paris: Presses de Sciences Po, 65–88.

Boy, Daniel, Agnès Rochem, and Vincent Jacques le Seigneur. 1995. *L'Écologie au pouvoir*. Paris: Presses de Sciences Po.

Boyer, Robert. 1995. "Wage Austerity and/or an Education Push: the French Dilemma." *Labour* (Special Issue): 519–66.

Boyer, Robert. 1986. *La Flexibilité du travail en Europe*. Paris: La Découverte.

Boyer, Robert, and Jacques Mistral. 1981. *Accumulation, inflation, crise*. Paris: Presses Universitaires de France.

Bréchon, Pierre. 2000. "L'Univers des valeurs politiques: Permanences et mutations." In *Les Valeurs des Français: Evolution de 1980 à 2000*, ed. P. Bréchon. Paris: Armand Colin, 105–15.

Brenner, N. 1999. "Globlization as Reterritorialization: the Re-scaling of Urban Governance in the European Union." *Urban Studies* 36 (3): 431–52.

Brubaker, Rogers. 2001. "Return of Assimilation: Changing Perspectives on Assimilation and Its Sequels." *Ethnic and Racial Studies* 24: 531–48.

Buchet de Neuilly, Y. 2001. "Les Cheminements chaotiques de la politique étrangère européenne." PhD. dissertation: L'Université de Paris I.

Bué, Jennifer, and Catherine Rougerie. 1999. "L'Organisation du travail: Entre contrainte et initiative." *Premières Informations et Premières Synthèses* 32 (1) (August).

Bunel, Jean. 1995. *La Transformation de la représentation patronale en France: CNPF et CGPME*. Paris: Commissariat Général du Plan.

Bunel, Jean, and Christian Thuderoz. 1999. "Le Syndicalisme entre participation et institutionnalisation." In *Syndicalisme et démocratie dans l'entreprise*, eds. Henri Pinaud, Michel Le Tron, and Alain Chouraqui. Paris: L'Harmattan, 117–46.

Caillosse, J., P. Le Galès, and P. Loncle. 1997. "Les Sociétés d'économie mixte locales en France: Outils de quelle action publique urbaine?" In *L'Action publique urbaine et les contrats*, CNRS (collectif). Paris: Descartes, 23–96.

Calvès, Gwenaèle. 2002. " 'Il n'y a pas de race ici': le modèle français à l'épreuve de l'intégration européenne." *Critique Internationale* 17: 173–86.

Calvès, Gwenaèle, and Daniel Sabbagh. 1999. "Les Politiques de discrimination positive: une renégociation du modèle républicain?" Paper presented at the Sixth Congress of the French Political Science Association, Rennes, September.

Card, D., and T. Lemieux. 2001. "Can Falling Supply Explain the Rising Return to College for Younger Men? A Cohort-based Analysis." *Quarterly Journal of Economics* 116 (2) (1 May): 705–46.

Casper, Steven, and Bob Hancké. 1999. "Global Quality Norms within National Production Regimes: ISO 9000 Norm Implementation in the French and German Car Industries." *Organization Studies* 20 (6): 961–85.

Castel, Robert. 1995. *Les Métamorphoses de la question sociale*. Paris: Fayard.

Catrice-Lorey, Antoinette. 1995. "La Sécurité sociale et la démocratie sociale: Impasse ou refondation?" *Prévenir* 29 (2ème semester): 61–79.

Chadelat, Jean-François. 1995. "La Sécurité sociale, un acteur du soutien de la croissance et du développement de l'emploi." *Revue française des affaires sociales* 49 (4): 79–89.

Charpentier, Pascal, Hervé Huyghes-Despointes, Michel Lallement, Florence Lefresne, Jocelyne Loos-Baron, and Nadège. Turpin-Hyard. 2004. "Gestion des temps et régulations sociales: Quelles incidences de la loi Aubry II sur l'organisation des entreprises et les conditions de travail des salariés." *Revue de l'IRES* 44 (1): 3–41.

Charraud, A. 1995. "Reconnaissance de la qualification: Contrats de qualification et évolution des règles." *Formation Emploi* 52: 113–32.

Chauvel, L. 1997. "L'Uniformisation du taux de suicide masculin selon l'âge: Effet de génération ou recomposition du cycle de vie?" *Revue française de sociologie* XXXVIII (4): 681–734.

Chauvel, L. 1998 (2nd edn. 2002). *Le Destin des générations: Structure sociale et cohortes en France au XXe siècle*. Paris: Presses Universitaires de France.

Chauvel, L. 2000. "Valorisation et dévalorisation sociale des titres: une comparaison France – Etats-Unis." In *L'État de l'école*, ed. A. van Zanten. Paris: La Découverte, 345–6.

Chauvel, L. 2003. *Génération sociale et socialisation transitionnelle: Fluctuations cohortales et stratification sociale en France et aux Etats-Unis au XXe siècle*. Mémoire d'Habilitation à Diriger des recherches, Paris: Sciences Po.

Chevrier-Fatôme, Carine, and Bernard Simonin. 2004. "Politique de l'emploi: un nombre croissant d'intervenants." *Premières Synthèses – Premières Informations* 30 (2) (July).

Chiche, J., F. Haegel, and V. Tiberj. 2002. "La Fragmentation partisane." In *La Démocratie à l'épreuve: une nouvelle approche de l'opinion des Français*, eds. Gérard Grunberg, Nonna Mayer, and Paul M. Sniderman. Paris: Presses de Sciences Po, 203–37.

Chiche, Jean, Brigitte Le Roux, Pascal Perrineau, and Henry Rouanet. 2000. "L'Espace politique des électeurs français à la fin des années 1990: Nouveaux et anciens clivages, hétérogénéité des electorates." *Revue Française de Science Politique* 50 (3): 463–88.

Chiche, Jean, and Dominique Reynié. 2002. "La France en Dépression électorale." In *SOFRES, l'état de l'opinion 2002*, eds. Olivier Duhamel and P. Méchet. Paris: Seuil, 35–82.

CNCDH (Commission nationale consultative des Droits de l'Homme). 1989–2003. *La Lutte contre le racisme et la xénophobie: Exclusion et droits de l'homme*. Paris: La Documentation française.

Coffee, John. 1999. "The Future as History: the Prospects for Global Convergence in Corporate Governance and Its Implications." *Northwestern University Law Review* 93: 641–707.

Cohen, E. 2001. *L'Ordre economique mondial: Essai sur les autorités de regulation*. Paris: Fayard.

Cohen, Elie. 1989. *L'État brancardier*. Paris: Calmann-Lévy.

Cohen, Elie. 1996. *La Tentation hexagonale*. Paris: Fayard.

Cohen, Elie, and Michel Bauer. 1985. *Les Grandes Manoeuvres industrielles*. Paris: Belfond.

Cole, A., and P. John. 2001. *Local Governance in England and France*. London: Routledge.

Colin, Thierry, and Benoît Grasser. 2003. "La Gestion des compétences: un infléchissement limité de la relation salariale." *Travail et emploi* 93 (January): 61–73.

Comité de Coordination. 1996. *Évaluation des politiques régionales de formation professionnelle*. Paris.

Comment, Robert, and Greg Jarrell. 1995. "Corporate Focus and Stock Returns." *Journal of Financial Economics* 37: 67–87.

Commission de la Nationalité. 1988. *Etre Français aujourd'hui et demain: Rapport de la commission de la nationalité*. Paris: 10/18.

Conference Board. Various years. "International Patterns of Institutional Investment." *Institutional Investment Report*.

Costa, O., J. de Maillard, and A. Smith. 2005. *Vin et politique*. Paris: Presses de Sciences Po, forthcoming.

Coutard, O. 2001. *Le bricolage organisationnel: Crise des cadres hiérarchiques et innovations dans la gestion des entreprises et des territories*. Paris: Elsevier.

Crettiez, Xavier, and Isabelle Sommier. 2002. *La France rebelle*. Paris: Editions Michalon.

Crozier, Michel. 1963. *Le Phenomene bureaucratique*. Paris: Seuil.

Crozier, Michel. 1964. *La Société bloquée*. Paris: Fayard.

CSA. 2003. *Comment va la France? Le point de vue des français*. http://www.csa-fr.com/fra/dataset/data2003/opi20031125e.htm.

Culpepper, Pepper D. 1998. "Individual Choice, Collective Action, and the Problem of Training Reform: Insights from France and Eastern Germany." In *The German Skills Machine: Comparative Perspectives on Systems of Education and Training*, eds. Pepper D. Culpepper and David Finegold. New York: Berghahn Books, 269–324.

Culpepper, Pepper D. 2003. *Creating Cooperation: How States Develop Human Capital in Europe*. Ithaca: Cornell University Press.

Culpepper, Pepper D. 2005. "Institutional Change in Contemporary Capitalism: Coordinated Financial Systems since 1990." *World Politics* 57 (2): 173–99.

Dalton, Russell, Scott C. Flanagan, and Paul Allen Beck. 1984. *Electoral Change in Advanced Industrial Democracies: Realignment or Dealignment?* Princeton, NJ: Princeton University Press.

Daniel, Christine, and Bruno Palier, eds. 2001. *La Protection sociale en Europe: le temps des réformes*. Paris: La Documentation française.

DARES. 1999. *Accords de la Loi Robien*. Paris.

Davezies, L. 2001. "Revenu et territories." In *Aménagement du Territoire: Rapport du Conseil d'Analyse Économique*. Paris: Documentation française, 173–92.

David-Aeschlimann, R. 2004. "France: Powers of the Regions Extended." *CEDEFOP Info* 3: 1–2.

Davis Global Advisors. Annual Publication. *Leading Corporate Governance Indicators*. Newton, Mass.

De Munck, Jean. 2000. "Les Métamorphoses de l'autorité." *Autrement* 198 (October): 21–42.

Dehousse, Renaud. 2004. "La Méthode ouverte de coordination: Quand l'instrument tient lieu de politique." In *Gouverner par les instruments*, ed. Pierre Lascoumes and Patrick Le Galès. Paris: Presses de la FNSP, 331–56.

DeJong, Henk. 1997. "The Governance Structure and Performance of Large European Corporations." *Journal of Management and Governance* 1: 5–27.

Denis, Jean-Michel. 2003. "Les Syndicalistes de SUD-PTT: Des entrepreneurs de morale?" *Sociologie du travail* 45 (3): 307–25.

Direction Générale des Collectivités Locales. 2003. *Les Chiffres des collectivités locales*. Paris: La Documentation Française.

Direction Générale des Collectivités Locales. 2005. *Les Collectivités locales en chiffres 2004–2005*. Paris: Ministère de l'Intérieur.

Dirn, Louis. 1998. *La Société française en tendances*. Paris: PUF.

Domart, Q. 2004. "Faire l'ENA" oui ... mais après? *Le Monde* 23 November.

Douillet, Anne-Cécile. 2003. "Les Élus ruraux face à la territorialisation de l'action publique." *Revue française de science politique* 53 (4): 583–606.

DRTEFP. 1999. "Analyse de la mise en oeuvre de la RTT par des entreprises alsaciennes ayant opté pour la loi de Robien." Report published by the regional direction of Alsace for work, employment, and professional training.

Duclos, Laurent, and Olivier Mériaux. 1997. "Pour une économie du paritarisme." *La Revue de l'IRES* 24 (printemps-été): 43–60.

Duclos, Laurent, and Olivier Mériaux. 1998. "Le Paritarisme, un fragment néo-corporatiste." In *L'Etat à l'épreuve du social,* eds. Philippe Auvergnon, Philippe Martin, Patrick Rozenblatt, and Michèle Tallard. Paris: Syllepse, 219–29.

Duhamel, Alain. 2001. *Chronique d'Alain Duhamel* (July). Paris: SOFRES.

Duhamel, Olivier. 2002, *Vive la VI[è] République*. Paris: Seuil.

Duhamel, Olivier, and Gérard Grunberg. 2001. "Systèmes de partis et Ves républiques." *Commentaire* 95 (Automne): 533–44.

Duhamel, Olivier, and Gérard Grunberg. 2002. "Les Partis et la Vè république: Post-scriptum." *Commentaire* 99 (Automne), 601–7.

Duhamel, Olivier, and Jean-Luc Parodi, eds. 1988. *La Constitution de la Cinquième République*. Paris: Presses de Sciences Po.

Duran, P. 1998. *Penser l'action publique*. Paris: LGDJ.

Duran, P., and J.-C. Thoenig. 1996. "La Gestion publique territoriale." *Revue française de science politique* 46 (4): 580–622.

Easterlin, R. A. 1966. "Economic-Demographic Interactions and Long Swings in Economic Growth." *The American Economic Review* 56 (5): 1063–1104.

Espinasse, Marie-Thérèse, and Catherine Laporte. 1999. *Des contrats d'agglomération aux contrats locaux pour l'accueil et l'intégration.* Notes et Documents 44. Paris: Direction de la Population et des Migrations.

Esping-Andersen, G. 1990. *The Three Worlds of Welfare Capitalism.* Cambridge: Cambridge University Press.

Esping-Andersen, Gøsta, ed. 1996. *Welfare States in Transition: National Adaptations in Global Economies*. London: Sage.

Esping-Andersen, Gøsta, Duncan Gallie, Anton Hemerijck, and John Myles. 2002. *Why We Need a New Welfare State.* Oxford: Oxford University Press.

Estevez-Abe, M., T. Iversen, and D. Soskice. 2001. "Social Protection and the Formation of Skills: a Reinterpretation of the Welfare State." In *Varieties of Capitalism: the Institutional Foundations of Comparative Advantage,* eds. P. Hall and D. Soskice. Oxford: Oxford University Press, 145–83.

Eurobarometer. 1989. *Public Opinion in the European Community: Special Issue on Racism and Xenophobia* 30. Brussels: Directorate-General Information, Communication, and Culture.

Eurobarometer. 1991–2000. *Public Opinion in the European Community* 35–53. Brussels: Commission of the European Communities.

Ewald, François, and Denis Kessler. 2000. "Les Noces du risque et de la politique." *Le Débat* 109: 55–72.

Eymeri, J.-M. 2002. "Définir 'la position de la France' dans l'Union européenne: la médiation interministerielle des généralistes du SGCI." In *Le Gouvernement du compromis: Courtiers et généralistes dans l'action politique,* eds. O. Nay and A. Smith. Paris: Economica, 149–76.

Fassin, Didier. 2001. "L'Invention française de la discrimination." *Revue française de science politique* 52 (4): 403–23.

Faure, A. 1997. "Les Apprentissages du métier d'élu local: la tribu, le système et les arenas." *Pôle Sud* 7: 72–9.

Faure, A., ed. 1997. *Territoires et subsidiarité*. Paris: L'Harmattan.

Faure, A., and A. Smith. 1998. "Que changent les politiques communautaires?" *Pouvoirs Locaux* 40 (mars): 31–40.

Favell, Adrian. 2001. *Philosophies of Integration: Immigration and the Idea of Citizenship in France and Britain*. Paperback revised edition. London: Palgrave, now Basingstoke: Palgrave Macmillan.

Feldblum, Miriam. 1999. *Reconstructing Citizenship*. Albany, NY: State University of New York Press.

Flauss, Jean-François. 2001. "L'action de l'Union européenne dans le domaine de la lutte contre le racisme et la xénophobie." *Revue trimestrielle des droits de l'homme* 36: 487–516.

Fleming, Charles. 2002. "French Candidates Agree on One Issue: the Civil Service." *The Wall Street Journal Europe* 18 April: A1, A6.

Fougier, Eddy. 2002. *La Contestation de la mondialisation: une nouvelle exception française?* Paris: Institut Français des Relations Internationales (IFRI).

Fouilleux, E. 2003. *Idées, institutions et dynamiques du changement de politique publique: les transformations de la politique agricole commune*. Paris: L'Harmattan.

Fouilleux, E, J. de Maillard, and A. Smith. 2002. "Council Working Groups: Their Role in the Production of European Problems and Policies." In *Committees in EU Governance*, ed. G. Schaefer. Report to the European Commission, 97–135.

Fourastié, J. 1979. *Les Trente Glorieuses ou la révolution invisible*. Paris: Fayard.

Freeman, R. B. 1976. *The Overeducated American*. New York: Academic Press.

Fridenson, Patrick. 1997. "France: the Relatively Slow Development of Big Business in the Twentieth Century." In *Big Business and the Wealth of Nations*, eds. Alfred Chandler, Franco Amatori, and Takashi Hikino. New York: Cambridge University Press, 207–45.

Friot, Bernard. 1999. *Et la cotisation sociale créera l'emploi*. Paris: La dispute.

Garbaye, R. 2002. "A Comparison of the Management of Ethnic Conflicts in British and French Cities." *International Journal of Urban and Regional Research* 26 (3): 555–70.

Gastaut, Yvan. 2000. *L'Immigration et l'opinion en France sous la Ve République*. Paris: Seuil.

Gaudin, J.-P. 1999. *Gouverner par contrat: l'action publique en question*. Paris: Presses de Sciences Po.

Gaxie, Daniel. 1995. *Rapport sur l'analyse secondaire des enquêtes d'opinion relatives à l'immigration et à la présence étrangère en France*. Paris: Université Paris I.

Gazier, Bernard. 2003. *Tous "Sublimes": Vers un nouvel plein-emploi*. Paris: Flammarion.

Geddes, Andrew. 2003. *The Politics of Migration and Immigration in Europe*. London: Sage.

Geddes, Andrew, and Virginie Guiraudon. 2004. "The Emergence of a European Union Policy Paradigm amidst Contrasting National Models: Britain, France and EU Anti-Discrimination Policy." *West European Politics* 27 (2) (Special issue edited by Vivien Schmidt and Claudio Radaelli): 334–53.

Géhin, J. P., and P. Méhaut. 1993. *Apprentissage ou formation continue?: Stratégies éducatives des entreprises en Allemagne et en France*. Paris: L'Harmattan.

Geld. 2000. *Une forme méconnue de discrimination: les emplois fermés aux étrangers*. Notes du GELD 1. Paris: Groupe d'études et de lutte contre les discriminations.

Geld. 2001. *Les discriminations raciales et ethniques dans l'accès au logement social*. Notes du GELD 3. Paris: Groupe d'études et de lutte contre les discriminations.

Genieys, W., J. Joana, and A. Smith. 2000. *Professionnalisation et condition militaire: une comparaison France/Grande Bretagne*. Research report for the C2SD and DAS., Ministère de la défense (September).

Giddens, Anthony. 1999. *Runaway World: How Globalization Is Reshaping Our Lives.* London: Profile Books.

Gilbert, G. 1999. "L'Autonomie financière des collectivités locales est-elle en question?" *Les 2ème entretiens de la Caisse des Dépôts et Consignations.* La Tour d'Aigues: Editions de l'Aube, 155–68.

Glaeser, Edward, Simon Johnson, and Andrei Shleifer. 2001. "Coase Versus the Coasians." *Quarterly Journal of Economics* 116: 853–99.

Glaude, Michel, and Catherine Borrel. 2002. "Immigrés et marché du travail: Regard statistique." In *Immigration, marché du travail, intégration: Rapport du séminaire présidé par François Héran,* Commissariat Général du Plan. Paris: La Documentation française, 105–19.

Goetschy, J. 1998. "France: the Limits of Reform." In *Changing Industrial Relations in Europe,* eds. A. Ferner and R. Hyman. Malden, Mass.: Blackwell, 357–94.

Goetschy, Janine. 1999. "The European Employment Strategy: Genesis and Development." *European Journal of Industrial Relations* 2 (July): 117–37.

Golden, M., P. Lange, and M. Wallerstein. 2002. "Union Centralization among Advanced Industrial Societies: an Empirical Study." Dataset available at http://www.shelley.polisci.ucla.edu/data. Version dated 19 September 2002.

Goldsmith, M., and K. Klausen, eds. 1997. *European Integration and Local Government.* Cheltenham: Edward Elgar.

Golub, J. 1996. "Sovereignty and Subsidiarity in EU Environmental Policy." *Political Studies* XLIV: 310–33.

Gordon, Philip, and Sophie Meunier. 2001. *The New French Challenge: Adapting to Globalization.* Washington: Brookings.

Gouldner, Alvin. 1971. *The Coming Crisis of Western Sociology.* London: Heinemann.

Gourevitch, Peter, and James Shinn. 2005. *Political Power and Corporate Control: the New Global Politics of Corporate Governance.* Princeton, NJ: Princeton University Press.

Goux, Dominique, and Eric Maurin. 2002. "Anatomie sociale d'un vote." *Document de travail La République des Idées* (May): 1–9.

Goux, Dominique, and Eric Maurin. 2004. "Anatomie sociale d'un vote: Elections régionales – 21 mars 2004." *Document de travail La Républiques des Idées* (April): 1–26.

Goyer, Michel. 2002. "The Transformation of Corporate Governance in France and Germany: the Role of Workplace Institutions." Max Planck Working Paper 02/10.

Goyer, Michel. 2003. "Corporate Governance, Employees, and the Focus on Core Competencies in France and Germany." In *Global Markets, Domestic Institutions: Corporate Law and Governance in a New Era of Cross-Border Deals,* ed. Curtis Milhaupt. New York: Columbia University Press, 183–213.

Grémion, Pierre. 1976. *Le Pouvoir périphérique: Bureaucrates et notables dans le système politique français.* Paris: Seuil.

Groux, Guy. 1998. *Vers un renouveau du conflit social?* Paris: Bayard.

Grunberg G., N. Mayer, and P. Sniderman, eds. 2002. *La démocratie à l'épreuve: une nouvelle approche de l'opinion des Français.* Paris: Presses de Sciences Po.

Grunberg, Gérard, and Etienne Schweisguth. 1990. "Libéralisme culturel et libéralisme économique." In *L'Électeur français en questions,* Daniel Boy and Nonna Mayer. Paris: Presses de Sciences Po, 45–69.

Guignier, S. 2004. "Institutionalizing Public Health in the European Commission: the Thrills and Spills of Politicization." In *Politics and the European Commission,* ed. A. Smith. London: Routledge, 96–116.

Guiraudon, Virginie. 1996. "The 1980s Reaffirmation of the French Model of Integration." *French Politics and Society* 14 (2): 47–57.

Guiraudon, Virginie. 2000. *Les Politiques d'immigration en Europe*. Paris: L'Harmattan.

Haegel, Florence. 2002. "Faire l'union: la refondation des partis de droite après les élections de 2002." *Revue Française de Science Politique* 52, 5–6: 561–76.

Hainsworth, P. 2000. *The Politics of the Extreme Right: From the Margins to the Mainstream*. London: Pinter.

Hall, Peter A. 1986. *Governing the Economy: the Politics of State Intervention in Britain and France*. New York: Oxford University Press.

Hall, Peter A. 1990. "Pluralism and Pressure Politics." In *Developments in French Politics*, eds. Peter A. Hall, Jack Hayward, and Howard Machin. London: Macmillan, 77–92.

Hall, Peter A. 1993. "Policy Paradigm, Social Learning and the State: the Case of Economic Policy Making in Britain." *Comparative Politics* (April): 275–96.

Hall, Peter A. 1999. "The Political Economy of Europe in an Era of Interdependence." In *Continuity and Change in Contemporary Capitalism*, eds. Herbert Kitschelt, Peter Lange, Gary Marks, and John Stephens. New York: Cambridge University Press, 135–63.

Hall, Peter A. 2002. "The Economic Challenges Facing President Jacques Chirac." *Brookings Institution US-France Analysis Series*. (June). www.brookings.edu/fp/cusf/analysis/hall.pdf.

Hall, Peter A., and David Soskice, eds. 2001. *Varieties of Capitalism*. Oxford: Oxford University Press.

Hancké, Bob. 2002. *Large Firms and Institutional Change: Industrial Renewal and Economic Restructuring in France*. New York: Oxford University Press.

Hancké, Bob, and Michel Goyer. 2005. "Degrees of Freedom: Rethinking the Institutional Analysis of Economic Change." In *Changing Capitalisms? Internationalization, Institutional Change, and Systems of Economic Organization*, eds. Glenn Morgan, Richard Whitley, and Eli Moen. New York: Oxford University Press, 53–77.

Hassenteuffel, Patrick. 1991. "Pratiques représentatives et construction identitaire – une approche des coordinations." *Revue française de science politique* 41 (1) (February): 5–26.

Hastings, D. W., and L. G. Berry. 1979. *Cohort Analysis: a Collection of Interdisciplinary Readings*. Oxford, Ohio: Scripps Foundation for Research in Population Problems.

Hayward, Jack. 1990. "Ideological Change: the Exhaustion of the Revolutionary Impetus." In *Developments in French Politics*, eds. Peter A. Hall, Jack Hayward and Howard Machin. London: Macmillan, 15–32.

HCI (Haut Conseil à l'Intégration). 1993. *L'Intégration à la française*. Paris: 10/18.

HCI (Haut Conseil à l'intégration). 1998. *Lutte contre les discriminations: Faire respecter les principes d'égalité*. Rapport au Premier ministre. Paris: La Documentation française.

HCI (Haut Conseil à l'intégration). 2004. *Le contrat et l'intégration*. Rapport au Premier ministre. Paris: La Documentation française.

Heller, D. E., ed. 2002. *Conditions of Access: Higher Education for Lower Income Students*. Westport (CT): Praeger publishers.

Héran, François. 2004. "Cinq idées reçues sur l'immigration." *Population et Sociétés* 397 (January): 1–4.

Hermet, Guy. 2001. *Les Populismes dans le monde: une histoire sociologique*. Paris: Fayard.

Heymann-Doat, Arlette. 1994. *Libertés publiques et droits de l'homme*. Paris: Librairie Générale de Droit et de Jurisprudence.

Hirschman, Albert. 1970. *Exit, Voice and Loyalty*. Cambridge, Mass.: Harvard University Press.

Hoepner, Martin. 2001. *Corporate Governance in Transition: Ten Empirical Findings on Shareholder Value and Industrial Relations in Germany*. Max Planck Institute Discussion Paper #01/5.

Hoffmann, Stanley. 1963. "Paradoxes of the French Political Community." In *In Search of France*, Hoffmann Stanley, Charles P. Kindleberger, Laurence Wylie, Jesse R. Pitts, Jean-Baptiste Duroselle, and François Goguel. Cambridge: Harvard University Press, 1–117.

Hoffman-Martinot, V. 1999. "Les Grandes Villes françaises: une démocratie en souffrance." In *Démocraties urbaines: l'état de la démocratie dans les grandes villes de 12 pays industrialisés*, eds. O. W. Gabriel and V. Hoffmann-Martinot. Paris: L'Harmattan, 77–121.

Holcblatt, N. (2002). "Privatisations et services publics: Cinq années de profondes transformations." In *L'État de la France, 2002*, eds. S. Cordellier and S. Netter. Paris: Éditions la Découverte & Syros, 242–7.

Hooghe, L., and G. Marks. 2001. *Multilevel Governance and European Integration*. Lanham, Md.: Rowman and Littlefield.

Hooghe, Liesbet. 1996. "Introduction: Reconciling EU-wide Policy and National Diversity." In *Cohesion Policy and European Integration: Building Multi-level Governance*, ed. L. Hooghe. Oxford: Oxford University Press, 1–24.

Howell, Chris. 1992. *Regulating Labor*. Princeton, NJ: Princeton University Press.

Hyde-Price, A., and C. Jeffrey. 2001. "Germany in the EU: Constructing Normality." *Journal of Common Market Studies* 39 (4): 97–114.

Inglehart, Ronald. 1997. *Modernisation and Post-Modernisation: Cultural, Economic and Political Change in 43 Societies*. Princeton, NJ: Princeton University Press.

Institut National de la Statistique et des Études Économiques. 2002. *L'Économie française*. Paris: Livre de Poche.

Institut National de la Statistique et des Études Économiques. 2003. *Tableaux de l'économie française, 2003–04*. Paris: INSEE.

Irondelle, B. 2002. "Europeanization without European Union? French Military Reforms, 1991–1996." *Journal of European Public Policy* 9 (3): 335–55.

Jaffré, Jérôme. 2001. "La Combativité se diffuse dans toute la socieeté." *Le Monde* (7 March): 18.

Jaffré, Jérôme. 2003. "Comprendre l'élimination de Lionel Jospin." In *Le Vote de tous les refus: les élections présidentielles et législatives de 2002*, P. Perrineau and C. Ysmal. Paris: Presses de Sciences Po, 223–50.

Jeanneney, Jean-Noël. 1995. "The Legacy of Traumatic Experiences in French Politics Today." In *Remaking the Hexagon*, ed. Gregory Flynn. Boulder: Westview, 17–29.

Jessop, B. 1995. "The Regulation Approach, Governance and Post-Fordism: Alternative Perspectives on Economic and Political Change." *Economy and Society* 24: 307–33.

Joana, J. 2001. "La Commune contre le municipalisme: Débat public et politiques municipales à Avignon sous la IIIe République (1884–1903)." *Genèses* 43: 89–111.

Joana, J., and A., Smith. 2002. *Les Commissaires européens: Technocrates, diplomates ou politiques?* Paris: Presses de Sciences Po.

Jobert, A., and J. Saglio. 2004. "Ré-institutionaliser la négociation collective en France." *Travail et Emploi*: 113–27.

Jobert, Annette. 2000. *Les Espaces de la négociation collective*. Toulouse: Octarès.

Jobert, Annette. 2003. "Quelles dynamiques pour la négociation collective de branche?" *Travail et emploi* 95 (July): 5–26.

Jobert, Bruno, and Pierre Muller. 1987. *L'Etat en action*. Paris: Presses Universitaires de France.

Jobert, Bruno, and Bruno Théret. 1994. "France: la consécration républicaine du néolibéralisme." In *Le tournant néo-libéral en Europe*, ed. B. Jobert. Paris: L'Harmattan, 21–86.

Joerges, Christian, and Jürgen Neyer. 1997. "Transforming Strategic Interaction into Deliberative Problem-Solving: European Comitology in the Foodstuffs Sector." *European Journal of Public Policy* 4: 609–25.

Johnson, Simon, Rafael LaPorta, Florencio Lopez-de-Silanes, and Andrei Sheifler. 2000. "Tunelling." *American Economic Review* 90: 22–7.

Join-Lambert, Marie-Thérèse. 1998. *Chômage: Mesures d'urgences et minima sociaux*. Paris: La documentation française.

Joppke, Christian, and Ewa Morawska, eds. 2003. *Toward Assimilation and Citizenship: Immigrants in Liberal Nation-States*. New York and London: Palgrave, now Basingstoke: Palgrave Macmillan.

Jordan A., et al. 2005. "Co-ordinating Environmental Policy: Shifting from Passive to Active Co-ordination?" In *Co-ordinating the EU*, eds. H. Kassim, A. Menon, and G. Peters. Forthcoming.

Jospin, Lionel. 2001. *Ma vision de l'Europe et de la mondialisation*. Les Notes de la Fondation Jean-Jaurès, 25 (October). Paris: Plon.

Jouve, B., and C. Lefèvre, eds. 1999. *Villes, métropoles: les nouveaux territoires du politique*. Paris: Economica.

July, Serge. 2002. "La Fracture politique." *Libération* 23 April: 3.

Kassim H., A. Menon, G. Peters, and V. Wright, eds. *The National Co-ordination of EU Policy*. Oxford: Oxford University Press.

Kastoryano, Riva. 2002. *Negotiating Identities: States and Immigrants in France and Germany*. Princeton, NJ: Princeton University Press.

Keating, M. 1998. *The New Regionalism in Western Europe*. Aldershot: Edward Elgar.

Keeler, John T. S. 1987. *The Politics of Neo-Corporatism in France*. New York: Oxford University Press.

Keller, Berndt, and Berndt Sörries. 1999. "Sectoral Social Dialogues: New Opportunities or More Impasses?" *Industrial Relations Journal* 30 (4) (October–November): 330–44.

Kepel, Gilles. 1987. *Les Banlieues de l'Islam*. Paris: Seuil.

Kessler, M.-C. 1982. "Le Cabinet du Premier ministre et le Secrétariat général du gouvernement." In *Administration et politique sous la cinquième République*, eds. F. de Baecque and J.-L. Quermonne. Paris: Presses de la FNSP, 156–80.

Kingdon, John. 1984. *Agendas, Alternatives and Public Policies*. Boston: Little Brown.

Kitschelt, Herbert. 1994. *The Transformation of European Social Democracy*. New York: Cambridge University Press.

Kitschelt, Herbert. 1995. *The Radical Right in Western Europe: a Comparative Analysis*. Ann Arbor: University of Michigan Press.

Knapp, A., and P. Le Galès. 1993. "Top Down to Bottom Up? Center-Periphery Relations and Power Structures in France's Gaullist Party." *West European Politics* 16: 271–94.

Krugman, Paul R. 1992. *The Age of Diminished Expectations: US Economic Policy in the 1990s*. Cambridge, Mass.: MIT Press.

Kuisel, Richard. 1995. "The France We Have Lost: Social, Economic and Cultural Discontinuities." In *Remaking the Hexagon*, ed. Gregory Flynn. Boulder: Westview, 31–48.

Kymlicka, Will. 1995. *Multicultural Citizenship: a Theory of Minority Rights*. New York: Oxford University Press.

Labbé, Dominique. 1996. *Syndicats et syndiqués en France depuis 1945*. Paris: L'Harmattan.

Labbé, Dominique. 2000. "La Désyndicalisation en France: Mesure, explication et consequences." In *Transformations des pratiques sociales et éléments émergents (relations professionnelles, syndicalisme)*. Paris: MBBC, 100–24.

Lagroye, J. 1997. *La Sociologie politique*. Paris: Dalloz.

Lallement, Michel. 1999. *Les Gouvernances de l'emploi*. Paris: Desclée de Brouwer.

Lallement, Michel. 2000. "Jeu, rationalité et négociation." In *La Négociation sociale*, ed. Thuderoz Christian and Giraud-Heraud Annie. Paris: Éditions du CNRS, 29–44.

Lallement, Michel. 2003. *Temps, travail et modes de vie*. Paris: PUF.

Lallement, Michel, and Olivier Mériaux. 2003. "Status and Contracts in Industrial Relations: 'La Refondation Sociale,' a New Bottle for an Old French Wine." *Industrielle Beziehungen* 10 (3): 418–37.

Lallement, Michel. and Arnaud Mias. 2005. "Flexibilité du travail et 'glocalisation' des relations professionnelles." In *La Société flexible*, eds. Matthieu de Nanteuil and Asseâd El Aksemi. Paris: Erès, 363–94.

Lamanthe, Annie, and Eric Verdier. 1999. "La Décentralisation de la formation professionnelle des jeunes: la cohérence problématique de l'action publique." *Sociologie du travail* 41 (4): 385–409.

Lamont, Michèle. 2000. *The Dignity of Working Men: Morality and the Boundaries of Race, Class, and Immigration*. Cambridge, Mass.: Harvard University Press.

Lanfranchi, Nicole, and Véronique Sandoval. 1990. "Le Déplacement du niveau de la négociation salariale." *Travail et emploi* 3: 25–32.

LaPorta, Rafael, Florencio Lopez-de-Silanes, Andrei Shleifer, and Robert Vishny. 2000. "Investor Protection and Corporate Governance." *Journal of Financial Economics* 58: 3–27.

Lascoumes, P. 1995. "Les Arbitrages publics des intérêts légitimes en matière d'environnement." *Revue française de science politique* 45 (3): 396–419.

Laurence, Jonathan. 2003. "Neo-Corporatism and Church–State Relations: the Case of Islam in France." Paper presented to the Annual Meeting of the American Political Science Association.

Laville, Jean-Louis. 1999. *Une Troisième Voie pour le travail*. Paris: Desclée de Brouwer.

Laville, Jean-Louis. 2005. *Sociologie des services*. Paris: Erès.

Le Galès, P. 2001. "Les Politiques locales." In *Le Droit au prisme de l'action publique*, J. Caillosse, and D. Renard. Paris: LGDJ, 285–303.

Le Galès, P. 2002. *European Societies, European Cities, Social Conflicts and Governance*. Oxford: Oxford University Press.

Le Galès, P., and J. Mawson. 1995. "Contract versus Competitive Bidding: Rationalising Urban Policy in Britain and France." *Journal of European Public Policy* 2 (2): 205–42.

Le Lidec, Patrick. 2002. *La République et ses maires, 1907–1997: 90 ans d'histoire de l'AMF*. Paris: Fouchier.

Le Monde. 2002a. 10–11 March: 16.

Le Monde. 2002b. 20–1 October: 7.

Le Monde. 2002c. 3 December.

Le Monde. 2002d. SOFRES/*Le Monde*/RTL, survey. 29 May. In *Ces Français qui votent*.

Le Monde. 2003. 12 February.

Le Pape, Y., and A. Smith. 1999. "Regionalizations and Agricultures: Rhône-Alpes and Pays de la Loire Compared." *Regional and Federal Studies* 9 (2): 16–31.

Le Saout, R. 2000. "L'Intercommunalité, un pouvoir inachevé?" *Revue Française de Science Politique* 3: 439–61.

Lefebvre Leclercq, Edwige. 1992. "Tiers-mondism: Bridge-Building and the Creation of the New Left in French Politics." Paper presented to the Eighth International Conference of Europeanists, Chicago.

Lequesne, Ch. 1993. *Paris-Bruxelles*. Paris: Presses de la FNSP.

Levine, Ross, and Sara Zeros. 1998. "Stock Markets, Banks, and Economic Growth." *American Economic Review* 88: 537–58.

Levy, Jonah. 1999. *Tocqueville's Revenge: State, Society and Economy in Contemporary France*. Cambridge: Harvard University Press.

Levy, Jonah. 2001. "Partisan Politics and Welfare Adjustment." *Journal of European Public Policy* 8: 2 (April).

Levy, Jonah. 2005. "Economic Policy: From the Dirigiste State to the Social Anesthesia State and Beyond." In *Developments in French Politics 3*, eds. Alistair Cole, Partrick Le Galès and Jonah Levy. Basingstoke: Palgrave Macmillan, 170–94.

Linhart, Daniele. 1994. *La Modernisation des Entreprises*. Paris: La Decouverte.

Livian, Yves-Frédéric. 1999. "L'Évolution de la relation d'emploi des cadres: une approche à partir du contentieux prud'homal." *Journées d'études pluridisciplinaires sur les cadres*, Aix en Provence, LEST (December).

Lolive, Jacques. 1999. *Les Contestations du TGV Méditerranée: Projet, controverse et espace public*. Paris: L'Harmattan.

Loncle, P. 2000. "Partenariat et exclusion sociale en France: Expériences et ambiguities." *Pôle sud* 12: 47–62.

Loriaux, Michael. 1991. *France after Hegemony: International Change and Financial Reform*. Ithaca: Cornell University Press.

Lorrain, D. 1991. "Public Goods and Private Operators in France." In *Local Government in Europe*, eds. R. Batley and R. Stoker. Basingstoke: Macmillan, now Palgrave Macmillan, 461–84.

Lorrain, D. 1993. "Après la décentralisation: l'action publique flexible." *Sociologie du Travail* 3: 285–307.

Lorrain, D. 1997. "France, Silent Change." In *The Privatization of Urban Services in Europe*, eds. D. Lorrain and G. Stoker. London: Pinter, 105–32.

Lorrain, D. 2000. "The Construction of Urban Service Models." In *Cities in Contemporary Europe*. eds. A. Bagnasco and P. Le Galès. Cambridge: Cambridge University Press.

Lorrain, D. 2001. "L'Économie paradoxales des réseaux techniques urbains." In *Concurrence et services publics: Actes des conférences Jules Dupuit*, eds. C. Henry and E. Quinet. Paris: L'Harmattan.

Mabileau, A. 1995. "De la monarchie municipale à la française." *Pouvoirs* 73: 7–17.

Maddison, A. 1982. *Phases of Capitalist Development*. Oxford: Oxford University Press.

Majone, G. 1995. *La Communauté européenne, un Etat régulateur*. Paris: Montchrétien.

Majone, Giandomenico. 1996. *Regulating Europe*. London: Routledge.

Mannheim, Karl. (1928) 1952. "The Problem of Generations." In *Essays on the Sociology of Knowledge*, ed. P. Kecskemeti. New York: Oxford University Press, 276–322.

Mannheim, Karl. 1990 (orig. 1928). *Le Problème des generations*. Paris: Nathan.

Marcel, Stéphane, and Didier Witkowski. 2003. "Il faut sauver le clivage gauche-droite." In *L'État de l'opinion*, eds. Olivier Duhamel and Philippe Méchet. Paris: Seuil, 95–122.

Marcou, G., F. Rangeon, and J. L. Thiebault, eds. 1997. *La Coopération contractuelle et le gouvernement des villes*. Paris: L'Harmattan.

Markides, Costas. 1995. *Diversification, Refocusing, and Economic Performance*. Cambridge, Mass.: MIT Press.

Marks, G., F. Scharpf, Ph. Schmitter, and W. Streeck. 1996. *The Governance of Europe*. London: Sage.

Marks, Gary. 1993. "Structural Policy in the European Community." In *Euro-politics*, ed. A. Sbragia. Washington: The Brookings Institute, 62–82.

Marsden, David. 1999. *A Theory of Employment Systems: Micro-Foundations of Societal Diversity*. New York: Oxford University Press.

Martin, Pierre. 2000. *Comprendre les evolutions électorales*. Paris: Presses de Sciences Po.

Masclet, O. 2003. *La Gauche et les cites: Enquête sur un rendez-vous manqué*. Paris: La dispute.

Mason, K. O., W. M. Mason, H. H. Winsborough, and W. H. Poole. 1973. "Some Methodological Issues in Cohort Analysis of Archival Data." *American Sociological Review* 38: 242–58.

Maurice, Marc, François Sellier, and Jean-Jacques Silvestre. 1984. "Rules, Contexts and Actors: Observations Based on a Comparison between France and Germany." *British Journal of Industrial Relations* 22: 346–64.

Maurice, Marc, François Sellier, and Jean-Jacques Silvestre. 1986. *The Social Foundations of Industrial Power: a Comparison of France and Germany*. Cambridge: MIT Press.

Mayer, Nonna. 1991. "Ethnocentrisme, racisme et intolérance." In *L'Électeur français en questions,* CEVIPOF (Centre d'études de la vie politique française). Paris: Presses de la FNSP, 17–43.

Mayer, Nonna. 2002. *Ces Français qui votent Le Pen*. Paris: Flammarion.

McArthur, John, and Bruce Scott. 1969. *Industrial Planning in France*. Boston: Harvard Business School Press.

McCormick, J. 2001. *Environmental Policy in the European Union*. London: Macmillan, now Basingstoke: Palgrave Macmillan.

Mead, M. 1970. *Culture and Commitment: a Study of the Generation Gap*. Garden City, NY: American Museum of Natural History – Natural History Press.

Mendras, H. 1984. *La Fin des paysans*. 2nd edn. (1st edn., 1967), Arles: Actes Sud.

Mendras, H. 1988. *La Seconde Révolution française: 1965–1984*. Paris: Gallimard.

Mendras, H. 1992. *La Fin des paysans suivi d'une réflexion sur La fin des paysans vingt ans après*. Arles: Actes Sud.

Mentré, F. 1920. *Les générations socials*. Paris: Éd. Bossard.

Mény, Y. 1974. Centralisation et décentralisation dans le débat politique français: (1945–1969). Paris: LGDJ.

Mény, Yves. 1992. "La République des fiefs." *Pouvoirs* 60: 17–24.

Mény, Yves, and Yves Surel. 2000. *Par le peuple, pour le people: le populisme et la démocratie*. Paris: Fayard.

Mériaux, Olivier. 1999. "L'Action publique partagée, formes et dynamiques institutionnelles de la régulation politique du régime français de formation professionnelle." Thèse de doctorat en science politique. Université Grenoble II.

Merrien, François-Xavier. 1990. "État et politiques sociales: Contribution à une théorie 'néo-institutionnaliste.' " *Sociologie du Travail* 3: 43–56.

MES. 1999. *Les Enseignements des accords sur la réduction du temps de travail*. Paris: MES (Ministère de l'Emploi et de la Solidarité).

Michel, Hervé. 1999. *Intercommunalités et gouvernements locaux*. Paris: L'Harmattan.

Milward, A. 1992. *The European Rescue of the Nation State*. London: Routledge.

Modood, Tariq. 2003. "Muslims and the Politics of Difference." *Political Quarterly* 74 (1): 100–15.

Monnot, Caroline. 2002. "Attac entend peser sur les débats à gauche sans participer à la recomposition." *Le Monde*, 3 December: 12.

Moravscik, A. 1998. *The Choice for Europe*. Ithaca: Cornell University Press.

Morin, François. 1974. *La Structure financiere du capitalisme français*. Paris: Calmann-Levy.

Morin, François. 1996. "Privatisation et devolution des pouvoirs: le modele français du gouvernement d' enterprise." *Revue Economique* 47: 1253–68.

Morin, François. 1998. *Le Modèle français de détention du capital: Analyse, perspective et comparaisons internationales*. Paris: Ministère de l'Économie, des Finances et de l'Industrie.

Morin, François. 2000. "A Transformation in the French Model of Shareholding and Management." *Economy and Society* 29 (1): 36–53.

Morin, François, and Eric Rigamonti. 2002. "Evolution et structure de l'actionnariat en France." *Revue Française de Gestion* 28: 155–81.

Morin, Marie-Laure. 1994. *Le Droit des salariés à la négociation collective, principe général du droit*. Paris: LGDJ.

Morin, Marie-Laure, Gilbert de Terssac, and Jens Thoemmes. 1998. "La Négociation du temps de travail: l'emploi en jeu." *Sociologie du travail* XL (2): 191–207.

Mueller, Dennis C. 1979. *Public Choice*. Cambridge: Cambridge University Press.

Muller, Pierre. 1990. *Les Politiques publiques*. Paris: PUF.

Muller, Pierre. 1992. " 'Entre le local et l'Europe: la crise du modèle français de politiques publiques." *Revue Française de science politique* 2: 275–97.

Muller, Pierre. 1995. "Les Politiques publiques comme construction d'un rapport au monde." In *La Construction du sens dans les politiques publiques*, eds. A. Faure, G. Pollet, and P. Warin. Paris: L'Harmattan.

Muller, Pierre. 2000. "Vers une sociologie politique de l'action publique." *Revue française de science politique* 50 (2): 189–209.

Muller, Pierre, Yves Mény, and Jean-Louis Quermonne, eds. 1996. *Adjusting to Europe: the Impact of the EU on National Institutions and Policies*. London: Routledge.

Myles, John, and Paul Pierson. 1997. "Friedman's Revenge: the Reform of 'Liberal' Welfare States in Canada and the United States." EUI Working Paper RSC 97 (30), Institut Universitaire européen.

Nay, O. 1997. *La Région, une institution: la représentation, le pouvoir et la règle dans l'espace regional*. Paris: L'Harmattan.

Nay, O. 2001. "Négocier le partenariat: Jeux et conflits dans la mise en oeuvre de la politique communautaire européenne." *Revue Française de science politique* 51 (3): 459–480.

Neumark, D. 2000. *On the Job: Is Long-Term Employment a Thing of the Past?* New York: Russell Sage Foundation.

Nivolle, Patrick. 1999. "Stratégie des acteurs locaux." In *Travail et emploi: Vers de nouvelles régulations*, ed. William Cavestro and Bruno Lamotte. Paris: La documentation française: 133–56.

Noblecourt, Michel. 2002. "Mondialisation, Europe, sécurité, institutions, retraite, services publics: ce qui divise les socialistes." *Le Monde* 22 October: 8.

Noiriel, Gérard. 1996. *The French Melting Pot: Immigration, Citizenship, and National Identity*. Translated by Geoffroy de Laforcade. Minneapolis/Saint-Paul: University of Minnesota Press.

Nye, Joseph, P. D. Zelikow, and D. C. King, eds. 1997. *Why People Don't Trust Government*. Cambridge, Mass.: Harvard University Press.

Oberti, M. 1999. "Formes et contenu d'une conscience sociale chez les jeunes des 'quartiers en difficulté.' " *Actuel Marx* 26: 69–83.

OFCE (Observatoire Français des Conjonctures Économiques). 2003. *L'Économie française* 2003. Paris: Editions de la Découverte.

O'Reilly, Jacqueline, Immaculada Cebriàn, and Michel Lallement, eds. 2000. *Working Time Changes: Social Integration through Transitional Labor Markets*. Cheltenham: Edward Elgar.

O'Sullivan, Mary. 2002. "The Stock Market and Corporate Investment: the Case of France." Paper presented at UNU/INTECH, October.

Ordeshook, Peter C. 1986. *Game Theory and Political Theory: an Introduction*. Cambridge: Cambridge University Press.

Organisation for Economic Cooperation and Development (OECD). 1997. "Is Job Insecurity on the Increase in OECD Countries?" *Employment Outlook*. Paris: OECD 129–60.

Organisation for Economic Cooperation and Development (OECD). 2004. *OECD Economic Outlook* No. 74. Paris: OECD.

Orren, K., and S. Skowronek. 1993. "Order and Time in Institutional Study." In *Political Science in History: Research Programs and Political Traditions*, eds. J. Farr, J. Dryzek, and S. Leonard. Cambridge: Cambridge University Press, 297–317.

Outin, Jean-Luc. 1997. "Les Politiques d'insertion." *L'Insertion professionnelle, analyses et débats*, ed. M. Vernières. Paris: Economica 120–37.

Padioleau, J. G. 1991. "L'Action publique urbaine moderniste." *Politiques et management public* 9 (3): 133–43.

Palier, Bruno. 1998. "La Référence au territoire dans les nouvelles politiques sociales." *Politique et management public* 16 (3), 13–41.

Palier, Bruno. 2000. " 'Defrosting' the French Welfare State." *West European Politics* 23 (2): 113–36.

Palier, Bruno. 2002. *Gouverner la sécurité sociale, les réformes du système français de protection sociale depuis 1945*. Paris: Presses Universitaires de France.

Palier, Bruno. 2003. "Facing Pension Crisis in France." In *Pension Security in the 21st Century: Redrawing the Public-Private Divide*, ed. Noel Whiteside and Gordon Clarke, Oxford: Oxford University Press, 93–114.

Palier, Bruno. 2005. "Ambiguous Agreement, Cumulative Change: French Social Policy in the 1990s." In *Beyond Continuity: Institutional Change in Advanced Political Economies*, eds. Kathleen Thelen and Wolfgang Streeck. Oxford: Oxford University Press: 127–44.

Perraudeau, Eric, and Xavier Timbeau. 2004. "Les Français face au ralentissement économique." In *L'Etat de l'Opinion 2004*, eds. Olivier Duhamel and Brice Teinturier. Paris: SOFRES/Seuil, 163–76.

Perrineau, Pascal. 2001. *Les Croisés de la société fermée. L'Europe des extrêmes droites*. La Tour d'Aigues: Editions de l'Aube.

Peters, G. 2005. "The Capacity to Co-ordinate." In *Co-ordinating the EU*, eds. H. Kassim, A. Menon, and G. Peters. Forthcoming.

Pew Research Center. 2003. *Globalization with a Few Discontents?* available at www.globalpolicy.org.

Pierson, Paul. 1994. *Dismantling the Welfare State: Reagan, Thatcher, and the Politics of Retrenchment*. New York: Cambridge University Press.

Pierson, Paul. 1996. "The Path to European Integration: a Historical Institutionalist Analysis," *Comparative Political Studies* 29 (2): 123–63.

Pierson, Paul. 1998. "Irresistible Forces, Immovable Objects: Post-industrial Welfare States Confront Permanent Austerity." *Journal of European Public Policy* 5 (4): 539–60.

Pierson, Paul. 2000. "Increasing Returns, Path Dependence, and the Study of Politics." *American Political Science Review* 94 (2): 251–67.

Pierson, Paul, ed. 2001. *The New Politics of the Welfare State*. New York: Oxford University Press.

Pinaud, Henri, Michel Le Tron, and Alain Chouraqui, eds. 1999. *Syndicalisme et démocratie dans l'entreprise*. Paris: L'Harmattan.

Pinson, G. 2004. "Le Projet comme instrument d'action publique urbaine." In *Gouverner par les instruments*, eds. P. Lascoumes and P. Le Galès. Paris: Presses de Sciences Po.

Pinson, G. 2005. "Nantes and Pays de la Loire Regional Governance: Problem and Project Driven Cooperation in the French Context." In *Urban-Regional Cooperation in the, European Union: Practices and Prospects*, eds. F. Hendriks, V. van Stipdonk, and P. Tops. London: Frank Cass, 119–41.

Pisani-Ferry, Jean. 2000. *Les Chemins du plein emploi*. Conseil d'analyse économique 30, Paris, la documentation française.

Platone, François. 1995. *Les Électorats sous la Cinquième République: Données, d'enquête 1958–1995*. 2nd edn., Paris: Cevipof.

Politique européenne. 2003. "Parlementarismes et construction européenne." *Journal special issue on national parliaments and the EU 9*.

Pollet, G. 1995. "La Construction de l'État social à la française: Entre local et national (19e–20e siècles)." *Lien Social et Politique* 33: 26–43.

Pollet, Gilles, and Didier Renard. 1995. "Genèses et usages de l'idée paritaire dans le système de protection sociale français: Fin 19ème–milieu du 20ème siècle." *Revue française de science politiqu: "la protection sociale en perspective"* 45 (4) (August): 644–67.

Pollet, Gilles, and Didier Renard. 1997. "Le Paritarisme et la protection sociale: Origines et enjeux." *La Revue de l'IRES* 24 sur le paritarisme, printemps-été: 61–80.

Prahalad, C. K., and Gary Hamel. 1990. "The Core Competence of the Corporation." *Harvard Business Review* 68 (3): 79–91.

Putnam, Robert D. 1993. *Making Democracy Work*. Princeton: Princeton University Press.

Putnam, Robert D. 2000. *Bowling Alone: the Collapse and Revival of American Community*. New York: Simon and Schuster.

Radaelli, C. 2001. "The Domestic Impact of European Union Public Policy: Notes on Concepts, Methods and the Challenge of Empirical Research." *Politique européenne* 5: 155–83.

Raffarin, Jean-Pierre. 2003. *Discours lors du vingtième anniversaire de la marche pour l'égalité. 03-12-2003*. Paris: Site du premier minister. http://www.premier-ministrre.gouv.fr.

Rappaport, Alfred, and Mark Sirower. 1999. "Stock or Cash? The Trade-Offs for Buyers and Sellers in Mergers and Acquisitions." *Harvard Business Review* 77: 147–58.

Renard, D. 1995. "Intervention de l'État et genèse de la protection sociale en France 1880–1940." *Lien Social et Politique* 33: 3–24.

Reynaud, Bénédicte. 1992. *Le Salaire, la règle et le marché*. Paris: Bourgois.

Reynaud, Jean-Daniel. 1973. "Tout le pouvoir au peuple ou de la polyarchie à la pléistocratie." In *Une Nouvelle Civilisation: Hommage à Georges Friedmann*. Paris: Gallimard, 76–92.

Rhodes, Martin. 2001. "The Political Economy of Social Pacts: 'Competitive Corporatism' and European Welfare Reform." In *The New Politics of the Welfare State*, ed. Paul Pierson. Oxford: Oxford University Press, 165–95.

Riker, William. 1986. *The Art of Political Manipulation*. New Haven: Yale University Press.

Rimac, Ivan, and Aleksadar Stulhofer. 2004. "Socio-Cultural Values, Economic Development and Political Stability as Correlates of Trust in the European Union."

Croation Accession to the European Union. Zagreb: Institute of Public Finance, 301–26.

Rivaud, P. 2001. "Leadership et gouvernance communautaire: la Commission européenne et l'idée de service universel des télécommunications (1987–98)." PhD. thesis: IEP de Paris.

Robert, C. 2004. "Doing Politics and Pretending Not to: the Commission's Role in Distributing Aid to Eastern Europe." In *Politics and the European Commission*, ed. A. Smith. London: Routledge, 17–30.

Roe, Mark. 1998. "Backlash." *Columbia Law Review* 98: 217–41.

Roe, Mark. 2000. "Political Preconditions to Separating Ownership from Corporate Control." *Stanford Law Review* 53: 539–606.

Rondin, J. 1985. *Le Sacre des notables: la France en decentralization*. Paris: Fayard.

Rosanvallon, Pierre. 1988. *La Question syndicale*. Paris: Calmann-Lévy.

Rosanvallon, Pierre. 1998. *Le Peuple introuvable: Histoire de la représentation démocratique en France*. Paris: Gallimard.

Ross, George. 1995. *Jacques Delors and European Integration*. Cambridge: Polity.

Rouart, Jean-Marie. 2003. *Adieu à la France qui s'en va*. Paris: Grasset.

Rouban, L. 2002. "L'Inspection générale des Finances 1958–2000: Quarante ans de pantouflage." *Cahiers de CEVIPOF* 31: 1–158.

Rozes, Stéphane. 2001. "La Popularité des mouvements sociaux ne se dément pas depuis 1995." *Le Monde* 7 March: 18.

Ryder, N. B. 1965. "The Cohort as a Concept in the Study of Social Change." *American Sociological Review* 30: 843–61.

Saglio, Jean. 1986. "Hiérarchies salariales et négociations de classifications: France, 1900–1950." *Travail et emploi* 27 (March): 7–19.

Saglio, Jean. 1990. "La Régulation de branche dans le système français de relations professionnelles." In *Les Relations sociales en Europe*. Paris: Ministère du travail et de l'Emploi, 96–111.

Sandholtz, W., and A. Stone Sweet, eds. 1998. *European Integration and Supranational Governance*. Oxford: Oxford University Press.

Sawicki, F. 1997. *Les Réseaux du Parti socialiste: Sociologie d'un milieu partisan*. Paris: Belin.

Schain, Martin. 2006. "The Impact of the Extreme Right on Immigration Policy." *West European Politics* 29 (2). Forthcoming.

Scharpf, F. 2000. *Gouverner l'Europe*. Paris: Presses de Sciences Po.

Scharpf, Fritz. 2000. "Globalization and the Welfare State, Constraints, Challenges and Vulnerabilities." Paper presented at the Cost A15 conference European Welfare States: Domestic and International Challenges, Cologne, 5–6 October 2000.

Schattschneider, E. E. 1960. *The Semi-Sovereign People: a Realist's View of Democracy in America*. New York: Holt, Rhinehart and Winston.

Schlesinger, Joseph A., and Mildred S. Schlesinger. 2002. "The Stability of the French Party System: the Enduring Impact of the Two-Ballot Electoral Rule." In *How France Votes*, ed. Michael S. Lewis-Beck. New York, London: Chattam House.

Schmid, Günther. 2002. *Wege in eine neue Vollbeschäftigung*. Frankfurt am Main: Campus.

Schmidt, Vivien. 1996. *From State to Market? The Transformation of French Business and Government*. New York: Cambridge University Press.

Schmidt, Vivien. 1997. "Economic Policy, Political Discourse and Democracy in France." *French Politics and Society* 15 (2): 37–48.

Schmidt, Vivien. 2002. *The Futures of European Capitalism*. Oxford: Oxford University Press.

Schnapper, Dominique. 1991. *La France de l'intégration: Sociologie de la nation en 1990*. Paris: Gallimard.

Schweisguth, Etienne. 2000. "Liberté, autorité et civisme, trente ans après mai 1968." In *Les Valeurs des français: Evolutions de 1980 à 2000*, ed. P. Bréchon. Paris: Armand Colin, 157–78.

Segrestin, Denis. 2004. *Les Chantiers du manager*. Paris: Colin.

Séguin, Philippe. 1993. *Ce que j'ai dit*. Paris: Grasset.

Shapiro, Martin. 1981. *Courts: a Comparative and Political Analysis*. Chicago: University of Chicago Press.

Shleifer, Andrei, and Robert Vishny. 1997. "A Survey of Corporate Governance." *Journal of Finance* 52: 737–83.

Simon, Patrick. 2000. "Les Jeunes de l'immigration se cachent pour vieillir: Représentations sociales et catégories de l'action publique." *VEI Enjeux* 121 (June): 23–38.

Skach, Cindy. 2006. *Borrowing Constitutional Designs: Constitutional Law in Weimar Germany and the French Fifth Republic*. Princeton, NJ: Princeton University Press.

Slama, Alain-Gérard. 1995. "Democratic Dysfunctions and Republican Obsolescence: the Demise of French Exceptionalism." In *Remaking the Hexagon*, ed., Gregory Flynn. Boulder: Westview, 49–68.

Smith, A. 1995. *L'Europe au miroir du local: les fonds structurels et les zones rurales en France, en Espagne et au Royaume Uni*. Paris: L'Harmattan.

Smith, A. 2003. "Multi-Level Governance: What It Is and How It Can Be Studied." In *Handbook of Public Administration*, eds. M. Painter and J. Pierre. London: Sage, 137–55.

Smith, A. 2004. *Le Gouvernement de l'Union européenne: une sociologie politique*. Paris: LGDJ.

Smith, A. 2005. "Shallow Institutionalization and Glaring Ommissions: the Co-ordination of EU Agriculture and Rural Development Policy." In *Co-ordinating the EU*, eds. H. Kassim, A. Menon, and G. Peters. Forthcoming.

Smith, Timothy B. 2004. *France in Crisis: Welfare, Inequality and Globalization since 1980*. New York: Cambridge University Press.

Smyrl, Marc. 1997. "Does European Community Regional Policy Empower the Regions?" *Governance* 10 (3): 287–309.

Sociologie du travail. 1996. Numéro spécial "Contrats et pratiques contractuelles: Approches pluridisciplinaires." XXXVIII (4).

Sociologie du travail. 1997. Numéro spécial "Grèves. Automne 1995." XXXIX (4).

SOFRES. 2002a. *L'État de l'opinion 2002*, 287. See also http://www.sofres.com/etudes/pol/180701_mondialisation_h.htm.

SOFRES. 2002b. *Les Français et l'Europe* 2002. http://www.sofres.com/etudes/pol/030102_europe_r.htm.

SOFRES. 2003. *Les Français et le Front National*. http://www.tns-sofres.com/etudes/pol/091203_fn_r.htm

SOFRES/*Le Monde*. 2001. Survey *Les français et la mondialisation*. http://www.sofres.com/etudes/pol/180701, 12–13 July.

Sorbets, C., and A. Smith. 2003. *Le Leadership politique et le territoire: les cadres d'analyse en débat*. Rennes: Presses Universitaires de Rennes.

Sorge, Arndt. 1991. "Strategic Fit and the Societal Effect: Interpreting Cross-National Comparisons of Technology, Organization and Human Resources." *Organization Studies* 12: 161–90.

Soskice, David. 1999. "Divergent Production Regimes: Coordinated and Uncoordinated Market Economies in the 1980s and 1990s." In *Continuity and Change in Contemporary Capitalism*, eds. Hebert Kitschelt, Peter Lange, Gary Marks, and John Stephens. New York: Cambridge University Press, 101–34.

Souriac, M.-A. 2004. "L'Articulation des niveaux de négociation." *Droit Social* 6: 579–89.

Soysal, Yasemin. 1994. *The Limits of Citizenship*. Chicago: Chicago University Press.

Spitz, Bernard. 2002. "Une Mondialisation: Deux France." In *SOFRES, l'état de l'opinion 2002*, eds. O. Duhamel and P. Méchet. Paris: Seuil, 113–27.

Stoleru, Lionel. 1969. *L'Imperatif industriel*. Paris: Le Seuil.

Stone, Alec. 1993. "Ratifying *Maastricht*: France Debates European Union." *French Politics and Society* 11: 70–88.

Stone, Deborah. 1989. "Causal Stories and the Formation of Policy Agendas." *Political Science Quarterly* 104: 281–300.

Streeck, Wolfgang. 1991. "On the Institutional Conditions of Diversified Quality Production." In *Beyond Keynesianism: the Socio-Economics of Production and Full Employment*, eds. Egon Matzner and Wolfgang Streeck. Brookfield, Vt.: Edward Elgar, 21–61.

Streeck, Wolfgang. 1995. "From Market-Making to State-Building? Reflections on the Political Economy of European Social Policy." In *European Social Policy: Between Fragmentation and Integration*, eds. Stephan Leibfried and Paul Pierson. Washington, DC: The Brookings Institution: 389–431.

Streeck, Wolfgang. 1998. "The Internationalization of Industrial Relations in Europe: Prospects and Problems." *Politics and Society* 26 (4) (December): 429–59.

Suleiman, E. 1974. *Politics, Power and Bureaucracy in France: the Administrative Elite*. Princeton, NJ: Princeton University Press.

Suleiman, E. 1978. *Elites in French Society: the Politics of Survival*. Princeton, NJ: Princeton University Press.

Suleiman, Ezra. 1987. *Private Power and Centralization in France*. Princeton, NJ: Princeton University Press.

Supiot, Alain. 1989, "Déréglementation des relations de travail et autoréglementation de l'entreprise." *Droit social* 3 (March): 195–205.

Supiot, Alain. 2000. "La Contractualisation de la société." Public conference, Université de tous les savoirs. Paris. 22 February.

Szreter, S. R. S. 1993. "The Official Representation of Social Classes in Britain, the United States, and France: the Professional Model and 'Les Cadres.' " *Comparative Studies in Society and History* 35 (2): 285–317.

Tallard, Michèle. 2004. *Action publique et régulation de branche de la relation salariale*. Paris: L'Harmattan.

Teinturier, Brice. 2004. "Les Français et la politique: Entre désenchantement et colère." In *L'Etat de L'Opinion 2004*, eds. Olivier Duhamel and Brice Teinturier. Paris: SOFRES/Seuil, 11–33.

Thatcher, Mark. 2004. "Varieties of Capitalism in an Institutionalized World: Domestic Institutional Change in European Telecommunications." *Comparative Political Studies* (September): 751–80.

Thernstrom, S. 1973. *The Other Bostonians: Poverty and Progress in the American Metropolis, 1880–1970*. Cambridge, Mass.: Harvard University Press.

Thibault de Silguy, Yves. 2003. *Moderniser l'Etat: l'encadrement supérieur*. Parliamentary Report on Reform of the ENA. http://lesrapports.ladocumentationfrancaise.fr/BRP/044000060/0000.pdf.

Tissandier, Hélène. 1997. "L'Articulation des niveaux de négociation: à la recherche de nouveaux principes." *Droit social* 12 (December): 1045–1051.

Tixier, Pierre-Eric. 1992. *Mutation ou déclin du syndicalisme? Le Cas de la CFDT*. Paris: PUF.

TNS-Sofres. 2002. "Evolution du clivage gauche-droite depuis 10 ans." Available at http://www.tns-sofres.com/etudes/pol/140202_clivage_r. htm.

TNS Sofres. 2005. *"L'Opinion française en attente d'une nouvelle gouvernance d'entreprise"*. http://www.sofres.com/etudes/corporate/040203_gouvernance.htm. Paris: TNS-Sofres. Accessed: 24 February 2005.

TNS-Sofres/EOS Gallup Europe. 2004. *The Future European Constitution (Wave 2)* Flash Eurobarometer 159 (2), 55. http://europa.eu.int/comm/public_opinion/flash/fl159_2en.pdf

Touraine, Alain. 1990. "La Crise du système des relations professionnelles". In *Les Systèmes de relations professionnelles*, eds. Jean-Daniel Reynaud, François Eyraud, Catherine Paradeise, and Jean Saglio. Paris: éditions du CNRS, 371–7.

Traxler, F., S. Blaschke, and B. Kittel. 2001. *National Labour Relations and Internationalized Markets: a Comparative Study of Institutions, Change, and Performance*. New York: Oxford University Press.

Trumbull, Gunnar. 2004. *Silicon and the State: French Innovation Policy in the Internet Age*. Washington: Brookings.

Turner, Ruth. 2004. *Turnout in Decline: a Global Picture*. London: Forethought.

Van der Elst, C. 2000. "The Equity Markets, Ownership Structures, and Control: Towards an International Harmonisation." Working Paper WP 2000–04, Financial Law Institute, University of Ghent.

Veltz, P. 1996. *Mondialisation, villes et territories: l'économie d'archipel*. Paris: PUF.

Vidal, J.-F. 2002. "Les Bouleversements du régime d'accumulation et les ajustements de la régulation: la croissance française sans mythes." *L'Année de la Régulation 2002* 6: 333–80.

Viet, Vincent. 1998. *La France immigrée: Construction d'une politique 1914–1997*. Paris: Fayard.

Wallace H. 1995. "Les Relations entre la Communauté et l'administration britannique." In *Les Politiques publiques en Europe*, eds. Y. Mény, P. Muller, and J.-L. Quermonne. Paris: L'Harmattan, 155–70.

Warin, Philippe. 2004. "La Gestion de proximité à l'épreuve des politiques publiques en France." In *La Concertation dans les politiques urbaines au Canada, en France et en Grande-Bretagne*, eds. Philip Booth and Bernard Jouve. Montréal: Presses de l'Université du Québec, 195–215.

Weaver, Kent. 1986. "The Politics of Blame Avoidance." *Journal of Public Policy* 6 (4): 371–98.

Weber, Eugen. 1976. *Peasants into Frenchmen: the Modernization of Rural France, 1870–1914*. Stanford, Calif.: Stanford University Press.

Weil, Patrick. 1991. *La France et ses étrangers: l'aventure d'une politique de l'immigration, 1938–1991*. Paris: Calmann-Lévy.

Weill, Nicolas. 2002. "Vers la fin de la 'mondialisation heureuse'?" *Le Monde* 8 October: 15.

Weir, M. 2002. "The American Middle Class and the Politics of Education." In *Social Contracts under Stress: the Middle Classes of America, Europe, and Japan at the Turn of the Century*, eds. O. Zunz, Leonard Schoppa, and Nobuhiro Hiwatari. New York: Russell Sage Foundation, 178–203.

Whittington, Richard. 1988. "Environmental Structure and Theories of Strategic Choice." *Journal of Management Studies* 25: 521–36.

Whittington, Richard. 2000. "In Praise of the Evergreen Conglomerate." In *Mastering Strategy*, ed. Tim Dickson. London: Financial Times Publication, 327–31.

Whittington, Richard, and Michael Mayer. 2000. *The European Corporation: Strategy, Structure, and Social Science*. New York: Oxford University Press.

Wieviorka, Michel. 2001. "Faut-il en finir avec l'intégration?" *Cahiers de la sécurité intérieure* 45: 9–20.

Williamson, Olivier. 1975. *Markets and Hierarchies: Analysis and Antitrust Implications*. New York: Free Press.

Worms, Jean-Pierre. 2002. "France: Old and New Civic and Social Ties in France." In *Democracies in Flux*, ed. Robert D. Putnam. New York: Oxford University Press: 137–88.

Wright, Vincent. 1983. *The Government and Politics of France*. 2nd. edn., London: Hutchinson.

WRR. 1989. *Allochtonenebeleid*. The Hague: Stu Uitgeverij.

Yakubovich, C. 2002. "Négociation collective des salaires et passage à la monnaie unique." *Premières Informations et Premières Synthèses* 48 (1): 1–8.

Zald, Mayer N. 1996. "Culture, Ideology and Strategic Framing." In *Comparative Perspectives on Social Movements: Political Opportunities, Mobilizing Structures, and Cultural Framing*, Doug McAdam, John D. McCarthy, and Mayer N. Zald, Cambridge: Cambridge University Press, 261–74.

Zappi, Sylvia. 2003. "Immigration: le virage à droite." *Le Monde* 28 April.

Zappi, Sylvia. 2004. "Le Haut Conseil à l'intégration fustige la discrimination positive." *Le Monde* 26 January.

Ziegler, N. 1997. *Governing Ideas: Strategies for Innovation in France and Germany*. Ithaca: Cornell University Press.

Zingales, Luigi. 1994. "The Value of Voting Right: a Study of the Milan Stock Exchange Experience." *Review of Financial Studies* 7: 124–48.

Zysman, John. 1977. *Political Strategies for Industrial Order: State, Market, and Industry in France*. Berkeley: University of California Press.

Zysman, John. 1983. *Governments, Markets, and Growth: Financial Systems and the Politics of Industrial Change*. Ithaca: Cornell University Press.

Index